Harrison Ford:
The Films

Harrison Ford: The Films

Brad Duke

McFarland & Company, Inc., Publishers
Jefferson, North Carolina, and London

LIBRARY OF CONGRESS CATALOGUING-IN-PUBLICATION DATA

Duke, Brad, 1969–
Harrison Ford : the films / Brad Duke.
p.   cm.
Includes bibliographical references and index.

ISBN 0-7864-2016-2 (illustrated case binding : 50# alkaline paper) ∞

1. Ford, Harrison, 1942–   I. Title.
PN2287.F59D85   2005   791.4302'8'092 — dc22   2004025793

British Library cataloguing data are available

©2005 Brad Duke. All rights reserved

*No part of this book may be reproduced or transmitted in any form
or by any means, electronic or mechanical, including photocopying
or recording, or by any information storage and retrieval system,
without permission in writing from the publisher.*

Cover: Ford as Indiana Jones (1981). *Insets (top to bottom):* in *What Lies Beneath* (2000); offscreen in *Patriot Games* (1992; U.S. Naval Academy, Nimitz Library); in *Blade Runner* (1982); in *Star Wars* (1977); in *The Last Crusade* (1989)

Manufactured in the United States of America

*McFarland & Company, Inc., Publishers
Box 611, Jefferson, North Carolina 28640
www.mcfarlandpub.com*

To all those who have assisted me in my research;
to the girlfriends who tolerated my mental and physical
absence as I wrote; to the travel companions whose destinations
were dictated by the previous shooting locations of Mr. Ford's
films; to *The Mosquito Coast* director Peter Weir for giving me
a reason to visit my now-favorite nation of Belize; to my patient
and polite friends and family who supported me throughout
my research and writing; to Amanda for being my informal
and unofficial secretary, agent, editor, provider of pats on the
back and speaker of words of encouragement; and finally, to
Harrison Ford for choosing to act — and in turn, providing
me the opportunity to write these very words. I thank you.

TABLE OF CONTENTS

Preface   1
Prologue: The Dawn of It All   3

1. An Ordinary Upbringing   5
2. The Origin of His Species   8
3. Finding His Calling   11
4. Have Wife, Will Travel   13
5. The Long and Winding Road   15
6. Odds and Ends   18
7. The Do-It-Yourself Man   23
8. Finally … Respect   26
9. Hanging with the Big Boys   31
10. A Star Was Born   34
11. A War Lost and a Wife Found   43
12. Getting Some Recognition   46
13. Little to Be Proud Of   50
14. Lose Some, Win Some   60
15. Destined for Success   62
16. The First George, Steven and Harrison Collaboration   74
17. Science Friction   88
18. Life Among the Aliens   100
19. Cracking the Whip (Again)   109
20. The Weir Years   119
21. Pregnancy, Paris and Polanski   138
22. Working Guy   144
23. Bonding with Connery   150
24. His Bad Hair Day   161
25. Time to Rehabilitate   169

26. At War with Irish Terrorists … and Tom Clancy	176
27. On the Run for the Money	188
28. Jack's Back	200
29. Something Wilder	212
30. A Devil of a Time	221
31. "America's Kick-Ass President"	233
32. Trouble Overseas	245
33. The End of an Era	252
34. The New Model Ford	257
35. Harrison Ford's Russian Perspective	262
36. The Buddy-Cop Flick Flop	267
37. All Cameras Aside	273
Filmography	289
Chapter Notes	293
Bibliography	307
Index	319

Preface

I recall glancing one day at the enormous pile of research amassed atop my desk, and asking myself, "Okay, what now?" Considering how much I had enjoyed the research and my continued admiration for the subject itself, I vividly remember declaring, "I'll write a book!"

Although it was conceived on a whim, moments later I found myself typing furiously into my now-prehistoric Magnavox Video Writer 350.

That was 1992....

In 1977, like every other kid my age, I was enthralled by all things *Star Wars*—most notably Han Solo. He was the coolest guy in the—well—galaxy, and he remained so for years.

In 1981, when Indiana Jones first appeared, and the name Harrison Ford flashed across the screen, I understood fully that there were fictional characters and the real individuals who portrayed them. For years, I furiously conducted research on Ford merely as a hobby—albeit a passionate one. The Internet was still in its infancy, so I had my work cut out for me. I was lucky to have benefited from a few well-connected friends—from a girlfriend who worked in the Harvard University microforms division, to a friend who was willing to lend me his Northeastern University ID necessary to infiltrate the school library's Lexis/Nexis database system. Ultimately, I found what I was looking for.

My goal was to document every written work about Ford. Where his name appeared in print, I would capture it in my word processor. But I did not rely solely on the written word.

Over the years, I carved out opportunities to further my research. While living in Boston without the benefit of owning a VCR, I would use my micro-cassette recorder to tape television interviews and documentaries. Later—as I and the technology around me matured—I was able to conduct online interviews with Ford's co-workers, observe firsthand the filming of some of his pictures, attend the Hasty Pudding Man of the Year press conference, and—more recently—hit the road to foreign locations to fill the gaps in my research. (An enormous *thank you* to Peter Weir for choosing to set *The Mosquito Coast* in Belize.)

That I left no stone unturned during my research was evidenced by my original manuscript, which came in just shy of 700 densely filled pages. After upwards of 20 years of research, each previously undiscovered film secret or revealing personal trait was invaluable to me. I had even come to know Ford's own mannerisms—the meaning imparted by a simple hand gesture or facial expression. In my enthusiasm, I wanted to impart everything to you, the reader, but there was understandably little interest in publishing such an oversized work. Hence the book before you today—a pared-down version—yet one that I am proud to say remains as rich with substantive detail as I'd originally intended.

In the first chapters, I have endeavored to describe Ford's early life—his youth, his fear of acting and his decision to act, and his early career hardships. I have intentionally strayed from lines of inquiry that might be considered purely based on gossip or speculation. My goal has never been to intrude upon Mr. Ford's privacy with an improper discussion of his personal life. Rather, my aim was to study and admire his films, to discuss in detail his long and successful career, and the effect that success has had on Ford himself. I focused heavily on the intricate details of his filmmaking, its successes, failures and difficulties. I included, wherever possible, direct quotes from the man himself and those who knew and worked with him, so that you might have the information directly—so to speak—from the horse's mouth.

So here they are—the fruits of *my* labor, courtesy of the fruits of *his* labor. From pre-production, through production, post-production and further on to the point of each film's release, I offer you insight into how some of the most memorable films and characters in cinematic history came into being.

Prologue: The Dawn of It All

As the Badger State disappeared beyond the horizon in the rearview mirror of the tiny Volkswagen van, its occupants steered it enthusiastically towards a destiny uncertain and a destination unknown. Determined by the simple flip of a coin, the future of the newlywed couple inside was set into motion.

The year was 1964 and winter had arrived in the American Midwest. Illinois native Harrison Ford and his college sweetheart Mary Marquardt—with all their worldly possessions tucked securely away within their Volkswagen bus—were heading west towards the Pacific Coast. Ford was in pursuit of a future in professional acting; considering the severity of winter in the Big Apple, he wisely chose the more pleasant alternative of Los Angeles.

"We'd just spent the last of the winter in the woods, and when the coin came up for New York we said: 'Shit. Do we really want another winter? Let's make it two out of three,'" recalled Ford. "If I was going to be poor, it's better to be poor in a warm place."[1]

And with that decision, 22-year-old Ford and his wife arrived 1,708 miles later just south of the City of Angels in the coastal town of Laguna Beach, California. There, he would settle in with the hopes of raising a family and of continuing a career that began during his days as a Ripon College student.

"I thought of acting like being in the Navy," said the actor. "I would travel around and meet interesting people. But I wouldn't have to kill them."[2]

Nearly four decades later, Harrison Ford is now enjoying a lifestyle far exceeding his original goals of a modest living from occasional television appearances.

Today, as a result of a 1979 divorce, he is without Mary Marquardt. In 2003, yet another marriage ended after he and *E.T.* screenwriter Melissa Mathison split following 20 years of marriage. In addition to being the proud father of four children, he is the grandfather of two and divides his personal time living in homes in California, Wyoming and New York City. Alongside his new love, *Ally McBeal* actress Calista Flockhart, he can't escape the watchful eyes of the paparazzi. Today, there is proof that he has lived up his dreams of decades ago. He now commands a substantial amount of income per film and all the luxuries that accrue. His résumé amounts to more than $5 billion of box office receipts worldwide, and he is without argument one of the most successful and sought-after actors in the world.

1

AN ORDINARY UPBRINGING

Named in honor of his maternal grandfather Harrison Needleman—a man who fell victim to influenza in the early part of the century—Harrison Ford was born on July 13, 1942, at Swedish Covenant Hospital in Chicago. He and his younger brother Terence, who was born in 1945 during the closing moments of World War II, led normal middle-class lives just outside the Chicago city limits. They were raised by their Irish Catholic father and their mother, a Russian Jew. Christopher and Dorothy Ford created a cultural and religious combination that offered widespread beliefs and methods of child rearing: His mother "was capable of guilt-tripping me as any Jewish mother can," recalled Ford, while his father "was perfectly capable of tanning my ass as every Irish Catholic kid raised by nuns might be."[1]

Although he enjoyed benefitting from both religions' holidays, Ford was not necessarily a willing supporter of either. In line with the liberal traditions of the time, his parents allowed them to attend services everywhere—from the local Protestant church to a Baha'i temple. Ford become fascinated with the idea of an all-powerful, all-knowing God and with the way people were affected by their faith. However, he never became absorbed by those beliefs himself.

Oddly enough, Harrison Ford grew up without the slightest desire to be an entertainer. "My first childhood ambition," remembered Ford, "was to be the guy who carried the coal from our house to the coal chute in a wheelbarrow. I remember there was this big pile of coal, and then he did his job, and then there was no coal. I liked the rhythm of his work. It was a job you could see getting done. My dad would come home from his job and talk about how unhappy everyone was there. And compared to that, I'd rather have shoveled coal. I was four or five."[2]

Recalling Walt Disney's *Bambi* as his first cinematic experience, Ford rarely went to the movies as a youth. Because of his brother Terence's interest in cinema, however, Ford ultimately discovered the magic that theaters were capable of providing. Yet Terence was not entirely responsible for exposing Harrison to Hollywood.

Harrison's family tree is filled with forebears in the entertainment industry. His grandfather, John William Ford, was in vaudeville as a blackface comedian—a stage performer who did song and dance routines as well as slapstick sketches during a period when that particular form of entertainment was considered entertaining. He passed away when he was 25 as the result of an alcohol-related illness.

Harrison's father Christopher worked in radio production as both a writer and an actor. He joined the touring group "Gangbusters," a group of tuxedo-clad actors who circled a single microphone and did their routine live over the airwaves. When his first son was born, Christopher Ford left the Gangbusters. Soon after, he switched careers entirely and became an executive at Needham, Louis and Brorby, one of the leading advertising agencies in the Windy City. He made his mark upon the world when he gave the public the ability to see soapsuds in action through a window on a washing machine door. He was also the first to employ the use of stop-motion photography techniques like those for the rosebud in the Parkay television commercials.

Harrison and his brother — or Harry and Terry, as they were known respectively by friends during their youth — started their schooling at Graeme Stewart Elementary. Despite his involvement with various extracurricular activities during his later tenures at M. S. Meltzer Junior High and East Maine Township High School in Park Ridge, Illinois, Harrison Ford was an extremely private kid.

"I never had a focused goal or ambition," claimed Ford. "I never set out to be held in esteem. I just wanted to be able to hold my head up in private. I couldn't even find a niche in high school. My classmates considered me an oddball, and they were probably right. Not that I cared much for what my classmates thought."[3]

Throughout the years, Ford maintained a C average. Although intelligent, he didn't apply his knowledge to academics. Instead, Ford's varied roster of high school credentials included president of the Social Science Club, member of the model railroad club, and representative of both the Boys Club and the Class Council. He was also a participant in the school's variety show program and a disc jockey for its radio station WMTH-FM. Additionally, the teenager was a member of the school's dance troupe, the Tower Trotters and, for a brief period, a member of the gymnastics team. On his third day, Ford unintentionally defied the laws of gravity and flipped off the trampoline, landing squarely on the gymnasium's parquet floor. He sustained a fracture to his tailbone, an injury he still suffers from today.

Before graduating in 1960 (five years ahead of the younger Hillary Rodham Clinton), Ford acquired a number of reputations for himself. The first was one that inspired envy throughout much of the school's male population. Preferring the company of women, Ford became extremely popular with members of the opposite sex, thereby creating undesired opposition by jealous members of the *same* sex.

Mistakenly labeled as "a wimp," Ford willingly lived up to his reputation by allowing himself to be bullied. For a long time, the future actor would participate in a daily ritual that involved being sacrificially thrown down the school's steep hillside.

"Eventually, my beatings were so inevitable that I'd just go to the lot and wait," said Ford.[4]

Rising each time only to be thrown down as an encore, Ford would react without argument or retaliation, causing frustration and dismay among his prepubescent aggressors.

"The entire school would gather to watch this display," recalled Ford. "I don't know why they did it. Maybe because I wouldn't fight the way they wanted me to. They wanted a fight they could win, and my way of winning was just to hang in there."[5]

This particular philosophy endured with Ford until — in a rather uncharacteristic moment of irrepressible aggression — he threw an antagonist down a flight of steps. From that point forth, the only individuals who would ever physically antagonize Harrison Ford were card-carrying members of the Screen Actors Guild or the National Association of Stuntmen. The future of Harrison Ford's pugilistic encounters would exclusively involve those events, dictated by the written lines of a screenplay.

2

The Origin of His Species

Submitting his application to Wisconsin's Ripon College, Harrison Ford was accepted and admitted into the Fall 1960 academic program.

Having applied to various other colleges in the mid-western region, Ford joked that his prior academic achievements had little to do with his ultimate acceptance to Ripon: "I think my high school adviser went skiing with their director of admission. I always got along with my adviser, even with his standard line, 'You're smarter than this, why aren't you doing better?'"[1]

Due in part to his ongoing questions concerning the complexities of religion and his boyhood interest in American history—namely his favorite subject, Abraham Lincoln—Ford focused on Philosophy and English.

While there, Ford was a brother in the Zeta Tau chapter of Sigma Nu, a now-defunct 29-member fraternity whose motto was to be "invincible against ignorance, regimentation, boorishness, and intolerance. Against confinement of mind or soul, against narrow or selfish views and against forces which would destroy Faith in God and Democracy."[2]

During the vacations nestled between each academic year, Ford found work in and around the Great Lakes region of Illinois. He took turns as a tree trimmer and a floral delivery boy. Claiming that his success stemmed from the initial interview process for each job, Ford fully admitted employing the very same talents he would later wholeheartedly apply to his future profession.

"I'm real polite," he declared. "I know how to sit straight and keep my head up. People think I'm not going to steal from them. Getting jobs is like acting."[3]

Because of a credit line he had taken advantage of and abused (compliments of a clothing shop he'd worked for on occasion), Ford found himself obliged to pay off a large debt he had accumulated during his academic tenure. On occasion, he could be found both on and off campus with a pool cue in hand. With it, he would challenge opponents willing to sacrifice their cherished pay to a game of nine-ball.

With his best friend, fellow fraternity brother and roommate Bill Haljum, he entered the publishing business with his informal answer to Ripon's official publication, *College Days*. *The Mug* offered line drawings by "Harry Ford" and contained text by Haljum and other classmates interested in offering their insights on campus life—how it *was* and the way it *should* be. To cover the cost of materials and printing, the two editors-in-chief solicited local businesses, selling them advertising space.

They accumulated enough money to keep *The Mug* out of the red — and pay off their personal debt as well.

One job that persists in Ford's memory was aboard a yacht on Lake Michigan. He was hired as a chef — a profession he knew next to nothing about. Stealthily he consulted his mother's hand-me-down of *The Joy of Cooking* and the daily culinary column of *The Chicago Tribune,* to which he became a routine caller for advice. Eventually, Ford became an entirely self-taught, seafaring cook.

"The people I worked for were heirs to the Swift meat packing family, and all they ever wanted was dead cow anyway," remembered Ford. "They were very easy to fool. Unfortunately, Lake Michigan can get very choppy. I was deeply seasick most of the time. In retrospect, managing to cook under those circumstances was probably the most heroic thing I've ever done."[4]

In his free time, Ford was a member of a musical trio consisting of himself, Haljum and friend Jeff Thompson. Known to the partygoers for whom they performed as "The Brothers Gross," the group played handmade instruments made from household goods and were likened by Haljum to "the poor man's Kingston Trio." Beer-drinking poker games rounded out the usual festivities, with the ever-goofy Ford holding his hand backwards for all to see.

Despite his eagerness to learn and a personal commitment to discipline himself until his college years were complete, Ford's interest in higher education weakened abruptly and significantly. Initially, Harrison was enlisted in the school's Reserve Officer's Training Corp (ROTC) program, only to drop out because of his refusal to cut his hair and his reluctance to live a regimented lifestyle.

In time, Ford realized he wouldn't be able to pragmatically apply his degree in Philosophy to anything later in life, and his attitude changed during the later months of his senior year. Having exhausted any desire to succeed academically, Ford reduced himself to existing on a diet of pizza and sleeping — even through his classes and exams.

"If it wasn't a clinical depression I was suffering, it was something very close, and for a couple of years," acknowledged the actor. "I was quite capable of sleeping for 20 hours, getting up and ordering a pizza to be delivered to my room, eating the pizza, putting the wrappers in the garbage, and going back to sleep for another 20 hours. The thought of facing classes, tests and other students seemed unbearable. It wasn't a high state of mental health I was in."[5]

Much to the dismay of his parents — who had enthusiastically reserved hotel accommodations just off campus for the graduation ceremony — Ford's opportunity to earn a college diploma was gone. With his poor attendance record and round-figured test scores, Ford learned that he would not graduate from Ripon College just three days before the commencement ceremony. (In 1985 he was offered an honorary degree by the institution, but has declined to accept it.)

"The usual," is what Ford attributed his failure to. "Total academic inadequacy. Lack of attention. Fraud. They had an independent study program, and my plan was to accumulate an entire semester's credits in four days or less, if possible. I remember doing a thesis on the plays of Edward Albee, who seemed like a good choice at that time, in the early 1960s, because he had only written four plays. Of course, my thesis was only four pages long."[6]

Over the immediate horizon was a future of student loans with nothing to show for them. Ford would return to Illinois, tugging along the expected shame and humiliation of failure. Despite this, his four years of enrollment at the small Liberal Arts college did yield one accomplishment from which he would benefit immeasurably: During the final quarter of his senior year, Ford faced his fear of confronting an audience by enrolling in Prof. Richard Bergstrum's drama course.

"All I knew about acting was what I had imagined," said Ford. "My decision to go into acting was mostly a reaction to my friends and college classmates who knew what they were going to do with their entire lives. They were all going off to work in the same office year after year, in the same job — maybe until they got a gold watch. That would be the limit of their life experience. Maybe they'd be doing fantastic things and be very successful, but I just couldn't imagine doing that, the same thing year after year. I thought acting would give me the opportunity to confront new and interesting challenges, to work with certain people on a finite problem within a finite period of time and then do it again with another set of problems, different people."[7]

Atop the wooden floor of the campus' Red Barn Theater, the young actor became involved in a handful of productions. They included the well-known *Three-Penny Opera* and *The Fantastiks*. Most notable was Thornton Wilder's *The Skin of Our Teeth* (March 6, 1964), in which he played a character named George Antrobus. For the role, he burrowed pillows beneath his costume, wore a fake mustache and added a half-pound of talcum powder to his hair for an aged, salt-and-pepper look. Ford recalled being "literally, pushed up there on stage. It scared me. It scared me something fierce."[8]

David Harris, Ripon's Dean of Men, recalled the young student as being "very likable — a fellow with a good sense of humor, unusually courteous, with an underlying seriousness.... Once he knew what was wanted of him, he could perform any way the director called for."[9]

"When I first started acting," remembered Ford, "the main satisfaction came from conquering the fear of actually getting up and doing it. I began to experience the fun of it."[10]

Although the fun would have presumably ended upon Ford's banishment from his graduating class, it did not. Accompanied by his girlfriend Mary Louise Marquardt — a Ripon College honors student — Ford joined the Belfry Players in June 1964 for a season of summer stock. In Williams Bay, Wisconsin, he would begin his journey toward professional acting.

3

Finding His Calling

Within the same walls of the former Mormon church where actor Paul Newman had performed ten years earlier, Ford became a proud and enthusiastic participant of the Belfry Players. Aside from playing bit parts and roles of substance, he helped with the design and construction of the sets. Marquardt worked as the head of ticket sales for the box office and also saw to the construction and painting of various sets. Together they resided in Crane Hall, the building adjoining the theater.

His less-than-luxurious Belfry Players income provided the actor and his girlfriend with little more than basic living accommodations. Yet Ford's chosen lifestyle demonstrated both his devotion to and his genuine passion for his craft.

Of the six plays in which he was involved, his first—a June 26, 1964, production of *Take Her, She's Mine*—marked the start of Harrison Ford's professional acting career.

"I was incredibly miscast, of course," admitted the actor. "Ridiculous. But I never thought it was ridiculous. I just thought if I didn't work my ass off, I was going to make a fool of myself in front of a given number of people."[1]

On the afternoon following his debut performance, Harrison wed Mary during a small ceremony at St. James Church in the town of Mequon, located just north of Milwaukee. Acknowledging his limited future prospects, Ford considered Mary's willingness to marry him to be nothing short of bravery. Attendees included Ford's two favorite college friends and their dates; his brother Terence; and Mary's sister. That night, instead of embarking on a traditional honeymoon, the dedicated Ford appeared in the second performance of *Take Her, She's Mine*.

Despite his participation in *Night of the Iguana* by Tennessee Williams (an amused co-star remembers him forgetting his lines), *Dark of the Moon*, *Sunday in New York*, *Little Mary Sunshine* and *Damn Yankees*, Ford's enthusiasm began to wane. He felt he wasn't able to fully demonstrate the extent of his acting capabilities because he was being offered only "ridiculous parts."

However, Ford undoubtedly appreciated what the Belfry had provided him: namely, on-the-job training. At the Belfry he received his first real "acting lessons" and his learning curve was immense.

Throughout the months of acting in consecutive nightly performances, Ford believed he matured significantly—from encountering and conquering his initial stage fright to the eventual desire to land more involved roles. By September of that year, he and his wife decided that he should take the next step and make the bold transition from stage to screen. It was a decision that meant a journey out of northern Wisconsin.

4

HAVE WIFE, WILL TRAVEL

When Harrison and Mary first arrived at the Southern California coastline in the winter of 1964, intimidation and fear were undoubtedly their prominent emotions. In the hills of Laguna Canyon, just 60 miles south of the city of Los Angeles, Harrison and Mary Ford successfully found employment, as well as an affordable ($75-a-month) apartment.

While a resident of the art community, Ford worked as a salesman at a local paint supply store, became a rigger aboard the America's Cup yacht *Columbia*, and was a late-night pizza maker in Hollywood. The latter job which provided him with just the right kind of stimulation he was seeking at that time in his life.

"Nobody cared or knew who I was," he would later explain. "I didn't have to make polite chat or pretend to be anything other than a chef. Nobody ever said anything more to me than, 'Deep crust with cheese and pepperoni.' That gave me a lot of time alone with my own thoughts."[1]

In nearby Santa Ana, he was an assistant buyer of knickknacks and oil paintings at the upper-crust department store Bullock's. "I must have said something that led them to believe retail sales would be my life," joked Ford.[2]

While employed at that store, an event occurred that left its mark upon the 21-year-old Ford. While attempting to fasten the seat belt of his newly acquired Volvo on the way to work, Ford inadvertently veered off the canyon road, over a curbside and into a utility pole. Ford was thrust face-first into the steering wheel.

"I remember vividly that although my car was in the middle of the road, no one would stop," said the actor. "They would just creep around me at five miles an hour and keep on going. I was just standing in the road, bleeding quite profusely. It pissed me off so much that no one would stop that I refused to gesture to them. So I stood there until somebody finally stopped and took me to the hospital."[3]

Ford was treated and soon released with several stitches and a bottle of painkillers. Because the wound was situated where movement occurred with each word spoken, it did not heal as Ford would have liked. The accident left him with a two-inch lateral scar on his chin. This reminder of that fateful day would evolve into his most distinguished and identifiable characteristic. In the years following, it would become his most frequently airbrushed feature and the one that is made most prominent in his caricatures.

In February 1965, Ford responded to an open casting call held by a local theater group at the Laguna Beach Playhouse. Ford won the coveted role of Southern soldier Clay Wingate in Stephen Vincent Benet's Pulitzer Prize–winning epic *John Brown's Body*. Due to the scarcity of actors in the area, he also took on two other less notable characters. *John Brown's Body* sold out performances for nearly two weeks. Throughout its run, Ford received many accolades, most notably from several of the area's newspapers.

Roy A. McCann wrote in his March 16, 1965, "McCanny Notes" that it was the simple presence of the young actor who so impressed him and kept his attention fixed: "The surprise of the evening for me was the tremendous talent of Harry Ford, who literally cast a shadow over all others on stage when he would speak. Here is a boy who looks like a youngster, but acts like a veteran. His speaking voice is such that we should be hearing it on TV or in professional theater before too long. He's a great talent."[4]

Critic Ellen Torgerson considered Ford's "a startlingly good debut" and wrote that he delivered his part "with the seemingly casual correctness and rich passion of the naturally talented actor. Handsome, debonair, arrogant, and elegant, Ford's Wingate is a neat pleasure to see and hear."[5]

Among the enthusiastic onlookers was Hollywood composer Ian Bernard, who lent his services to the production. Bernard contacted an associate at Columbia Pictures and suggested that Ford be granted an interview with a studio executive. Immediately upon Ford's arrival at the studios (then located on Gower Street in Los Angeles), he was sent into a waiting room, where he anxiously sat before being called into an office where the head of Columbia's casting department awaited.

Ford was greeted by Barry Gordon, a gentleman stereotypical of the Hollywood moguls of that era — squat, bald, and smoking a cigar. Greeting the 21-year-old actor, Gordon and his assistant asked Ford about his height, weight, whether he could speak any foreign languages, and whether he was capable of riding a horse. Then he was abruptly shown the door, with the assurance that if his services were ever required, he would be contacted.

Discouraged, Ford began his somber journey through the studio corridors toward the building's elevators. From there, his intent was to continue through the main entrance out into the fresh California air, where he would clear his head. But a brief detour to the men's room turned out to be a timely stroke of luck: On his way back to the elevators following the stop, he was ecstatically approached by one of the individuals who had interviewed him just moments earlier. Greatly relieved, the assistant requested that Ford return to the very office from which he had been trying to escape.

"I knew right from the beginning," claimed Ford, "that if I had gone down to the elevator instead of going to take a pee, it wouldn't have been worth chasing me down the street."[6]

5

THE LONG AND WINDING ROAD

Harrison Ford had become the newest member of the Columbia Pictures team. In the spring of 1965, he signed a contract entitling him to $150 a week for seven years, thus officially classifying him as a "contract player." Admitting to a complete ignorance of the system, the naïve young actor was initially under the impression that it was *he* who had to pay the *studio*.

"I started at Columbia Pictures at $150 a week," he said, "and I enjoyed all the respect that it implies. I think mail clerks were making more money. I wasn't worth more than $150 a week, to tell you the truth."[1]

Ford enrolled in Columbia's "New Talent" program. Along with 11 other young members, he underwent a series of morally debilitating trials which were intended to create talent by means of what he considered a "horrible" and "factory-like" atmosphere and attitude.[2]

"It was 1964–65 and Columbia was still playing 1920–30," recalled the actor. "You had to come to the studio every day attired in jacket and tie, go to acting class, eat in the executive dining room, submit yourself to photo layouts—six starlets and six fellas playing football on a Malibu beach in front of a Chevrolet Nova for *Argosy* magazine.... Nobody knew your name or cared a damn about you. I went nuts! ... All the studios were making their biggest films in Europe, everybody in Hollywood was taking acid and smoking dope, and I was a baby actor getting nowhere."[3]

His daily grind consisted of attending classes which completely eliminated any opportunity to exercise individuality with their "don't think, just do" approach—and having his hair cut in a pompadour style as part of an obvious tribute to Elvis Presley. Early publicity photos were touched up to eliminate the scar on his chin, hoping to make his mug more presentable.

"They gave me enough money to pay the rent," remembered Ford, "but the attitude that they could manufacture a star from raw material was silly. Styling your hair, dressing you—it was all so deadly wrong, calculated to remove all those particularities which made you interesting in the first place ... I was sure that the most important thing for an actor was to hold on to what was individual about himself."[4]

It was also during this period that the studio recommended that Ford change his screen name, because they felt that "Harrison Ford" sounded too pretentious. Fighting fire with fire, he offered his own suggestion: Kurt Affair.

The studio—and the Screen Actors Guild—also put pressure on Ford to change his name because of another actor named Harrison Ford, who had passed away years earlier. (Much like the Harrison Ford of our generation, this handsome silent screen actor was described by Hollywood insiders as one who couldn't be any less interested in the industry in which he was employed. The first Harrison Ford, who died in 1957 at the age of 73, was immortalized with a star honoring his place in film history on Hollywood's Walk of Fame.)

Due to the complexities of having two people with identical names in the same business, SAG insisted that the living Harrison Ford rethink his moniker. Ford appeased their insistence by offering to include a bogus middle initial in his name. As a result, his first two cinematic appearances credited him as Harrison J. Ford.

Just when all hope for showcasing his acting skills seemed to fade, Ford learned that he had a shot in an upcoming motion picture. As it turned out, the young, down-and-out actor won the role of a bellboy in the 1966 film *Dead Heat on a Merry-Go-Round* starring James Coburn.

Upon its release, the film did reasonably well — about $3 million in ticket sales. Based on its $2 million budget, it was deemed profitable. *Dead Heat* told the story of Eli Kotch (Coburn), a con man who employs his ingenious scheming and charming personality to the fullest in an attempt to pull off a bank heist at Los Angeles International Airport.

Ford's role as a bellboy required him to walk onto the scene and deliver a few lines of dialogue to the waiting Coburn — which amounted to less than one minute of screen time. Dishearteningly, in the end it was not significant enough to even earn him a mention during the closing credits. However uneventful the role or the film was then — and no matter how inconspicuously it now stands in the history books — *Dead Heat on a Merry-Go-Round* was an historic occasion in that it marked the motion picture debut of Harrison Ford.

Excited at the idea of finally being considered for the big screen, Ford's elation was short-lived. Before the film was released, a copy was sent to the studio vice-president, who called Ford into his office to chastise him for his performance. Ford can recall the conversation vividly. It marked the first and only time anyone verbally told him that professional acting was a waste of his time and efforts.

The executive proceeded to tell Ford the tale of the first time anyone had seen Tony Curtis. In Curtis' debut film, he was charged with the simple job of delivering a bag of groceries. The talent scout who had been watching this delivery boy made the distinction that Curtis was in fact not a delivery boy as he was meant to portray, but in fact a genuine movie star.

Stupefied, Ford leaned forward and stated that he thought Curtis was supposed to act like a grocery delivery boy — and not a movie star.

Considering the period and manner in which the actor stated his case, Ford's words were undoubtedly viewed as sarcasm and not an innocent translation of what he honestly believed to be true. Whether or not Ford was correct, he was wrong in the opinion of the executive.

"Crime pays," as they say. And for Ford's refusal to act like a movie star while delivering Coburn his message, he was subjected to another six agonizing months of classroom training.

A young Harrison Ford and unidentified actress on the set of *Dead Heat on a Merry-Go-Round* (Columbia, 1966).

Years later, when Ford's visage was just as recognized throughout Tinseltown as his name, a waiter approached him during a party with a silver tray. On the tray was a card, which the waiter handed to him. Written and signed by the executive who dismissed the young actor years earlier, it contained one simple sentence: "I missed."[5]

6

ODDS AND ENDS

The crisis in Vietnam had young men nationwide considering their future—some with optimism, others with fear of the unknown. For those who were able, it was only a matter of time before they were called to duty.

As he was no longer a student and didn't yet have children, next to nothing would render Harrison Ford exempt from the draft. So he tried to dream up ideas to avoid service. He submitted a letter to the draft board with an onslaught of thoughts involving his moral and religious beliefs that more than likely left the board unable to grasp just what his true intent was. Although he had always believed it, he was about to find out whether the pen was, in fact, mightier than the sword.

"I confused them so badly that they never took action on my petition. My conscientious objection wasn't based on a history of religious affiliation, which made it difficult at the time. I went back to my philosophy training from college. I remembered Paul Tillich's phrase, 'If you have trouble with the word God, take whatever is central or most meaningful to your life and call that God.' I always had trouble with the notion of God in a stand-up form. So I developed a thesis and took the Biblical injunction to love thy neighbor as thyself as the central and most meaningful thing in my life. I combined it all and typed for days and sent it off and never heard a word. Never got called in."[1]

During the ensuing months, while still at Columbia, Ford was cast in a handful of uninspiring and publicly ignored movies, two of which appeared in 1967: *Luv* and *The Long Ride Home* (a.k.a. *A Time for Killing*).

Luv starred Jack Lemmon, Peter Falk and Elaine May. Considering its inspiration, the hugely successful 1964 Broadway and international play of the same name by Murray Shisgal, the film version became the antithesis of the romantic stage comedy. In the film, Ford portrayed a hippie (complete with a beret and a fur vest) whose convertible is accidentally backed into by a vehicle driven by May. Ford's character approaches May's, says hello to the woman, reaches over and punches her passenger (Lemmon) square on the nose before returning to his car. When the closing credits rolled, Ford's name was nowhere to be seen.

A Time for Killing was filmed on location along the dusty trails of Kanab, Utah, during the autumn of 1966. It was a Western headlined by Glenn Ford, George Hamilton and Inger Stevens. Initially released as *The Long Ride Home*, it told the story of an escaped prisoner (Hamilton) who is determined—despite his knowledge that the

Civil War has officially ended—to exact revenge on his captor, Major Charles Wolcott (Glenn Ford).

Sentimentally significant as Glenn Ford's one hundredth motion picture, *Killing* was Harrison J. Ford's third role. In it he portrayed Lt. Schaffer, a Union officer reluctant to follow through with his orders to execute a Confederate prisoner by firing squad, enticing the other prisoners to riot and escape. Despite providing Harrison with his largest amount of screen time thus far, he was limited to mostly physical acting, since his only dialogue was the word "Fire."

Killing marked the first time a Harrison Ford character died (albeit off-screen). It was another film that succumbed at the box office because of poor reviews and the fact that it was the bottom half of a double-bill in theatres.

Like many movie actors, Ford was looking for his big break to propel him out of auditions and minor acting roles and into the lifestyle of a successful actor. To audition for director John Schlesinger, Ford flew 3,000 miles to New York City, hoping to land the role that would enable him to display his talent and subsequently prove his worth to the industry. Hopeful that the director would at least consider him after paying for the flight himself, the young actor was again turned down. The role of Joe Buck in a project later known as *Midnight Cowboy* went to actor Jon Voight.

Eighteen months after Ford signed up at the studio, Columbia elected to terminate his tenure prematurely. As Ford recalled, the way the studio let him go was neither professional nor pleasant. While studio head Mike Frankovich was dealing with business in Europe, he assigned the reevaluation of Ford's contract option to Jerry Tokovsky. As Ford recalled, Tokovsky, an agent-turned-producer, said, "Kid, when Frankovich is back, I'm going to tell him we ought to get rid of you. I don't think you're worth a thing to us. But I know your wife is pregnant, you need the money, so I'll give you another couple of weeks. Just sign the piece of paper my secretary has. Okay, boy? Now, get out of here."[2]

Retaliating with a barrage of verbal insults (and refusing to sign the paperwork), Ford was terminated from his short-lived status as a "contract player" at Columbia Pictures. No more than three days later, Ford signed under a similar contract deal with Universal.

During the late 1960s and early 1970s, Ford was often dissatisfied and, as a result, unemployed in both television and motion pictures. Despite the lack of work, he did manage to maintain a close relationship with the industry through trade contacts.

The former manager of the Rolling Stones, Earl McGrath (who owned and operated a Los Angeles–based art gallery at the time Ford met him), suggested that Ford put his profession in front of the camera on hold and temporarily take on work *behind* one.

In 1969, director Paul Ferrara hired the struggling actor to serve as his second unit cameraman for *Feast of Friends*, an upcoming documentary on Jim Morrison and the Doors. For the band's fans, it was a welcome offering of behind-the-scenes and on-stage antics of the most notorious Southern California band since the Beach Boys. For Ford, it was a foray into professional photography that would not be soon forgotten. "When it was over, I was one step away from joining a Jesuit monastery.

I couldn't keep up with those guys: it was too much! ... I don't think any of it was in focus—not a bit of it."[3]

While the quantity of Hollywood Westerns remained consistently strong throughout the 1960s and early to mid–1970s, the quality of Western roles that Ford was offered did not improve over time. Ford knew he had to pay his dues to succeed. So he persevered and continued to accept them.

By March 1967, when he was assigned a role in Universal's Western drama *Journey to Shiloh*, Ford had another reason to graciously accept *anything* sent his way: The previous autumn, his first son Benjamin had been born. With that came the need for an increased income to support a family of three.

Originally intended for television, *Shiloh* (based on a novel by Will Henry) suffered from below-average production values. In fact, the filmmakers ventured no farther than the film studio's back lot to shoot it. When the film was released in March 1968, those viewers who remained in their seats long enough for this bottom half of a double-bill saw a long-haired Harrison Ford playing Willie Bill Bearden. Along with the six other actors who made up *Shiloh*'s group of young Texans (advertised as "The Unstoppable Seven"), Ford follows Confederate Gen. Hood in pursuit of fighting glory, only to become disillusioned by the insanity of war.

Working with an actor like James Caan (in his first starring role) was a new experience for Ford. But his collaboration with actor Paul Petersen made the experience more bearable (they had previously worked together on *A Time for Killing*). Although both were still residing at the base of the Hollywood totem pole, Petersen saw something in Ford that convinced him that Ford's success would come with time and patience: "He was there and he was paying attention. Even in rehearsals he was intense. Harrison would practice throwing a knife until he was perfect each time."[4]

Released in April 1970 was Columbia Pictures' *Getting Straight*. Elliot Gould—known for his roles in *M*A*S*H** and *Bob & Carol & Ted & Alice*—led the cast as a thirtysomething former activist named Harry who returns to college as a student to earn his Masters degree. There he becomes embroiled in a student uprising against the government. Beside him is his fellow activist-girlfriend Jan, played by Candice Bergen.

Getting Straight was filmed on location on the Lane Community College campus in Eugene, Oregon, where hundreds of members of the student body and faculty were cast as students, National Guard Members and in other bit roles. Ford, 27, played Jake, a student who hosts a party attended by Harry and Jan.

The film was a relative success, considering the underlying subject matter dealt with topical themes like Communism and the Vietnam War. Grateful for the college's cooperation, Columbia Pictures introduced a new course to the college's roster involving the study of film theory and cinematic history. Its premiere meeting was hosted by the film's cast and crew.

In addition to acting in films, Ford made several TV appearances between 1967 and 1974. The actor guest starred on such popular titles as *The Virginian* and *Ironside*. In 1969 he appeared in "The Hazing" episode of *My Friend Tony*. And in 1971 he acted in an episode of the short-lived *Dan August* series alongside Burt Reynolds and an actor with whom he would appear in a certain film nine years later, Billy Dee

Williams. He was also on *Kung Fu*, *Petrocelli* and two episodes of *Gunsmoke*. But Ford has especially fond memories of his part in *Love, American Style*.

He recalled that he had been given little time to prepare his wardrobe for the role of a philosophical hippie in the November 24, 1969, installment "Love and the Former Marriage." Ford appeared on the set with long hair and a beard, thinking both were appropriate for the role. He was surprised when he was told he required a haircut and trim, then outfitted with a navy blue shirt with a high collar and contrasting white stitching and a pair of vinyl burgundy jeans supported by an oversized belt.

"They even had a scarf with a little ring to put around my neck," remembered Ford. "And I thought, 'Somebody has clearly made a mistake here.' So, rather than argue with the wardrobe people, I just put on these clothes and went looking for the producer to point out that I'd been mis-costumed. I walked onto the set and somebody directed me to a man standing with his back to me. I tapped him on the shoulder and, when he turned around, I saw he was wearing the same thing I was. He was a hippie producer, I guess. A Hollywood hippie. At least the check went through when I got paid."[5]

In 1966, Italian director Michelangelo Antonioni graced the predominantly European art film world with his now-legendary vision, *Blow Up*. When the announcement came that he was following up that film with his first movie in America, the feeling among the American film industry was pure excitement. The new film, *Zabriskie Point*, dealt with Southern California's counterculture of the late '60s.

Fred Roos, a Hollywood producer who had faith in Ford and believed him to be enormously talented, approached Antonioni and suggested Ford for the disillusioned and angry lead role. Roos thought that the young actor was "on-the-money perfect for the part."[6]

Unimpressed with Ford's resumé, the director did recognize what Roos' young apprentice embodied but hadn't yet been able to show on film. As Roos explained, "He was not a leading man in the way they thought of leading men at the time. The strongest quality I saw was his great sense of masculinity. There was a kind of dangerous intensity that he had, and combined with all that was this droll sense of humor. And then he had extreme confidence, but nothing braggadocio, just an air of confidence. I was so bitterly disappointed when I couldn't convince Michelangelo."[7]

Despite Roos' assurance that the actor would eventually rise to greatness, Roos did have reservations about Ford's attitude: "Harrison was not conventionally good-looking," said Roos. "He was also tight-lipped, standoffish, and most people though he had an attitude. He's an incredibly cranky guy. But I though he was going to be a star. And we got along famously."[8]

Remaining respectful of Roos' consideration for the casting, Antonioni — who wrote the initial screenplay before up-and-coming playwright Sam Shepard fine-tuned it — saw to it that Ford received a role in the film. Ford was summoned for a few days' worth of work as a character in the film's airport sequence.

The muddled *Zabriskie Point*, a $7 million investment, failed to grasp audiences as firmly as his previous film, earning a pathetic $1 million. The entire sequence in which Ford appeared was completely eliminated in the film's cutting stages.

Ford contributed somewhat more successfully to television movies, including *The Intruders* (1970), author James Michener's nineteenth-century pioneer tale *Dynasty* (1976) and *The Possessed* (1977).

In 1975, acclaimed director Stanley Kramer (*The Caine Mutiny*; *Judgment at Nuremburg*; *High Noon*) personally selected Ford to take part in *Judgment: The Court Martial of Lt. William Calley* (a.k.a. *The Trial of Lt. Calley*) a courtroom drama. It was based on the true account of an American officer on trial for questionable actions involving the destruction of an entire village in the My Lai province during the Vietnam conflict.

Impressed by Ford's film and television work, Kramer allowed Ford to choose whichever un-cast role he wanted. Initially, the actor took a liking to the role of Calley himself, but it had already been assigned to Tony Musante. Ford ultimately selected the role of a G.I. under Calley's command who takes the stand as a witness to the atrocities. Kramer singled out that character as the most difficult to portray.

"I couldn't comprehend it," the actor would later remark about Calley's actions. "I could never imagine it happening to me. What I could imagine was being under his command, seeing it happen and not being strong enough to stop it."[9]

Critics singled out Ford's performance as the emotional highlight of the entire production. Director Kramer was startled to find his young player "absolutely wonderful. He was an intense, tremendously sensitive actor [who] "hasn't even scratched the surface yet."[10]

In *The Possessed*, Ford played college biology professor Paul Winjam, who was simultaneously seeing both his boss (the institution's principal) and one of his students. Before his character was scheduled to spontaneously combust into a ball of flames, Ford offered to add his own dash of realism.

During a scene in which he was to lecture his predominantly female class on spiders, the actor realized that "real fear of the spiders was a crucial element. So I read up about spiders and I bought a tarantula. But when I took it to the set in a coffee tin, the director went wild."[11]

So Ford played the scene as it was written. In it, he gallantly impressed his students with his fearless handling of the deadly spider–courtesy of a ball of knitting wool the prop man had concocted.

7

The Do-It-Yourself Man

By 1970, the Fords had two sons—Benjamin, born in 1967, and Willard, born two years later—and a home in the Hollywood Hills. (They purchased their split-level, three-bedroom house on Woodrow Wilson Drive for $18,500.) The house needed repairs and Ford chose to tackle the job himself.

"I decided I would take down all of the things I didn't like," he told Larry King in 1995, "and when I finished, there wasn't much house left ... a few windows and whatever was necessary to hold up the outside. Everything else was gone."[1]

Visiting nearby Encino Public Library, Ford studied and eventually mastered the art of carpentry. "To me, one of the attractions of carpentry is that it's simple and logical," said Ford. "You start at one place and step by step you end up with the finished project. It's a functional science, and it becomes a form of meditation—the mind is absorbed in simple tasks, you are no longer wrestling with your mind."[2]

With his income remaining unchanged despite the escalating costs of supporting his growing family, the actor elected to pursue his carpentry skills to supplement his acting paycheck. Having this alternate stream of money coming in would allow Ford to pick and choose the acting projects he felt would ultimately advance his career. While he understood the basics of woodworking, the actor recalled intentionally starting jobs high above the homeowners, perched on their rooftop out of sight, with book in hand.

"I was more dependent on my library card than I was on my actual known skills," admitted the actor.[3] But by the mid–70s, Ford was known as the "carpenter to the stars."

His first job of substance came in 1972 following a request by Brazilian composer-producer Sergio Mendes to convert his three-car garage in Encino into a recording studio. Budgeting the project at $100,000, Ford hired a crew (who embarrassingly knew more than he did) and oversaw both its construction and assisted in its overall design.

The studio took nearly six months to construct. Its interior consisted of soundproofed walls, handcrafted hardwood floors and stained glass windows purchased from a Tennessee mausoleum. As Mendes recalled: "A friend of mine had recommended him for the job. He seemed to know what he was talking about, even though he had no papers that indicated that he was a carpenter. He seemed to take a lot of care in what he was doing, and I like that. I hate to use the word 'perfectionist,' but he was very careful and neat and did a great job. During his break time, he would read books about carpentry, as well as film scripts...."[4]

No sooner had Ford completed the studio than phone calls for more work started coming in. "Carpentry gave me something to do so that when I did go to auditions, I went as a busy person with only a few moments to spare, rather than as a hungry man with all the time in the world."[5]

Ford's brother Terence was also a struggling actor at the time. As a favor, he worked for his brother on various jobs and was astonished at Harrison's professionalism and craftsmanship: "He was one of the best finish carpenters I've ever seen. Cabinetry, molding, hanging doors. And he was a builder. He poured the foundations and framed the houses. He went from beginning to end on a project, and he wouldn't do anything wrong. He was meticulous."[6]

Eventually Ford's clientele roster included Richard Dreyfuss, Sally Kellerman, James Caan, Glenn Ford, Talia Shire, Fred Roos, Doors keyboardist Ray Manzarek, James Coburn, John Gregory Dunne, Joan Didion, Valerie Harper and others.

The ornate wall-to-wall bookcase constructed for director Richard Fleisher stands today as "The Harrison Ford Memorial Library" in homage to the man who built it decades earlier. For actor and neighbor David Sommerville, Ford assisted in preventing his home from falling down a hill, courtesy of a structure jokingly named "The Ford Foundation."

While Ford was honing his woodworking skills, he was also nailing down his other career. At the suggestion of producer Fred Roos, he reluctantly made an appointment to meet with a professional manager. Connecticut-born former model Patricia McQueeney was then an accomplished Hollywood agent, representing actors on behalf of Compass Management. There she maintained a clientele list of newcomers including Cindy Williams, Teri Garr, Charles Martin Smith, Frederic Forrest, Candy Clarke and Mackenzie Phillips.

Ford's misgivings were obvious when he arrived at her office in his carpenter clothes. "He sat on the couch in my office with his hands clasped between his knees and his head down," said McQueeney, "and I sat there looking at him thinking: 'What in the world am I going to do with him?' And I knew he was sitting there thinking: 'What has Fred Roos gotten me into?'"[7]

Ford eventually committed to McQueeney, allowing her to take the reins of his professional life. Ford and McQueeney are still partners. One thing has changed, however: Ford is now her sole client. In January 2000, Ford and McQueeney hired United Talent Agency (UTA) to better assist them in discovering worthy projects for the actor.

In 1987, she was honored for her services by the Conference of Personal Managers. She claims that the simple term "manager" does not fully cover all the groundwork it actually entails: "There is more to being a manager than suggesting career choices. We provide a personal service, which sometimes involves decisions about marriage, divorce, investments, lifestyle, living arrangements and a hundred other things."[8]

Looking back, McQueeney said, "Harrison always had enormous dignity and was extremely smart. If he didn't like a role that I gave him, he would just turn it down. And sometimes they were good jobs, very lucrative. But they were television jobs, and he wouldn't tie himself up with a series. He had two little boys and a mortgage, but he'd say: 'No, I'm not going to do it. I'll go build a cabinet.'"[9]

Ford became quite good at his alternate profession. Despite his admiration for carpentry work, though, thoughts of acting were never far from his mind: "Through carpentry I fed my family and began to pick and choose from among the roles offered. I could afford to hold out until something better came along. But I never gave up my ambition to be an actor. I was frustrated but never felt defeated by my frustration."[10]

As the actor passed on several roles offered to him throughout the late '60s and early '70s, he prepared a substitute plan to open a furniture factory as a remedy for the worst case scenario; he was ready to begin production at a moment's notice, if need be. Yet, in 1972 one script sent via Fred Roos made such an impact on him that he actually took the time to meet with the film's up-and-coming director, George Lucas.

Although enthused by the quality of the material Lucas presented, Ford still had reservations. Realizing that if he were to submit to their offer of $485 for the 28 nights of principal photography, he would suffer a 50 percent loss of pay from what he might otherwise make in his carpentry business in that same amount of time.

Lucas increased his rate of pay by a then-considerable $15 per week.

The film was *American Graffiti*. Soon industry executives would have a new outlook on Ford as a serious actor.

8
FINALLY ... RESPECT

The year 1973 provided cinemagoers with temporary relief from the tumultuous reality surrounding them. With Richard Nixon's resignation and the American public's refusal to support the escalation of military force in Vietnam, local cinemas became the ideal form of escape. *The Exorcist, Enter the Dragon, Magnum Force* and *Mean Streets* all premiered that year. And director George Lucas released *American Graffiti,* a movie that would ask all of its viewers, "Where were you in '62?"

"I decided it was time to make a movie where people felt better coming out of the theater than they did when they went in," said Lucas. "It had become depressing to go to the movies."[1] Lucas claimed his other reason for doing the film was to prove to his father that the years spent cruising Tenth Avenue in Modesto as a teen weren't all for naught.

Graffiti was based entirely on Lucas' experiences as a wide-eyed youth in a small Northern California town. Lucas, Gloria Katz and Willard Huyck wrote the screenplay depicting people Lucas knew at one time and situations he was once a part of.

Fresh off the commercial failure of his 1971 science fiction film *THX-1138*, Lucas realized that it was make-or-break time. If *Graffiti* proved to be the creative and financial miscarriage its predecessor had been, the likelihood of again setting foot in Hollywood as a director would be diminished, if not altogether eliminated.

Ceaseless 1950s rock 'n' roll, complemented by vintage cars of the same era, were the driving forces behind the film. "*American Graffiti* is a musical," the director explained in his first proposal. "It has singing and dancing, but it is not a musical in the traditional sense because the characters in the film neither sing nor dance."[2]

Initially, Lucas had great difficulty finding a studio willing to financially back his project. But the director convinced Universal Pictures to agree to do the film. Lucas had to meet certain criteria: An established individual would assist in producing it, and its cost would not exceed $1 million.

Francis Ford Coppola, who attended the University of Southern California film school with Lucas and acted as executive producer on Lucas' *THX-1138*, was elected to act as *American Graffiti*'s producer. The budget was approximately $750,000 — $50,000 of which went to Lucas for his writing and directing efforts. The director originally intended to include about 80 songs, but only 45 songs made it in. Lucas used up nearly $90,000 of the given budget for the music rights.[3]

Coppola balked at spending that amount of money on the soundtrack, but eventually submitted to Lucas' insistence that the film's score was vital to telling the story. The producer also disliked the film's title and urged Lucas to change it to *Rock Around the Block*, again to no avail.

Lucas and Coppola spent a great deal of time and effort casting the film's central circle of friends. When the initial casting was complete, the individuals in front of the camera were relative unknowns. *American Graffiti* would prove to be the launching pad for many famous faces.

Eighteen-year-old, freckle-faced Ron Howard (former child star of TV's *The Andy Griffith Show*) was selected to portray the college-bound Steve. Today, he is one of the industry's most successful directors. His girlfriend Laurie was portrayed by 25-year-old *Laverne and Shirley* co-star Cindy Williams. Acclaimed actor Richard Dreyfuss lent his services as Curt, and Charles Martin Smith portrayed the bespectacled dork Terry. Other actors included former professional boxer Paul LeMatt as John Milner; Bo Hopkins as Joe, the tough leader of the Pharoahs; Wolfman Jack as the late-night deejay; 12-year-old Mackenzie Phillips as Carol; Kathleen Quinlan as Peg; Suzanne Somers (in her first credited professional acting assignment as Blonde in T-Bird); and Chicago native Harrison Ford as the built-for-speed bad-ass, Bob Falfa.

American Graffiti began principal photography in the town of San Rafael, California, on June 26, 1972. Because most of it took place at night, filming had to be done in the late hours while the city slept. The cameras rolled from 9 P.M. until dawn on thruways blocked off by the city (for $300 per night). The vintage automobiles seen throughout the film were gathered from collectors all over the state, who rented them for $25 per evening of filming.

At the outset, things seemed to go just as planned. The first of many problems came up during the second night, when a local bar proprietor complained that the filming was affecting his business. As a result, five days after the commencement of principal photography, Lucas and his crew relocated 20 miles north to the town of Petaluma. Petaluma's citizens and business owners were more than proud to play host to a genuine Hollywood production.

Other problems plagued the production, however. There was the expected equipment failure; one crew member was arrested for growing marijuana. A fire shut down the production and forced a temporary relocation. And an assistant cameraman fell off the back of a trailer and landed beneath the moving wheels of Paul LeMatt's yellow 1932 Deuce Coup Roadster (license plate THX-1138 — an homage to Lucas's first film). Fortunately, he survived to tell his tale.

By the last day of photography, the cast and crew were exhausted — just as the film's characters who had spent the night socializing were to be portrayed. "It was fun," recalled Ford. "It was like a party, but not a Hollywood party. It was a real low-budget movie, even for those days. I only got a couple hundred dollars a week. There were no dressing rooms. The actors sat in the same trailer as the costumes."[4] The budget was so tight, in fact, that Ford was once chastised when he took a second doughnut from the catering table.

The actor recalled how hard Lucas worked — and how stressful it was for him not to have the most basic camera equipment. The budget was so controlled that the

Ford's first collaboration with George Lucas, as hot-rodder Bob Falfa in *American Graffiti* (Universal, 1973), shown here with Debralee Scott.

director rented a U-Haul trailer to pull a car with a cameraman crouched in its trunk due to the lack of an actual camera car.

Harrison Ford was the oldest and most experienced cast member. He served as the "unofficial den daddy" to the other actors as they waited long hours to appear before the cameras. They would vent their anxieties by racing to the top of the local Holiday Inn sign and urinating in the ice machines (Ford has sworn he did not take part in the latter). They would also toss empty beer bottles off their balconies onto the hotel's parking lot below. At one point, the director recalled, one of the actors set his motel room aflame. Frustrated and concerned for their property, the hotel management demanded that Ford be transferred to the nearby Howard Johnson motel, removed from the rest of the crew.

When not filming, Ford would sometimes be found drinking beer while relaxing in the comfort and safety of his character's 1955 Chevy.

"He was a little bit on the wild side," recalled Lucas. "We shot all night — it was pretty boring — and he had a tendency to drink a few beers and get in the Chevy ... and race up and down the streets. The police who were on the picture kept threatening to impound the car and take him downtown."[5]

Although Ford and LeMatt's on-screen characters were rivals, their relationship off-camera was the exact opposite. Their hijinks included pushing an unsuspecting Richard Dreyfuss into the hotel pool from a balcony. Dreyfuss connected with the shallow end of the pool, resulting in an awkward and inconveniently located scratch on his forehead.

"I was a bit of a carouser in those days," admitted Ford. "And I was in the company of other hell-raisers. If I'd been in the company of priests, I would have behaved differently."[6]

Although Ford's activities angered the young director, Lucas saw something special in the young hellion. From the early moments of the film's pre-production, Lucas was impressed with Ford's passion for the project. While discussing how the character of Bob Falfa should present himself, Lucas and Ford were at odds. Lucas envisioned Falfa's head as close-cropped in true military fashion. But Ford thought it would be more appropriate for Falfa to be topped with a white cowboy hat. He felt the hat would successfully promote a "sort of shit-kicker–cowboy–truck driver-type" appearance.

"Yeah," the director ultimately said, "I knew guys like that in high school— guys who always wore those hats. Yeah, that's a good idea. Let's try it."[7]

In his desire to add yet more depth to his character, the actor chose to sing a song to woo his passenger Laurie (Williams) in the film. As a friend of Don Everly of the famed Everly Brothers, Ford elected to sing one of their songs. Following several unsuccessful attempts, however, the actor settled on a song from the musical *South Pacific*.

And so Harrison Ford sat in his 1955 Chevy and belted out "Some Enchanted Evening." Some criticized the rendition as an insult to the original lyricist Ezio Pinza. It was apparent that Ford suffered from severe tone-deafness, and he was further ridiculed for his poor attempts to ad-lib the lyrics he didn't know. Furthermore, the song's original composer and writer, Richard Rodgers, denied Lucas permission to use it, as he felt that the scene besmirched his (and his late partner Oscar Hammerstein's) talents. Despite the pleading of many concerned parties to remove the entire sequence, Ford's cinematic singing debut made its way into the film's 1978 theatrical re-release. (It was not in the film's original 1973 release.)

American Graffiti opened in theaters on August 1, 1973. Almost instantly, word of mouth attracted so many filmgoers that it became the highest grossing film in history. *Graffiti* eventually sold nearly $117 million worth of tickets domestically. One analyst claimed that for each dollar Universal spent on its production, the film earned back $50. The soundtrack was also a phenomenal success; it sold an estimated 100,000 copies during the first two weeks of the film's release.[8]

"It didn't actually explode," said Universal Pictures executive Ned Tanen. "It was never that huge a hit. It just stayed in theaters for, like, two years. They had birthday parties for it. It just ran and ran forever."[9]

Lucas' former USC classmate Steven Spielberg (who would later collaborate with Lucas on the creation of the popular *Indiana Jones* trilogy) summed up his feelings about *American Graffiti* following an advance screening: "It hit a chord of nostalgia, because it was such a warm nod backward. It was for George's, mine, everybody's generation."[10]

Graffiti won Golden Globe awards for Coppola as producer and for Best Comedy. The screenwriters were awarded with the awards for the best writing of the year by both the New York Film Critics Association and the National Society of Film Critics. Although it was nominated for five Oscars (Best Film, Best Director, Best Supporting Actress (Candy Clark), Best Screenplay and Best Editing), it was awarded none.[11]

More than two decades later, on December 27, 1995, the film was one of 25 honored by the Library of Congress and included among 25 others as an entry under the National Preservation Act. Each year, 25 films are selected and placed within special climate-controlled vaults to protect them from aging and deterioration. There *American Graffiti* resides with other films—*Psycho, 2001: A Space Odyssey, Chinatown, The Godfather, Star Wars, Gone with the Wind, The Deer Hunter,* and more—all of which, says Librarian James H. Billington, "have enduring cultural, historical or aesthetical significance."[12]

For the first time in his film career, Harrison Ford felt as though he was a contributor whose suggestions and opinions hadn't fallen upon deaf ears. Gone were the days of such responses to his on-set queries as, "'Don't bother me, I'm trying to make a movie here.'"

"It was as if the whole world changed," said Ford. "For the first time people had listened and for the first time I was in the company of people who cared enough about things to do them the right way."[13]

Ford and Lucas would go on to collaborate in a plethora of films.

9

Hanging with the Big Boys

The success of *American Graffiti* provided Harrison Ford with his first role in a film of great appeal and enabled him to form important personal and professional alliances.

(His relationship with George Lucas would not resume until he was considered for a role in the director's science-fiction epic *Star Wars*, which *Graffiti* helped finance.)

Ford moved into his next film with the help of *Graffiti*'s casting agent, Fred Roos. Written by its director-producer Francis Ford Coppola, the script for *The Conversation* told of a surveillance expert, Harry Caul, who is approached by a mysterious businessman simply known as The Director. Caul is hired to keep tabs on The Director's wife because she may be having an affair. As Caul comes closer to discovering the truth behind the couple's relationship, his professional scruples and his personal life are unavoidably garbled and ultimately collide.

The Conversation initially stemmed from a conversation that Coppola had with fellow director Irvin Kershner in 1966. Kershner had learned of a new technology utilizing powerful microphones so effective that they were able to select a target and focus on it while eliminating all background interference. Said the director at the time: "I was fascinated to learn that bugging was a *profession*, not just some private cop going out and eavesdropping with primitive equipment."[1]

Immediately following the completion of his script in 1969, Coppola turned heads when he estimated it would cost a mere $400,000 to produce, have Marlon Brando as its star, and be filmed within a four-week period.[2] Then along came Coppola's *The Godfather*; Coppola's Mafioso masterpiece would consume much of his time. As a result of that film's worldwide success, the asking price of its star Marlon Brando rose, making him unaffordable for *The Conversation*. In 1972, Coppola presented a more realistic budget of $1.1 million for the film, and a far longer shooting schedule. But without Brando's involvement, he was back to square one.

Gene Hackman—an actor Coppola classified as "ordinary" and "unexceptional in appearance"—was hot off the success of his Oscar-winning performance in the 1971 William Freidkin film *The French Connection*.[3] Without hesitation he signed on to Coppola's project in the lead role of Harry Caul.

When Harrison Ford arrived to audition for his role, he was originally reading for the part of a character named Mark, the male half of the couple whom Hackman was hired to observe. In a surprising turn of events, Coppola chose actor Frederic Forrest instead. Fortunate for Ford, Fred Roos — Coppola's co-producer on *The Conversation* — insisted that Ford be considered for another role, one which had not yet been incorporated into the script. Eager to work with Coppola and Roos again, Ford agreed to accept the then-unwritten role of corporate henchman Martin Stett.

By the end of filming *American Graffiti*, actress Cindy Williams had become friendly with Ford and his wife. In *The Conversation*, the two would again work alongside one another. She was cast in the role of Ann, the female half of the targeted couple. For the rest of the roles, Coppola chose from the cast of *The Godfather*. John Cazale was selected to portray Stan, Caul's partner in wire-tapping. And in an unaccredited performance, Robert Duvall portrayed The Director.

Shooting began on schedule on the morning of November 26, 1972. When Ford was summoned to join the cast and crew on location in San Francisco, he set his creativity to work on the two-dimension character he would be portraying. Believing that Stett would be far more interesting if he were subtly homosexual, Ford made the decision to portray Stett that way without the consent of others.

Arriving on the set in a newly purchased $900 green flannel suit, Ford approached his director, who was hardly able to contain his astonishment. When Ford described his intentions to the bewildered Coppola, the director happily granted the actor permission to play his first screen homosexual. As a result, the office set was modified to better suit the film's latest personality.

Coppola chose San Francisco's Union Square as the location where the conversation between the couple would take place. To achieve more realism, extras were not employed during this sequence. While Williams, Forrest and Hackman went about their business of acting, most of the passersbys had no idea they were being filmed. Incidentally, the pedestrians were not the only individuals affected by Coppola's desire to keep a low profile. In their attempt to surreptitiously record the action, the sound technicians were accosted by the local police, who feared that the people suspiciously lurking in the shadows were there to assassinate the famed director.

Filming wrapped on March 23, 1973, and came in just over its scheduled budget at $1.9 million.[4] Ironically, just days prior, the headlines of the nation's newspapers described an event strikingly similar to Coppola's tale. Those involved in the production would view the director as a modern-day Nostrodamus as the shocking news of President Nixon's Watergate crisis unfolded around them.

"This movie will say something significant about the nightmarish situation that has developed in our society," said the director nearly a year before the scandal broke, "a system that employs all the sophisticated electronic tools that are available to intrude upon our lives."[5]

Released on June 4, 1974, the film quickly became the most talked-about picture since Coppola's own *Godfather* two years earlier. Although the adjectives used by critics to describe the film were "grim" and "eerie," all were in total agreement that Coppola had succeeded in creating an outstanding motion picture. The film went on to be nominated and to become the eventual recipient of several awards, including four Golden Globes, and it was nominated for three Oscars. *The Conversation* won the Grand Prize at the 1974 Cannes Film Festival and was deemed the Best

Film of 1974 by the Committee on Exceptional Films of the National Board of Review. In 1995 (alongside *American Graffiti*), it was included in the National Film Registry under the Film Preservation Act.[6]

Although Ford walked away from the critical success of the film virtually unrecognized for his efforts, he felt as though the role, however small, had advanced his abilities as an actor yet again. But, despite his optimistic feelings, it would be nearly three years before he was able to prove his passion for his craft. Resorting back to carpentry, Ford would not act in a motion picture again until 1976.

With his friend Fred Roos keeping a constant eye out for worthwhile work of any form for him, Ford was (perhaps sympathetically) hired to install an elaborate doorway in Coppola's office at Goldwyn Studios. Ford was shamed and humiliated as actors he had worked with in the past greeted him as he labored on his hands and knees. To remedy his discomfort, Ford rescheduled his work until the evenings when the bulk of the foot traffic was gone and he would be left alone to perform his craft.

Just down the corridor, George Lucas and director Brian DePalma were sharing an office and jointly conducting interviews of hopeful actors to be considered for Lucas' upcoming science-fiction project. Sympathetic to his current situation, Lucas asked if Ford would help by reading the part of a character named Han Solo opposite the auditioning actors.

After a week of reading opposite hundreds of other actors, a minor miracle took place in the 34-year-old actor's life. Perceptive to the undeniable chemistry between Ford and two other actors in particular, Lucas ultimately hired Ford (on February 26, 1976 — exactly one month before shooting officially began), along with Mark Hamill and Carrie Fisher, for *Star Wars*.

"I pretty much badgered George [Lucas] into casting him in *Star Wars*," recalled Fred Roos. "He wasn't high on George's list. He didn't know him like I did."[7]

The film became the most successful motion picture in box office history, grossing more than $500 million worldwide. With his salary and a percentage of the film's profits guaranteeing him a lifetime of financial security and the creative freedom that accompanies it, Ford resigned from the business of professional carpentry forever.

10

A Star Was Born

Auditions to find the perfect trio of actors for *Star Wars* lasted nearly two months. Before the director settled upon his now world-renowned choices, serious consideration was given to actors Christopher Walken (as Han Solo), Will Selzer (as Luke) and former *Penthouse* Pet Terri Nunn (as Princess Leia).

However, 24-year-old television actor Mark Hamill (who, coincidentally, had attended Lucas' casting call for *American Graffiti*) seemed a definite possibility. Described by Lucas as more of a "gosh and golly kid," Hamill had the qualities that the director envisioned in young Luke Skywalker.

Amy Irving was considered a potential fit for Princess Leia, before director Brian DePalma cast her in his film *Carrie*. *Graffiti* alum Cindy Williams and child actress Jodie Foster were also possibilities. Instead, the daughter of Debbie Reynolds and Eddie Fisher, 19-year-old Carrie Fisher, won the part.

And long before Ford was hired, actors Nick Nolte and William Katt—and reportedly Al Pacino—were in the running for Han Solo. But as the result of his irritation with reading the part against hundreds of other actors, and his self-professed "grumpy by nature" attitude, Ford unintentionally presented George Lucas with the very characteristics inherent in Han Solo. By the time Fred Roos and the film's casting agent Diane Crittenden finally convinced Lucas that Harrison Ford was Han Solo in the flesh, the start of filming was less than one month away.

"I don't think he saw me for *Star Wars*," claimed the actor, "until he'd seen every other living actor between the ages of 7 and 35 ... and then he asked me ... and I tested like everybody else...."[1]

The opportunity came at just the right time in Ford's life. With the infrequency of acting assignments, he stood an excellent chance of having his family removed from the benefits the Screen Actors Guild health care plan. If the actor was not grossing $1,200 a year from various acting jobs, all would be lost.

Ford signed on to *Star Wars* and agreed to a salary of $1,000 a week, and another $1,000 per week for expenses while shooting on location in England. In addition, Lucas promised his actors a portion of the film's final gross in the belief that, aside from the writer and director, actors make the biggest contribution to a film. Ford and his co-stars, Mark Hamill and Carrie Fisher, were given a quarter of one point.

Although it was gracious of Lucas to consider the well-being of his actors, the amount allotted (based on an average film's earnings) would ordinarily not even be worth the effort of computing. However, the theatrical release and subsequent re-releases of *Star Wars* amassed well over $300 million in domestic ticket sales alone, making 34-year-old Harrison Ford a millionaire virtually overnight.

When the film was finally released in the spring of 1977, it was considered to be the most revolutionary piece of filmmaking ever made — from both from a technical standpoint and its plotline. The story is a simple one — a tale of good versus evil. Despite the fact that the film's premise had been used countless times before, it had never been told by such unique characters in equally unique surroundings.

Even for some of the film's major players, the attempt to adequately verbalize just what their film was about proved difficult. "I never felt that I knew my character," said Ford, "until I saw everything that was going to be around him, how the other people were going to be, and what the tempo of the thing was."[2]

Relating to his human co-stars was simple. To relate to the film's non-human characters, the actor was more pragmatic: "Surely the job was to relate to them as one would relate to a human being, but one with a tin mind. You meet people like that all the time anyway."[3]

The actor found himself a stranger in an even stranger land even as photography moved towards completion: "This guy came to interview me in London from the BBC," recalled Ford. "I walked off a set at lunchtime and he said, 'What's this picture about?' And I sat there with this microphone in my face and realized I didn't know what the fucking picture was about ... but I knew what it was about in my head."[4]

Just what was in Ford's head during the film's 1976 filming is unknown. What was ultimately presented on-screen nearly a year later, though, is known the world throughout.

At that point in film history, the science fiction genre was an unpopular one with the exception of Stanley Kubrick's *2001: A Space Odyssey*. Other respectable entries were *Forbidden Planet* and *Planet of the Apes*. Lucas was an enthusiast of science fiction and fantasy films and novels, and he felt he had what it would take to bring the genre to the next level and, he hoped — if all went according to his plan — far exceed it.

"When I was young," remembered the director, "I used to love *Flash Gordon*, *Buck Rogers* and *Tommy Tomorrow* on television. When I was older and went back and looked at them and saw how really awful they were, I realized that if I were to do one of those in a more sophisticated manner, it would probably be a great way to develop a modern myth. Mythology usually takes place in a far-off land, and the only area left was outer space."[5]

The first screenplay handed to the actors was entitled *The Adventures of Luke Skywalker as Taken from the Journal of the Whills: Saga One: The Star Wars*.

A screenplay's contents are not carved in stone. Changes occur from the first moments of principal photography, as the cast and crew congregate for the first time, to the final stages of the editing process. With *Star Wars*, its contents had changed radically from its original creation in 1973 up until the time photography began.

Initially, its story was completely different. The last name of Luke, his brother Biggs and sister Leia was Starkiller. At first, the film told of the daring rescue of their father Kane. Kane Starkiller and a 60-something general named Luke Skywalker were the only two humans to share a belief in "the Force of Others." Their nemesis was Prince Valarium, the Dark Knight of the Sith. If all had gone according to Lucas' earliest vision, Harrison Ford would not have been required; the character of Han Solo had little screen time. Solo was originally presented as a large alien complete with green-colored skin, gills and no nose.

Many changes were made up until Lucas's final screenplay. Originally, his vision was so expansive that the only feasible way to faithfully adapt it to a screen format was to divide it into nine separate episodes.

The fourth episode is what Lucas decided to tackle first. Subtitled "A New Hope," it relates the adventures of Luke Skywalker. Reluctantly living on the desert planet of Tatooine with his aunt and uncle, Luke happens upon a pair of robots (otherwise known as droids) who sweep him into a world far more interesting than his daily chores. Aware that a beautiful princess has been held captive by the evil Galactic Empire, Luke embarks on a journey to fight the galaxy-wide oppression. Along the way he meets up with Ben Kenobi, who becomes his Jedi Knight mentor. Eventually they meet Han Solo, the captain of a spaceship that they hire to locate and rescue the princess. Together, the band of freedom fighters—aided by the droids R2-D2 and C3-PO and Solo's co-pilot, Chewbacca the Wookie—combat the ominous Darth Vader and his evil Empire.

Lucas consolidated the essentials of his lengthy 160-page script and created a 12-page treatment that he presented to the various studio heads he hoped would accept and finance the project. Before the writer-director signed with 20th Century–Fox, he approached and was turned down by Universal Pictures—just one month before his film *American Graffiti* proved him to be a major Hollywood director.

Lucas hired Boeing Aircraft employee Ralph McQuarrie to create illustrations that Lucas strategically inserted into his treatment with the hopes of enhancing his proposal to the studios. Miki Herman, a Lucas employee, claimed that it was McQuarrie's artistic translations of the script that ultimately influenced 20th Century–Fox to put their faith and money into the picture. With the agreement made between Lucas and studio head Alan Ladd, Jr., Lucas received a $100,000 directing fee. To sweeten the deal, he was given 40 percent of the film's net profits, an immense percentage from all merchandising profits (which the executives believed would amount to nothing) and complete control over the film's sequels, if any.

The events of *Star Wars* took place in three different settings. The first was the surface of the sun-scorched desert planet of Tatooine. The second setting was the cold exteriors of the Death Star and the various star ships that fly through space, and the third environment was the unlimited boundaries of space itself.

Star Wars began principal photography on March 25, 1976, in the southern region of Tunisia. In an area called Tozeur, the bone-chilling winds and sand storms of its winter season plagued the cast and crew with poor visibility conditions. The airborne sand not only attached itself to camera lenses, but also lodged within the gears and joints of the film's central robots, R2-D2 and C3-PO, making movement laborious.

Difficulties arose for R2-D2 (whose name was conceived while Lucas was doing the sound mix for *Graffiti* and noticed a recording reel labeled "Reel 2, Dialogue 2") and Kenny Baker, the 3'8" actor in the unit. Tempers flared when the unit did not respond to the remote control commands because of mysterious radio signals that ran rampant through the North African winds.

For English radio actor Anthony Daniels, playing C3-PO under these conditions proved brutal. Apart from the physical discomfort of performing in the form-fitting, gold-colored suit made up of molded plastic and Fiberglas, his lack of peripheral vision caused him to regularly stumble into unseen hazards. And, on the second day of filming, the riverbeds that were supposed to be dry were just the opposite, when — for the first time in 50 years — it didn't rain, it *poured*.

Despite nearly five weeks of Tunisian photography, Ford's services were not required until filming resumed at Elstree Studios. Situated on a 28-acre lot a half-hour drive from London, EMI Elstree (selected after Paris and Rome soundstages were considered and ultimately rejected) was the largest soundstage in Europe. (Elstree was where legendary director Alfred Hitchcock had shot some of his classic thrillers.)

Lucas and his team occupied all nine of its stages and built an estimated 45 sets there. The production design was such an enormous undertaking that an auxiliary soundstage was reportedly rented from nearby Shepperton Studios.

Lucas didn't want the sets to be futuristic, overly designed or noticeable. Acting upon his director's wishes, production designer John Barry proceeded with the task of intentionally corrupting the sterilized sets, which he had previously spent months painstakingly perfecting.

When George Lucas directed *American Graffiti*, he had an easily manageable 18 employees under his command. With *Star Wars*, a total of nearly 900 people were employed by the time the production was complete. Of that figure, almost 75 percent were British. The American members of the cast and crew found their rigidity unsettling and unhealthy for morale.

The English crew did not find Lucas easy to work with. Ford recalled having to resort to his dry wit in an attempt to lessen the tension that was prevalent throughout the set: "The only damper on the pure fun of that set was the almost-unanimous attitude of the English crew that we were totally out of our minds, especially George," recalled the actor.[6]

While Lucas had to deal with adversity within the ranks, the film's principal actors dealt with being frowned upon by the English crew by relishing in their friendships with one another. It was this feeling of brotherhood and camaraderie that Lucas considered the key to the film's overall success.

"Very little time was wasted," Ford said of his director's approach. "George didn't have an authoritarian attitude like many directors: 'Kid, I've been in this business 25 years, trust me.' He was different. He knew the movie was based so strongly on the relationship among the three of us that he encouraged our contributions."[7]

Mark Hamill recalled being both "scared to death" and "fascinated" by Ford upon their first meeting. Ultimately, he was proud of the relationship that formed between he and his co-stars throughout the difficult times experienced during the ten-week studio shoot.

"We were like a family, the three American kids versus 'them,'" recalled Hamill. "There were times when we got pretty silly together, especially when we had to do lots of takes in the Death Star. It got pretty close and tight in there, and we'd get giddy and do stupid jokes I wouldn't care to repeat."[8]

The film was originally slated for a Christmas 1976 release. Its completion was delayed (and it ultimately came in over budget) due to the logistical difficulties of photographing scenes with extremely complex physical sequences coupled with dialogue that would tax the concentration of any trained professional.

During a scene in which Han Solo was required to deliver the line "It'll take a few moments to get the coordinates from the navi-computer," Ford discovered the difficulty of such wordy dialogue. Because of its tongue-twisting attributes, Ford involuntarily endured nearly a dozen failed attempts before he finally nailed it.

"It was a matter of getting the words out," admitted the actor. "It was about a five-page scene, and I blew it about four or five times, and then I got really pissed at myself. It took me about four or five takes to come out of that, and then we got it. That was the most takes I've ever done. I'm usually about a four-take actor, and they end up right the first and the last. The first one is usually right on but spoiled in some technical way. And the second two are an attempt to get back to the spontaneity of the first one."[9]

Carrie Fisher recalled that the dialogue she was given to read for her audition was even more complex than what was in the final script. But apart from the verbal difficulties, there were logistical glitches that presented challenges.

Unlike spontaneous American filmmakers, English crews were accustomed to working for a finite period of time. At precisely 5:30 each night, they would customarily cease all filmmaking functions, leaving Lucas and his crew helplessly in the middle of a given scene whether or not it was an acceptable take or not. This meant that the next morning was spent setting up shots that were prepped and ready to be filmed the night before.

Despite this, the production's problems were not solely the fault of the British. Because of the mental and physical toll of filming, Lucas ultimately collapsed from exhaustion and hypertension. Former London hospital porter Peter Mayhew, who wore the yak-fur costume of Chewbacca the Wookie (and who also appeared as the Minotaur in *Sinbad and the Eye of the Tiger*) suffered from heat exhaustion and dehydration after many hours under the intense stage lighting. Without the presence of sand in its joints and wheels, the remote-controlled R2-D2 still suffered from an array of technical glitches. Ultimately a lighter Fiberglas mold was made and it was maneuvered via an out-of-sight cable. Carrie Fisher was none too pleased at having her breasts taped against her chest to avoid excess "jiggling." Makeup artist Stuart Freeborn was hospitalized due to illness after only two weeks of production. As a result, the 20 characters required for the cantina sequence were never completed to the degree that Lucas desired. (Until the director had the opportunity to fix some of the inadequacies for the release the Special Edition of the film 20 years later, he felt that that particular sequence was the most flawed of the entire film.) Sir Alec Guinness initially bad-mouthed his director when he discovered that both his screen time and dialogue as Ben Obi-Wan Kenobi would be greatly reduced. Quarreling between

10. A Star Was Born 39

The film that made motion picture history — and forever changed Harrison Ford's life: *Star Wars* (Lucasfilm, Ltd., 1977).

Lucas and the actor who portrayed Darth Vader, David Prowse, erupted when Prowse discovered that the character's voice would later be dubbed in by actor James Earl Jones (who was paid $10,000 for his vocal services). Notorious for his roles in classic films of horror and supernatural tales, Peter Cushing (Grand Moff Tarkin) was insistent that no long shots be taken of him due to his refusal to wear the uncomfortable boots the wardrobe department provided. Instead the space despot who destroyed Princess Leia's home world of Alderaan wore slippers. Special effects crews accidentally destroyed John Barry's sets as a result of the improper detonation of explosive charges used to simulate laser-blast hits.

And, the most considerable setback, the team of young hopefuls hired to handle one of the most integral components of the film — its special effects — was going nowhere fast.

The miniature and optical effects required for *Star Wars* were relatively difficult considering that they had yet to be invented. The first step in the process was to hire *2001: A Space Odyssey* special effects assistant John Dykstra. With Dykstra's talents at their disposal, Lucas and producer Gary Kurtz rented an abandoned warehouse in an industrial park in Van Nuys, California, for the special effects work. When work officially began in July 1975, what is now known throughout the world as *the* most advanced special-effect house — Industrial Light and Magic (ILM) — had found its first home.

In addition to professionals like Richard Edlund (who oversaw the creation and handling of the miniature and model effects), Lucas hired a staff numbering almost 100 — and whose average age was 20. For nearly 22 months (including six additional months spent prior to production on the design and development of the special cameras and equipment), the team was composed of a wide variety of individuals ranging from seasoned veterans to recent college grads. Early on, ILM (then jokingly nicknamed "The Country Club") spent a great deal of time experimenting with unfamiliar equipment and untested techniques.

Nearly $2.5 million of the film's final $10.5 million budget was spent on its special effects. Long before the Academy Award for their achievements in *Star Wars*, the technicians labored seven days a week painstakingly photographing the various models seen throughout the film. The 75 creations included the Death Star, a multitude of X-Wing fighters, Y-Wing fighters, Star Destroyers, TIE (Twin Ion-Engine) Fighters, an escape pod, a Sandcrawler and the Millennium Falcon. The completed film contained roughly 363 special effect shots.

To help photograph the movements of the "spaceships," John Dykstra developed the first-ever computer controlled camera, aptly christened the "Dykstraflex." It had the ability to track around a stationary object and recall its precise movements time and again without ever losing focus. With that, Dykstraflex gave the appearance that the various ships seen hurtling through space in the film were moving. In reality, the models were completely stationary; only the camera moved.

With the film over schedule and budget, the pressure from the studio to wind it up grew intense. Complications arose when funding was terminated and Lucas was forced to make do with what he had before him. His wife Marcia oversaw the editing of the film. Lucas himself tended to the film's final details. There was last-minute photography in Death Valley, California (which doubled for Tatooine), and among the historic Mayan temple ruins of Tikal National Park in Guatemala (which served as the location for the hidden Rebel outpost situated on the fourth moon of Yavin).

Mark Hamill was in a high-speed car accident while cruising along the Pacific Coast Highway. His nose was nearly eradicated and required drastic plastic surgery, as did one of his cheeks. Lucas was forced to film him from behind and use a double at a distance and at angles where his face was not in plain sight. Ironically, the accident proved convenient, considering that Hamill's character would later be ravaged by a fierce snow creature known as a Wampa during the early moments of the sequel, *The Empire Strikes Back*.

As time progressed, even Ford began to entertain doubts as to the validity of the project: "I really wasn't sure how [*Star Wars*] would do. I thought it would either reach a wide audience who would recognize it as a fun, space-age Western, or it would be so silly that my two kids would be embarrassed for me to even leave the house."[10]

With so much of their money invested in Lucas' project and the success of their studio hanging in the balance, the executives at 20th Century–Fox demanded proof that *Star Wars* existed. Assembling a rough-cut (minus John Williams' triumphant score and the final sound effects), Lucas unleashed his film on an audience made up mostly of financiers and skeptical Fox executives. With the exception of Alan Ladd, Jr., none were impressed. Devastated, Lucas continued fine-tuning his labor of love.

The second time, the audience consisted largely of Lucas' own friends and business acquaintances. In attendance were Lucas' friend Steven Spielberg, Willard Huyck and Gloria Katz (both of whom contributed to the comedic portion of the script involving the relationship between Solo and Leia), screenwriter John Milius, *Time* magazine film critic Jay Cocks, Brian DePalma and writer-producer Hal Barwood, among others. Only Spielberg and Cocks were overwhelmed at the incomplete film they'd seen.

"They were all my real close friends and they felt sorry for me more than anything else. There were a lot of condolences, which is even worse than saying you don't like the movie," Lucas recalled.[11]

The majority of the group considered the film to be deficient on most levels. DePalma and Cocks even lent a hand to their friend by rewriting the film's opening crawl.

"I figured, well, it's just a silly movie," said Lucas. "It ain't going to work."[12]

His mood changed for the better when he released the film to its first test audience screening at San Francisco's Northpoint Theater on May 1, 1977 — where four years earlier he had screened *American Graffiti*. As the opening crawl concluded and the seemingly infinite bulk of the Imperial Star Destroyer cruised overhead, thrilled audiences made it perfectly clear to Lucas that his four years of faith and dedication would, in fact, pay off.

Prior to the screening, Alan Ladd, Jr., was a non-smoker. As a result of the audience's overwhelming response during and after the screening, he walked into the theater's lobby, lit a cigarette and has made an unhealthy hobby of lighting up since.

Following the Sunday morning screening, countless thoughts were running through Lucas' mind: "It was a very high moment — I knew the film worked," admitted the director. "But I had no idea of what was going to happen. I mean, I had no idea."[13]

Recalling the moments of frustration on the set of *American Graffiti*, director Lucas considered the experience of *Star Wars* to be the defining moment in Ford's life, the moment when he matured into a professional actor. Spending nearly three months in the presence of British actor Sir Alec Guinness and others "mellowed him out a lot as an actor," as Lucas firmly asserted.

"He began to see how it was a real profession — in terms of how you act professionally on the set — by being around a lot of actors who did their job and didn't cause a lot of difficulties and didn't take a lot of time and did their homework before they came on the set," said Lucas. "All the kinds of professional things you expect caught him at the right moment and made him realize how important the job of an actor is and how everybody depends on everybody to do their job well and not to be self-indulgent. He became a very good professional actor from that point on. He disciplined his talent in a much different way...."[14]

Taking advantage of the freedom to change dialogue which he didn't feel comfortable delivering, Ford offered the memorable line "Great, kid. Don't get cocky," to Mark Hamill during a highly charged space battle between the Millennium Falcon and a group of Imperial TIE Fighters. The actor also ad-libbed dialogue for the "conversation" he had with a communications console during the scene in which the heroes attempt to rescue Princess Leia from the Death Star's detention center.

"We did it in one take," said Ford, "and I never learned the dialogue for it because I wanted to show how desperate I was. I told George I wanted to do it all the way through the first time. I said, 'Stop me if I'm really bad,' but he didn't."[15]

No one in the world (George Lucas included) knew what to expect of the movie that posters announced was coming to their galaxy that summer.

On May 25, 1977, *Star Wars* made its official debut. Because of the 20th Century–Fox non-believers, the film arrived at only 32 theater doorsteps across the entire nation.

Its first week saw only $3 million in ticket sales. Yet by the July 4 holiday weekend, word of mouth had circulated at such an astounding rate that the film reaped nearly $30 million in box office receipts. Just two weeks later — not even two months after its official opening — the film garnered a grand total of $68 million. By the end of August, it crossed the $100 million mark and earned the distinction of making that sum faster than any other picture in the 80-year history of Hollywood. Soon Lucas' film surpassed his friend Steven Spielberg's *Jaws* as the biggest all-time moneymaker in motion picture history.

The influence of its success was undeniable, from the average filmgoer who experienced *Star Wars* on numerous occasions, to the parents and children who were responsible for the merchandising empire resulting in hundreds of additional millions of dollars in revenue, to the wise investors who saw the film's possibilities. Prior to the release of *Star Wars*, 20th Century–Fox stocks were dormant at 11⅛ per share. By September of that year, their value had more than doubled, soaring to 24⅝ each. The film maintained such a consistent pace at the ticket booths that it was re-released in 1978 and 1979 to eager audiences, which ultimately brought the film over the finish line with $322.7 million in total sales. Worldwide, the film earned an unprecedented $524 million.[16]

As an added bonus, it was nominated for ten Academy Awards, including Best Picture, Best Director and Alec Guinness for Best Supporting Actor. While it ultimately lost to Woody Allen's film *Annie Hall* for Best Director and Picture, it didn't go unrecognized. *Star Wars* received several technical achievement Oscars, including Best Art Direction, Sound, Editing, Visual Effects and Original Score. The Academy presented sound designer Ben Burtt with a Special Achievement Award for his sound effects. And, like *American Graffiti* and *The Conversation*, *Star Wars* was later included as one of the motion pictures to be forever safeguarded under the Film Preservation Act.

11

A War Lost and a Wife Found

In 1975, Francis Ford Coppola announced that he would resurrect a film project based on a script originally written in 1969, called *Apocalypse Now*. This pronouncement would startle everyone — including his original collaborators and fellow USC alums George Lucas and John Milius.

When it was eventually released on October 1, 1979, the film was unanimously considered by critics as *the* film to see concerning the Vietnam War. Wonderfully acted, majestically photographed, and successfully rattling the emotions of viewers, *Apocalypse Now* — then and now — is considered a masterpiece in every aspect of filmmaking.

The now-infamous story behind the film is worthy of mention. With its budget having skyrocketed beyond its initial estimation, its shooting schedule expanded by nearly a full year, the difficulty in preserving mental stability among all those involved in its genesis, and the incessant damning of it by all those in Hollywood, the hardships of the project had become a testament to Coppola's dedication to it. He became obsessed with it and was sure that he was making the first film to ever receive a Nobel Peace Prize.

"My film is not a movie," the director would state to a preview audience at the 1979 Cannes Film Festival. "It is not *about* Vietnam. It *is* Vietnam. It's what it was *really like* — it was *crazy*."[1]

Considered an extremely loose interpretation of a classic literary work, *Apocalypse Now* credits the 1901 novella *Heart of Darkness* by Joseph Conrad as its sole source of inspiration. Coppola originally planned on making the film (which George Lucas was to initially direct) in the early 1970s. But his dream project was unavoidably put on the back burner when artistic differences arose. Lucas and Milius were interested in making a small, low-budget film with stock footage provided from previously documented conflicts of Vietnam. Coppola demanded a traditional Hollywood production — a generous budget, exotic locales and familiar actors whom the public could readily relate to.

Interest in the project dwindled. Lucas proceeded to work on his film *THX-1138* and Coppola on his own *Godfather* films and *The Conversation*. Despite appearances, Coppola's interest never diminished.

In 1975, Coppola accepted $13 million from United Artists for the film's distribution rights and proceeded with the pre-production phase of *Apocalypse Now*. Securing permission from Ferdinand Marcos to film in the Philippines, where military resources were made available to him, Coppola and his newly formed American Zeotrope production company went on to cast the characters described in-depth in Milius' script.

The film, whose title was originally inspired by a peace-pin of the late '60s era which read "Nirvana Now," tells the story of Martin Sheen's Capt. Benjamin Willard (which ironically could be broken down into the names of Harrison Ford's two children at the time). Willard was an Army officer assigned to journey into the heart of Vietnam to locate and "terminate with extreme prejudice" a highly decorated Special Forces officer named Col. Kurtz (Marlon Brando) — a man who had seemingly gone insane by abandoning his family and career and taking military matters against the enemy into his own hands.

From catastrophic typhoons and unrecognizably overweight actors to drug usage and serious health issues, the production was one of the most difficult shoots in filmmaking history. After a grueling 238 days of location photography, the question "Apocalypse When?"—as asked by the legions of anxious critics and Hollywood moguls alike—would soon be answered. At the film's May 1977 wrap party, Coppola said he'd never seen so many of his former staff members happy to be unemployed.

When the film was released, the public and critics who were sympathetically expecting a sub-par Coppola film were startled.

"This film is the best I could do," justified the director. "You are going to be thinking and talking about it tomorrow. And the day after tomorrow."[2]

Apocalypse Now was awarded the esteemed Palmes d'Or (the Golden Palm) at the Cannes Film Festival months before the film's final cut was prepared for public consumption. This honor was just the beginning of its long list of accolades. Aside from earning several Golden Globe Award nominations, the film went on to be nominated for several Academy Awards including Best Picture, Director, Adapted Screenplay, Production Design, Editing, Sound and Art Direction—and one for Robert Duval's Supporting Actor portrayal of the fearless, surfing-fanatic Lt. Col. Kilgore. In the Best Picture category it lost to *Kramer vs. Kramer*, but Oscars did go to Vittorio Storaro's stunning cinematography and the Walter Murch's sound.

Its budget had escalated from the original $13 million to more than $30 million. But *Apocalypse Now* grossed more than $150 million in the United States alone.

Based on the amount of screen time he had in the final print, Ford's role could have been considered nothing more than an extensive cameo. Suggested by Fred Roos, Ford joined Coppola's cast amidst the lush environs of the Philippines.

Ford had agreed to play even a very small part, because he loved the challenge of working with Coppola. He appeared in only one (long) scene with Martin Sheen. This scene was, however, a crucial one — telling the audience everything they needed to know for the remainder of the film. In the sequence—found at the start of the film—Ford shared the screen with Sheen, G.D. Spradlin and assistant director Jerry Ziesmer as the civilian.

Ford equipped his character with a lethargically monotone and apprehensive manner (exemplified by the dropping of his papers) and the nervous clearing of his throat to indicate his character's discomfort. He subtly paid tribute to George Lucas by having the wardrobe department apply an identification patch to his character's uniform with the name "Lucas" emblazoned upon it in capital letters.

Ford blended into the scene and his character so successfully that George Lucas was unable to detect the usage of his name upon the character's breast pocket — and didn't even realize who the actor was until the scene was nearly half over.

"I'm an actor," responded a proud Ford. "You weren't supposed to recognize me."[3]

Ford's services were required for only nine days, but it ended up taking only four. Filming took place within a trailer that served as a compact, mobile Army office — seedily decorated and equipped in an effort to represent the war-weary soldiers' home away from home. (Why this interior scene was not filmed on a sound stage to conserve money is unknown.)

Despite his relatively minor role, the actor's name would eventually appear on completely re-designed posters promoting Coppola's new Director's Cut — entitled *Apocalypse Now Redux*— when it hit select theaters during the spring-summer film season of 2001.

Despite the exotic setting, a mere week was hardly enough time to form new alliances among the many faces circulating around the set — with the exception of one. Coppola's executive assistant (and former babysitter) made such a positive impression upon Ford that even after his return to the States, the relationship between the two would continue — and flourish. By participating in a film of immense importance, he not only added to his list of diverse credits, but he also found himself his future Mrs. Ford.

12

Getting Some Recognition

It would have been grossly uncharacteristic for Harrison Ford to settle on the lifestyle of the Hollywood elite. However, the actor did indulge in a few amenities after the tremendous wealth and overnight fame *Star Wars* brought him.

Aside from purchasing the latest model Porsche 911SC, Ford elected to leave his household problems high above the Hollywood Bowl and move to an entirely new home.

While scouting for a new abode, Ford discovered an ad in *The Los Angeles Times* describing a house that seemed to suit his personality and needs perfectly: "The ad was all about how it was only five minutes from the Beverly Hills Hotel," recalled the actor. "I guess so you wouldn't have to miss your pages. A real plus."[1]

Virtually constructed into the lush hillside of Benedict Canyon in Beverly Hills, the Ford home was the perfect setting for the actor to raise a family and was the ideal geographic location for an actor to be situated. The last house on a private narrow drive (rendering sightseeing bus passage fundamentally impossible), it was peacefully nestled on a cul-de-sac concealed by bushes. Ford was delighted that the house was built in 1941, since he believed the construction of homes in that era was superior to those built following World War II.

About as fast as the furniture could be moved in and the boxes unpacked, Ford made space in the garage for his woodworking shop. There, he would continue with his carpentry trade, only this time his only customer was himself.

In 1977, George Lucas' *Star Wars* forever altered the history of motion pictures. Harrison Ford's life was also altered, resulting in a higher public profile and consistent job offers.

"Both the success of the film — which gave me the opportunities to work — and George's generous contribution to my bank account, both helped change my life," proclaimed the actor. "But the most significant thing was not the money but the opportunity to work."[2]

Discouragingly, most of the offerings were tasteless regurgitations of the science-fiction character that had given his face worldwide recognition. Although *Star Wars* had yet to reach its pinnacle of success, Ford sensed the need to find a character entirely different from Han Solo—or else risk being forever pigeonholed by the role.

So Ford chose an unconventional path that would not lead him to more fame

Putting his carpentry skills to work for *Heroes* (Universal, 1979).

in the public eye, but rather one which he took solely to establish himself as a true actor in the eyes of film executives and critics: He elected to portray a secondary character in a small film by director Jeremy Paul Kagan.

Heroes was a low-budget film about human relationships. Studio executives felt it had promise because of its two headlining stars, Henry Winkler and Sally Field.

An enormous success as the leather-clad cool cat in the 1970s TV sitcom *Happy Days*—a direct descendant of *American Graffiti*—Winkler teamed up for the film with actress Field (after Talia Shire rejected the part). Field's '60s television hits *Gidget* and *The Flying Nun* made her a star of immense appeal in the hearts of the American public. All three used the film to put an end to the string of stereotyped roles offered to them.

As a Vietnam veteran and recent mental institution escapee, Winkler's character—the disturbed but excitable Jack Dunne—finds himself hitchhiking across country, bound for Eureka, California, where he plans to regroup with his fellow Army friends and live up to his post-war dreams of opening a worm farm. En route to his destination, he happens across Ann (Field), a woman escaping from the pressures of her own indecision to commit to marriage. At his side throughout the course of their journey across the Midwest, Ann must deal with Jack's idiosyncrasies as he still struggles mentally with the memories of horrors experienced during the war. The two fall in love.

Kenny "The Ace" Boyd is elected by Dunne to raise rabbits, whose droppings provide nourishment for the worms. Described by Dunne as a "renowned farmer and fighter," Ford's Boyd is a loner who lives in relative squalor in a trailer on his grandparents' property.

First-time director Kagan told *People Profiles* writer Robert Abele of the impression the 36-year-old actor made: "He was quite shy and quite good in the casting session, but he was not very communicative. He stayed in my mind, though, and I called him back and he told me a little bit more about himself. I thought I'd take a chance. There was something special about him. Something honest, simple, that came from the heart."[3]

Suggesting to the director that he would enjoy playing Boyd as a Missouri farmer, Ford played a mentally impoverished but lovable man whose devotion to racecars is his sole hobby and his own therapeutic means of dealing with the war. Ford traveled from his California home to Missouri to record conversations between himself and various locals in bars and auto parts stores, to research his character's accent. Because of his fear that no one would take him seriously if he divulged that he was an actor researching a role, Ford said he was a professional writer.

While Ford walked about the familiar streets of Petaluma, California, as a relative unknown (principal photography for *Heroes* took place prior to the release of *Star Wars*), Winkler and Field were continuously bombarded by fans. Kagan remembers walking over to Ford, who was shielding himself from the rain as his co-stars signed autographs, and stating, "You know, someday, Harrison, that's gonna be you." And Ford looked up with hair matted to face, and said, "Not a chance."[4]

Singled out by the critics for his portrayal of Kenny Boyd, Ford's performance was the predominant saving grace of the film when it was released in November 1977.

"We worked together like bread and butter," said co-star Henry Winkler. "There was never a problem of actor's ego between us. Harrison has volcanic energy. Even when we were out on the prairie, he always seemed as if he were confined. He was like a caged lion! ... Harrison doesn't do anything halfway. You had to be on your toes, because he acts with the same intensity that he lives...."[5]

New York Times regular Vincent Canby wrote that he was "effective in a supporting role too small to make the picture worth seeing."[6]

The critics who made the effort to mention Ford in their reviews generally commended him in a similar fashion, as did David Ansen of *Newsweek*: "Ford gives us an inkling of what this movie might have been. Behind his good-old-boy bravado, you feel the toll the war has taken on this man — his soul has been gutted, his juices turned off. When Ford is on-screen, the tiny echoes of old movies die away and *Heroes* takes on — briefly — the resonance of real life."[7]

The actor succeeded in what he originally set out to do with *Heroes*. Admitting that the role was not as "well rounded" as he had hoped it would become when he first read the script, Ford remained pleased with his decision to play it.

With his low-key (if not lethargic) approach to Kenny Boyd, Ford successfully made a radical departure from the high-flying personality of the space pirate Han Solo. The actor was well aware that the comparison-happy world expected a follow-up film whose success would either equal or surpass that of *Star Wars*, and he was conscious from the moment he signed on that his decision to participate in *Heroes* would indeed create a step back in his career. In the instance of the wildly unpopular *Heroes*, Ford deemed his decision a necessary evil in order for his career to advance one step.

"I didn't really care if people went to see the movie," claimed Ford. "I was doing it for people in the industry, so that they would understand that it wasn't the only string in my bow ... and that I was fiercely determined to do that kind of thing."[8]

"Harrison did a very small part in it, a marvelous part," recalled his proud agent, Patricia McQueeney. "He plays a Vietnam vet with a worm farm. [His part was] a very small, very showy, excellent piece of film. I sent it out like crazy, and got a lot of work for him."[9]

13

LITTLE TO BE PROUD OF

With the exception of Lucas' *Star Wars*, Steven Spielberg's 1977 film *Close Encounters of the Third Kind* and Francis Ford Coppola's 1979 epic *Apocalypse Now*, the late 1970s offered few memorable movies. The year 1978, in fact, passed by with nothing substantial to offer the eager public from this circle of USC film school friends. Joining the list of unmentionables that year was the World War II adventure film *Force 10 from Navarone*, starring Robert Shaw, Edward Fox and Harrison Ford.

Force 10 was meant to live up to the enormous box office appeal of its 1961 predecessor, *The Guns of Navarone*, starring Gregory Peck and David Niven. Despite the general enthusiasm for the return of British officers Major Mallory and Sgt. Miller (albeit with different faces), *Force 10* was a disappointment, both commercially and artistically. It also marked the first time in Ford's career (both amateur and professional) that his performance received derogatory notices.

Assigned to eliminate traitorous double agent Nicholai Lescovar (Franco Nero), United States Army Lt. Col. Mike Barnsby (Ford) leads two British officers through the war-torn countryside of Yugoslavia. With his team of commandos, Barnsby has also been assigned to destroy a key bridge and thus thwart the progression of the German army, turning the tide of the war.

Force 10 found Ford working for the first time with Shaw, Fox and the man behind "Rocky" Balboa's fierce opponent Apollo Creed, Carl Weathers. It was the second film out of three in which he would appear with actor Angus McInnes. In *Star Wars*, McInnes portrayed a doomed rebel pilot whose scenes were set in the main briefing room and in his X-wing fighter high above the Death Star. In *Force 10* there would be much more dialogue between Ford and McInnes with the latter as Lt. Doug Reynolds, a soldier and friend under Barnsby's command. The two actors would be reunited seven years later in the Peter Weir film *Witness*.

Enthused by the possibility of another high-profile, exotically set adventure to be directed by Englishman Guy Hamilton (whose four previous James Bond affiliations—*Goldfinger*, *The Man with the Golden Gun*, *Diamonds Are Forever* and *Live and Let Die*— displayed his cinematic worth with style, class and, most importantly, talent), the project was given the appropriate financial backing without second thought.

Acknowledging the film's budget, its American producer, Oliver A. Ungar, stated exactly what the theme of the film would be when questioned during filming in January 1978: "With ten-and-a-half million invested, it's got to be success."[1]

Clowning around in the Yugoslavian countryside with Barbara Bach while filming *Force 10 from Navarone* (Columbia, 1978).

Unlike Ford's rationale for accepting his previous film *Heroes* (to exhibit his talent and versatility), the reason he signed on to *Second Guns*—as it was known initially—was materialistic gain.

Although excited to have his name above the film's title for the first time in his career, it was the money that spurred Ford's decision. In a rare moment of displaced priorities, the actor deemed the situation "important, because in order to be considered for certain parts in Hollywood, you have to have a certain price tag attached to your name. If you're in the high-priced category, you've got a head start."[2]

At the onset, Ford had been promised a script rewrite as one of the stipulations before finally agreeing to the project. By the end of the shoot, Ford and the others involved would fall victim to Hamilton's direction and Robert Chapman's (*High Noon, The Bridge On the River Kwai*) screenplay. The script was based on the original 1968 book by famed genre novelist Allistair MacLean—the author who also penned *The Guns of Navarone*.

Shooting in the mountains of Yugoslavia became unexpectedly troublesome—a warning that things would not unfold as planned. Yugoslavia's unpleasant weather forced the entire cast and crew to relocate to the English countryside. England's infamous dreary weather conditions eventually became a nuisance as well. The moviemakers persevered, filming when the weather permitted. This grossly inflated its budget, and its schedule was extended beyond where a financial profit was considered a reasonable expectation.

With the insufferable weather, the Yugoslavian food (which Ford considered to be the most "strenuous" facet of the production) and the rigorous shooting requirements, the only positive aspect of filming *Force 10* was the friendship he fostered with his co-star, Robert Shaw.

Shaw was a veteran of the literary world, the stage and screen, having starred in such popular film adaptations as *Jaws* and *The Deep* (in addition to playing the heavy to Sean Connery's James Bond in *From Russia with Love*). Shaw maintained a notorious reputation for being unapproachable and disagreeable, intensified by his constant alcoholic intake.

Shaw died at the age of 51 as the result of a sudden heart attack prior to the theatrical release of *Force 10*. Ironically, during one conversation with Ford, the Scottish-born actor demanded that whichever one of the two was living would be present at the other's funeral. (Due to a scheduling conflict, Ford was unable to attend.)

"It was a tough job and it was tough for both of us," recalled Ford. "We got to know each other quite well and it was quite a shock, his death. I liked him. It was well worth the experience."[3]

Other locations were the island of Malta and, in England, the Jersey Channel Islands and Shepperton Studio Centre in Middlesex where the film's not-so-special special effects and miniature work were done. (The construction, and later destruction, of the miniature dam consumed a full one-tenth of the budget.)

During the production, Hamilton viewed the business of making films with uncertainty. "If you make a lot of successful pictures, after that you could make the telephone directory," claimed Hamilton. "But after two flops you couldn't even get arrested."[4]

With *Force 10*'s December 1978 release, Hamilton had his first failure. The prospect of making "the telephone directory" had become even more remote.

Earning a mere $7.1 million in the United States, *Force 10 from Navarone* (which then–President Jimmy Carter selected as the feature film for Thanksgiving Day at Camp David) closed out the year with a whimper instead of the anticipated bang.

"It was a job I did for the money," admitted Ford. "I can't do that, and I won't ever do that again. It wasn't a bad film. There were honest people involved making an honest effort. But it wasn't the right thing for me to do."[5]

The same year *Force 10* was released, Ford participated in three other film projects: *Hanover Street* with Christopher Plummer and Lesley-Anne Down; Robert Aldrich's *The Frisco Kid* with comic actor Gene Wilder, and—thanks to Fred Roos and as a favor to George Lucas—*More American Graffiti* (in an unaccredited cameo role).

Due to the startlingly tremendous success Universal Pictures experienced with Lucas' *American Graffiti*, executives were greatly excited by the option of a follow-up. As a nod to Jimi Hendrix's signature song, the project was initially entitled *Purple Haze*. Weary of being associated with the hallucinogen on which Hendrix had based his own classic, however, Lucas finally settled on the title of *More American Graffiti*.

Lucas had no involvement in the project due to a lack of "emotional investment."

He readily handed the reins over to writer-director B.W.L. Norton, whose credits up until that point included writing the script for the 1978 film *Convoy* and directing the 1972 horror television film *Gargoyles*. (Since *Graffiti*, Norton has been responsible for nearly two dozen television productions and — with the exception of *Baby ... Secret of the Lost Legend*—has not strayed from the small screen.)

Delegating himself the job of executive producer, Lucas sought to line up the original film's principal players. He was able to secure all of them with the exception of Richard Dreyfuss, an actor with exceptional industry clout since he was awarded the Oscar for *The Goodbye Girl*.

Lucas also approached Ford. Initially uninterested, Ford reconsidered and accepted the role of Officer Falfa primarily out of a deep respect and appreciation for what his friend Lucas had done to his career and life. With the sole condition that his appearance in the film remain uncredited, Ford worked one day during August 1978.

Dressed as a leather-clad warrior of law enforcement, Ford was virtually unrecognizable on-screen. The film's costume department outfitted him in full-throttle motorcycle cop garb. He delivered his lines complete with a helmet and sunglasses—the combination nearly enveloping his recognizable mug.

"I was in full regalia," recalled the actor, "I mean with the helmet and the Harley [motorcycle], you know? All day long, people would come up to me, taking me for a policeman, 'Scuse me, Officer — how do you find a taxi around here?' 'Well, sir,' I'd say, 'you put your hand up in the air and then you yell "Taxi!" It's like that.' One lady asked me nervously, 'Is it all right if I turn here?' I waved my arm and bowed, 'Lady, the city is yours.' I tell you, you get that uniform on and something happens to you."[6]

Released on August 3, 1979, *More American Graffiti* failed to deliver the emotional wallop its predecessor did six years earlier. The film depicted unpleasant settings and situations all shot in different film formats and crosscut from story to story. There were tales of Vietnam (which Lucas insisted on filming himself), John Milner's (LeMatt) life on the race track circuit, the now-married Laurie (Williams) and Steve's (Howard) domestic struggles, and Debbie's (Candy Clark) wild trip through San Francisco's psychedelic music and drug-drenched underworld. In all, *More* was a film reliving a period of time no one cared to relive.

In the end, Universal's $7.5 million budget became the mother lode of angst for its investors. They would only experience relief two long years after its release when cable television managed to help the film break even financially.

For Ford, if there were one film in which to appear both uncredited and incognito, *More American Graffiti* was the one.

The same year, 1979, Ford contemplated a starring role in writer-director Peter Hyams' *Hanover Street*. The actor envisioned himself in the role of U.S. Army Lt. David Halloran. The actor would disregard concerns of stereotyping and commit himself to a film that, in the beginning, he thought would be exceptional.

The role of Lt. Halloran was originally offered to Kris Kristofferson, and Genevieve Bujold was going to portray his love interest. Because of prior contractual obligations, the producers were forced to look elsewhere to find the ideal couple who were never meant to be. During the final days of filming *Force 10 from Navarone*, Ford briefly considered commandeering the role of Butch in the prequel to the popular *Butch Cassidy and the Sundance Kid*. Ford ultimately declined, not wanting to court comparisons with actor Paul Newman (who originated the role in the 1969 film). Later, he was approached by Peter Hyams with a new offer. The two spent an entire evening of discussion in Ford's trailer while on location for *Force 10*. With that film running over schedule and Ford's weariness at being away from his home for such an extended period of time, he again declined. It was only after detecting Hyams' passion for the project that Ford finally offered his commitment based on his admiration for what he called the director's "monomaniacal attitude."[7]

Categorized as an action-adventure–romance, *Hanover Street* marked the third consecutive critical and commercial miscarriage for Harrison Ford. Although he had intended to continuously expand his abilities with a variety of roles, the poor reception for the film was a painful indication that his final decisions were not always the most appropriate.

Despite having "flown more mythical miles than I care to imagine"[8] in accepting *Hanover Street*, the most significant attraction for the actor was that it allowed him to play a romantic lead for the first time in his acting career. All previous films had him act in what he called "totally sexless" environments—both in content and characterization.[9] So Ford chose the role despite his reluctance to film overseas—far removed from the long-sought-after creature comforts of his home and family.

"At that state in my career," recalled the actor, "I'd made *American Graffiti*, *Star Wars*, *Heroes* and *Force 10 from Navarone* and I'd yet to kiss a girl or be involved romantically. Then along came this love story and I agreed to do it, expecting that the script, which I didn't have total faith in, would be changed as we went along...."[10]

Unfortunately, the promised revisions never were done. Furthermore, Ford inadvertently overlooked the issue of filming two consecutive films set in World War II Europe—let alone portraying his second consecutive aircraft pilot.

"It's a coincidence that I'm playing a pilot again," said Ford. "Han Solo was a straight-out action/adventure guy, but this is really a love story set in wartime. I get the girl but I give her back, the noble thing to do. What a guy."[11]

The story unfolds in wartime (1943) London. The "girl" is British Red Cross worker Margaret "Maggie" Sellinger (Lesley-Anne Down). American B-25 pilot Lt. David Halloran (Ford) falls in love with her on Hanover Street and complications arise when he discovers that Margaret is a married woman. Halloran is sent off on a mission to transport a British intelligence officer who is infiltrating a German Gestapo stronghold. Problems arise in midair and the two are unexpectedly the flight's only survivors and inevitably become comrades in arms. Matters become even more complicated when Halloran learns that this man is the husband of his forbidden love.

Hanover Street was filmed on location in London, the English countryside of Herts and at EMI Elstree Studios (where Ford had previously spent several months filming *Star Wars*). In an impressive display of successful set design (and one of the film's few positive attributes, apart from composer John Barry's tear-inducing score), the film's title street was designed and constructed with great realism by production

Ford and Christopher Plummer as German officers in disguise in *Hanover Street* (Columbia, 1979).

designer Philip Harrison's crew in full scale over a period of 12 weeks and filmed on Elstree's back lot.

Five fully restored and operational B-25 bombers were leased to the production and flown to England courtesy of an American outfit known as the Confederate Air Force. As an homage to his own wife, director Hyams christened Ford's lead plane as "Gorgeous George-Ann." (The remaining planes were named after the wives of various other key production members.)

Ford's dissatisfaction with the script, coupled with behind-the-scenes personal strife involving the painful closing moments of his marriage to Mary, resulted in a lack of enthusiasm that was apparent on screen.

Los Angeles Times film critic Charles Champlin — who was as impressed with Ford's performance in *Star Wars* as he was with *Heroes* (where he believed Ford "excelled" as Ken Boyd) — felt a sense of betrayal. In his review, he claimed the actor gave his latest screen character "a kind of glum, almost sour intensity."[12]

Ford predicted the eventual critical upheaval even during the making of the film. His remedy? "Keeping a straight face gets you through a lot of things."[13]

Originally, director Hyams (who previously directed the 1978 hit *Capricorn One* and who would go on to direct *Outland, 2010, The Presidio, The Star Chamber* and *Timecop*, among others) described his leading man as possessing "a fierce, burning, sexual energy."[14] He looked upon that attribute as a benefit to his project.

Unexpectedly, that "energy" seemed to fizzle before the eyes of audiences. Despite the lack of on-screen chemistry between the Ford and Lesley-Anne Down characters, there was apparently an abundance of it off-screen. (*Playboy*'s Bruce Williamson noted, "Hyams gives us a pair of lovers who seldom appear to enjoy each other very much."[15])

In his DVD commentary on the film, Hyams—a self-professed "obsessive-compulsive"—shared his less-than-sentimental sentiments: "It's impossible to look at a movie you've made and not really wish you could re-shoot every frame of it. All I really see now are things I've done wrong and they seem to outnumber the things I've done right."[16]

Soon after the film's May 18, 1979, release, Down publicly yet respectfully blamed her co-star's personality for their stunted on-screen relationship. "He doesn't say a lot," she recalled, "which is interesting for an actor, because they tend to talk a lot. It was difficult to get to know him—he's a very insular, private person. But the instant the cameras turned on, I was in love with him."[17]

At the time of the filming, there were rumors that Ford and Down were carrying on a secret affair, which became a significant contribution to the actor's eventual divorce. Those rumors were not confirmed, however, until a November 1997 interview in *People* magazine, when the actress revealed a few secrets of her relationship with Ford. Apparently, the reported affair was known only to a few members of the Columbia Pictures payroll in 1978.

Filming generally began on the bed-and-breakfast set at eight in the morning. The couple would spend two full days on top of and under the sheets filming their scenes: "We used to fall asleep at lunch," said Down, who was 25 years old at the time. "The crew would leave the set, and we would wake up and say, 'Oh, they're back.'"[18]

The film's critical reception did nothing to entice people to rush into theaters; its box office tally was only $3 million. Despite the rumors of Ford's extramarital affair and his personal and professional clashes with his director, some good came out of the experience. Finally he had been given single billing above the film's title, and he had put behind him the stressful task of confronting a woman beneath the sheets on screen.

"Making that film was not a happy experience for me," the actor stated in 1981. "I haven't seen it so I don't like talking about it. I keep saying that if 50 people tell me they liked it, then I may change my mind and see it. But so far I'm just up to 18 so there's no immediate danger of that happening...."[19]

Following the completion of *Hanover Street*, Ford acquainted himself with a number of activities. He tended to various tasks around his Beverly Hills home, spent long-overdue time with his children and, strangely enough, quarreled with none other than "The Duke" himself.

Around that time, Ford discovered that he was wanted for a feature film. The project's title was *No Knife*. Its director was Robert Aldrich, the man responsible for such popular films as *The Dirty Dozen* and *The Longest Yard*. Its star was supposed to be comic actor Gene Wilder, whose leading roles in Mel Brooks' *Young Frankenstein* and *Blazing Saddles* won him the admiration of the filmgoing public.

Set in the Wild West of the 1850s, the film tells the amusing tale of orthodox Polish Rabbi Avrim Belinski. Belinski is sent from Poland to San Francisco to tend to his fellow believers and to meet a beautiful young woman who awaits his vows of marriage. During his journey, he happens upon Tommy Lillard, a tough but undereducated cowboy who supports Avrim's beliefs and relishes his companionship. Together, the two make their westward trek despite many unexpected obstacles.

Ford's previous co-star Henry Winkler hoped to land a role in the film. Declining Winkler's offer, the producers instead found just what they needed in their cowboy in Harrison Ford. As the producers began to seriously ponder their casting options and just weeks after Ford was initially considered, legendary actor John Wayne was approached and showed interest in the film. This conflict reportedly caused a minor commotion between the two leading men. Known primarily for his manly cowboy roles set in the Wild West, "The Duke" ultimately bowed out, noting that the comedic elements of the script would not attract his archetypal fan base.

When first approached with the project, Ford didn't deliberate long. Not only did he readily accept due to his son Willard's coaxing (as he likened the character of Tommy Lillard to that of his father's then-favorite leading man Bud Abbott of Abbott and Costello fame), but because it was scheduled to be filmed in the United States— a considerable relief after having filmed in Europe on his last two films.

With Ford securely aboard as Wilder's co-star, filming began at locations including Colorado, Arizona and the California coastline. Some exterior locales and all interiors were filmed on rented soundstages at California's Burbank Studios.

The producers assembled an assortment of actual tribesmen, including members of Navajo, Papago and Apache tribes, for the film's Native American characters. Production designer Terrence Marsh previously supervised the art direction of *Lawrence of Arabia* and *Doctor Zhivago*. For *The Frisco Kid* (the new title for *No Knife*), Marsh oversaw the set's overall design and construction. Just outside of Tucson, Arizona, in Patagonia Park, a replica teepee village was constructed. Many of the exterior town sets designed by Marsh were shared by the cast and crew of another, more dramatic Western of yesteryear: *The Villain*, starring Kirk Douglas.

Ford had always felt as though he was in competition with Wayne. Although Ford had played a plethora of cowboy roles during his episodic television years, his director jokingly harassed him with constant comparisons as to how Wayne would have done the job.

The film's producer Mace Neufeld recalled, "I think Harrison always felt when Aldrich was shooting a scene, that Aldrich was looking at him and seeing the picture of John Wayne, and he gave him a pretty hard time on the film...."[20]

On July 6, 1979, *The Frisco Kid* was released to theaters nationwide. Gene Wilder's name above the title was a stronger selling point than Ford's. Audiences were beginning to lose faith in Ford's ability to portray memorable characters in memorable films.

Time magazine said that the film "just misses being very good."[21] Vincent Canby of *The New York Times* believed the territory was foreign for director Aldrich, claiming that he was "not much at home in the kind of lovable comedy this film wants to

Stepping into the shoes of "The Duke" for *The Frisco Kid* (Warner Bros., 1979).

be. The comic timing is always a couple of beats off.... There's no shortage of talent in *The Frisco Kid*, but it's the wrong talent for the wrong material...."[22]

Notwithstanding its modest accumulation of only $12 million at the box office, *Frisco Kid* was yet another disappointment on Ford's resumé. But it proved to be the *final* chapter in Harrison Ford's book of unexceptional films. From this point forth, the term "commercially unsuccessful" would rarely be read or heard in connection with his films.

14

Lose Some, Win Some

Despite his new commercial viability, Ford's private life began to falter. As the offers of roles with overseas locations increased, his relationship with his wife Mary declined. With shooting locations including Yugoslavia (where *Force 10* was filmed) and London (for *Star* Wars and 1979's *Hanover Street)*, the actor was rarely with his family.

"I had to go all over the world, and Mary and I were dragged apart more and more," he recalled. "Slowly but surely our relationship began to break up. Although she tried to keep us together, traveling to see me whenever possible, the situation became unbearable. I'm not the easiest guy to be married to, but it was the outside pressures that finally drove us apart."[1]

Provoked by all of the publicity and promotional tours, premieres, and parties, rumors that he was romantically involved with his *Hanover Street* co-star Lesley-Anne Down began to circulate. Coupled with the overall change in attitude Ford was inescapably undergoing, Mary and Harrison drifted apart and eventually separated in 1978. They signed the divorce papers in 1979.

Today, Ford claims with certainty his greatest regret in life to be "the failure of my first marriage and the pain it caused."[2] Following the divorce settlement, Ford relinquished custody of Benjamin and Willard to Mary — who conveniently ended up living only minutes away from his own Hollywood Hills home. The actor respectfully remained on amicable speaking terms with the mother of his children, both out of a genuine appreciation for her and being sincerely indebted to her for his success as an actor.

"I would have never accepted the role in *Star Wars* if Mary hadn't been right behind me all the way. She goaded me on by dealing with all the problems connected with getting back into acting and was a tremendous support all along."[3]

Ford soon discovered that he would not spend his life as a Hollywood bachelor with an ex-wife and two sons.

"I'd always thought that life was for couples, not singles," explained the actor. "A man alone hasn't the strength to overcome all the obstacles in front of him. He needs support to help him when he's down, or perhaps it's a question of mutual assistance...."[4]

Melissa Mathison was employed as a script supervisor to Francis Ford Coppola when she first met Ford on the Philippine set of *Apocalypse Now* in 1977.

Their second meeting took place later that same year over a dinner arranged by Fred Roos in Toronto, where Mathison was at work on Coppola's *The Black Stallion* and Ford was busily promoting *Star Wars*.

Until the early 1980s, the two maintained their professional relationship by phoning one another and meeting in social settings. But their mutual respect for one another developed far beyond their original expectations and into a serious, loving relationship. Before long, the two shared their lives as a couple in Ford's Shaker mansion.

"I was captivated," declared Ford. "But I knew that I was going to have to change my way of life completely or risk losing her."[5]

Part of Ford's new regimen included insisting that both Melissa and his children accompany him on his distant shooting locales as often as possible. As Ford continued his work as an actor and a newly improved boyfriend to Mathison, she became an accomplished screenwriter.

Melissa Mathison was born in Los Angeles on June 3, 1950, the daughter of Richard Mathison, former journalist with *The Los Angeles Times* and the West Coast bureau chief for *Newsweek* magazine. Her journey into the world of filmmaking began when she took the job as babysitter to Francis and Eleanor Coppola's children. Soon after, she found herself as his assistant on the set of 1974's *The Godfather II*. ("I just got coffee and Cokes for people. Bringing coffee to Al Pacino was exciting.")[6] Her first foray into screenwriting as a Berkeley graduate was *The Black Stallion*, which she completed in 1977 for Coppola, its executive producer. In between that and her script for another Coppola executive produced film (1982's *The Escape Artist*), she wrote for both *Time* magazine and — like her brother Dirk before her — *People*. (Ford jokingly referred to the magazine as "Peephole," because it "absorbs, digests and shits personalities like yesterday's prunes."[7])

Her most significant contribution to the film industry came while accompanying her boyfriend to his desert shooting location for *Raiders of the Lost Ark* in 1980. There she made the acquaintance of director Steven Spielberg, who — based on his admiration for *The Black Stallion* — approached her to write the script for *E.T. The Extra-Terrestrial* (then entitled "A Boy's Life"). Mathison agreed to write the story (and also served as an associate producer on the film). She won the 1982 Academy Award for Best Original Screenplay. She also won a "Best Screenplay Written Directly for the Screen" award from the prestigious Writers Guild of America.

In 1983, Mathison wrote "Kick the Can," the second segment of the film *Twilight Zone: The Movie*, under the pseudonym Josh Rogan. The sequence was directed by Spielberg in a fleeting six days.

Now a well-known screenwriter with a celebrity boyfriend, Mathison went from being an observer to one observed, and was forced to adapt to life under the looking glass. But she understood it was part of the package deal that she shared with Ford. Ford was sympathetic: "She suddenly finds herself a celebrity writer, and she doesn't want to be a celebrity writer. She just wants to write...."[8]

15

DESTINED FOR SUCCESS

George Lucas, the creative force behind the *Star Wars* phenomenon, had always envisioned that the show would continue. It was originally written as an enormous space saga, too elaborate to be condensed into one film, so the writer-director dissected the work into nine different episodes. The first film, *Star Wars*, was subtitled *Episode IV: A New Hope*.

At the time, the film's worldwide viewing base didn't anticipate a sequel. After all, the film had a beginning, middle and end, with the Rebels celebrating a decisive victory over the evil Empire. Viewers got closure, and were able to exit theaters completely satisfied. It was a black-and-white tale of good vs. evil.

But, for those who closely followed George Lucas during the late '70s, it was general knowledge that more could be expected. Come 1980, the Empire would indeed strike back.

The intent of the 1979 *Star Wars Holiday Special* (which aired on CBS on Sunday, November 7) was to reinvigorate the public interest in *Star Wars* and give audiences a taste of what was to come. The program featured the original cast members amidst the Imperial-controlled environs of Chewbacca's home planet of Kashyyyk. For the first time, the Wookies' daily family life was shown in their home atop the enormous trees that blanketed the Wookie-dominated planet.

Seemingly photographed on a budget rivaling a junior high school stage production, the program was brutally painful to endure. Featuring the chintziest of props, the lamest of special effects, the most obnoxious application of makeup (reminiscent of Tammy Faye Baker) the cheesiest dialogue and the most careless acting, *Holiday Special*—which also featured Art Carney, Beatrice Arthur and Harvey Korman—was broadcast on that evening for the first and final time.

The program (complete with musical interludes performed by Carney, Jefferson Airplane and Carrie Fisher) was so poorly received that it remains undocumented in virtually any and all publications on TV programming history.

Luxuriating in the success of *Star Wars* and recovering from both the physical and mental turmoil of bringing the film to the screen, Lucas decided against directing the new film. It was time for him to hand over the reins of complete control and settle in as the executive producer.

Considering the complexities of the script and the amount and variety of the special effects required, Lucas was excited at the technical challenges. But his priority was to develop and strengthen the relationships among the film's central characters.

Written by Leigh Brackett, a prolific author of screenplays and science-fiction novels, a rough draft of *The Empire Strikes Back* began circulating in the early months of 1978. Shortly after completion, however, Brackett was hospitalized and died due to complications from an unforeseen bout with cancer. The task of fine-tuning the script came to a standstill.

"After Leigh died, I did a draft in between before we were able to hire another writer," said Lucas. "I was faced with going into production and you just can't come up with somebody just on the spur of the moment who would be right."[1] Lawrence Kasdan was ultimately chosen to do the revisions. (A former ad copywriter, he was later employed by Lucas on another writing project *Raiders of the Lost Ark*.)

Lucas was quick to offer Irvin Kershner (whose resume included *Loving*, *The Return of a Man Called Horse* and *The Eyes of Laura Mars*) the director's chair based on his ability to bring human relationships to the screen. Lucas was once under the tutelage of Kershner, who taught photography and film design classes at the University of Southern California during the 1960s. To any director, an offer to take command of the sequel to a staggeringly successful film is the opportunity of a lifetime. But getting Kershner to commit was difficult, despite their prior relationship.

"I told George I didn't want to do a sequel," said Kershner. "He said, 'I don't blame you. Neither would I, but this isn't. It's the second act of the second trilogy of nine films I plan to make on this theme. I want it to be better than mine.' I still was unconvinced. My director friends told me to stay out of it. I realized now that I was concerned about what others would think if I came in on the heels of something great."[2]

Kershner ultimately agreed to be in charge of the film. Along with Lucas, producer Gary Kurtz was similarly jubilant following a 1978 meeting with Kershner.

Empire would be Kershner's first foray into science fiction, but Kurtz and Lucas noted his positive attitude, enthusiasm and lack of cynicism. Kershner proved that he was legitimately interested in the genre. Kurtz was relieved, as he had discovered that it was a rare thing to find a director with the appropriate attitude towards the project.

By the start of negotiations for his return, Harrison Ford had already established himself as a lucratively employed actor with an eclectic body of work. His career went on despite the moderate box office success of his films. Fearful of becoming stereotyped and tired of reading every science fiction script that followed *Star Wars*, he carefully weighed each project offered to him.

When approached by Lucas to reprise Han Solo, Ford was justifiably prudent. Assured that the script would focus on the further development of the characters, Ford soon signed on. He would join fellow castmates Carrie Fisher and Mark Hamill in completing the most anticipated sequel in cinematic history.

"It's part of the natural progression, really," stated Ford. "You'd expect development of the characters in a second act. I was expecting it and wasn't surprised when I saw a different version of Han Solo in the script. We get to know him better."[3]

The fans' expectations for *Empire* were nothing less than stratospheric, so the producers avoided the potential for flawed special effects and sets by coming up with a fascinating opening sequence on a planet whose environment was Earth-like.

It was no easy task to find the ideal location — one that had the look of a treeless, barren icecap but was also reasonably accessible to the filmmakers. They wanted to avoid recognizable alpine terrain, but could not conceivably film above the Arctic Circle. So they scoured the countries of northern Europe (including Finland, Sweden and Norway), northern Canada and Alaska in search of a previously undiscovered location that would meet their needs.

Accessible only by a single-track electrified railroad linked between the Norwegian capital of Oslo and the port city of Bergen, the town of Finse, Norway (which was home to the railway station and a single hotel), would become the ice planet Hoth, where filmmakers would film the opening moments of *The Empire Strikes Back*.

Two days prior to the March 5, 1979, commencement of principal photography, the production created a base camp for the 70 members of the cast and crew 30 miles east of Finse at a ski lodge at Geilo. All of its rooms were booked and its storage areas, railroad buildings and tents were used to house additional equipment, from props to camera booms and cranes to the 15 tracked vehicles required for the transportation of hardware and personnel.

Instead of importing extras to pose as the Rebel ground troops, the casting department hired members of a more-than-willing Finnish alpine rescue team — a sensible choice considering they needn't be pampered to withstand Norway's icy environment.

Upon their arrival, the filmmakers were given candid insight into what lay ahead meteorologically. In one of the most treacherous winters in Norwegian history, the temperature would regularly drop to 20 degrees below zero. Cast and crew contended with hostile winds, frostbite and even avalanches.

"Some days the weather would change on the glacier very quickly," recalled director Kershner. "Our Norwegian guides would say we'd have to quit early because we wouldn't be able to see to get back to the hotel. Halfway down the glacier the storm would return and cause a whiteout. You couldn't see the front of your own vehicle. During a whiteout sometimes it would take an hour and a half to return to the hotel with men walking in front of the vehicles to identify the flags [which would mark the safe route of travel]. The unpredictability of the weather made working on this location very difficult. The most amazing thing about filming in the snow is that it never photographs as cold as it really is."[4]

The weather interfered with photography on a daily basis, causing setbacks in the shooting schedule. The eyepiece of the camera would cloud up from condensation created by the eyeball of the photographer, thereby creating doubts as to whether or not a shot was in focus or if the camera was in fact tracking the action. Additionally, the 20- to 30-mile-per-hour winds allowed for only 20- to 30-second intervals of footage before the lens would require manual cleaning.

On the first day of filming, the weather became so intolerable that scenes of Mark Hamill trudging through the snow were accomplished by setting the camera up just two feet outside of a hotel room door, with Kershner and crew utilizing the room as safe shelter.

Just as one troublesome issue was dealt with, another would appear. Unable to escape the lenses of the paparazzi even in a location as remote as the Hardanger Plateau, the moviemaker's activities were captured by a photographer from a British newspaper. The photojournalist, who apparently bribed a helicopter pilot from the Norwegian Air Force, successfully acquired the first-ever "in production" photo of *The Empire Strikes Back*. The pilot, however, was not as fortunate. The Royal Air Force dealt with him accordingly, and he was left with nothing but a small wad of cash and a photograph to view during the unexpected vacation forced upon him.

Because of the tremendous amount of public curiosity, the producers went to great lengths to ensure that *Empire*'s secrets would remain just that. The main provision — apart from the expansive on-set security — was that several of the principals were given only portions of their scripts with their co-stars' dialogue completely obliterated with magic marker.

While filming its conclusion, only a handful of individuals — including Lucas, Kershner, Kasdan and Mark Hamill — knew the dialogue of the scene in which Luke discovers that Vader is, in fact, his father.

Having delivered a bogus line at filming, actor David Prowse (Darth Vader) discovered only at the film's premiere that his character was related to Luke.

Hamill remembered feeling both privileged and amused to be in on the secret: "Before we filmed that moment in *Empire*, they took me aside and said that they were going to film the dialogue as Vader saying 'You don't know the truth. Obi-Wan killed your father,' instead of what everyone eventually saw. It was fun knowing all along that James Earl Jones would later dub in 'I am your father.' It was that line I was actually reacting to, instead of the cover line...."[5]

Ford himself was not given a complete shooting script until three weeks before the start of principal photography. "One of George's real strengths is not giving you all the information you need, yet at the same time not denying you anything essential. You have a feeling that you want to know more at all times."[6]

Immediately upon his arrival to film the scenes of Luke Skywalker's rescue — a sequence that was conceived while Kershner overcame the boredom of waiting during the whiteouts — Ford was introduced to the environment's unmerciful conditions. En route to the shooting location, the actor was stranded in his train, delayed by an avalanche.

Summoned via radio by the railway authorities, a special train equipped with a plow made a path through 50-foot-high snowdrifts and safely delivered the actor. Ford spent the journey in the vehicle's engine compartment and arrived at his destination at midnight.

Following his ordeal, Ford recalled the experience, defining it as an ordinary occupational hazard: "Part of professionalism is showing up on time and knowing your lines," said the actor, "but I have never before learned them in an avalanche or reached a set in a snow plow."[7]

Alan Arnold, the film's publicist, chronicled each day of the production and later published them in *A Journal of the Making of "The Empire Strikes Back"* to coincide with the film's release. He wrote of the occasion and the manner in which Ford presented himself in an interview immediately following his journey to the Norwegian set: "He looked a bit dazed and bleary eyed. He had gotten very little sleep, but he could not have been more courteous. His manner reminded me of something I had not encountered since dealing with actors from the past, romantic stars like Cary Grant, in particular, who were trained in the old studio style attitude to publicity. I have seldom seen it in the younger generation of actors who tend to be self-conscious, probably because a fair number of them are inarticulate. Yet here was Harrison — urbane, self-assured, and charming after having been up half the night. What a pleasant change."[8]

The inclement Norwegian weather was not the only factor responsible for delays: On January 24, 1979, Elstree Studio's Stage 3 — which was then occupied by the sets of director Stanley Kubrick's *The Shining*—was consumed in a flash fire. Because of the rescheduling, tension began to mount.

But, by March 12, the cast and crew — with the exception of Mark Hamill, who was required to stay in Norway a while longer — assembled their equipment at Elstree Studios, where every sound stage was by then filled with the film's elaborate sets—a total of 64 in all. Director Kershner (referred to as "Kersh" by cast and crew) said, "To build these giant sets, shoot them, take them down and build another one and keep going was difficult. I think, at one point, there were up to 400 people working. They had every carpenter, every bricklayer, etc. They had everyone who could lift up a hammer hammering and making plaster, etc. It was amazing. I would finish shooting and the next day, the set would be rubble and by noon it would be swept clean and they would be laying out the next set...."[9]

Despite the number of laborers, the studio's eight stages were not enough to house the enormous production. Requiring a space large enough to house the sets for the swamp planet Dagobah *and* the Rebel base's ice hangar, construction crews were summoned to create what would become the largest sound stage in the world.

At 250 feet long, 120 feet wide and 45 feet high with a capacity of nearly 1.25 million cubic feet, the stage could host a game of regulation soccer. With construction completed in May, the stage began its transformation from a vacant four-walled wood, steel and concrete edifice to the icy laser-carved caverns of the Rebel hangar. (The effect of the stronghold's "icy" walls was achieved through administering hot wire-cutters to large sheets of polystyrene.) Full-scale mock-ups of the Rebel fleet — including several X-wing fighters and snow speeders — were dwarfed by the structure that accommodated them.

One prop in particular was the most involved undertaking on the entire set and perhaps for the entire production itself. At nearly 70 feet in diameter, 16 feet high and an overall length of 80 feet stood the full-scale Millennium Falcon, the largest prop built for the film. Weighing in at 23 tons, the ship was constructed by the same contracting company that built the stage and was transported in 16 separate components. From its point of creation 250 miles west of London at Pembroke Docks in Wales, it traveled across southern England to the studio in a convoy of trucks.[10] Once there, the sections were assembled like an enlarged jigsaw puzzle by lifting them into place with compressed air pads much like those found on hovercraft.

To make up for the production delays, a second unit was initiated under the direction of John Barry, the Oscar-winning production designer of the original *Star Wars*. On May 3, 1979, 43-year-old Barry was suddenly struck with a normally

The 1980 return of Han Solo, Princess Leia, Luke Skywalker and Chewbacca (Lucasfilm, Ltd., 1980).

treatable case of infectious meningitis and tragically passed away. What was most unusual about the incident was the fact that those who worked alongside Barry for his two weeks of direction were mysteriously not infected. For one afternoon the production halted all activities to pay respect to their fallen comrade, resuming work later that evening in true "time is money" fashion.

Just when the filming of the Hoth interior sequences was completed, the set was struck and in its place sprang forth a totally new environment. There, on what was soon thereafter dubbed the "*Star Wars* stage," lay the planet Dagobah, where Yoda trains Luke Skywalker in the ways of the Force. Aiding Yoda is the ghostly apparition of Ben Kenobi, played by returning actor Sir Alec Guinness. Due to a lengthy period of recuperation from eye surgery, Guinness was not able to guarantee his appearance in the sequel until just weeks before the conclusion of photography — much to the delight of cast, crew and (ultimately) the fans.

While preparing to design Yoda's surroundings, the producers speculated what would be appropriate considering the physical appearance and personality of the 800-year-old Jedi Knight (brought to life by Muppets puppeteer Frank Oz). What was agreed upon was the murky, densely forested swamp planet Dagobah.

Sitting atop an elevated stage (in order to make room for the planet's swamp) were gnarled steel-framed trees that blocked out daylight, perpetually encompassing the planet in darkened mist. Crews spread fallen leaves on the several tons of soil that had been brought in. High above hung authentic lianas and Spanish moss.

"There were trees, and hills, and bushes, and four feet of water and it was slippery and pretty dangerous," recalled Kershner. "That set was pretty impressive, though. When you smoked it up and you had clouds hanging in the air, it was magnificent! We closed all the doors and stopped all the air movement and then they sprayed this vegetable stuff and you actually had the mist hanging in layers. We all had to stand still quietly until the air settled and then blow the stuff in. We would shoot the scene and then the mist would all go to hell as soon as we started moving. But the scene was impressive."[11]

The remaining sound stages of Elstree studios housed the sets for the interior tunnels and smaller chambers of the Rebel base on Hoth; the Wampa cave on Hoth (where Hamill hung upside down for a six-day period for only a few moments worth of footage); the interiors of the Millennium Falcon and the various Star Destroyers; and the sleekly designed, brightly lit interiors of Cloud City, the Tibanna gas-mining colony administrated by Han Solo's old acquaintance Lando Calrissian (Billy Dee Williams).

Towering 30 feet high, the carbon freezing chamber set proved to be a difficult environment for both cast and crew. The absence of guardrails and the shape of the set made the task of camera set-ups and actor placement difficult. Above was nearly 50 tons of recycled junk purchased from a nearby scrap yard and dressed to look like functional gadgetry. Midget actors portrayed the boar-like Ugnaughts. For them, difficulties arose due to the excessive amounts of steam emanating from the floor panels below.

Kershner considered the sequence to be the most satisfying one in the film — enhanced by what the director calls an abundance of "emotional color."[12]

What was additionally impressive to the director was the presence and interaction of virtually every character in the film, all on one stage: Darth Vader, Boba Fett, Han Solo, Princess Leia, Chewbacca, C3-PO, several Stormtroopers and various other Imperial officers. They were assembled to witness the carbon freezing and delivery of Han Solo into the hands of bounty hunter Boba Fett (portrayed by English actor Jeremy Bulloch).

Meanwhile, in Northern California, Lucas was busy overseeing the building of an extension to his home.*

Lucas would keep up with Kershner's activities by viewing videotape of the rushes that were flown in daily from London. Contributing as much as he could despite the distance separating him from the project, Lucas provided the footage of R2-D2's encounter with the exposed spine of one of Dagobah's more hostile inhabitants. By standing waist-deep in his as-yet-unfinished swimming pool in California, Lucas and a small crew photographed the scene themselves. It would later be inserted into the actual Elstree set footage with no visual inconsistencies.

According to Kershner, Lucas's subsequent involvement was limited to visiting the England sound stages on three occasions. Lucas would remain virtually unrecognizable on the sidelines, refusing Kershner's continuous invitations to stand camera-side by simply stating, "It's your picture." He also refused to have a personalized director's chair on the set waiting for him.

"I was shocked one day," recalled the director. "I'm shooting, and I look over and way in the back of about 50 people is George standing there. And I said, 'George, come over here!' He was sort of embarrassed, he's so shy! So he came over and watched the shooting. That was the morning that we shot a scene that ended up about six seconds on film and it took us ten hours to shoot! Everything kept breaking! Nothing worked!"[13]

For all involved, the frustrations of coping with such an uncooperative environment began to wither morale. "It was a bit grueling," recalled Carrie Fisher. "You were like one of the best-paid hostages in the world, sitting there for hours and never knowing when they were going to film."[14]

To cope with the boredom while technicians did their troubleshooting, the cast would await their cue in their respective dressing rooms or congregate and discuss the scene at hand. Occasionally, such fervent discussions would result in an unintended insult to Brackett's and Kasdan's screenwriting efforts.

"But you always have changes when you come to play a scene," claimed Ford. "We all know about other films where that gets out of hand, but not in this case, though a lot of lines were the result of invention at the time. When you know your characters as well as we do, some of the best lines come out."[15]

The new material would not be performed before the cameras until it met the final approval of the director. Throughout the film, Ford's contributions were frequent and greatly appreciated by Kershner, who began to confide in the actor when he thought of dialogue reconstruction.

"Harrison I adored because he was so creative and so much fun," said the director. "We really had fun making the picture. We would try things. I would have an idea at the last minute and would go running up to Harrison and say, 'Harrison, listen to this: Instead of running down the steps, you just stand there and let them come at you. And then you'll jump!' And he would say, 'Yeah, yeah, let's try it!'"[16]

---

*The property would eventually facilitate any and all post-production requirements for the projects on which he and his company were involved. Ultimately, Industrial Light and Magic would settle in, becoming the world's largest and most sophisticated special effects facility. The newly christened home base was commemoratively named "Skywalker Ranch."

One scene was a major improvisation entirely attributable to Ford. The sequence in which Han and Leia say their final farewells to one another in the carbon-freezing chamber was originally written with the two characters exchanging the overexploited "I love you"s. Ford persisted in his discussions with Kershner, hoping to find a response that would more appropriately represent his character and make Solo's predicament more poignant and memorable.

Ford insisted that he be shackled so their final kiss would be "rough and brisk and over with," and that he respond to Leia's "I love you" with a very sarcastic and sobering "I know."[17]

"I was very interested in that moment and how it works," said Ford. "We never even shot 'I love you, too.' We just went ahead. It gave George pause. He had not written the scene with a laugh. But that laugh opens you up emotionally. You don't have another emotional outlet in that scene. The kiss, as the Princess and I are pulled back, is visually strong, and there'll never be a payoff for the scene without a laugh."[18]

Writer Kasdan later claimed that he was displeased by the way his work had been sabotaged: "Han and Leia's relationship is not at all what I had envisaged. I could be the only person who feels this way, but I thought their romance had a touch of falseness about it ... [Han and Leia's originally scripted scenes] being changed had a lot to do with the circumstances of filming, Kershner and the actors' feeling about doing their roles again. I was one of the people who wasn't crazy about Harrison Ford in *Empire*."[19]

"I regarded that scene as entirely Ford's," said director Kershner, "which is why I gave him so much opportunity to tell me how he thought we should treat it. That led to a little tension with Carrie, who thought I was giving him too much head. Professional jealousy is very healthy, incidentally, and natural. But it was his scene, and I think he handled it quite beautifully."[20]

In the corporate world, Ford and Fisher's relationship would have been technically classified as a conflict of interest. While filming *Star Wars*, the two became so close that their relationship could easily be called "intimate." While being interviewed for a 1999 biography of Lucas, David Prowse revealed that the two co-stars "had a nice little relationship going. Whenever anyone couldn't find Harrison, you'd say, 'Have you tried Carrie's changing room?'"[21]

Their intimacy was not as evident during the filming of *Empire* as the result of Ford's new relationship with Melissa Mathison and Fisher's own bout with drug and alcohol dependency (baggage she'd had since filming *Star Wars*). She would later speak for the Lucas biography, claiming that her fondest moments during the filming of *Empire* were those in which she "felt like slapping" Ford.[22]

In 1990, Fisher penned her first novel, *Postcards from the Edge*, loosely based on her own experience as both the child of celebrities and an actress with an addiction. Fisher never forgot her personal alliance with Ford, making mention on her novel's acknowledgment page of both he and Mathison and their concern and support during the difficult periods throughout her life.

Ford's co-star Mark Hamill heartily agreed with Kershner's praise of Ford, recalling not only that particular moment on the carbon-freezing set but numerous other contributions. "Harrison's ideas are usually superb," said Hamill. "He has more freedom to bring bits to Solo, there's no question that he's added much to the role. When the story gets a little too arch, too corny or old-fashioned, Harrison will express exasperation or skepticism. He represents a portion of the audience that's too sophisticated to see the story from a young person's viewpoint."[23]

The $20 million-plus *Empire Strikes Back* entered its third and final stage at George Lucas' ever-expanding Northern California special effects facility, Industrial Light and Magic. There, model builders and cameramen created and filmed the various vehicles seen in the film. Animators photographed the Imperial snow-walkers (AT-ATs— or All-Terrain Armored Transports) and the Tauntauns using stop-and-go animation (a process in which the object is repeatedly moved and photographed one frame at a time). Artists created background matte paintings and plates. And sound-effects technicians supervised by Ben Burtt created and integrated the required otherworldly noises.

While most of this is customary during a film's post-production process, the scope of the visual effects required for *Empire* was so overwhelming that they were considered a major, if not *the* major requirement of principal photography.

At a 1979-estimated cost of between $5–8 million, the film's special effects shots totaled up to nearly 414, compared to the 380 shots involved for *Star Wars*. (To appreciate and understand the expense of the special effects, consider that the creation of Darth Vader's Star Destroyer, *The Executioner*, cost over $100,000 alone.)

While the special effects took on an almost supporting role in the end, director Kershner wanted the audience to focus their attention on the story and its characters.

"I hate to do things for the sake of making them look pretty," said Kershner. "I do like everything to be in the service of communicating a story so I tend to become very economical in my shooting."[24]

Ford also relates to Kershner's concerns involving the superfluous use of effects. While addressing the moments in the film that do not showcase the presence of actors, Ford admitted that even its non-human inhabitants are capable of depicting an emotional depth.

"If you look at the film again," said Ford, "I think you'll see that there's not one special effects scene in the whole movie. Every scene is about people. Sure, there are special effects in the background, there are scenes that are full of special effects but you'll never see a scene where you come into the scene or go out of the scene without some attachment to a human being. Look at the robots. The robots are not robots; they have human personalities. That's the hook, always....

"I know that people don't go into movie theaters to watch mechanical things. They go to the theaters to have a human experience. In fact, critics ask that question all the time: 'Are you upstaged by special effects?' And it's really pretty insulting, because it implies that the filmmaker has somewhere lost control. Let's face it, if you're being upstaged by the special effects, then someone somewhere has made a God-awful mistake."[25]

Based upon the box office results, audiences were indeed captivated by the film's look. But it was primarily the emotional elaboration of the characters that attracted viewers in droves.

"People who are expecting a repetition of the emotional experience of the first film are not going to find exactly that," vowed Ford. "The audience that saw the first film is more sophisticated now, three years later, in the same way the techniques are more sophisticated. And the demands upon them are slightly more than they were in the first film."[26]

To generate excitement and awareness among the public, the film's cast (needlessly) participated in a worldwide publicity tour. Accustomed to such painstaking rituals, Ford, Hamill, and Fisher were able to cope with the exhausting process—sometimes participating in 160 interviews or more a day—by using humor in front of the microphones and television cameras.

"The last time we were on tour together, Harrison was the publicity sheriff," recalled Hamill. "He would give us report cards: 'Humility: B. I like what you said about not being in the business for the money—A for that.'"[27]

Opening on May 21, 1980, in 126 theaters with round-the-clock screenings, *The Empire Strikes Back* earned an impressive six-day gross of nearly $9 million. Initially, industry analysts were skeptical of the film's long-term popularity.

For a film to become a certified blockbuster, the $100 million barrier must be broken. With its first week results coming in under $10 million, the film would reach blockbuster status only if it had "legs"—a term that film industry analyst Harold Vogel at Merrill Lynch uses to describe repeat business.

"You can't really determine the success of a film until after the fourth week," said Vogel. "With a film like *The Empire Strikes Back* all the buffs want to see it the first week. Later you see how it holds up in the wide distribution and if it gets much repeat business. Repeat business is what makes a film."[28]

Much to the delight of the would-be and repeat viewers who grew increasingly frustrated with the regularity of sold-out screenings, *Empire* went into an additional 575 theaters on June 2. Proving that it did indeed have "legs" and that each was alive and kicking, the picture eventually amassed an estimated grand total of $223 million in the United States alone.

Newsweek's David Ansen claimed that "even the most earthbound eyes can't deny that what they're watching is a celestial class act."[29] *Variety* praised the film, lauding it as "a worthy sequel to *Star Wars*, equal in both technical mastery and characterization."[30] (The film was subsequently presented with an Academy Award for its outstanding achievement in sound by Ben Burtt and additionally given a Special Achievement award for its visual effects.)

Janet Maslin of *The New York Times* focused her attention on Ford's performance and character as one of the film's selling points: "This time Harrison Ford's Han Solo steals the show. Mr. Ford slips easily into the film's comic-book conversational style, and he also brings a real air of tragedy to Han's fate, which is another thing we won't exactly know about until next time."[31]

Ford, too, felt that his performance in the film was the best he'd ever given to date.

The unexpected, serial-like conclusion of the film was noted. "I have no real defense for that argument, but what obligation is there to tie up every question with an equal answer?" questions the actor. "The cliff-hanger is because the trilogy is really constructed in the classic form of a three-act play. Naturally, there are going to be questions in the second act which have to be resolved in the third.[32]

"I guess it really depends on what you go to a movie for. I figure there was at least 11 dollars' worth of entertainment in *Empire*. So if you paid four bucks and didn't get an ending, you're still seven dollars ahead of the game."[33]

16

THE FIRST GEORGE, STEVEN AND HARRISON COLLABORATION

In 1981, movie theater marquees began displaying 27 × 41 posters with the bold caption "INDIANA JONES — THE NEW HERO FROM THE CREATORS OF *JAWS* AND *STAR WARS*."

Below the caption stood the lone figure of a leather jacket–clad, fedora-topped man with the most peculiar of accessories strapped over his left shoulder. With the release of the film, the face of Hollywood and popular culture would be forever changed on a global scale.

The origins of *Raiders of the Lost Ark* stemmed from a casual conversation between Steven Spielberg and George Lucas while building sand castles on vacation in Hawaii. There, on the beach of the Mauna Kea Hotel, the two discussed the possibility of bringing to life the Saturday matinee action-adventure series of the 1930s, '40s and '50s that they remembered being fascinated by as kids. Given the energy and talent at their disposal, the subject went from friendly (and presumably inconsequential) oceanfront chatter into a real commitment.

"I'm really doing it more than anything else, so that I can enjoy it," admitted Lucas. "Because I just want to see this movie. You know, you sit back and you say, 'Boy, why can't they make movies like this anymore?'"[1]

Lucas — who would serve as the film's executive producer tried to decide who would be best suited to write a story about the archaeologist-adventurer named after his wife Marcia's Alaskan malamute. After consideration, he chose screenwriter Lawrence Kasdan, from *The Empire Strikes Back*.

"George and Steven and I sat for a week of meetings [from January 23–27, 1978] about the story, really outlined the thing into a tape recorder," Kasdan recalled. "It was a constant process of an idea coming out and another person saying, 'Yah, that's pretty good but it doesn't quite fit. Let's try this.' And the third person saying, 'How about this for a capper?' We wound up with about a 100-page transcript of the story outline. I left those meetings feeling I was in pretty good shape and then realized, 'Uh-oh, this is going to be hard.'"[2]

By April 1980, the approved fifth revision of the collaboration provided what ultimately became the shooting script for *Raiders of the Lost Ark*. The screenplay described the heroics of a character named Indiana Jones (initially designated by

16. The First George, Steven and Harrison Collaboration

Lucas as Smith) — a professor and archaeologist racing against Hitler's Nazis in their quest for the Lost Ark of the Covenant. In Biblical times, the Ark was the chest rumored to contain the Ten Commandments.

With the final blessing of Paramount Pictures, director Spielberg and producer Frank Marshall were granted time and budget guidelines. Recalling Spielberg's filmmaking history — which tended to regularly suffer from extended shooting schedules and escalating budgets— Paramount President Michael Eisner warned of severe penalties if Spielberg's production didn't specifically comply. Agreeing to the studio's terms, Spielberg's prompt decision piqued the curiosity of Paramount. Eisner signed on, figuring either they didn't care or they had it all figured out.

While location scouting and the hiring of the film's crew took place, Spielberg, Lucas and Marshall began casting in February 1980 in the kitchen of Lucasfilm headquarters. The team spent nearly six months in their efforts to discover a living, breathing Indiana Jones.

"We wanted an unknown originally — a total unknown," said Spielberg. "Conceitedly, George and I wanted to make a star of Johnny the construction worker from Malibu. We couldn't find a construction worker in Malibu, so we began looking at more substantial people in the film industry."[3]

Contenders ranged from Tim Matheson to Tom Berenger to Peter Coyote to Tom Selleck. Had it not been for the studio's inability to allow a breach of contract for his television series *Magnum P.I.*, the face of Indiana Jones would have undoubtedly sported Selleck's trademark mustache.

With three weeks to go for the final casting decision in order to make their projected June start of principal photography, an air of desperation entered the production's atmosphere. Then, while watching his partner's film *The Empire Strikes Back* just prior to its initial release, Steven Spielberg had a startling revelation.

"I called George Lucas," recalled Spielberg, "and said, 'He's right under our noses.' George said, 'I know who you're going to say.' I said, 'Who?' and he said 'Harrison Ford.' 'Right.' 'Let's get him,' he said. And we did."[4]

Ford, who had developed an outstanding working and personal relationship with Lucas, had only met Spielberg once before socially. He was not only interested in the project, but also at the idea of collaborating with the industry's most prominent director.

Ford enlisted his youngest son Willard and girlfriend Melissa Mathison to accompany him to Spielberg's home. As they chatted and played video games, Ford took to the director and accepted the project, providing one condition be met: "The only question I had in my mind about it was because both *Empire* and *Raiders* were written by Larry Kasdan," said Ford, "that there was some little similarity in the characters. Or, in the dialogue, not the characters. Steven agreed we should make a definition between the two and not give Indiana Jones the kind of snappy dialogue which, in cases, was a little Han Solo."[5]

Aware of the improbability of a globetrotting adventurer battling Nazis for relics of supernatural powers, Ford admired the character of Indiana Jones due in part to the ordinary personality traits he possessed.

"Indiana has human frailties, fears, and money problems, which make him more down to earth. Indy doesn't have any fancy gadgetry keeping him at a distance from enemies and trouble. He's right in there with just a bullwhip to keep the world at bay."[6]

Satisfied with the changes made to his character, Ford enthusiastically agreed not only to the contracted $400,000 paycheck, but also to the supplementary seven percent of the film's net profits, which he felt — based on his intuition — would be considerable. (Spielberg's salary was $1.5 million, while Lucas' was $4 million.) Furthermore, he verbally agreed to act in any sequels that might arise if the first installment became a financial success.

La Rochelle, France, was selected as a location for its proximity to England's Elstree Studio, where the group occupied production offices and soundstages. La Rochelle would provide the filmmakers not only with the appropriate geographical location, but also two significant props which were considered too large to transport anywhere and yet too impractical to duplicate with miniatures.

Principal photography began June 23, 1980, where it spent one week filming three miles off the coast of France atop the churning waters on board two extremely diverse oceangoing vessels. The first was an old freighter recently converted into a 1930s-era tramp steamer named the *Bantu Wind*. The second was a German U-boat named the *Wurffler*. Originally constructed for the film *Das Boot*, the submarine was made available to the production when *Das Boot* came to a standstill.

Frank Marshall understood the importance of thrilling the audience with sets and sounds they might otherwise never experience. A massive German submarine was sure to impress. No matter the difficulty involved in filming a full size sub, a mere model would never suffice.

The crew was pleasantly surprised by the holding area where the submarine was contained. Originally constructed by the German Army during World War II, the interiors of the virtually impregnable pen provided the exact desired location for the sequence involving a Nazi stronghold.

However, shooting in La Rochelle had its price. For nearly their entire stay, the production fell victim to troublesome weather.

"The first two days the weather was very rough," recalled associate producer Robert Watts, "and we had limitations on the height of waves we could take the submarine out in. So we shot the interiors. We shot everything at sea Wednesday and Thursday. Thursday got very rough. We managed to stay out even though a lot of people got seasick."[7]

It seemed that no matter where a Lucasfilm Production touched down, the weather was always a factor. In the filming of *Empire, American Graffiti* and now on *Raiders* in both La Rochelle and in the sky above England's Elstree Studios, the weather had never before been as bad.

The filmmakers went ahead with filming on the deck of the *Bantu Wind* and with the seafaring shots of both vessels. In his first exposure to the environment and the maiden test of his physical capabilities, Ford elected to swim the distance between the freighter and the sub — an act that he claimed was more uncomfortable than dangerous.

Leaving France behind, the next stop on the itinerary was England.

On June 30, the production shot the interiors of the house of Imam, the Egyptian scholar who aids Indy and Sallah (South Wales–born actor John Rhys-Davies) in the translation of a medallion's inscriptions. It's these inscriptions that hold the clue to the Lost Ark's whereabouts.

While unfortunate conditions in France may have lessened morale among the cast and crew at the onset, the footage was shot on schedule and under budget — a factor that made an impact on the schedule's remainder.

"If you start out like that," said Kathleen Kennedy, associate to Mr. Spielberg, "the crew is pretty hyped up, and you come back to the studio ready to go right into shooting again. The momentum kept up...."[8]

Scheduled for two days of filming, the scene in Imam's home required only *one* day — a turn of events that brought universal relief.

Elstree's Stage 4 was the setting for the film's exciting opening moments of Indiana's escape from the booby-trapped South American temple. The plaster-constructed walls were adorned with souvenirs of old. Recalling the storage facilities containing props used on previous productions, production designer Norman Reynolds nostalgically used "Old Man's Beard" — a network of vines his department had utilized on the Dagobah set of *The Empire Strikes Back* — to decorate the temple walls.

Out with Tom Selleck. In with Harrison Ford — as Indiana Jones (Lucasfilm, Ltd., 1981).

Although the temple is littered with both natural and man-made booby traps, Indiana Jones illustrates during the film's opening moments his intelligence, agility and bravery as he skillfully eludes every obstacle before him.

The first is a brush with insects. Brought to Indy's attention by his partner Satipo (Alfred Molina), a horde of tarantulas clings to the back of his leather jacket.

Although seemingly fearless, then 37-year-old, not-so-tough Ford admitted to at least one moment of trepidation: "Ordinary spiders I don't mind, but tarantulas are so vile-looking, so hairy, and well, some animals just seem so disgusting or evil. I got goose bumps on the tarantula set."[9]

As Indy progresses, the traps become more prominent and deadly. Arrows were launched toward Indy following his theft of the Idol of the Chachapoyan Warriors.

(Ford was struck by several arrows and darts during his "escape" but they caused no physical harm, as they were rubber-tipped.)

Constructed of nearly 800 pounds of plaster, Fiberglas, and wood, the last obstacle was a 12-foot-high boulder not only capable of crushing Indiana Jones but (more significantly) actor Harrison Ford as well. Standing on the sidelines and out of camera range, assistants could, if necessary, attempt to slow the boulder with long poles. A mechanical arm was attached to the prop for additional control.

Each time the boulder was rolled down the hill, the set had to be redressed. It was time-consuming because of the number of stalactites that had to be replaced. To provide the menacing sound of a rolling boulder, Ben Burtt taped the sound of a Honda station wagon rolling down a gravelly hillside with its motor off.

Despite the ten attempts it took (two takes from each of the five different camera angles), the scene was filmed without incident or bodily injury. Reflecting on the tense moments during filming, Spielberg recalled his leading man's dexterity and fleet-footedness.

"He was lucky. And I was an idiot for letting him try. I mean, the absolute worst time to eliminate your leading man is in the second week of shooting."[10]

The production moved on to Elstree's Stage 5, for the filming of the exquisitely detailed Map Room. There, the collective talents of production designer Norman Reynolds' artistry, Ford's acting, Spielberg's direction and Douglas Slocombe's cinematography were coupled with one additional ingredient for dramatic results—music. Spielberg utilized background music as an emotional aid for Ford during the filming of that scene.

"Harrison does this well because he has a wonderful ability to imagine how he should feel," said the director. "But music makes it easier. You let the music direct you. You let the beats and measures of the score tell you how to feel. It just so happened we found a couple of wonderful numbers for the interior Map Room sequence that were as if written for *Raiders*, as if written for Harrison."[11]

Encompassing nearly all of Stage 3 was the film's most impressive of sets.

As described in Kasdan's script and later visualized in simple, thumbnail sketches by Steven Spielberg, the sacred Ark of the Covenant was held in an elaborately detailed temple known as the Well of Souls. There, the Ark was eternally preserved and confined—buried by a centuries-long sandstorm.

The set interior was embellished with intricate hieroglyphic markings on its walls and the podium on which the Ark rested. The chamber's most impressive features were the three nearly 37-foot-tall jackals that served as the Ark's mythic guardians.

Designed and constructed by Reynolds and his crew of artisans, the set's historic accuracy was overseen by Howard Kazanjian, who had always maintained a personal fascination with Egyptology.

The day following Ford's thirty-eighth birthday, the actor rapelled down the length of the enormous jackal. Ford's Irish-born stunt double Martin Grace rode atop the Jackal during its collapse into the chamber wall.

The production warily filmed among an estimated 6,500 Denmark-imported snakes (supposedly including 2,000 artificial ones), such as grass and rat snakes, copperheads, asps, pythons, cobras and constrictors for nearly two weeks. Animal handler Mike Culling claimed it would require the strength of five men to uncoil the constrictor if it wrapped itself around someone. One cobra was 12 feet long and required four people to reposition it.

All were undoubtedly intimidating; some were deadly. For those who ventured into the snake den on a daily basis, all that stood between them and a venomous death were the high rubber boots and reinforced pants and jackets they wore. An ambulance, a doctor and two nurses stood by with anti-venom serum.

While Ford was comfortable with the snakes, his co-star — New York–bred stage actress Karen Allen, who portrayed the tough Marion Ravenwood (after Debra Winger turned down the role), was reluctant.

While most of the cast and crew members who came in contact with the snakes were provided with protective clothing, the scenes required that she be dressed only in a skirt and short-sleeved shirt — thus leaving her legs and arms exposed. As filming progressed, however, Allen was able to overcome her fear of the snakes.

When moments of discomfort interfered with her ability to perform, stunt double Wendy Leach would bravely step in to assist. But even a brave stuntwoman has moments of apprehension. When Leach was unprepared, animal handler Steve Edge would remove all traces of manly leg hair, don her dress and relieve her.

Initially, Allen was so intimidated by the reptiles that at times she was unable to react on cue. Spielberg — who was originally dismayed at the difficulties this posed — had a solution: At one point during the production, he dropped a snake on her from high atop a scaffolding. From that point forth, the actress screamed on cue for a week — and whenever her director was nowhere in sight, she would look to the ceiling.

The snakes proved to be somewhat uncooperative. They took a liking to the light and warmth of the torch fires, which they were supposed to fear. Additionally, the pythons did not strike on cue. The moviemakers overcame the problem by tempting them with an arm or pant leg, or by simply waving handkerchiefs off-camera.

For the scene of Indy and a hooded cobra, the production was faced with the challenge of keeping Ford protected from the reptile. Ultimately they propped a thin sheet of Plexiglass between him and the snake.*

On Stage 2 was the Raven Bar, where Indiana Jones and Marion Ravenwood reunite after several years. One of the film's largest fight sequences took place there. The scene was complete with elaborately choreographed fisticuffs between the heroic couple and sinister German agents led by Toht (Ronald Lacey). Filmed over two weeks, the scene also involved the spray of machine gun fire and hits — made possible by the use of tiny charges implanted into the walls, called squibs. While all this was happening, the bar was also supposed to be afire.

Kathleen Kennedy recalled that the plan was to burn the set piece by piece — allowing for control of the flames and photography of them. First, the bar area would be burned, then the door and so forth. Editing would create the illusion of the entire

---

*At Ford's home months after the completion of filming, during a backyard party, the actor reportedly was the victim of a bite from a garden-variety snake — a very unlikely turn of events for Indiana Jones.

building being engulfed in flames. Plans went awry, though, when the building actually did burn down. Camera control was lost, the sets was rebuilt and the scenes were filmed again.

Additional soundstage photography involved the filming of the hidden, corpse-filled catacomb/exit from the Well of Souls, the cabin of the *Bantu Wind* (where Ford offered the line "it's not the years, it's the mileage"), and the secret German altar set to be used for the Jewish Ark–opening ritual (humorously referred to by those at ILM as the "God's reply to evil men" sequence).

Another phase of the *Raiders* production would take the cast and crew to an entirely new continent for five weeks. There, in an entirely different world, the crew worked around strange customs, foreign languages, and harsh environments.

According to executive producer Robert Watts, "When I heard that this picture was set in Egypt, I asked three questions: 'Do we see the Sphinx? Do we see the Pyramids? Do we see the Nile?' And when the answer was no, I said, 'Well, then, we don't have to go to Egypt.'"[12]

The filmmakers chose the desert landscape of an area near Tozeur, Tunisia (1980 population — 13,000), for the Nazi-overseen archeological dig where the Well of Souls lies. For accuracy, the filmmakers hesitantly decided to film within the region of the Sahara Desert where temperatures regularly reached 130 degrees in the direct sunlight. Shaded areas—where the mercury dropped a mere ten degrees—offered little relief.

Paying a daily rate of ten dinars (equivalent to $2.38 in 1981 American dollars), the casting department rounded up nearly 600 locals to portray the Arab diggers scattered about the 70-acre set. In addition, roughly 30 German and French tourists who were willing to accept 20 dinars a day, sacrifice their vacation and withstand the intolerable temperatures were hired to play members of the German Army. Soon, logistic hardships arose. Producer Marshall explained: "One of the things about shooting in a studio is that it's controlled—it doesn't rain, you can shoot all day. And you have everything you need. When you're in the middle of the desert and a light burns out, you can't go get a bulb from the electrical department; if the camera breaks, you don't have a camera department to fix it."[13]

The efforts of continuity handler Pamela Mann were never more vital than in the Sahara: "When one's working with amateur extras," explained Mann, "that brings great problems with continuity. If someone wants to put on a sun hat because the sun's burning his head, and he didn't have it on in the last shot, he sees no reason why he shouldn't put on the sun hat. One tries to keep an eagle eye out for that sort of thing, and hopes that one doesn't see something horrible in rushes that one's missed."[15]

One event that plagued filmmakers was the incessant pointing and laughing by the Arabs toward the rolling cameras. Furthermore, extras were given their marks so that each time they would return to the same place as previously instructed. But the utterly confused extras would pick up their marks and tote them along wherever they went.

While the cast, crew and European extras quenched their thirst with cold bottled water, the Arab extras began their short-lived careers as actors without any form of liquid relief. To remedy the situation, the production brought in a fire truck as a mobile thirst-quencher, and distributed nearly 5,000 gallons of water each day. However, as a result of the number of Arabs frantically attempting to get at the truck's precious cargo, near-riots broke out.

"Steven was real angry," recalled David Wisniewitz, who was on hand for the creation of his studio-sanctioned making-of documentary. "The water was almost too hot to touch anyway, out of a fire truck that had been out all day in the heat. Steven said he doesn't care who they are or how they have been treated before, they are going to get proper food and drink. You know [the locals] treat the horses better than they treat the people out here on this location. Even the goats are better off."[15]

Yet, despite all the setbacks, Spielberg aimed to complete the filming in an efficient, but high quality manner. He never let on that he was bothered by the suffocating hear or dust, or distressed by the inevitable illnesses he and his crew contracted. His positive attitude was a fine example for the crew, and saved them from burying themselves in a negative mindset.

Ford, too, lacked enthusiasm for the North African country. "After a couple of weeks in Tunisia I matched Steven's enthusiasm to get out. I try not to say bad things about entire nations but parts of Tunisia made me sick."[16]

Situated on the same 70-acre compound as the dig area was the airfield that housed the German Army's uniquely shaped *Flying Wing*. Constructed by the Vickers Aircraft Company and painted at Elstree — and subsequently disassembled and shipped to the Tunisian location — the $60 million plane was an example of Spielberg's desire to emphasize the advanced state of Germany's military might and to help demonstrate the ongoing conflicts between man vs. machine.

During this sequence, the extreme heat did have its advantages. While filming a spectacular brawl between Indy and a muscular German mechanic (played by the late Birmingham, England, wrestler Pat Roach, who passed away in 2004, who also portrayed a Sherpa during the Raven Bar fight sequence and would later appear in both of the *Raiders* sequels), one of the plane's heat-softened tires rolled over one of Ford's legs. The actor received minor damage to his anterior cruiate ligament.

Although it was one of the production's largest and most intricately detailed props, it was to be destroyed in a cataclysmic explosion. On the sidelines stood the local fire department in case of danger.

For producer Frank Marshall — who played the pilot of the plane — witnessing Tunisia's unsung heroes in action was one of the joys of his filmmaking experience. "The Tunisian fire department's hoses not only pulled apart at the joints," said the producer, "the hose caught on fire and the fire department had to put out their own hose. It was like a slapstick comedy, with the fire department falling down, and the hoses breaking and running out of water. They'd say, 'Fire it up!' and this little dribble would come out of the hose."[17]

While Spielberg oversaw the direction of various insert shots and dialogue-laden scenes with Karen Allen and Paul Freeman's Belloq, second unit director Mickey Moore directed Ford and a virtual army of stuntmen in German uniform out on the dusty roadways of the Sahara Desert.

During the first three weeks of filming the sequence (Spielberg directed the closeups during the last two), Moore concentrated on working with the stunt people atop, around and under the four specially built vehicles in the German convoy. All were constructed to mount camera equipment and rigging for stunts. The closeups of the interior cab fight between Indy and various truck drivers were filmed in a mock-up of the cab portion constructed atop a flatbed truck, to facilitate camera placement and operation. The most dangerous stunt of the entire film took place with a car-mounted camera filming the action from a few feet above the ground.

Ford was responsible for nearly 75 percent of the horseback riding (excluding the horse-to-truck "transfer," which stuntman-coordinator Terry Leonard performed). Ford hung precariously on the front grill and on top of the wheel well following his forced removal from the driver's seat (which he says was the most unsettling experience of the whole production). And it was Ford who was dragged behind the truck for closeups. But it was the courageous Terry Leonard who was dragged dangerously beneath the truck.

Having luckily walked away from a stunt during the making of *The Legend of the Lone Ranger* that had nearly crippled him the year before, Leonard certainly had his reservations. He agreed to the stunt only if the film's stunt coordinator and his longtime associate, Glenn Randall, drove the vehicle.

"I don't give him [Randall] one thought," said Leonard. "That's why he's here. I've got confidence in him; we've done many things together. I just eliminate that from my mind because if I were going to concentrate on what I think he's doing then I'd have a split second under that truck where I am not paying attention to what I'm doing."[18]

A trench was dug so that there would be adequate room beneath the truck, which went 25 m.p.h. The filmmakers got the needed footage in three days and without incident.

In the end, the entire truck chase sequence took five weeks to film, required more than 50 stunts and involved 13 stuntmen — all for a highly charged and furiously paced six minutes of screen time.

Ford claimed that what he does cannot be classified as stunt work. "I am informing every man in every bar from here to the East Coast," said the actor, "that I intend to back up nothing I have ever said or did in a movie. Indiana Jones is tough. I am not tough."[19]

Glenn Randall would disagree: "There are probably actors who would be more than willing to try a lot of things, but they would possibly not possess the physical attributes that it takes to do them. Harrison just happens to be capable of doing them. Yet, if you ask him, he'll say, 'Not me! I'm the biggest coward in the world.' But in actual fact, he is not. He will go for a lot of things, and he'll spend the time to learn what he has to do to get the job done, instead of just going out and trying it."[20]

Ford believed that the more he was involved, the more an audience would believe it is Harrison Ford as Indiana Jones and not a stunt person. The producer insisted that Indy's fedora — which Ford kiddingly claimed to have firmly fastened on with carpet tacks — remain on at all times to easily disguise whomever was sporting it.

Furthermore, the actor admitted to having a trace of guilt. "I know I'm overpaid in some ways, so I expect to do my share or more on a film."[21] (Following the release of the film, Ford narrated and appeared in a documentary describing the film's stunt work, *Great Movie Stunts: "Raiders of the Lost Ark,"* which was aired and later released on videocassette.)

Although he mentally prepared for his role by reading up on archaeology, the actor admitted to minimal physical preparation prior to the production: "In fact, I haven't been fit for about 13 years.... Now I don't do a thing. I don't work out. I don't jog. But I have to say I do have a good constitution."[22]

He related the condition of his body following the completion of filming to that of a "55-year-old linebacker."[23] His constitution, however, was not enough to prepare him to use his trademark accessory. For weeks, the actor withstood self-inflicted bodily punishment while preparing to master the art of the bullwhip.

"I had very little instruction," said the actor. "There's not a lot you can do. Glenn Randall, the stunt coordinator, showed me how not to whip the hell out of myself. But half an hour after he started training me, he finished because it's really something you have to do for yourself."[24]

The task was made more difficult by an injury to his right wrist from falling off a ladder at Valerie Harper's house during a carpentry job in the '60s. Between takes and during down time, the actor would practice with ropes and whips of varying size and thicknesses. He would exercise his wrist using a heavy steel sphere ergonomically designed to strengthen the muscle and bone.

The last Tozeur natural resource used was a rocky, less barren area known as "*Star Wars* Canyon."

Years earlier at that location, Lucas filmed several scenes of *Star Wars'* Tatooine scenes. For Spielberg's purposes, the canyon served as the setting where Indy threatens to destroy the Ark if Marion isn't released from the clutches of the Germans.

The next stop was nearly 200 miles northeast of Tozeur, in a town called Kairouaun, Tunisia. It was selected because of its resemblance to Cairo circa 1936, and the filmmakers found all the locations needed for the home of Sallah and the city streets where Indy and Marion are pursued.

The filming went off without a hitch. The city surprised him by allowing unprecedented use of its resources. The production was even permitted to close off the main street with little incident—a feat impossible in most any other city.

The monkey ("portrayed" by primate actor Snuff) was so unpredictable and unwilling to conform to Spielberg's direction that up to five hidden wires maneuvered it wherever and whenever desired.

For Frank Marshall, the experience left him feeling defeated—both professionally and personally. "I ended up not liking the monkey because he was impossible to work with," recalled Marshall. "Didn't listen to me at all."[25]

Suffering from dysentery, virtually unable to walk, Ford (and his visiting girlfriend Melissa) was stricken for nearly the entire stretch of desert shooting. Spielberg recalled that his leading man spent a considerable amount of time unable to stand up straight, stooped over. (The director himself wisely avoided illness by importing his own canned food to the location.)

"What really keeps you excited in this business," explained Ford, "is when you come upon those moments in filming when you don't know what to do. Once production starts there are problems—and opportunities—you never dreamed of. You must then make haphazard decisions and play them through audaciously. That's the challenge."[26]

Prior to Ford's confrontation scene with an Arab swordsman, Ford suggested that he deal with the attacker in a time-efficient and economic manner.

"I was into my fifth week of dysentery," recalled the actor, "and I was riding in at 5:30 A.M. with nothing to do but submit to wild imaginings. So I stormed Steven with the idea of just dismissing this maniac. I'd never unholstered my gun in the whole movie, so I said, 'Let's just shoot the fucker.' And we did...."[27]

As the production went on, Ford and Spielberg's relationship matured. Although each always made a heartfelt effort to consider the other's suggestions, there were times when the two disagreed. "Steven Spielberg and I did a lot of arguing," admitted Ford, "but we both profited from it. People put up with me because I'm sincere, because I don't do it for ego gratification. I may have more to say about the wardrobe than the wardrobe person wants me to, but that's the way I am about it. If things make sense to me, chances are they'll make sense to an audience."[28]

Ford again deviated from the script for the sake of character development for the scene in the Nazi sub pen. Initially, the actor was to remain incognito among the enemy in a uniform of the soldier he'd recently strong-armed. Ford suggested that this had become all-too-common in his films (*Force 10 from Navarone*, *Hanover Street*, etc.). The actor suggested that the filmmakers add a dash of realism by making the uniform a couple of sizes too small. A tighter-fitting Nazi uniform got incorporated into the daily call sheet.

"He was involved in a lot of decision-making about the movie as we went along that wasn't by contract," claimed Spielberg. "It was because I sensed Harrison's exceptional story mind and that he was a very smart person, making me want to call on him time and again."[29]

On September 30, 1980, the *Raiders* production moved to its final location on the island of Kauai, Hawaii, for the film's Peruvian jungle scenes.

As Robert Watts recalled, the task of filming the South American temple exterior (with Old Man's Beard used yet again) was done with great difficulty. Although the area selected was abundant with natural beauty—including a cliff face with a waterfall cascading into a pool—the amount and size of equipment proved troublesome.

Cumbersome equipment had to be lowered down by crane. Mosquitoes swarmed throughout the area, and everyone involved suffered endless bites. Daily mosquito foggers and bug spray offered little relief.

The next Hawaiian location (the area where Indiana Jones and his Peruvian entourage search for the temple) proved to be equally difficult. A portion of the location was accessible only by boat, the remaining portion by helicopter.

An airplane capable of landing on water and resembling those of the 1930s was needed, and the production was fortunate to discover a Junction City, Oregon, family willing to loan out their own antique single-engine Waco biplane. The production paid homage to Lucas by giving it the identification letters of OB-CPO — referring to two of his *Star Wars* characters, Obi-Wan Kenobi and C3-PO. (During the construction of the Well of the Souls set, likenesses of the *Star Wars* droids were incorporated into the ancient Egyptian hieroglyphics.)

Though no one could guess it from the end result, the scene where Indy swung from a vine to the floating plane nearly resulted in disaster. While Ford clung to the moving plane's pontoon, the plane careened out of control after gaining only 20 feet of altitude, struck the shoreline embankment and tipped violently to its side. Fortunately, no one was injured. After a few repairs, the filmmakers captured what they needed.

Following the film's official wrap party, on the *Raiders of the Lost Ark* cast and crew boarded their flights back home and took a much-deserved rest while waiting anxiously for the final product. It arrived only months after post-production work involving Industrial Light and Magic's special effects.

Raiders was completed in 73 days and for a relatively reasonable $20 million. More than 11,000 shots were photographed (many of which were unscripted and unscheduled). Nearly 300,000 feet of film were ultimately exposed before being edited by Michael Kahn into a piece of celluloid history.

"The crew worked faster than any I've had," said Spielberg, "which is one of the main reasons we finished the film 12 days ahead of schedule. We were averaging, outside, 40 set-ups a day and inside, under difficult lighting conditions, 15 shots a day. That's the fastest I've ever shot next to my experience in television. I never shot a picture this quickly without having to compromise quality. And it proved to me that you *can* make a movie that should have cost $35 million for $20 million."[30]

Spielberg claimed that his new leading man was a "remarkable combination" of Humphrey Bogart and Errol Flynn. "It was even great directing Harrison Ford, because he's a big kid," said Spielberg. "He's a little more serious and he's a little more sobering but he is a big floppy kid. I kind of have an easier time directing people like that, who still have a little bit of the kid stuff left over from childhood."[31]

Raiders was instantly heralded as "one of the most deliriously funny, ingenious and stylish American adventure movies ever made" by Vincent Canby of *The New York Times*.[32] Critics around the globe attributed the film's success to Ford's flawless execution of its hero, stating that no other actor had a right to even consider the role knowing he existed. *The Village Voice* confessed that it "had not thought that Ford had it in him to convey such a marvelously weary doggedness of spirit as he confronts the inexhaustible wiles of the world's villains."[33]

Soon after *Raiders*' June 12, 1981, release, it became the most commercially successful film of that year. In its first weekend, it earned $4,347,401 on 1,078 screens. The film was in such demand that after 44 weeks of continuous screenings, new prints were struck and sent to theaters because the original prints were so worn. In the end (and following its 1982 re-release), *Raiders* earned an impressive final box office tally of $242,374,454 ($363 million worldwide). As of March 2001, the film was 38 on the list of the top money-making films worldwide (#18 within the U.S.). It also gained notoriety for becoming the biggest-grossing film in Paramount Pictures' history up until that point.

Nominated for eight Academy Awards including Best Director, Best Score (John Williams) and Best Picture (which was ultimately awarded to *On Golden Pond*), the film was honored with four — all within the technical categories. They included Best Visual Effects (Richard Edlund, Kit West, Bruce Nicholson and Joe Johnston); Art Direction (Norman Reynolds, Leslie Dilley and Michael Ford); Film Editing (Michael Kahn) and Sound (Phil Varney, Steve Maslow, Gregg Landaker and Roy Charman). In addition, Ben Burtt and Richard Anderson received a special Oscar for Best Sound Effects Editing. In 1999, it was inducted into the National Film Registry.

Indiana Jones instantly became Hollywood's newest hero. "Indy" became a household name and worldwide sales of leather bomber jackets and fedoras increased significantly — and Harrison Ford became one of Hollywood's top leading men.

Talking about the next step in his career, Ford jokingly touted his next project to the press as "a $150 musical about a homosexual priest that takes place entirely in a 6-foot-by-6-foot, stark white room. At the end of the movie, I open the door, and a mob of Tunisians pulls me off my horse and kills me."[34]

As with most enormously successful films, a follow-up was deliberated. Ford's response to the idea of a sequel was impulsive: "Why not? We've got the clothes."[35] But despite its enormous box office success, Ford was also hesitant to consider a sequel until he knew the public approved: "Here's how you know when you've done your job: It says 'The End' and they [the audience] climb up on their seats and yell for more."[36]

Just as the actor anticipated, audiences climbed onto their seats and, with wild enthusiasm, yelled until the year 1984, when its "prequel" *Indiana Jones and the Temple of Doom* was released.

For Mark Hamill, Ford's former co-star in the first two *Star Wars* films, *Raiders* was proof of the theory of actor evolution. "He did Carrie [Fisher] and me a great favor in the sense that he answered the question, 'Is there life after *Star Wars*?'"[37]

While the 1980s blockbuster sequel to *Star Wars* elevated Ford's income and position in Hollywood, nothing would have a greater impact on his celebrity status than *Raiders of the Lost Ark*.

"As for being recognized, so far that hasn't been too much of a problem," said the actor in late 1981. "I've got a very plastic sort of face which seems to change with each movie I make. So I'm not your instantly recognizable type, like, say, Dustin Hoffman. However, with *Raiders* currently being such a worldwide smash, I think from now on it's going to be impossible to maintain my anonymity...."[38]

Almost overnight, Ford was forced to adapt. Being in Hollywood made the art of camouflaging himself from the public all the more difficult.

"I find I can go to the beach and so on," clarified the actor. "Unless people are expecting you, you're gone before they actually realize it's you. I try to avoid recognition wherever possible because it destroys the natural order of things. Sure, living in the public eye is hard but I don't take it personally and I don't resent it. I'm practical enough to realize that it's the by-product of incredible good fortune in other fields. I certainly wouldn't go around with bodyguards. The interest in me is of a generally benign nature. People are enormously kind."[39]

Gladly willing to chat or provide his autograph, Ford remained receptive to fans, claiming that through the years he had encountered very few individuals "who have not appeared to be totally in possession of all their marbles."[40] He knew that if it weren't for the ticket-buying public, his success as an actor would not exist.

"I can't be annoyed," said the actor years later. "That's just not possible. I'll draw the line where I think things are getting out of hand. But these people are supporting my family, my ambitions, and my dreams. They're my customers, and I treat them that way."[41]

17

SCIENCE FRICTION

After roles ranging from an archaeologist to a space pirate, and from a United States colonel to a sensitive cowboy, Harrison Ford — even with his aversion to being typecast — chose the science fiction genre once again. Yet on this occasion, science fiction would be redefined, as would the actor's idea of "a day's work."

At the hands of respected director Ridley Scott — whose 1979 film *Alien* terrified viewers (its tag-line was "In Space, No One Can Hear You Scream") — Ford committed to a unique vision, portraying a futuristic bounty hunter in a project then entitled *Dangerous Days*. The actor was unaware of the hardships he would experience. In retrospect, Ford considered that film — later re-titled *Blade Runner* — the most physically and mentally unsettling of his career.

The film was released to general acclaim. It survives not only as a cult film but as one of the most influential science fiction films ever made.

Blade Runner's beginnings dated back to 1978 when screenwriter Hampton Fancher suggested to actor Brian Kelly (of the television series *Flipper*) that he purchase the rights to the 1968 novel *Do Androids Dream of Electric Sheep* by prestigious science fiction author Philip K. Dick.

Throughout 1978, the screenwriter committed himself to converting the novel (the rights were purchased by Kelly for $2,000) into screenplay format. He eventually produced a script that soon attracted the interest of Oscar-winning producer Michael Deeley (*The Deer Hunter*).

"What ultimately sold me on the project was Hampton Fancher's script," recollected Deeley. "I've read a lot of screenplays and produced a lot of pictures, but Fancher's script really was the most driving and interesting and original piece of writing I'd ever seen...."[1]

During the rewrite stages, title choices included *Android, Mechanismo, Dangerous Days* and *Blade Runner*. The latter was arrived at with the approval of William S. Burroughs, who coincidentally authored a novel of the same name — as did Alan E. Nourse, who also permitted the name to be used for the movie's title.

However, director Ridley Scott was still not content. He was partial to the title "Gotham City," but was denied permission to use it by *Batman* creator Bob Kane. In the end, Scott yielded and abided with the now universally known choice.

Scott — who originally read the script in April 1979 and declined due to his reluctance at directing back-to-back science-fiction films — became interested in the project following Michael Deeley's consideration of directors Adrian Lyne, Michael Apted, Bruce Beresford and Robert Mulligan. Fancher felt Scott was the ideal director for the film. Fancher ultimately influenced Deeley, who would finalize his decision by stating that Scott, in his opinion, had "the best eye for moviemaking in the world."[2]

Ridley Scott instantly admired the script's many qualities. He decided it was an "extraordinary piece of work with marvelous design possibilities," and officially signed on to the project as director on February 21, 1980.[3]

Despite Scott's initial approval of the script, he was not in total agreement with Fancher on several aspects. Deeley saw that Scott wanted to stray from Fancher's softer tone and give the script a harder edge.

Criticizing those who might attempt to deface his work, author Philip K. Dick called Fancher's screenplay "a bumbling effort from start to finish."[4]

Scott became more and more dissatisfied with the script's rewrites and allowed the professional relationship to spoil the personal one. Fancher was ultimately replaced by screenwriter David Peoples at the suggestion of Ridley's brother, director Tony Scott (*Top Gun*, *Crimson Tide*).

Scott, Deeley and Peoples worked to provide an acceptable script not only to appease themselves, but also the film's financial backer, Filmways. In the end, Filmways reneged, concerned that their $13 million investment would not prove profitable.

Seeking a new financier, the producers hit pay dirt with three separate entities, for a combined $21.5 million total budget. Those three backers were Alan Ladd, Jr.'s, Ladd Company, Far-East film magnate Sir Run-Run Shaw and Jerry Perenchio and Bud Yorkin's Tandem Productions.

Harrison Ford's involvement as a "Blade Runner" began when the actor was on Steven Spielberg's London *Raiders* set. Actress Barbara Hershey was responsible for involving Ford.

Recalling a mid–1980 phone conversation with friend Steven Spielberg, she told her screenwriting friend Hampton Fancher that Spielberg predicted Ford would become the world's biggest box office sensation.

Other actors considered for the role included Robert Mitchum, Gregory Peck, Tommy Lee Jones and Christopher Walken. Ridley Scott favored actor Dustin Hoffman at some point during 1980 for the role of protagonist-antagonist Rick Deckard.

Hoffman wanted points throughout the script drastically rewritten. Concerned that the actor would convert the film into a political and social commentary, Deeley and Scott reevaluated their choice. In the end, neither were willing to see the film follow such a course and sought another option.

With the projected start date for filming fast approaching, Scott and Deeley were skeptical of Ford's professional aptitude.

"Ford had not been given much of a chance, particularly since *Star Wars*, to show what he was made of," said Deeley. "Both Ridley and I felt Deckard's curious mixture of emerging sensitivity and hard-boiled bureaucracy would offer an excellent chance for Harrison to do that."[5]

Ford as Rick Deckard in the cult classic *Blade Runner* (Warner Bros., 1982).

Scott found upon viewing both *The Conversation* and *Apocalypse Now* that his would-be leading man had "a strange, slightly sinister side, very low key and somber. Almost a different Harrison Ford. Very dangerous."[6] These traits were ideal for what the director envisioned for the character.

Scott and Deeley visited the actor at his London set, and were both impressed *and* distressed upon first meeting the actor.

"He drove into London, and I think he still had the goddamn hat on he wore as Indiana Jones," recalled Scott. "I thought, 'Oh, shit!' Because up to that point, we'd seen Deckard wearing the same kind of hat. The kind they used to sport in those old noir thrillers."[7]

Ford suggested Deckard's short-cropped haircut: "Ridley had envisioned a big felt hat in his first visual concept of the character at a time prior to seeing *Raiders of the Lost Ark*. It was important to me not to wear the same hat in one movie after another. I didn't want to drag the baggage of one project to the next. You can't do that. So the hat was out. Ridley still wanted something to distinguish the character and I wanted something easy-care. So I got that haircut [which itself was an event with Scott directing the stylist over a four-hour period], figuring it would give the character definition, a certain look."[8]

Ford wanted the remaining hair to be unkempt, and suggested beard stubble. He also wanted his character to remain in the same shirt throughout the entire film — offering filmgoers a man who was not concerned with vanity.

Ford officially signed on to the project during the last week of October 1980.

"Our main character, Deckard, is a detective, like Sam Spade or Philip Marlowe; a man who follows a hunch to the end," said Scott. "He's in trouble because he's begun to identify with his quarry, the Replicants. [Harrison] possesses some of the laconic dourness of Bogey, but he's more ambivalent, more human. He's almost an anti-hero."[9]

Ford was captivated by Deckard's internal struggle — his reluctance to shoot and kill vs. his inborn talent for doing so. Such complexity made for an interesting character — and one that the actor was anxious to portray.

"Other than Harrison Ford," recalled producer Deeley, "we decided early on not to choose familiar faces for *Blade Runner*—particularly in the case of the Replicants. This made for quite adventurous casting; we had to find new people so that audiences wouldn't say, 'Oh, look, there's old so-and-so playing an android. Isn't that sweet?'"[10]

Sean Young was selected as Rachel, the Replicant Deckard falls in love with; Dutchman Rutger Hauer was chosen (based on the director's fascination with his appearance) as Roy Batty, the leader of the Nexus 6 Replicants that Deckard is hunting; Daryl Hannah as Batty's love interest and fellow Replicant, Pris; Edward James Olmos as Gaff, Deckard's covetous, promotion-thirsting fellow Blade Runner; E. Emmett Walsh as Bryant, the police captain who lures Deckard out of retirement; William Sanderson as Sebastian, the genetic designer deceivingly befriended by Pris; Joe Turkel as Tyrell, the godfather of genetic engineering and creator of the Nexus 6 Replicants; Brion James as Leon, the doltish, deadly Replicant and companion of Batty, Pris and the sexy nightclub dancer Zhora (portrayed by actress Joanna Cassidy).

Following the film's release, virtually every actor flourished in their professions.

Ford lived just minutes away from the Burbank Studios where the majority of the film would be made. The actor relished the idea of commuting in local traffic — only to return after his shift to the comfort of his own bed.

Originally built in the 1920s, Burbank Studios — later designated Warner Bros.

Pictures— was the home to countless classic productions. But when those older films were conceived, it was the intent that its back lot New York sets provide the appearance of routine life among the streets of that city— thus requiring minimal set-dressing.

"Most films depict the future as pristine, austere, and colorless," claimed Scott. "We were determined to avoid shiny buildings, underpopulated streets, and silver suits with diagonal zippers. ... "Our city is rich, colorful, noisy, gritty, full of textures, and teeming with life— much like a major city of today. This is a tangible future, not too exotic to be believed. It's like today only more so."[11]

It would take more than the application of a coat of paint and props to transform the New York of the past into the Los Angeles of the future. Courtesy of the industry's most talented set designers, art designers and construction crews, that backlot set would be virtually reconstructed and later respectfully dubbed "Ridleyville."

"Not only did we have hundreds of extras, we had 50 to 60 vehicles, lighting effects and moving mannequins," said production executive Katherine Haber. "We had to create a red light district, a hustle bustle scene, so it was a huge amount of coordination with background action, cars moving, lights flashing and people moving. With Ridley's eye on detail, everything had to be perfect. The wardrobe was incredible."[12]

Thanks to the costume design team of Charles Knode and Michael Kaplan, the inhabitants of *Blade Runner* were appropriately outfitted to provide a "multinational, multiracial society." The wardrobe department looted every second-hand clothing resource available.

Knode and Kaplan costumed extras as punks in Russian and Chinese Army uniforms, nuns and Hari Krishnas— an eclectic assortment of every part of a city's demographic magnified endless times—for their vision of the future.

The socialist agenda of Scott's future dictated that the set be retrofitted to bring twentieth century consumerism in line with the daily practical needs of the future. Function becomes the sole rationale behind the city, and style is forgotten as a ghost of days long past.

To provide a sobering ambiance for the (presumably) post-apocalyptic environment, seven overhead sprinkler systems (installed 20 feet above the set) provided "rainfall," which, coupled with the omnipresent neon lighting, eerily illuminated the city streets. A crew of seven was hired full-time to maintain the neon lighting.

Another ingredient necessary to create a palpable nightmarish environment was night itself.

Backlot filming officially began on April 23, 1981. Required to arrive at the set by mid-afternoon, the cast and crew would work through the night, lunch during the witching hour and wrap the day's work between five and six in the morning.

On that date, Ford, Young and Turkel filmed the sequence of Rachel's interrogation at Tyrell's office. Shot on Soundstage 4, the 80' × 80' structure—complete with an enormous picture window and 20-foot-high columns— was considered by its production designer to be one of the highlights of the film's many impressive sets.

Yet another impressive set was Deckard's apartment. Set decorators effectively combined the hi-tech gadgetry of the film's 2019 setting with antiques of the early twentieth century to demonstrate Deckard's existence in the present while conveying a nostalgic yearning for the past.

To complement the overpopulated, archaic city streets far below, the apartment was furnished with an excessive amount of furniture and enclosed with gray textured blocks of Mayan influence. In addition, low (6'8") ceilings were installed to help create a claustrophobic atmosphere.

The interior spaces of apartment 9732 were scarcely lit. The set's predominant illumination — which dramatically filtered through the dwelling's vertical blinds — came from neon lights and searchlights from neighboring structures. This use of light signified the landscape's invasion upon Deckard's privacy.

Blatantly harkening to lighting schemes popularized in the film noir period of the 1940s, the production also paid homage to Bernardo Bertolucci's 1971 film *The Conformist*, which served as an outstanding example and guideline for the look of the film.

The production also shot on location throughout Los Angeles.

The police station where Deckard is brought early on in the film to meet with his ex-employer, Bryant (Walsh, who would later land a role alongside Ford in 1999's *Random Hearts*), was filmed on four consecutive nights (to avoid excess crowding) at downtown Los Angeles's Union Station.

During that time, Ford and Walsh would alleviate their anxiety and boredom by befriending one another; Ford's youthful ability to let loose was evident as he and Walsh cavorted around. One evening, he and his co-star even gleefully crowded into an instant photo booth to have their pictures taken together.

For two days in May 1981, the production utilized a fully operational meat packing plant in the Los Angeles suburb of Vernon to film scenes set in Chew's (James Hong) "Eye Works" lab. While the Southern California weather on the blacktop reached a scorching 98 degrees, the interior of the plant was seven degrees below zero. Between takes and during the moments when the camera equipment began to freeze due to the severe cold, Hauer, Hong and the crew would seek relief outdoors.

While the interiors of Deckard's apartment were shot on a soundstage at Burbank, the exterior was filmed at the 1920 Frank Lloyd Wright "Ennis-Brown House" in the Los Feliz hills of L.A.

Ending their search for an appropriately decrepit building, the filmmakers settled upon downtown's architecturally celebrated Bradbury Building. Admired for its foyer area — complete with open staircases and elevators accentuated by elaborate iron work — the structure has regularly been utilized in an abundance of film and music video productions. Lawrence G. Paull and his production design team gave the glamorous building the aged and decayed look necessary for the scene.

"What we did to that building you wouldn't believe," recalled a proud Paull. "On a superficial level we trashed it with hi-tech, then filled it with smoke on the inside and shot it at night. We also added a canopy with big columns to make it look like it was an old apartment building [for the film's exterior entrance scenes]. All of a sudden, we had a very gothic, eerie environment."[13]

Returning to Burbank's backlot for the final two weeks of shooting, the crew found itself on top of the Lawrence G. Paull–designed "Rolling Rooftop" set. The set — named because of its construction atop wheels and stage jacks — was constructed in three weeks and stood 22 feet above the ground. It served as the top three stories and rooftop of the Bradbury. It was further complemented with castings of actual cornices reproduced from downtown's Rosaling Hotel and Rowan Building, in addition to an abundance of enormous windmills, which to Scott represented waning power generators.

Adjoining the "Rolling Rooftop" was yet another rooftop which was constructed to provide Ford's character with his escape route. As the script dictated, Deckard was to jump from the Bradbury's roof to the rooftop of the neighboring building with Batty doing likewise in pursuit. Originally, the distance between the two was to be a 20-foot span (complete with a safety net). Ultimately, the gap was closed to only ten feet.

Following the stuntman's successful leap, Ford situated himself between the steel girders that extended beyond the side of the building. He hung precariously from the I-beam, secured by a waist tether.

Throughout the filming, Ford voluntarily offered his physical capacities — often crossing the line between actor and stunt person. To Ford, the scenes requiring a physical confrontation must have seemed manageable. Upon signing, the actor soon discovered that working with Ridley Scott meant the actor would receive more than he bargained for. During his citywide pursuit of the Nexus 6 Replicants, Leon ambushes Deckard in a darkened alley. It was filmed in three consecutive nights on the backlot, Ford and Brion James participated in all aspects of the scene without the involvement of any stuntmen or doubles.

As stunt coordinator Gary Combs recalled from the sidelines of the shoot, "That's why Harrison got so sore and so stiff. You can do something two or three times and survive, but after you do something maybe 17, 18 or 20 times, it finally gets you."[14]

In a similar incident exemplifying Scott's sadistic knack for achieving perfection at all costs, Ford's character is unmercifully battered down by the female Replicant, Zhora (Joanna Cassidy). The actress recalled the three nights of filming. Choreographed by Combs, herself, and Ford, the scene was also shot without the use of any stunt double.

"Harrison really needed to get some stress out," said the actress. "He enjoyed fighting with me because I'm strong and capable...."[15]

As capable as both individuals appeared, various portions of the scene required many takes. The strangulation scene (Deckard's own necktie proves to be a formidable weapon for Zhora) reportedly required nearly two dozen attempts before Scott was satisfied. The on-set pressure was significantly reduced due to his gentlemanly attributes.

"Harrison Ford was always around when I did my stunts and was very protective," recollected Cassidy. "He always wanted to make sure I was okay. 'Can you do this?' he'd ask. 'How many times do you want to do it again?' He was very good with me. I loved working with Harrison."[16]

Ford's physicality was again required in the scene in which he confronts the

Replicant Pris (Daryl Hannah). Pris proves to be a unique challenge due to her acrobatic capabilities. Pris cartwheels across the room and onto the back of Deckard and proceeds to strangle him with her inner thighs while simultaneously clamping down on his temples and dealing vicious blows with her balled-up fists.

"Glutton for punishment" Ford insisted on intensifying Pris' onslaught by allowing her to inflict further suffering upon him — namely by suggesting that Pris detain him further by raising his body above the ground by his nostrils before he is dropped.

"The fight between Harrison and her is quite vicious and we all cringed when she put her two fingers in Harrison's nostrils to haul him up," recalled producer Michael Deeley. "Harrison came up with that idea and, even though all of us found it very painful to watch, he insisted on doing it."[17]

Despite his classification of stunt work as "something you're silly enough to think isn't going to hurt the next day," Ford, in fact, did participate in technical terms as stunt coordinator Combs recalled.[18]

During a conversation that Ford and Combs had during the filming, the actor inquired whether he was eligible for "adjustments"— a pay increase per the amount and difficulty of stunts one performs. Combs affirmed that Ford was indeed eligible and as a result he was paid for his supplemental contributions.

Prior to *Blade Runner*, Ridley Scott was respected throughout the industry as having a keen sense of (and stubborn insistence for) detail. Characteristically stepping beyond the boundaries of what a director's typical responsibilities are, Scott's enthusiasm meant unequivocal commitment to a production. Deeley maintained that Scott assumed both the roles of production designer and art director for the film — albeit unofficially.

During the production, Scott's peers went from advocates pledging their undivided support, to virtual mutineers. The production as a whole was "a monument to stress,"[19] according to high-ranking members of Scott's staff.

"Ridley was very tough on his crew," stated Hampton Fancher. "But that was because he was toughest on himself. He had a very clear vision of what he wanted on *Blade Runner*. A lot of the crew didn't understand that."[20]

One individual whose lack of understanding created further dissension on the set was Harrison Ford. Although the actor today admits a total awareness and appreciation of the film's success, Ford has deliberately withheld any information regarding the experience, with the exception of laconically revealing, "*Blade Runner* was not one of my favorite films. I tangled with Ridley."[21]

"I think it's honest to say," contended the director, "that doing *Blade Runner* wasn't tremendously smooth in terms of a working relationship with Harrison.

"Harrison's a very charming man," he continued. "But during the filmmaking process I think we grew apart, mainly because of the logistics of the film I was trying to make. In concentrating on getting *Blade Runner*'s environment exactly the way I wanted it, I probably short-changed him."[22]

Secluded in his trailer when his services weren't required, Ford would display his chagrin on the set by reportedly evading human interaction. Exhaustive round-the-clock filming had also taken its toll on him. These factors would result in the corruption of fruitful relationships— both professional and personal — with his co-stars.

Having been required to work with Ford solely during the concluding moments of principal photography atop the "Rolling Rooftop" set, Ford's co-star Rutger Hauer recalled: "It's just that I never really got to know him. Even though he was very polite and professional, I always felt as if there was a three-foot sheet of glass between us."[23]

During the production's last night of filming, in which Batty explains to Deckard the meaning of life upon the rooftop (courtesy of Hauer's own last-minute "Tears in Rain" contribution), Ford's character was expected to be fatigued from the physical and mental torment Batty had imposed upon him. On that particular evening, an exhausted and rain-soaked Ford was required to sit upon the garbage-strewn and rain-soaked set for filming closeups in reaction to Batty's lament.

"People have told me since that Harrison's particularly convincing during that moment," said Katherine Haber. "That he looks beaten up and exhausted. Let me tell you, Harrison was beaten up and exhausted. He was also half asleep!"[24]

No person conflicted with the actor more than his cinematic love interest, Sean Young.

"I think the reason there was friction between Sean and Harrison was clashing personalities," explained Haber. "You also have to remember that Harrison is the consummate professional, and here he was working with someone who was very green. That couldn't have been easy for him, given the other stresses Harrison was under."[25]

This animosity that swelled between the two was most evident during the scene jokingly referred to by perceptive crew members as "the hate scene."

"Harrison hated Sean," accentuated Haber. "That was not a love scene, that was a hate scene. When he pushes her up against those blinds? Uh! He hated her. He hated her."[26]

Screenwriter Hampton Fancher's original intention for the scene was to be "a very tender, erotic moment." Yet, when it came time for the cameras to actually roll, the relationship between the two actors provided a startlingly different variation. Later, even the screenwriter admitted he was oddly drawn to the violent love scene that transpired on screen.

Costume designer Michael Kaplan recalled, "Just before their love scene, Sean freaked out — how was she going to kiss this man who never even gave her the time of day? The whole crew was waiting to see what would happen. When they shot the scene, Harrison threw her against the Venetian blinds so hard she later said he'd hurt her. Then he grabbed her, kissed her, and tears started running down her face. At that point in her career, I don't think she was a good enough actress to fake that; besides, she was still crying in our dressing trailer afterward."[27]

"There's considerable tension between our characters," explained Young. "Harrison carried that through both on and off the set in a way that we were able to act together very well. He knew what buttons to push to make me so frustrated — and that's what my character was. Harrison's behavior towards me really shaped my character."[28]

On July 9, 1981, *Blade Runner* completed principal photography. During the two months of post-production — aside from the traditional aspects of mixing the sound, instituting Greek-born Vangelis' score, dubbing and editing — the film's special effects were integrated into the final print.

The effects were supervised by a team of effects pioneers including Douglas

Trumbull, art director David Dryer and matte painter Michael Yuricich. The crew actually began their work prior to principal photography. Finally, on December 19, 1981, they completed their task with a total expenditure of $3.5 million. The movie was originally intended to have 38 special effects shots—a massive undertaking—and the technicians ultimately brought the total number of shots in at 90 (65 of which were used in the final film).

Trumbull was intensely proud of the complex visual effects they produced. Never before had they been presented with such a wide range of moving opticals in each scene—vehicles and pedestrians whizzed past, lights flashed and signs glowed as rain fell down upon it all. Each of these elements called for new and different techniques to bring it into harmony with the movements of the camera.

In the opening sequence, an industrial landscape with a miniature city appears in the seemingly unreachable horizon, lit only by the towering chimneys that belch flames up toward the perpetually dark sky. To provide this eerie environment (christened the "Hades Landscape"), model builders painted their special effects canvas on top of a waist-high platform measuring 13 feet deep by 18 feet wide. There the miniature metropolis was scantily illuminated by more than 2,000 points of light—provided by an impressive seven miles of fiber optic cable.

For the various close up shots of the cityscape scattered throughout the film, model-makers laboriously created an infinitely more detailed environment. To provide the miniature city, models (the tallest of which stood eight feet tall) were generally constructed from scratch by gathering different kits from various toy stores. Additionally, the art department would purchase previously built constructs that were originally designed for television commercials and film productions (including some from John Carpenter's *Escape from New York*). Builders would apply components onto the existing structures, thereby maintaining the film's universally recognized retrofitted look.

In an effort to stay within the special effects budget, the effects department improvised by creating buildings out of common raw materials, such as cardboard boxes. Furthermore—and perhaps in a premeditated tribute to the film's leading man—a five-foot-tall model of the Millennium Falcon constructed by Bill George was inserted on its end and covertly placed into the cityscape.

With the tremendous time and effort put into the film, Scott and Deeley were anxious to exhibit the final product. Considered by the director as "the workprint," a rough cut of the film was assembled and released to test audiences in Dallas and Denver on March 6 and 7, respectively.

Scott and Deeley were dismayed upon receiving the generally negative polling results distributed in questionnaire form to each audience. Although dazzled by the visual brilliance and technical ingenuity of its production design, the audience was disenchanted with the movie's slow pace and overall lack of clarity. Some attendees actually left before the end.

Retreating to the theater's office following the first test screening, Scott and Ford (who, because of his inability to remain anonymous in public, was smuggled into the rear of the theater with girlfriend Melissa after the house lights went down) sat in silence, mourning the film's visibly poor reception.

Offering consolation to her real-life leading man and his director, Mathison approached Scott and softly stated, "I just wanted to tell you how much I loved your movie."[29]

Scott and editor Terry Rawlings deleted scenes and restructured what remained — including livening up the movie's bleak original ending, thus providing closure for the film's viewers.

To achieve this, Scott borrowed aerial photography footage from Stanley Kubrick's *The Shining* and inserted his own footage of Ford and Young in Deckard's sedan as it motors through the vast and radiantly lush mountain landscape. Reassembling his cast and crew two hours northeast of L.A., in Big Bear, California, in late March of 1982, Scott filmed the couple's escape to their optimistic yet uncertain destiny.

Contractually obligated to provide an explanatory monologue dubbed over the completed film if need be, Ford reluctantly agreed.

"In fact, Harrison disliked the entire idea of a voice-over from the start," said Katherine Haber. "He thought it was overkill, that it was too overemphatic and disruptive."[30] Admitting that he approached the procedure "kicking and screaming,"[31] the actor recorded what some insiders considered to be a deliberately careless dubbing session — thinking it would never be used in the final film.

At a screening at which Scott, Deeley and Rawlings presented their new cut to officials at Tandem in late January 1982, the team was taken aback with the reactions. One executive questioned whether drugs were present during the recording sessions.

Whether or not narcotics were used during the session was never revealed. But, the third version Ford recorded (intentionally droning or not) was the version that was added to the final cut of *Blade Runner*, which was widely released to American audiences on June 25, 1982.

Genre magazines made the film their focus, books were published, conventions were organized and talk-show spots were scheduled. Press conference attendees were delighted to see no trace of the reported ambivalence between Ford and Ridley Scott. The two appeared in unison and enthusiastically touted their film around the globe.

Blade Runner opened to a weekend tally of $6.1 million on a total of 1,290 screens. Released on a date uncomfortably close to that of Spielberg's *E.T. The Extra-Terrestrial*, the film garnered mostly negative reviews. David Denby of *New York* magazine claimed the film was "all visuals and no story ... terribly dull."[32] Peter Travers of *People* magazine nixed the film with "[T]his is a slothful movie, dim both literally and figuratively...."[33] *Variety* stated, "On every level, the technical brilliance of the achievement is continually compelling ... a stylistically dazzling film."[34] *Playboy*'s Bruce Williamson considered it a "sumptuously styled but ultimately soul-less morality play...."[35] Richard Corliss of *Time* commented in a questionably complimentary manner, stating: "*Blade Runner*, like its setting, is a beautiful, deadly organism that devours life."[36]

Despite the negative press, the film was rewarded with a host of honorariums paying tribute to its visual attributes (an aspect that is foolishly minimized as having no relevance to the function of a meaningful film).

Blade Runner was named the best science fiction film of 1982 and given the Hugo Award. The British Academy of Film and Television Arts also honored the film for its cinematography and production design-art direction. It received a special technical award from the British Critics' Circle. The film was also awarded the L.A. Film Critics Award for best science fiction film.

The film was nominated for two Academy Awards, Best Art Direction (by Lawrence G. Paull and David Snyder, with set decoration by Linda DeScenna) and Best Visual Effects (by Douglas Trumbull, David Dryer and Richard Yuricich).

After 31 days of release, *Blade Runner* earned precisely $25,443,381 on 539 screens. By the time it had outlived its welcome in theaters, the film accumulated an estimated $28 million — an unsatisfying amount considering the amount of blood, sweat and tears sacrificed on its behalf.

"*Blade Runner* was before its time," recollected Haber. "It came out at the height of the Reagan era, when everyone was rich and having a good time and there was light in the future. People said, 'Who needs to think that the future is going to be like this?'"[37]

Original author Philip K. Dick tragically passed away due to complications from a stroke on March 2, 1982 — months before the visual equivalent of his thoughts officially came to life on the big screen. In December 1981, however, the author was treated to a 20-minute reel of completed footage. Recalling the uncomfortable silence during the screening, David Dryer ultimately considered the conversation that followed to be one of the most successful moments of his career. It was then, when a stupefied Dick questioned how what he'd seen on screen was possible.

"Those are not the exact images," reported Dick, "but the texture and tone of the images I saw in my head when I was writing the original book! The environment is exactly how I'd imagined it! How'd you guys do that? How did you know what I was feeling and thinking?!"[38]

The author was also taken aback when he was shown still photographs of the actors who would bring his fictional characters to life. When Rutger Hauer's photo was presented, Dick said: "Seeing Rutger Hauer as Batty just scared me to death, because it was exactly as I had pictured Batty, but more so."[39]

He had a similar reaction when shown a photograph of Rick Deckard. "Of course Harrison Ford is more like Rick Deckard that I could have even imagined," claimed the author. "I mean, it is just incredible. It was simply eerie when I first saw the stills of Harrison Ford.... Ford radiates this tremendous reality when you see him. And seeing him as a character I created is a stunning and almost supernatural experience to me."[40]

18

LIFE AMONG THE ALIENS

Home life for Ford and Mathison was strikingly similar to that of any ordinary couple. When not tending to the duties of stardom, the actor preferred to remain home. There he exercised his green thumb, tended to minor repairs, experimented in the kitchen with what he called "'meals in minutes,' simple food, mostly fish,"[1] or constructed furniture in his woodworking shop in the garage.

"I've had tastes of what they call the 'Hollywood life,'" claimed Ford, "but I don't stay indoors all the time. I'm not a hermit for heaven's sake. There are occasions when I can be compelled to attend some kind of function for something or someone I believe in. But no one needs to be part of that circus they call the Hollywood scene. It's a fallacy that you have to be. It's bull that it has helped anyone. In this game you can take or leave that kind of stuff. I leave it, thank you very much."[2]

Admitting his membership in Los Angeles' own "underground of anti-joggers," Ford partook in little exercise (at least not until the late 1980s).[3] Lacking what he dubbed "the sports gene," the closest the actor ever got to an athletic facility was the area's baseball diamond — where the proud father would watch his oldest son Benjamin in the Babe Ruth League. On other occasions, Ford would go to the indoor arena to watch son Willard practice Kung Fu. Any other time spent with his children generally entailed relaxing around his home and watching videos as a family.

While some children of the industry choose to live in their parents' shadow, both Benjamin and Willard were far removed from that lifestyle — viewing their father not as a worldwide superstar but simply as their father.

"Oh, they're not steeped in the myth," claimed Ford. "They knew me when I was a bad actor and a poor carpenter. They've grown up with me through the process. So I don't think that they relate to what they see on the screen."[4]

While producing the script for *E.T.*, Mathison used Ford's children as the prime inspiration for the characters, from the dialogue they spoke, to the background littered with a bevy of *Star Wars* toys, to the pajamas they wore. Mathison claimed it was her ability to effectively relate to the younger generation that allowed her to create the film's believably everyday characters.

"All the boys in the movie are based on boys I know, including Harrison's," claimed the screenwriter. "In the back of my mind I was always writing this movie for a 14-year-old boy. And if he wasn't embarrassed and felt it wasn't condescending, then nobody would."[5]

18. Life Among the Aliens

Had the story of *E.T.* gone according to Steven Spielberg's original plan, her boyfriend would have been involved in the picture. Following the scene in which Elliot, the main character, becomes inebriated at school as the result of his symbiotic connection with his new houseguest (who is drinking beer from the fridge), he is brought to the principal's office.

Mathison was cast as the nurse attempting to subdue the disgruntled Elliott. Ford appeared in the film as the school's principal, participating as a favor to Steven Spielberg under the sole condition that his role not be credited in the final film's release.

"So we have Harrison Ford playing the principal, very strict, sitting back in a tweed suit," recalled Spielberg. "I didn't show his face that clearly, I just showed the back of his head and his hand tapping and his legs; I wasn't showing adults in the movie. That's why I think he did it, because he didn't really have to be on camera."[6]

However, Mathison's nervousness in front of the camera was so apparent that Spielberg was forced to eliminate the entire sequence and, as a result, made a promise to Ford that he'd be given more closeups during their next collaboration.

In the summer of 1981, the screenwriter of *The Empire Strikes Back*, Lawrence Kasdan—celebrating the box office success of his work on *Raiders of the Lost Ark*— was eager to embark on a new career path. With the idea of moving from behind a desk to behind a camera, Kasdan hoped to direct films instead of write them. His 1981 directorial feature film debut *Body Heat* showed that he truly was multitalented.

In the meantime, jack-of-all-cinematic-trades George Lucas was mentally preparing for the development of his final beloved *Star Wars* film, then entitled *Revenge of the Jedi*. Intending to temporarily relieve Kasdan of his directorial duties, Lucas approached Kasdan to write the screenplay based on their prior relationship during the creation of both *Empire* and *Raiders*. Kasdan acquiesced, recognizing the debt of gratitude he owed to Lucas. Moreover, though, he genuinely enjoyed working with him, and looked forward to the satisfaction — and financial rewards— that was sure to come with the completion of the trilogy. And so, he put aside his directorial hopes.

Together, the two plotted out the final installment of the saga. *Jedi* told the triumphant story of the gathering of all the Rebel forces into a giant armada to wage final war upon the evil galactic Empire. The Empire's power had never been more deadly, with the presence of the Emperor and an all-new Death Star to intensify their threat.

Long before Lucas and Kasdan spent countless hours in script meetings, though, Lucas had hired his upcoming project's director. Lucas sought the expertise of a newcomer, hoping to instill a fresh approach not only in the material at hand but also in the working environment itself.

After narrowing down a long list of considerations, Lucas had to decide between American cult film director David Lynch and Englishman Richard Marquand. Lynch (*Eraserhead, The Elephant Man*) was well respected in the industry for his unique method of presenting material. But he wasn't accustomed to answering to another producer, and respectfully declined. Marquand, whose previous feature films were *The Legacy* and *Eye of the Needle* (and the Emmy Award–winning series *Search for the Nile*) enthusiastically signed on, fulfilling his desire to become part of cinematic history.

The director credited Lucas with "a great sense of pace and sense of humor," and admired his illustrations of the "warm relationship side of the characters that play the major roles."[7]

Marquand felt Irvin Kershner had been best suited for *Empire* "because he was more interested in the darkness and the danger and the doom"[8] — which is what the script dictated and he so successfully translated on screen.

"In *Empire* there are not many gags," said Marquand. "You rarely see the gang together, and that means you have a sense of loneliness and possible despair and certainly danger. You're worried all the time — and of course you should be...."[9]

Demonstrating his good intentions, Marquand asserted: "I'm going to bring back that pace — and keep the danger and the action and the gang back together for the final adventure...."[10]

Thanks to Kasdan's script and the understanding that Lucas would be present significantly more on the *Return of the Jedi* set than on *Empire,* the pace, danger, and action came easily. Marquand's challenge of getting "the gang back together" proved to be a more difficult task, however.

Just as he had been concerned during the developmental stages of *The Empire Strikes Back*, Ford again was initially skeptical about the evolution and maturation of his character Han Solo in *Jedi*.

Believing that Solo was nothing more than flesh-and-blood window dressing, Ford suggested two ideas to Lucas. The first was for Solo to remain in the carbon freezing state that he was placed in at the conclusion of the previous film. And the second — and to Lucas, the more absurd of the two — was that Solo be killed off.

"I didn't think I was really involved in the story," said the actor, "so I had no idea of what to do with my character. We had tough discussions about that. Part of the brouhaha was that I thought my character should die. Since Han Solo had no momma and poppa and wasn't going to get the girl anyway, he may as well die to give the whole thing some emotional resonance. But George wouldn't agree to it."[11]

For the first time in their working history, Lucas vetoed Ford's suggestions. Lucas didn't feel that Ford was overstepping his bounds; but the absence of Han Solo would have drastically altered the spirit of the series.

The script was amended to appease Ford. The actor later stated: "I'm well satisfied with what the character has become and the way his usefulness has been completed, because this story is really the adventures of Luke Skywalker." The actor felt Solo was an ideal role because it was "the most contemporary voice in the film, but he designs himself only by his relationship to Luke and Leia. It's no secret that Luke is a kind of alter ego for George Lucas, and that's what's philosophically important in this story."[12]

Given the wholehearted commitments from Mark Hamill (Luke), Carrie Fisher (Princess Leia), Billy Dee Williams (Lando Calrissian) and others, the process of casting the actors was complete.

The film's projected budget of $32.5 million came from Lucas' earnings from previous successes. The production prepared for principal photography at Borehamwood,

England's EMI-Elstree soundstages, and, for the first time in the entire trilogy, on American soil.

On January 11, 1982, cast and crew reunited at Elstree Studios. All nine of its soundstages were occupied by the production's elaborate sets and every vacant area was utilized for storage. Lucasfilm Ltd. became the sole inhabitant.

What was created for the filming of *Empire* and known as the "*Star Wars* Stage" was employed once again. Stage Six was used for the exterior gate entrance to Jabba the Hutt's Tatooine palace and the enormous docking bay of the Empire's all-new, under-construction Death Star. There, a full-scale prop of a new Imperial-class vehicle known as the Imperial Shuttle—complete with its five-ton undercarriage—was constructed and photographed.

Another stage housed the massive Throne Room of Jabba the Hutt. With four walls, a ceiling and a floor elevated four feet above the stage floor to accommodate the puppeteers hidden beneath, the fully enclosed set was host to myriad life forms and to the most impressive ILM creature creation, Jabba the Hutt.

Jabba was nothing more than an enormous mass of inert foam and latex. It was brought to life by nearly a half-dozen technicians cleverly concealed behind, beneath and—because of his size and shape—within.

Director Marquand considered Jabba's Throne Room set the most trying to film within because of the complications inherent in choreographing the movements and timing of numerous actors, aliens and accompanying staff and crew involved. The set's logistic problems were exacerbated by the attention required simply to keep the costumed actors conscious.

The sheer weight of the materials used for the creature costumes posed an enormous risk of suffocation for the actors within the heavy outfits. Creature handlers were frequently found cooling the suffering participants by crouching on their hands and knees, blowing cold air from hair dryers up the mouths of each alien.

Other sequences involved the Rebel Main Briefing Room (filmed on Stage Five), the brief scenes of Dagobah (where Yoda, his abode, his environment's vegetation and Luke's X-Wing Fighter were retrieved from storage at ILM) and Stage Four's complete dedication to the Emperor's Throne Room.

After nearly 78 days of interior photography in London, Ford and the other homesick members of the American cast and crew were eager to return stateside.

"You gotta travel on, travel on," said the actor. "I've had the same dressing room at Elstree for four films and it's beginning to feel pretty old. This is a wonderful country, very pretty and I admire the people but London is obviously a tourist economy and I'm quite prey to it. Generally it ain't what it used to be, is it?"[13]

In late March, the production relocated to the desert regions of the U.S. where, for the next two weeks, they would remain for location shooting.

The Buttercup Valley—just outside of Yuma, Arizona—represented the arid wastelands of Tatooine where the film's heroes are held captive and condemned to death by the gangster Jabba the Hutt. Located near the Colorado River along the California-Arizona border, the locale the "dune-buggy capital of the world" at times—was chosen for its immense and beautiful sand dunes.

Constructed over a period of nearly five months, Jabba's 212 × 80-foot-high

Carrie Fisher and Harrison Ford reprise their roles as Princess Leia and Han Solo for the last time in *Return of the Jedi* (Lucasfilm, Ltd., 1983).

anti-gravity "Sail Barge" required more than $100,000 worth of lumber, 4,000 yards of fabric for its sails and more than 16,000 pounds of nails.

Encompassing the 30,000-square-foot set with a four-acre stockade fence was not enough to prevent dune riders from occasionally appearing as in the background. To guarantee the secrecy of the most anticipated film of all time, local police and a 24-hour security force were hired to keep the curious at bay.

What's more, scripts were not distributed in their entirety and call-sheets were prepared on a day-to-day basis— never to divulge too much information should they get into the wrong hands. The names of the principals were listed as "Harry," "Martin" and "Caroline" as misleading substitutions for Ford, Hamill and Fisher respectively. Hypothetical sequences were also filmed to disorient the actors— including three different finales.

Producer Howard Kazanjian also reduced the number of crew allowed on set from 100 or more, to a mere handful of four to five people who were truly crucial to the filming of that scene. Moreover, he required frequent turnover of those few — so the next plot twist would be seen by the eyes of less informed crew members, further cloaking the storyline in mystery.

In addition, T-shirts, baseball caps and jackets distributed to cast and crew members were emblazoned with the words "Blue Harvest (Horror Beyond Imagination)" on them. Those who ventured beyond the fence for supplies and accommodations sported this attire, in the hopes of confusing outsiders as to their purpose in the desert.

The crew also had a helicopter warding off any aerial interlopers. During one security breach, a handful of people stealthily infiltrated the perimeter by cutting through the fence and photographed the extraordinary set.

Pictures of a *Star Wars* model appeared in the media. Kazanjian insisted that it was a "Blue Harvest" set, pointing to the aforementioned T-shirts and caps as proof of his statements. Overall, Kazanjian felt the production's secrets had remained largely intact.

Selling the set as scrap to a company in Mexico, the production was able to compensate for some of its $1.2 million dollar expense under the provision that none of it be re-sold as souvenirs.

After having introduced nearly $2 million of revenue into the local economy, the production wrapped and relocated to the northernmost part of California for the forest moon of Endor sequences.

The production could not film within the national park due to the amount of pyrotechnics required for the sequence and associated fire hazard, coupled with the unavoidable damage that would result from the presence of hundreds of people in a relatively undisturbed environment.

Unit production manager Miki Herman claimed that the biggest difficulty was in attempting to persuade landowners to allow them to utilize their acreage for battle scenes.

Locating land owned by a private lumber company, the unit began filming among the giant Sequoia trees of the fishing and lumber community of Crescent City (1982 population of 2,500), in California's Redwood Forest, during April 1982.

Standing as high as 400 feet, with an average circumference of nearly 20 feet, the giant trees served as the ideal backdrop for the forest moon, where the battle between the Empire and the Rebellion continued.

Several weeks worth of clearing and replanting were done to achieve the required look. This was no simple feat, considering the indigenous animals and insects, including the rather daunting presence of a territorial bear. The moviemakers were relieved to accomplish their set dressing without incident.

What also made the Endor set unique was the peculiarity of its fictitious native inhabitants. Originally it was intended that the area be populated by a society of Wookies (Chewbacca's breed), but Endor's inhabitants ended up being pudgy-faced "Teddy bear" warriors known as Ewoks.

More than 200 local residents portrayed the various Stormtroopers, Imperial Officers and Rebel soldiers seen about the forest. The casting of the Ewoks had been tended to months earlier due to the difficulty finding dozens of dwarfs and midgets from both England and the United States.*

---

*The sequence involving the Ewok village high atop the treetops was filmed earlier at Elstree Studios. There, elevated 20 feet above the stage floor and surrounded (360 degrees) by a painted forest backdrop, the scene was shot with the film's principals and a separate cast of English-bred "little people" portraying the Ewoks. A handful of actors used their spare time to make another film project, "Return of the Ewok." Ford (who decades later professed his distaste for the creatures — likening their scenes in the film to a "Teddy [cont.]

Following the completion of filming among the four different locations throughout the forest, the production wrapped principal photography for the final chapter of the trilogy on May 28, 1982. As Tomblin jokingly remembered, "a good seven seconds ahead of schedule."[15]

Coming in relatively on time and on budget, the production then moved to the special effects workshops at Lucas' Industrial Light and Magic.

Consuming roughly $8 million of the movie's total budget, the number of special effects in *Return of the Jedi* were what Lucas had originally intended for the first of the three films but was unable to incorporate with limited technology and funding in 1976. Intending to overwhelm viewers with an all-out visual assault, Lucas spared no expense. With upwards of 900 separate effects, *Jedi* outnumbered its predecessors by a staggering amount (1977's *Star* Wars had 545; *Empire* had 763).[16]

"We have to make each film better than the one previous," claimed visual effects art director Joe Johnston. "The public demands a special-effects extravaganza, something that will blow them away for their five dollars. We were never sure whether the movie was a vehicle for the effects or for the story."[17] Involving optical integration, animation, miniature work, blue-screening techniques and matte painting, the film's final touches took nearly a year to produce.

The effects (which won an Academy Award in the Best Visual Effects Achievement category) were such a monumental endeavor that certain moments during the final ship-to-ship battle above Endor involved as many as 67 layers of separately photographed elements per shot. Some of the ships were built, some were brought out of their dormant state from ILM's storage facilities, and some were actually purchased from local toy stores, their intricate details sufficient enough for the model builders to include among their own.

While the cast and crew were in Crescent City, a cameraman walked through the recently forged paths with a mercury-balanced camera — otherwise known as a Steadicam — strapped to his chest. Filmed at 1/30th of normal speed, the speeder bikes — which were later integrated using the miniature and blue-screen work of Industrial Light and Magic — attained high velocity when the footage was projected at normal speed.

To prepare for the release, Lucasfilm Ltd. dispatched contingents of technicians throughout the country to upgrade each theater's audio and video capabilities by installing Lucas's own hi-fidelity THX Sound System (named after his first cinematic excursion, *THX 1138*).

Released on the sixth anniversary of the debut of *Star Wars*, *Return of the Jedi* burst onto 950 theater screens throughout the United States and Canada. It was originally entitled *Revenge of the Jedi*, but Lucas reconsidered, believing that a Jedi Knight's character wouldn't include vengeance.

While fans in Philadelphia stood in quarter-mile-long lines awaiting the first screening, some Tucson, Arizona, residents didn't hesitate when asked to pay a then-

---

bear prom"),[14] Fisher, Hamill, Daniels and co-producer Robert Watts created a 24-minute short film — shot by assistant director David Tomblin and his own 16mm camera — with Wicket (Warwick Davis) as the central character. Reportedly Davis possesses the only VHS copy of that endeavor, which he hopes to one day release to convention audiences.

unheard-of $6 for entry. In the Big Apple, one impatient female enthusiast faked pregnancy with a stuffed pillow tucked beneath her shirt to remedy the long wait. Elsewhere, a print of the film was stolen by a gun-toting thief in the hopes of saturating the black-market with bootlegged video tape copies.

The first day of business generated $6,219,629, entering the record books with the largest single-day total in history. Two days later, on Friday, the film beat its own record, bringing in $6,437,005. On Sunday, that record was beaten again with one-day receipts of nearly $8.5 million. At the conclusion of the week, *Jedi* had earned $45,311,004 — beating the previous record held by Steven Spielberg's *E.T. The Extra-Terrestrial*, which had earned $25 million during its opening week the summer before. To the surprise of no one, *Jedi* eventually took the top slot in the year-end recaps, with more than $249 million worth of ticketholders passing through theater doors.

Audiences may have approved of the film, but critics felt otherwise.

Daily Variety's Jim Harwood applauded the film's visual achievements: "George Lucas and Co. have perfected the technical magic to a point where almost anything and everything — no matter how bizarre — is believable...." In that same review, however, he chastised the performances of its key players: "Harrison Ford, who was such an essential element of the first two outings, is present more in body than in spirit this time, given little to do but react to special effects...."[18]

Director Marquand disapproved of any negative critique of his star. Claiming that his film "brings you back to basic good things," Marquand explained that Ford was an "intrinsic part" of how the film and its complications came together.[19]

"Unlike some stars," said the director, "Harrison is a craftsman who understands the needs of the movie as well as understanding and protecting the needs of his own part. There are times in making a movie when things just get very rough. But Harrison is always there to rely on.... He has a very warm heart, and he's very loyal. I hope I can work with him again. I like his company."[20]

From the director right down to the technicians whom he respectfully referred to as "sir" on the set, Ford won the admiration of all those he worked alongside.

Likening the making of the trilogy to "senior year in high school,"[21] Mark Hamill was saddened to recognize that *Jedi* marked the trilogy's conclusion, and would likely be his last opportunity to work with Ford.

"You approach it with a mixture of emotions," explained Hamill. "You are very relieved to be finished with it, but at the same time, you're going to miss all your friends. It was nostalgic...."[22]

Hamill considered Ford a friend, but also somewhat of a mentor to him. "I think he'd be a great director," said the actor, "because he naturally understands the direction a scene should go in. Harrison has probably made more changes in his lines. He's good at turning phrases and making them his own.... Harrison plays his changes as if they were in the script, and often no one notices. I admire him for that."[23]

"We've become something of a family," said Carrie Fisher. "I especially liked working with Harrison. He and I have the same sort of sparring relationship off-screen that you see in the films, so we work well together. He's good at rewriting dialogue and coming up with ideas for scenes."[24]

"I love working with Mark and Carrie and everyone," admitted Ford, "but it will be a bit sad, because this second sequel is the last one for the foreseeable future, that I will appear in...."[25] In the future, I could return, but the next three installments will most likely feature completely different characters. Of course, George [Lucas] is a good friend, not just an employer, and I trust his instincts and good taste...."[26]

Producer Kazanjian viewed the individual films as chapters within a single book. "Now the book is finished, and I have put it on the shelf. ... *Star Wars* has grabbed my life and taken it over against my will. Now I've got to get my life back again — before it's too late!"[27]

For Ford, the longing for the progression of his acting career was much like Lucas' desire to reacquaint himself with his personal life. Having committed his upcoming services to Lucas and Spielberg for another Indiana Jones film, the actor began to realize that his involvement in *Return of the Jedi* was primarily based on two things. The first was maintaining his relationship with George Lucas, to whom he owed a great deal of his success. The second was allowing his appetite for financial gain to outweigh his passion for quality projects where he could display his true acting abilities.

With the phenomenal success of *Jedi* further confirming his clout as one of Hollywood's major players, Ford was anxious to move beyond the stereotypes: "I'm amazed," said the actor, "when people ask me, 'Well, have you ever done comedy?' What do they think I've been doing for the last five or six years?"[28]

19

CRACKING THE WHIP (AGAIN)

Inevitable. Unavoidable. Inescapable.

These perfectly describe the situation regarding the sequel to 1981's *Raiders of the Lost Ark*.

Yet Steven Spielberg did not agree to participate because of public demand. The thought of another adventure had been in his mind since the days when he and Lucas discussed the original concept of *Raiders*. From the beginning, Spielberg intended to act solely as a behind-the-scenes advisor, primarily overseeing it in the pre-production phase.

Congregated for a three-day retreat, Lucas and Spielberg invited *American Graffiti* screenwriter–husband-and-wife team Gloria Katz and Willard Huyck to produce a basic synopsis for the tentatively titled *Indiana Jones and the Temple of Death*.

Upon receiving the completed first draft, six weeks after Katz and Huyck began writing it in June of '82, Spielberg's level of interest changed drastically. He wanted complete creative control. Running through his mind was the possibility of setting box office records, but more significantly was the sheer joy of the work itself.

Lucas spoke on behalf of Spielberg when he stated: "You have to enjoy making a good movie and entertaining an audience. And both Steven and I are like that."[1]

The shooting script three months later told a darker tale of adventure, complete with new characters set against a backdrop of an evil cult—a premise opposite that of its predecessor.

Returning as executive producer, Frank Marshall claimed that the new film was a more personal story for Indy. Set in 1935—a prequel to *Raiders*, which took place in 1936—it featured Indiana Jones and his sidekick Short Round attempting to recover sacred stones. The stones—which were believed to possess magical powers—were stolen and hidden among the caverns below an Indian palace, where a cult called the Thuggees maintained a work force of child slave labor in an effort to discover the remaining stones.

The screenplay was shootable, but the issue of whether it would actually go before the cameras was yet to be determined by the involvement of Harrison Ford.

The actor—who had recently been considering the lead role in Elmore Leonard's *Stick* before Burt Reynolds claimed it—was approached by Spielberg, but refrained from any involvement until the writing had reached the revised first-draft stage. Then Ford was instantly swayed: "Of course I'm doing the second *Raiders* film. With great pleasure.... [T]his is very exciting for me. It was one of the best working relationship experiences of my life working with Steven."[2]

For the new adventure, Indiana would not be joined by *Raiders* veterans Sallah, Brody or Marion. Indy's new love interest, nightclub singer Willie Scott (named after the director's dog), was actress Kate Capshaw. Indy meets Scott at a Shanghai nightclub as she sings a Chinese version of Cole Porter's "Anything Goes."

Capshaw was a high-school teacher in Missouri before she moved to New York to pursue modeling. From there, she took on various motion picture roles, such as *A Little Sex*. Just days prior to working on the new Indiana Jones film, Capshaw wrapped on *Dreamscape*, Natalie Wood's final picture.

The guidelines for the script required that Spielberg find an actress "who's full of life, vulnerable, energetic, [and] rambunctious with a sense of humor."[3] Capshaw won the role following her impressive interview with casting director Mike Fenton and Spielberg.

For Huyck and Katz, the character of Willie Scott offered comic relief to the somber tone of the film.

"Not only did we name her after Spielberg's dog, we made her an anathema to all feminists," explained Willard Huyck. "Her squeamishness is funny, a counterpoint to Indy's machismo."[4]

With a previously pampered lifestyle, Willie Scott's change in situation is made apparent by her constant whining, bickering and screaming. "In a way," says Gloria Katz, "Willie represents the audience's realistic viewpoint of what they would be like if they were normal persons thrown into a jungle. True, she's not the brave, strong woman, but she is a different kind of woman and, in certain respects, a more realistic one."[5]

The role of Short Round — named for Willard Huyck's dog, which was named after the orphan in the film *The Steel Helmet*— was played by 12-year-old Vietnamese-born Ke Huy Quan (pronounced key-way-quwan). Quan, who came to America in 1979, had no prior acting experience when he responded to an open casting call held in Los Angeles' Chinatown. Receiving high marks, Quan was called in again to act alongside Ford in a scene that was not in the final draft of the script. Together the two enacted a poker scene in which Indiana was accused of cheating. The scene made such an impact on Spielberg that it was later photographed and added to the final cut of the film.

For Ford, there was much to celebrate aside from his much-anticipated reunion with the now legendary fedora, whip, and leather jacket.

Since his initial meeting with Melissa Mathison during the 1978 filming of *Apocalypse Now*, they had shared their lives in Ford's Benedict Canyon home (the couple had been described by the press as "Ford and his live-in girlfriend.") On March 14, 1983, 41-year-old Ford and 33-year-old Mathison exchanged white roses and marriage vows in a judge's chamber during a private ceremony in Santa Monica Superior Court. They honeymooned for nearly an entire month at an undisclosed location. It lasted until April 18, 1983, when Ford's presence was required in Sri Lanka for principal photography for *Indiana Jones and the Temple of Doom*.

Sri Lanka — an island nation off the coast of India — was not the first choice for the location. Having initially decided on mainland India, the production was ultimately denied permission to film there for fear of social and religious complications. Indian officials believed it sacrilegious for the word Maharaja to be mentioned. The production decided to relocate rather than rewrite the script. It took nearly a month to transport equipment (including enormous power generators) from England to Sri Lanka via cargo boats. There, among the tea plantations (Sri Lanka's largest export), the production photographed several key sequences within a three-week period.

The return of Indiana Jones (Lucasfilm, Ltd., 1984).

The mountainside Mayapore village is where Jones, Short Round and Willie learn of their responsibilities from the village elders. Created by production designer Elliot Scott, the village sets were made of mud. At first the commune is in ruins. Throughout the film, the village goes through a physical improvement, most notable during the film's final moments.

By photographing the sequence in reverse, the crews were able to "de-construct" the dwellings by casually tearing away the intact buildings until they reached the point of natural-looking decay.

Nearby, the British government was overseeing the development of Victoria Dam, which was in its fourth year of construction. When the production found it, they deemed it an ideal location to shoot a scene where Indiana Jones is trapped on a rope bridge high above an alligator-infested river. The British dam overseers were hired to handle all aspects of the bridge set.

Located near the dam, the bridge was constructed high above a gorge formed by Sri Lanka's largest river. Situated 350 feet above the ground, the 200-foot-long bridge swayed there, much to director Spielberg's unease. Apart from his concern for the cast and crew's safety on and about the set, the agoraphobic director was forced to drive nearly two miles down, around and up the canyon every time his services were required on the opposite side.

"That bridge was real," recalled Ford, "and that was a real river 300 feet below. Everyone, including Steven, was sort of tenuous about it when we first saw it. But I felt we had to establish a proper disdain for the rope bridge. So, before anyone could do anything, I just ran across it. I convinced Steven that there was no danger. In fact, it was dangerous as hell."[6]

Because of his relationship with Spielberg, Ford was able to persuade him to let him partake in much of the physical action. What Ford called physical action others would call stunts—most notably Englishman Vic Armstrong, Ford's stunt double and friend since *Raiders of the Lost Ark*.

For stuntmen like Armstrong, a project like *Temple of Doom* was a double-edged sword. "[H]ere was Harrison trying to do all my stunts for me," recalled Armstrong. "Obviously, for insurance reasons, there's a limit to how far stars are supposed to go. When you have 500 people working on a $20 million movie, and the star gets a busted ankle, you have problems. But whatever job I was called in for, Harrison would always find some way of trying it too. And Spielberg wasn't going to stop him. He went along with everything Harrison wanted to do."[7]

Even Armstrong was uncomfortable with the idea of Ford assuming responsibility for the bridge sequence. "Sure, he had a safety cable and harness on," said Armstrong. "But safety cables have been known to snap and nothing is foolproof. Yet there was no way that guy was going to leave it all to me. There was nothing between him and the rocks 250 feet below, yet he wasn't nervous. He's the most fearless actor I've ever come across."[8]

The bridge sequence was photographed at two different locations. The first was the gorge location in Sri Lanka. There the confrontation between Indy and the Thuggees took place up to the point of the bridge's collapse. The production constructed another bridge 15 feet above the ground for the subsequent shots.

To film on the rope bridge set, Spielberg used a Steadicam camera. To make sure the job was done properly, the director had the camera's inventor, Garret Brown, personally handle the photography of the sequence.

Spielberg decided not to have stunt personnel fall from the bridge. So special effects supervisor George Gibbs came up with several life-like dummies taken from molds of tailors' mannequins. The mannequins were stuffed with foam and pneumatic motors for realistic bodily movements during their descent.

The remaining action involving the struggle along the bridge's broken half was photographed on the EMI–Elstree Studios backlot. There a 60-foot-tall mock-up of the set was erected, with mats below.

Meanwhile, a 25-man second-unit team—commanded by second unit director Mickey Moore—was busy photographing the film's opening car chase sequence. It was originally going to be shot in Hong Kong, but that was nixed because of the city's architectural modernization. The filmmakers settled 60 miles outside of Hong Kong, in the Portuguese colony of Macao. There, the car chase following Indy's daring escape from Saigon's "Club Obi Wan" (an homage to *Star Wars*) took place during a six-night period of post-midnight photography. In his second cameo appearance of the film series, executive producer Frank Marshall stood in as a rickshaw driver complete with eye makeup, hauling Lucasfilm senior vice-president Sidney Ganis in tow. (Ganis is now president of worldwide marketing for Columbia Pictures.)

The six-day stint also produced one of the film's most involved stunt sequences. Exiting in grand fashion, Ford and Capshaw's characters crash through the nightclub's window and plummet through three awnings and bounce off the last two before safely landing in a rickshaw far below. Grateful that Ford was in Sri Lanka, Vic Armstrong took the near 80-foot plunge himself with Wendy Leach in one successful take.

Having completed location photography on time and under budget, the production resumed photography in mid–June at EMI-Elstree. There they would film the interiors of Club Obi Wan and Pankot Palace. On Stage 6 — specially constructed for the ice hangar sequence in *The Empire Strikes Back*— were the enormous mining tunnels and Thuggee ceremonial chamber of the Temple of Doom.

Not long into soundstage photography and with nearly two-thirds of the film to go, there was an unscheduled three-week hiatus. Their leading man experienced severe back pains undoubtedly brought on by elephant riding during Sri Lankan shooting. While the pains persisted, the actor temporarily abandoned the project for an emergency flight to Los Angeles to remedy the discomfort.

"The only fun thing about riding elephants is the getting off," admitted the actor. "You ride with your legs in a hyper-extended position to accommodate the girth of the animal right over its shoulders. First one leg, then the other is pulled forward, which tends to spread you apart — like being stretched on a medieval rack, I imagine."[9]

Treated by sports medicine specialists at Centinela Hospital, Ford underwent surgery to treat a ruptured disc. Normally a painful operation called a laminectomy is performed, but Ford underwent a treatment called chymopapain. This procedure involved the injection of papaya fruit enzyme into the damaged area, which served as a corrosive agent and slowly ate away at the infected area.[10] (His back would never fully recover, as the subsequent necessity to sleep upon a board with regularity would prove.)

Prior to and during the production, the actor trained with fitness guru Jake Steinfeld in a rigorous "Body by Jake" regimen designed to create muscle mass necessary for scenes in which he would bare his upper torso. By the time filming was complete, Ford was able to bench press 360 pounds, up from only 80 at the outset. (Spielberg earned high praise for his ability to do 1,000 consecutive sit-ups.)

Following what doctors considered to be an unusually brief recovery period, Ford reunited with cast and crew at Elstree on August 8, 1983. The success of his recovery would be put to the test during the sequence in the subterranean caverns of the Temple of Doom where Indy parries with a Thuggee guard (played by *Raiders* veteran Pat Roach). Ford and Roach choreographed a long and brutal battle of fist, foot and stone, much to Harrison's dismay.

"At one point the guard throws me into the mine car," said Ford, "and since I'd just come back from surgery, I had second thoughts about being the throwee."[11]

Ford willingly called on Armstrong, who had a nearly identical physical build. The actor would later jest that his wife Melissa would often get confused and make the wrong decision of whom to go to bed with.

Another sequence involved nearly 100,000 insects. In the sequence, christened the "bug tunnel" scene, 50,000 cockroaches, 30,000 beetles and thousands of other insects including locusts, spiders and crickets. There were also millipedes and centipedes, whose teeth were filed to prevent them from biting the actors. The moviemakers used 2,000 to 3,000 at a time per shot. The bugs (the bulk of which had a three-week life span) proved to be the most difficult to film. Placed in cold storage to make them lethargic, the hordes of insects were still not on cue. They would scurry away the moment the set was lit, leaving only a few seconds for the cameras to capture a usable image. Frank Marshall, who acted as a second unit director for closeups during the sequence, recalled the discouraging moments of painstaking photography — the bulk of which resulted in unusable footage. Up to seven actresses were used during the filming, thereby lessening the emotional burden on Kate Capshaw's shoulders.

"Steven was very sympathetic, and only did as many takes as he had to," explained the actress. "He had a Bug Patrol wait between each take to take them off and reapply them, so I never had to stand around with bugs on me for more than a couple of minutes."[12]

Despite the care and precautions taken, Capshaw recalled the few that escaped unnoticed. "You'd go home and think they'd gotten up your pants legs or were crawling in your hair. There were times I didn't feel like an actress, I felt like a prop."[13]

Comparing the bug tunnel of *Temple of Doom* to the serpent scenes in *Raiders*, Marshall revealed that snakes were the preferred nuisance of cast and crew.

"I found that people were much more scared by the insects than they were by the snakes," said the executive producer. "Every once in a while I'd hear this shriek because one of the bugs crawled through from the bug tunnel to the tap dance rehearsal stage next door. Of course, this was a bad place for any bug to be — 32 girls tap dancing away — so both the insects and the girls would run like hell. Mutual fear!"[14]

The exciting "mine chase sequence" was also filmed on the soundstages at Elstree with photography consisting of both live action with real actors and stop-action with miniatures, meticulously spliced together during the editing process for a seamless and realistic effect. The sequence proved to be the production's most technically involved, time-consuming, and costly. It was described by Spielberg as a "roller coaster ride" constructed on the soundstage. Production designer George Gibbs oversaw the creation of the gigantic tunnel set. There, the actors were whisked around a circular track at 10 miles per hour (made to look dangerously fast by under-cranking the camera) in specially built mine cars. Each car had its own self-contained acceleration and braking system discreetly controlled by the actors. Cinematographer Douglas Slocombe photographed each rotation from a different angle using a variety of colored gels that he would apply to the camera lens, thus creating the illusion of an endless network of subterranean tunnels.

A 50-foot-long miniature of the mineshaft was also constructed and photographed. Returning from his tour of duty on *Return of the Jedi*, Phil Tippett was assigned to the production as creative consultant. His job was to oversee the creation of the miniature puppets of Indiana, Willie, Short Round and their Thuggee pursuers — all of them under 10 inches tall. The task of bringing the miniatures to life with movement was made possible by the painstaking and tedious efforts of stop-motion animators Tom St. Amand and Mike McAlister, who — working for hours on a cold, fog-filled set — were able to provide only a few seconds worth of usable footage.

Another example of movie magic on the soundstages was the sequence involving the lowering of sacrificial victims into a churning pit of molten lava. The "victim" was a three-foot-tall, motor-maneuvered latex foam puppet. The "lava" used was pump-circulated, colored glycerin. It was contained within a half-scale, bottom-lit mock pit.

The crew completed its European soundstage photography with the interiors of Club Obi Wan around August 22, 1983. They returned to the United States to film two remaining sequences before concluding post-production work at Industrial Light and Magic in Northern California.

Frank Marshall recalled how several scenes intended for *Raiders* were never brought before the cameras, but — given the filmmakers' new financial freedom — were integrated into the new script: "We felt we were going too far," explained Marshall. "With this movie, we knew we could stretch things further, and so we put them in."[15]

For an airplane crash into a mountainside, an Industrial Light and Magic team constructed a miniature of the plane (with a three-foot wingspan) and guided it with wires into an artificial snow-capped Himalayan mountaintop. All of the airplane miniature effects scenes were photographed on the ILM complex roof so that the blue skies of Northern California could be used as a natural backdrop.

To film the live-action sequence, the second unit team (headed by *E.T.* cinematographer Allen Davieau) spent two weeks in early August in Northern California. The first week was spent at Mammoth Mountain, where ski patrol head Cliff Mann was hired to provide the filmmakers with footage of the life raft plummeting down the slope. This was made possible by placing a camera positioned between his legs as he descended the mountainside on skis. The second week was devoted to the creation of the white water raft ride, which was filmed on the Tuolomne and the American Rivers.

On September 8, the production ventured to Hamilton Air Force Base in Marin County, California, for the final two days of principal photography. The filmmakers gave the previously abandoned base new life as the Shanghai Airport, with a plane awaiting Indy and his entourage for safe transport from the clutches of Lao Che.

The plane, a vintage (late '20s) Ford Tri-Motor, was the first of its kind ever to land at the air base. The scene also featured Dan Aykroyd in a small cameo role as Indiana's English-imported protégé. Three (very distant) background extras in missionary costume were none other than George Lucas, Steven Spielberg and producer Robert Watts.

Despite the three-week delay and the complexities of a production spanning three continents, *Indiana Jones and the Temple of Doom* was completed with a final budget of $28 million and only one week behind schedule.

Executive producer Frank Marshall considered the filming a reunion — with many of the same faces back to reprise their roles from the first Indiana Jones outing. Additionally, the warmth, humor and, as Marshall jests, "lots of foo-foo rice" thrown among the cast and crew on the set, made for an effortless way to overcome the tension of the production's grueling requirements.

The best example of humor on the set was during the scene where Ford is shackled to a stone and slashed with his own bullwhip by Pat Roach's Thuggee character. Catching Ford off guard, Roach was replaced by Barbra Streisand, who was sporting a sexual dominatrix outfit. Administering the "punishment" with Indy's whip, Streisand — who apparently was given the assignment while Spielberg helped her during the editing stages of *Yentl*—could be heard saying between each whip crack, "That's for *Hanover Street*, the worst movie I ever saw." Adding to the wackiness of the prank, friend and former *Star Wars* co-star Carrie Fisher threw herself upon Ford in an effort to protect him, just as former *Empire* director Irvin Kershner caught sight of the entire incident and exclaimed, "Is this the way you run your movies? I would never let this happen on one of my sets!"[16]

For Harrison Ford, acquainting himself with the film's new members was a rewarding experience. He and Quan befriended one another during the film's Sri Lankan location with swimming lessons at the hotel following the day's photography.

"It really hurts an actor to see a kid walk on a set and be great without any training or experience," said Ford. "And it also reminds an actor where this stuff really comes from 'cause kids don't bring in stuff from outside to use ... it all comes from inside. It's fascinating to watch a kid work."[17]

Quan considered Ford to be "a generous man, and a noble actor," while Kate Capshaw observed a more private person, taken aback by the actor's penchant for solitude.[18]

"Harrison is very internalized, quiet, private," recalled the actress. "It was a new experience for me, because I'm such a jabbermouth. If someone doesn't jabber with me, I begin to think they hate me."[19]

As she recalled, the actor spent much of his off-camera time schmoozing with the crew or bound for the privacy of his dressing room. The actor nevertheless made a unique impression on his co-star.

"I began to fall in love, a little bit, with a quiet man, because he is wonderful," declared Capshaw. "The interesting thing is that Harrison was traveling with his wife, and I was swooning with homesickness over my boyfriend [producer Armyan Bernstein], who was back in the States. So you know, there was no danger of any on-set romance. We were just partners — acting partners."[20] (Capshaw found a more appropriate partner in director Steven Spielberg, who was then in a struggling marriage with actress Amy Irving. Capshaw and Spielberg created and maintained a relationship during the filming that would later result in marriage on October 12, 1991.)

Indiana Jones and the Temple of Doom opened on Memorial Day weekend. It held the Paramount record of being shown on 1,687 screens with the earliest of shows beginning at 12:01 A.M. In its first week, the film earned an estimated $46 million. According to Paramount Motion Picture Group President Frank Mancuso, it set a box office record for the largest single day total of $9,324,710 million, with nearly 13 million people seeing the film.

However, controversy over the film's violence spread throughout like wildfire. Audiences were repulsed by cuisine consisting of chilled monkey brains and beetles, the thrashing of enslaved juveniles and the removal of a human heart from a living patient.

"I personally liked the idea of exploring the dark side," admitted Ford, "but the same thing that gave me pleasure might be frightening to a 12-year-old kid, and that was never our intention."[21]

Openly considering the film "noticeably inferior to *Raiders*" and admitting that it was not necessarily appropriate for children under ten, Steven Spielberg defended himself and his directorial efforts. "The film isn't called "Indiana Jones and the Temple of Roses" ... there are parts of this film that are too intense for younger children, but this is a fantasy adventure."[22]

"To whatever degree," stated Ford, "we missed the mark and occasionally I rose to protest, but moviemaking is a collaborative effort and, while my attitude was noted, it did not prevail. I would assume George thought that it was the best way to go."[23]

Vincent Canby of *The New York Times* stated, "The movie, in addition to being endearingly disgusting, is violent in ways that may scare the wits out of some small patrons."[24] Gene Siskel of *The Chicago Tribune* told parents that it was unavoidable that their children would attend the film, and suggested that they themselves be present to cover their eyes. Furthermore, *The Los Angeles Times* critic Sheila Benson jokingly warned, "They're going to have to scrape youngsters out from under their seats."[25]

Another critic went so far as to classify both the film and Spielberg's tastes as "racist," an accusation the director was quick to dispel: "I feel that *Indiana Jones and the Temple of Doom* is a sexist film, not a racist," said Spielberg, hoping not to alienate his female audience. "The problem is that when you have bad guys in a movie, unless they're Nazis or terrorists, you can't be considered a racist. If they are Chinese or Japanese or if they're American Indians, then you're a racist...."[26]

Considering that Prince Charles and Lady Diana (among other royals) would be in attendance, the British Board of Censors introduced a few editorial revisions for the June 11, 1984, European premiere of the film, cutting minute's worth of footage which was deemed inappropriate for children under the age of 15.

In the U.S., the National Coalition of Television Violence (NCTV) cataloged 194 acts of violence. The Motion Picture Association of America responded to the graphic nature of the film by reconsidering the film's initial PG (Parental Guidance) rating. Had the rating been upgraded to the proposed R (Restricted) rating, the film's earnings would surely have plummeted.

In the end, a decision was made in favor of money over morality. Spielberg and Paramount prevailed in their efforts toward maintaining *Temple of Doom*'s PG status. But highlighted at the bottom of its theatrical posters was the warning, "This film may be too intense for younger children."

As a direct result — made possible with the assistance of the questionably rated film *Goonies*— the MPAA rating board introduced the PG-13 rating, affectionately nicknaming it "The Indiana Jones Rating." (The film *Red Dawn* would bear the industry's official first PG-13 rating.)

Temple of Doom went on to earn $179,870,271 at the North American box office. It was nominated for two Oscars, Best Original Score by longtime Spielberg collaborator John Williams, and Best Visual Effects (which it went on to win).

Temple of Doom was the third most successful film of 1984, trailing behind *Ghostbusters* and *Beverly Hills Cop*. Concerning its rating, Ford said, "This is a completely moral tale," claimed the actor, "and in order to have a moral resolve, evil must be seen to inflict pain. The end of the movie is a proof of the viability of goodness....[27]

"I think what you have to be concerned about in films is behavior that causes people to imitate it, and there are very few people who have had their hearts plucked out of their chests as a result of someone having seen that film."[28]

20

THE WEIR YEARS

In 1985, in what was undeniably the biggest decision of his career, Harrison Ford broke free of the action-adventure genre and headlined a film that would earn itself and its actor several Golden Globe and Academy Award nominations.

That film was *Witness*.

The original screenplay, entitled "Called Home," made its way into the hands of the actor in 1983, while he was filming *Indiana Jones and the Temple of Doom*. Conceived and written by the husband-and-wife television-writing team of Earl W. and Pamela Wallace (with assistance from William Kelley), the screenplay was submitted to producer Edward S. Feldman.

Feldman, whose production credits included *The Other Side of the Mountain* and *Save the Tiger*, welcomed the script with enthusiastic optimism. Always looking for a story that hadn't been done a hundred times before, Feldman praised the screenplay's originality despite the need for whittling out a lot of unnecessary moments.

Those moments that made the cut told the story of an Amish boy who witnesses a murder in a Philadelphia train station while traveling with his mother. Sent to investigate the murder is detective John Book (Ford). Having discovered that the crime involved police corruption, Book becomes sought after, too, and hides out on the Amish farm where the boy and his mother live. There, amid the undisturbed countryside, he begins to fall in love with the boy's mother.

The first draft of the screenplay sent to 20th Century–Fox was denied on two occasions. Working closely with the writing team, Feldman decided to option the film himself. He approached Paramount Pictures with the newly revised script and the idea of casting Harrison Ford — a decision brought about by the producer's vision of Gary Cooper in the older film *Friendly Persuasion*.

"I thought of Gary Cooper wearing that Quaker outfit," recalled Feldman, "and I asked myself, 'Who today is a reactive kind of actor who would also look funny in an outfit like that?' Harrison Ford came to mind, and the movie was on its way."[1]

Luckily for Feldman, Ford had just declined involvement in both *Quigley Down Under* and *The River*, which went on to star Tom Selleck and Mel Gibson, respectively. (Selleck, by now becoming a predictable consideration for films ultimately selected by Ford, was reportedly also considered for the role of Book.)

"It was the kind of film that I thought was about 90 percent there," recalled Ford, "which is a much higher grade than I give most film scripts when I first get them.

But I felt that, if we didn't have a really good director, it wouldn't gain anything — in fact, it would most likely lose something in the translation."[2]

In addition to contacting Feldman to confirm his involvement to the tune of $4 million, Ford attached a list of directors he felt would best suit the project. Considering the contents of the script, Feldman agreed that a foreign director was appropriate.

Australian Peter Weir (*Fearless, The Truman Show, Master and Commander: The Far Side of the World*), whose previous directorial credits included *Gallipoli, Picnic at Hanging Rock, The Year of Living Dangerously*, and *The Last Wave*, was about to start filming *The Mosquito Coast* when the financing for that project fell apart. (Weir would direct that film the following year with Ford as his leading man.)

"I came home and said to my agent, 'I need work. Find me what they call in Hollywood a "go" project.' The thought of 12 months of gardening, puttering about, and going to the supermarket was too much to bear," said Weir.[3]

When Feldman discovered that Weir's current project was terminated, he sent the "Called Home" screenplay to Weir via his agent. Weir officially signed on to the project three days later.

Despite his average of two years spent in pre-production on past works, Weir was allowed a mere seven-week period for pre-production work. Weir claimed that the film presented him the "extraordinary opportunity of doing a period film within a contemporary film.

"The very fact that there is a group of people living here ... much as they lived ... more than 200 years ago is positively fascinating. It's rare that you can get another perception of time," he added.[4]

"Called Home" eventually became *Witness* as a result of Paramount's $400 offer to any employee who could devise a more suitable name. To avoid the film evolving into a cliché-packed police melodrama, Weir and Ford chose to fine-tune the screenplay at hand — collectively reveling in its unique page-to-screen potential.

"The material represents a unique opportunity I had not seen this movie before. Eighty-five percent of the scripts I read I know where they came from. It's a second-generation effect. This was more or less a literate script for adults. I saw a movie when I read it. It felt like a movie to me, and many things do not."[5]

The script had a similar alluring effect on others in the eventual cast.

Kelly McGillis was selected to portray Rachel Lapp, the Amish widow who shares forbidden love with Book. A graduate of the Juilliard School of Music in New York, McGillis' first credit was the 1983 film *Reuben, Reuben*. She would later appear in the enormous 1986 box office hit *Top Gun* alongside Tom Cruise.

The 27-year-old McGillis recalled her surprise when Ford and Weir told her the news that she had won the role. She was then working her shift as a waitress in a Greenwich Village coffee shop.

"They picked me up at work, and I wasn't done yet," recalled the actress. "And so I made them wait for about 20 minutes. And the whole time, everybody is going, 'Harrison Ford is in here.' And then after my shift, I sat down with them, and they all said, 'Who the hell does she think she is sitting with Harrison Ford?' It was just unbelievable. There was just this attitude I could feel coming over me in waves."[6]

In his debut screen performance, Russian-born Alexander Godunov portrays Daniel Hochleitner, the Amish farmer and would-be suitor of Rachel, who discovers unintended competition from the "outsider" Book. Given political asylum in the United States in 1979, Godunov (who passed away in 1995 from complications stemming from alcohol abuse) was the star of the Moscow Bolshoi Ballet. Remaining dedicated and true to his original passion, the actor maintained a daily training routine at a rented dance studio in Lancaster.

"What we wanted for the role of Hochleitner was a person who could convey the simplicity of a farmer, and the virility and masculinity of a person who would make a worthy opponent for Harrison Ford's character to contend with. Alexander surpassed our expectations," claimed Feldman.[7]

Completing the cast is Lukas Haas, the eight-year-old actor who plays Samuel. Prior to *Witness*, Haas appeared in *Testament*, which won him critical acclaim, and in the ABC movie-of-the-week *Love Thy Neighbor* alongside John Ritter.

Witness also features Josef Sommer as Book's corrupt police officer–employer Schaeffer; Jan Rubes as Rachel's father Eli Lapp; Patti Lupone (from Broadway's *Oliver*) as Book's sister Elaine; Danny Glover as McFee, the corrupt policeman who commits the film's murder; and Angus MacInnes as McFee's partner Fergie.

Ultimately convinced that Ford would be appropriate and capable of carrying the film, Paramount decided to green light the project by granting Feldman an $11.5 million budget. While locations were being scouted, members of the film's cast — particularly Ford and McGillis — participated in character research.

Ford spent part of February and March 1984 with the Philadelphia Police Department's homicide division. Detective Capt. Eugene Dooley — who was subsequently given a role in the film and was given credit as an honorary technical advisor — tutored Ford. Ford virtually became a member of the unit as he observed and participated as far as the law would allow.

"All I knew about cops was what I had seen on television and in the movies," admitted Ford. "And suffice it to say, it ain't like that."[8]

One of the more eventful moments of his research (apart from the sobering experience of viewing the coroner's slides of previous unsolved homicides) was when he participated in two actual raids to serve warrants to suspected murderers.

"I sort of held all the liberal predispositions against the use of unreasonable force, but I did come to understand what the value of 'up against the wall' was," said the actor. "When these guys kicked in the door and went in, all of them screaming, a cacophony, I couldn't believe it. And it totally disarmed the people who were inside to the point where they offered no resistance, which is exactly the idea."[9]

Ford walked away from his experience with a new education. "You can hold onto ideas as a moral point of view of how you'd like to see things in a perfect world. But it's not perfect out there," he said.[10]

Ironically, during Ford's research, the department discovered corruption and sentenced a deputy chief to 15 years in prison.

Aside from reviewing literature and viewing many documentaries, McGillis participated in every aspect of the daily routine of the Amish lifestyle. At one point, she became a guest of honor for several days, joining an Amish family at their home.

At play in the fields of Amish Country in *Witness* (Paramount, 1985).

There she helped with household chores and made regular shopping visits to the town. She recorded conversations on her Walkman so that she could study the Amish dialect at later (and more private) moments.

"Besides speaking English," noted McGillis, "they used lot of words and phrases that we don't, since what they call 'Dutch'— actually a low form of German — is spoken in the home. The youngest child, a four-year-old, spoke only Dutch, so it was a great learning experience trying to communicate with him."[11]

The family felt betrayed upon discovering that their guest was actually researching a role for a motion picture and was not actually a hopeful recruit, and they insisted that she vacate the premises for fear of their own excommunication.

Respecting the customs and lifestyle of the Amish was a delicate effort throughout filming in Lancaster County. As outsiders, the last thing Weir and Feldman wanted was to upset the tightly knit community. While the incident with McGillis may not have been the best start, a Paramount spokesman maintains that permission was given.

"At no time did we ever expect to get cooperation from the Amish," claimed producer Feldman. "They have no interest in us, and we decided to stay clear and respect their wishes."[12]

On more than one occasion, Weir refrained from photographing Amish groups during their daily farming activities. This technique would have not only saved the production money, but also would have provided a look of realism. And while the Amish belief excluded them from any involvement, individuals did offer their services by selling items from self-owned shops and renting horse-and-buggies and other props.

Despite Paramount's inability to get any Amish as behind-the-scenes advisors, the filmmakers hired some Mennonites who would prove to be assets to the production. Mennonites (ex-members of the Amish faith chastised due to their inability to maintain the religion's disciplined guidelines) do utilize modern conveniences like telephones, televisions, automobiles and, on the rare occasion, the right to participate in the making of motion pictures.

John King was a sales representative for the local lumber company that supplied Paramount with all the materials required for the sets. He offered his services as the film's consultant regarding all aspects of the Amish lifestyle. Aside from providing invaluable theological insight, King advised the crew on Amish fashion, dialect and concerns regarding decor and details for the interiors and exteriors of residences.

One residence in particular where King offered insights was the film's central location — the dwelling and yard representing the home of the Lapp family.

Having considered several locations, Lancaster location scout Tom Scott (who passed away prior to the film's release) ultimately decided on an enormous stretch of farmland in nearby Strasburg. It was nestled behind a vast hill connected to the world only by a long stretch of driveway. The Mennonite family willingly surrendered their home for the several weeks that filming required.

To ready the home for the start of filming on May 8, slight alterations took place. The production enlisted carpenters from the Local 287 in Harrisburg to oversee construction within the century-old dwelling. They removed doors and painted over interior walls in muted shades. Crews in the yard removed all overbearing vegetation and all signs of convenient living — including television aerials and power lines. An addition to the five-bedroom home was installed; it included a kitchen and living room where the funeral of Jacob Lapp was held. And finally, a water wheel was installed to accentuate the small pond in the front of the home.

The silo on the property would be the setting for a violent confrontation between Ford's character and one of the corrupt officers. But the producers deemed the existing silo as too dangerous, due to its uncontrolled environment. Nicknamed the "sealed death chamber" sequence, the actual scene was filmed at the former Posey Iron Works building in Lancaster. Similarly, the early scenes involving the murder in Philadelphia's 30th Street Station's rest room were also filmed there because the train station's rest rooms were recently renovated and considered inappropriate.

Filming the sequence in the barn brought about one of screen history's most cherished moment of non-sexual chemistry. There Rachel and Book dance to Sam Cooke's "(What a) Wonderful World." Because of Rachel's faith and recent status as a single mother, she is conflicted between her emotions toward Book and maintaining her faith. It was Ford's suggestion to use that particular song and liven up the script by introducing the couple's near-kiss. This sequence featured the film's first moment of chemistry between the two characters.

Director Weir had faith in his leading man. "He has two sides to his nature. He has the very careful eye of the craftsman, and he has a kind of wild, uninhibited side — the artistic side. And he can be very funny inside that reckless area."[13]

"Peter lets me interpret ideas intellectually rather than kinetically," said Ford. "Before *Witness*, all directors ever seemed to want from me was the forward propulsive action and the sly wink."[14]

Once Ford was satisfied with the details of the screenplay, recalled Weir, "then it was like: 'Let's be loose about it. Let's see what happens but not be uptight about it.' So we'd ad-lib or invent scenes as we went along, knowing we had a solid structure to bounce off."[15]

"We were veterans of a campaign," continued Ford. "We'd been in the same place and seen the same things. Our visions of the film were mostly consistent, and when they were not we were able to influence each other without destroying our enthusiasm. My relationship with Peter worked more than it ever has with a director before...."[16]

Weir rewrote nearly the entire barn-raising sequence. Originally the script called for Hochleitner to fall from a high rafter into the arms of Book, depicting Book as a sort of Amish savior. Weir instead developed the relationship between Hochleitner and Book by making Book the better carpenter of the two. Book's multidimensional qualities are displayed, impressing both Rachel and the other laborers to the point where they are not as quick to label him as "Yankee," but as a member of their community.

The barn-raising took place on a 90-acre residential lot in the town of Christiana, Pennsylvania. The location was chosen due to its isolated area, leaving nothing in the background but nature's sweeping hillsides.

Though the ritual is an Amish one, the production improvised by making it a Mennonite one. All of the actors used for the scene were Mennonite extras on Paramount's payroll, paid to look Amish. An Amish individual who advised the production off the set on the issue of the barn's frame construction was soon excommunicated for participating. The film's dialogue states "we have a barn to raise, and a day to do it," when in actuality, the 40' × 60' structure was constructed (with less durable and less expensive spruce lumber) and photographed over a period of five days and filmed at multiple angles. To help visualize the final product, Weir played classical music over loudspeakers and used it as an audio aid to motivate his actors while photography took place.

Ford — who claimed "I always knew someday I'd make more than $12.50 an hour for doing this!"[17] — was particularly fond of working alongside individuals of similar expertise and interests. He was described by an extra as being in his glory, despite suffering from the occasional bout of vertigo.

Said Weir: "The writers swore they'd made the policeman an expert in carpentry before they had any idea Ford would play the part. It was a happy coincidence. It was wonderful to film that sequence and to see your leading actor become an organizer and leader of carpenters."[18]

During the down time between filming takes of this scene, an extra conceived the concept of "Indiana Stoltzfus and the Temple of Tobacco." Ford was so amused by the idea that he had 22 dozen shirts printed and distributed them as parting gifts to the cast and crew when filming concluded.

Soon after filming, the owner of the property on which the barn was built had it dismantled and the materials sold.

The sequence would later be considered by critics to be one of celluloid's most visually and emotionally enchanting. Nearly every reviewer noted the scene as a flawless whole. They were quick to commend Weir's impeccable choreography and direction, the beautiful cinematography of John Seale and the theme composed by Maurice Jarre.

Following photography in Lancaster, the production moved to the town of Intercourse, Pennsylvania, for two days of shooting in June 1984. There they filmed at W.L. Zimmerman & Sons, Inc.— the grocery store where Ford's character visits to use the public phone and to contact his partner Carter (Brent Jennings). Across the way on Queen Street was where filmmakers staged the fight between Book and a group of local ruffians.

Zimmerman's has provided for the needs of the Amish since 1909. The religious group accounts for nearly 80 percent of the clientele. Paramount offered store manager Jim Zimmerman a small amount of money for the use of his establishment. In the end, he refused any compensation because at the time he was already receiving pressure from his Amish customers not to participate.

"We already heard the Amish were upset," recalled Zimmerman, "because people were taking money for this. In fact, that was part of it. They thought we were tempted to betray them for all this money."[19]

Despite the apparent displeasure at Zimmerman's relations with the filmmakers, the Amish did not boycott the store. In fact, business in general improved due to the unintended effort of advertising the store name.

While the filming significantly increased the number of visitors to Amish country, the one location most frequented was the store and its public phone. For years after, tourists would visit for an unscheduled phone call and a photo opportunity.

Principal photography began in Philadelphia on April 27 and lasted until May 6. Various locations throughout the city were used for filming. The first was the parking garage of an apartment complex where Book is initially shot. Another was 30th Street Station. And finally, an area of Chinatown was the backdrop for Book's confrontation with a murder suspect at a fictitious bar called Happy Valley.

Leaving the city behind, the production relocated to the Lancaster area. From there the crew continued its shooting at the depot of a non-functioning train station in the town of Parkesburg, at the Strasburg farm and in the town of Intercourse.

Completed under schedule (52 days) and under budget ($12 million), *Witness* concluded principal photography in early July 1984.

The Lancaster Chamber of Commerce estimated that the filming contributed an additional $6.5 million or more into the local economy, and significantly increased the number of tourists (which until then was estimated at nearly four million a year). But *Witness* also left in its wake a tremendous amount of undesired controversy.

After denouncing the film during its production, the Amish community issued a more ferocious verbal assault just prior to its world premiere.

In an effort to boycott the film, the sect sought advice from the National Committee for Amish Religious Freedom (NCARF), who issued this statement to Paramount: "For the Amish, the movie represents immoral and unlikely behavior portrayed for profit and laughter in such a way that it appears sympathetic."[20]

The committee, composed of lawyers, scholars and clergymen — none of whom were Amish — had one representative who was most outspoken on the issue. Born into the Amish faith, John Hostetler converted to the Mennonite church at the age of 18. He eventually became a professor of anthropology at Temple University. There he would become the nation's leading authority on the Amish lifestyle, authoring numerous books and making documentary films on the subject.

"This film is the high-water mark of commercial exploitation and harassment of an innocent people," claimed Hostetler. "It is an intrusion into their religious space and symbols, uninvited and endured in silence."[21]

Hostetler went on to accuse the production of creating a "psychological invasion"[22] of the Amish people, constantly clashing with the production throughout filming. Weir considered it hypocritical of him on the premise that he himself was exploiting the Amish for profit with his published past. Whether it be for entertainment or education, the concept of creating what the Amish consider to be "graven images"— or any type of visual likeness— is frowned upon.

"[The film] may not be violating any statutes but it is violating gross sensitivities," said Hostetler. "It is breaking the hearts of the people. They feel that copying their customs and dress is a mockery."[23]

Ford spoke out against these accusations: "It is the very moral nature of the Amish that makes them useful to our story," explained the actor. "We would never violate that because it would diminish our story."[24]

The NCARP requested formally to the Pennsylvania governor's office that the film ultimately not be released. "We hope that the public — as silent expression of respect for our Amish, and as a pocketbook reprimand to all who would exploit them for gain — will refrain from patronizing *Witness*," stated a representative.[25]

Partly honoring the Amish requests, Pennsylvania state officials declared that banning the film was unconstitutional but in a statement offered to the Amish, the state proposed that it would not participate in the encouragement or promotion of any future films dealing with the Amish, in addition to giving filmmakers fair warning that they needn't expect cooperation from the Amish.

The Pennsylvania Dutch Visitors Bureau found the entire incident beneficial. In its spring 1985 advertising campaign, the bureau printed advertising encouraging tourists to "Visit Another Country ... Pennsylvania Dutch Country — As Seen in the Movie *Witness*."[26]

During the controversy, director Weir summed up his feelings: "No art, no creative endeavor — which this is— should be subject to the censorship of the state or of any individual. The freedom of creativity is as vital as the freedom to be an Amishman or not to be an Amishman."[27]

Hostetler believed that if the Amish faith had a more rigid policy regarding dealing with outside conflicts, the outcome of the debate could have resulted in postponing the film's release, perhaps indefinitely.

"The Amish people were justifiably outraged by the movie, but you didn't hear much about it, because they don't fight back," he said. "If the Amish would vocalize how they feel, Lancaster County would have been in an uproar."[28]

Despite the effort on behalf of the Amish community, Paramount released *Witness* on February 8, 1985. One day prior, Paramount held a special black-tie premiere screening at Lancaster's Fulton Opera House to benefit both the Opera House's restoration and the Historic Preservation Trust of Lancaster County. Onlookers gathered for the arrival of Ford and others. Unexpectedly, Ford did not attend — destroying the dreams of all those who wished for a photo opportunity with Indiana Jones. Those who didn't possess the $60 and $100 tickets were consoled by the ability to buy souvenirs outside the theater — the most popular of which were the "Indiana Stoltzfus" T-shirts.

The actor later proved that he appreciated his stay in Lancaster. In 1989, he contacted officials with the Lancaster Farmland Trust, and supported the project with both a financial contribution and permission to use his name to help solicit others.

The trust was founded in 1984 and developed to help "preserve the richest and most productive farmland in Lancaster County, to support the farmers who are good stewards of the land and to encourage the growth of agricultural industry, recognizing that our farm heritage has enriched the lives of all citizens."[29]

"Apparently," said the trust's executive director Alan Musselman, "his stay in Lancaster County was much more than a job assignment to him. Here is a man who travels worldwide. Yet, he recognized Lancaster County for the natural treasure that it is and wishes to help protect it."[30]

In a letter Ford submitted to the Trust, he stated:

> I have had the firsthand opportunity to experience a special place and an extraordinary community in Lancaster County, Pennsylvania. An important part of America's heritage, this area of exceptional resources is home to a culture of wholeness and productivity that must be preserved. It is under enormous pressure. Farms, countryside communities and cultures are threatened with being over-whelmed by suburbanization, highways and commercialization. This is too important a part of America to lose by default. Please join with me in supporting the Lancaster Farmland Trust in our mission to preserve Lancaster County farmland resources and to move toward a more sustainable and agriculture community. Together we can save an important part of America's heritage.[31]

"We thank Mr. Ford for his tremendous endorsement," said Daniel Herr, the Trust's president. "It is through the support of people like him and others that we are able to pursue our mission of preserving this countryside and way of life."[32]

It is usually a conscious effort for a studio to release a film deemed worthy of Oscar nominations close to the nomination period — which is generally November or December. The early release date of *Witness* was considered to be well out of range for possible Oscar contention and reflected Paramount's lack of confidence in the film. Paramount also had the final word on the film's advertising campaign. The film's one-sheet depicted Ford without his leading lady. Actress Kelly McGillis' character was removed from the original poster for fear of alienating the audience with her untraditional attire.

Director Weir was concerned that ticket buyers would expect the Harrison Ford of the past. He was pleasantly surprised at the audience's reaction to the film during its initial test screenings.

"The anticipation for a *Raiders* Mark III was terrifying," said Weir. "At first, one could sense that they were puzzled because they were expecting more action; but by the middle of the film, they were loving the humor. Whether that became some sort of substitute for the expected shootings, I don't know, but they got lost in the story and were obviously entertained."[33]

Witness opened on February 8, 1985, on 876 screens nationwide to an impressive $4.54 million in its first weekend. It continued strong, ultimately becoming 1985's fourth-most successful motion picture, eventually accumulating a total domestic gross of $65,532,576.

Despite his popularity with the public, Ford was yet to be taken seriously by some critics. Having been classified up to that point as being upstaged by the special effects and stunt work in his films, Ford grew weary of being typecast as a cinematic hero only and not being noted for his ability. After *Witness*, that stereotype was no longer accurate. Apart from the film's apparent mass and critical appeal, virtually all critics suggested the possibilities of an Oscar nomination for the actor.

Weir and Ford were in pre-production on *The Mosquito Coast* when the 1985 Oscar nominations were announced. (By that point, the Golden Globe nominations that went to Ford, McGillis and Weir were old news.) The news was a welcome surprise and offered temporary relief from the difficulties of filming in the jungles of Belize. Not only would director Weir be immensely proud that his film had earned eight nominations (including Best Director and Best Picture), but his leading man Ford was also recognized. (The other contenders were Jack Nicholson, James Garner, John Voight and William Hurt.)

"The nomination was a surprise because it hadn't occurred to me," claimed Ford. "But I wasn't surprised by the reaction to the film."[34]

Flattered by the consideration of the Academy members, Ford readily admitted his distaste for the entire proceeding: "I don't believe in the competition. You can't compare two different efforts in two different movies and say one is better than the other. Nonsense as far as I'm concerned."[35]

Unable to attend the ceremony, Ford, Weir and John Seale watched the 58th Annual Academy Awards via satellite from Ford's boat on March 24, 1986. In the end, the film won two Oscars, both in the technical field. The first was awarded to the trio of Kelley and the Wallaces for their original screenplay and the second was awarded to Thom Noble for Best Achievement in Editing. Ford ultimately lost to William Hurt for his performance in *Kiss of the Spider Woman*.

Ford—that year's only no-show Best Actor nominee—was proud just to be nominated, to be recognized as one the world's greatest actors—at least for that year.

"The reviews are among the finest I've had as an actor, although that's what I've always been doing," he stated.[36]

Witness marked the first time the actor had been nominated for a major award. He was ultimately awarded neither the Golden Globe nor the Academy Award for his portrayal of John Book; the British Academy of Film and Television Arts also nominated him but ventured no further.

"It wasn't frustrating not to win," admitted Ford. "I can't even remember the other people who were nominated that year. It's a high honor, I don't disdain it, it's just not the most important thing in my general scheme."[37]

Ford profited from the rejection: "All my life, I've tried not to take things too personally. When I got an Oscar nomination, my friends told me I should feel vindicated for all the critics who said I walked through the Spielberg-Lucas movies. Well, I don't feel vindication. It's just not in my repertoire. Besides, no one could criticize me as harshly as I do myself."[38]

The following year, Ford's five-year box office winning streak came to an abrupt conclusion with the release of *The Mosquito Coast*. It was a commercial failure, although Ford was hailed and ultimately awarded a second Golden Globe nomination for his performance.

Written as a novel in 1982 by Cape Codder Paul Theroux, *The Mosquito Coast* instantly became a hot publication. Producer Jerome Hellman (*Coming Home, Midnight Cowboy*) admired the novel's originality and complexity. The story tells of Allie Fox, an inventor who dropped out of Harvard University because he is sickened by the corruption of the modern world, uprooting his family and relocating to the unspoiled jungles of Central America.

"I like the issues it explores," said Hellman, "which aren't really treated often enough — man's imperfectability, the fact that it's foolhardy to bring technology to primitive cultures thinking you can improve them, and the perils and beauty of obsession."[39] The novel made such a positive impression on Hellman that he was adamant to purchase the rights.

"I didn't want anyone else to produce this movie," said the producer on his decision to buy the rights to the novel for $250,000. "There were several people who were interested in the book when it was first published, circling, making offers. I didn't negotiate at all. I simply met the asking price — which was a great shock to the agent."[40]

Hellman searched for a studio to support his project. Warner Bros. President Bob Sharpio gave the go-ahead to develop a screenplay. Hellman employed a personal favorite of his, famed screenwriter Paul Schrader (*Taxi Driver, Raging Bull*), to adapt the novel into script form. The script, a "terrific, trailblazing first draft," was approved and immediately shown to Hellman's first choice, director Peter Weir. (The novel was initially brought to its ultimate director's attention by Sigourney Weaver during the 1982 filming of *The Year of Living Dangerously*.)

"I think the material needed a romantic director like Peter to soften the harsher aspects of the book," said Hellman.[41]

Following a week of intense examination by Hellman and Schrader at Weir's Sydney, Australia, home, Weir committed to the project. The three then traveled to the East Coast to scout various New England locations.

Just as things were looking up, Bob Sharpio left Warner Bros. His successor apparently did not share his enthusiasm for the project and declined to support it.

"It was a period," recalled Hellman, "when in a few months' time, every studio had a change: no sooner had an executive approved us for production, then he or she headed elsewhere, leaving Peter and me to start shopping for another home."[42]

Next on the list of hopeful backers was Goldcrest, a small, independent, English production company who ultimately agreed to fund the project.

Although Theroux's novel was set in Honduras, the producers considered Jamaica, Costa Rica, Guatemala, Mexico and Hawaii as more practical locations for filming. Then staff members of Norman Jewison's *The Dogs of War* suggested Belize to Hellman and Weir, who financed a reconnaissance trip there in late 1983. Located on the Caribbean coast of Central America between Mexico and Guatemala, the country formerly known as British Honduras provided the filmmakers with the conveniences of English as its speaking language and close proximity to the U.S.

Within a matter of days, the location scouts discovered all the sites required for filming. Mountains, jungle, ocean and rivers—everything the production called for was within an hour of Belize City.

Returning from the trip, the filmmakers discovered that Goldcrest had undergone staffing changes, and once again Hellman and Weir were out. Unpredictable New England weather in the early months of 1984 also postponed the project indefinitely. Then Weir committed to *Witness*, further delaying the project.

Continuing to present his pitch at the various studios, Hellman met with Oscar-winning executive producer Saul Zaentz (*Amadeus*). Zaentz unhesitatingly agreed to finance and distribute the $18 million project, closing the deal in one day in early March 1985.

With Weir finally obligated to the project, the production was confronted with complications with the film's central character. Jack Nicholson had originally been chosen to portray Allie Fox, but was no longer a possibility. Aside from his disinterest in the role, Nicholson based his final decision on his inability to watch his beloved Los Angeles Lakers while on location deep in the jungles of Belize. Further scheduling conflicts led to his final decision before the actor had to officially decline involvement and bow out of the project.

Enter Harrison Ford.

"When we were working on *Witness*," recalled Peter Weir, "it just occurred to me that [Ford] would make a perfect Allie Fox. He evokes a very American quality—strength, leadership—just by walking onto the screen. All of which made me believe we would follow him to the jungle and believe what he said."[43]

Ford had just recently declined an offer to star in *Terms of Endearment*. (That film ultimately starred Jack Nicholson, who won the Oscar for Best Supporting Actor.) Another project he turned down was *Beverly Hills Cop*, which during its early stages was no more than a crime drama without the humor. Fresh off the success of *Witness*, Ford welcomed the opportunity to collaborate with Weir on a project he hoped would advance his career.

"I was looking for something that would contrast with what I'd done in *Witness*, something that would offer the audience something different and something with some ambition, some aspect of uniqueness," explained Ford. "I found it in this screenplay."[44]

What so strongly attracted the determined actor to Schrader's screenplay were his own similarities to the character.

"I think he's easy enough to understand," said Ford. "His criticisms are not all that different from those many of us have. It's a matter of degree. In his case, the degree of criticism was extreme. And the ends to which he is willing to go to create a new beginning are extreme. I haven't the courage or the industry to be an Allie Fox, but I can understand him."[45]

Weir also agreed that confronting the challenge of presenting Fox to an audience was exciting.

"I've never had a character like Allie in my films before that I like and dislike in equal measure," admitted the director. "Men like Allie have obviously changed the course of the world's history in certain instances—they've become great statesmen or great dictators. They have a cause and if people must suffer for that cause, then that must be the price."[46]

In the novel, Fox is a great deal more abrasive, eccentric and, quite simply detestable. During script discussions, the film's producers realized that if they were to present the Allie Fox of the novel, the audience would not have responded positively.

"So the Allie of the film is a different Allie from the book," said Ford. "His cruelty, for example, is mitigated at the beginning, for fear of alienating the audience."[47]

Together, Hellman, Weir and Ford concentrated on Fox's human qualities, focusing on making a film about relationships: about humanizing the character. A researcher was employed to extract and anthologize Allie's countless verbal commentaries on the spoils of mankind from the novel. This research resulted in a 52-page collection of quotables entitled "The Thoughts of Chairman Allie."

One individual who did not support Ford's decision was his agent, Patricia McQueeney. "Harrison is very much into the environment and anti-pollution and all of those good things that Allie Fox was also into," explained McQueeney. "But what I didn't like was the torture that he puts his wife and his kids through. And I said, 'The audience thinks you're a hero. They aren't going to want you to be this mean guy who drags these people through the jungle.'"[48]

Selected to portray the Fox clan were Helen Mirren as Mrs. Fox (oddly referred to by Allie as "Mother"); 15-year-old River Phoenix (who spent the bulk of his childhood traveling and living throughout Central and South America with his siblings and parents, who were then Christian missionaries) as the oldest son, Charlie; 11-year-old veteran performer Jadrien Steele as Jerry Fox; and Rebecca and Hillary Gordon as the eight-year-old Fox twins, April and Clover.

They were loaded into a van to visit the film's Georgia locations, and Weir felt an immediate comfort with his principal actors. Witnessing a natural bonding between the actors, the director partook in the first "Fox Family outing."

"I sat way in the back, Harrison drove, and all of the other actors were up in front with him, chatting away," recalled Weir. "It was the first time they were all together, and I didn't say anything; I just listened and watched them. Then I noticed Helen and Harrison starting to use the dialogue or ideas from the movie. The girls would start doing something, and Helen would shush them, saying, 'Don't distract Harrison. He's concentrating.' Or she might say to him, 'Are you lost?' And he'd reply, 'I'm never lost!' It was almost Mother and Allie. Right from that first drive, the casting worked. We had one of those moments that you sometimes get when

As Allie Fox in Peter Weir's *The Mosquito Coast* (Warner Bros., 1986).

making films: in a flash, the power of creating, of true creativity. It was a tangible feeling."[49]

Supplementing the cast were Andre Gregory as Allie's theological opposition, Reverend Spellgood; Martha Plimpton (the daughter of actor Keith Carradine) as Spellgood's daughter Emily, an admirer of Charlie Fox; Dick O'Neill as Tim Polski, the Fox's New England neighbor and employer of Allie's inventions; and a cameo appearance by *Gone with the Wind*'s 75-year-old Butterfly McQueen (that film's frightened maid, Prissy) as Ma Kennywick, a woman who resides on the Fox family's land.

Filmed out of sequence due to seasonal conditions, *The Mosquito Coast* began in Belize during the week of February 7, 1986. Weir reassembled his Oscar-nominated key production team from *Witness*— John Seale, Maurice Jarre and Thom Noble — to confront the new challenges of *The Mosquito Coast*.

"Here on location, we have that kind of intimacy that only comes on a set. It doesn't generally exist in peacetime, you might say," said the director. "On location in the jungle, you don't have the nine-to-five mentality that you have in city shooting. I like the concentration that results from everybody being at hand and from the ideas that abound in the surroundings. The atmosphere of the film is within the setting all around you. You disappear into the film."[50]

"After a while, you get used to it," Ford said on how being a stranger in a strange land could take its toll on both body and spirit. "It just becomes part of the job. One of the great disappointments in my life, though, is that I go to these fascinating places, but I don't have very much time to see them. Or, by going there, you sometimes change the place so much that you don't get a chance to see it as it really is. Making a film is a very technological event to impose an unsophisticated environment."[51]

Stage trained Helen Mirren recalled her curiosity and fascination upon her arrival in Belize: "It's a desperately poor country, a place right out of a Graham Greene or Somerset Maugham story — decaying, tropical, miserable and poor.... If you read the book you can't imagine there being anywhere in the world like the setting Theroux describes. Yet the moment you arrive in Belize, there it is."[52]

Filming on location in the harsh jungle environment held both advantages and disadvantages for the filmmakers and their performers.

"It's a beautiful country," claimed Ford, "very poor, primitive to say the least, and when you're trying to do something as complicated as doing a movie, the biggest difficulty is logistics, getting supplies and stuff down there. But the advantage of it is that it lends something to the atmosphere that you don't have to act."[53]

There were an abundance of cuts and bruises, unwanted visitation by local wildlife, the unavoidable necessity for suntan lotion, and the biggest nuisance of all — mosquitoes.

"To actually experience the heat, the bugs, the mud, and the rain," said Mirren, "was a million times better than playing it on a studio back lot with a few palm trees."[54]

To overcome cultural isolation, the production flew in via the local TACA airlines (humorously designated as "Take a Chance Airlines") nearly two dozen televisions, videocassette recorders and a large selection of videotapes. A cappuccino machine, home stereo systems, computers, brand-name toiletries, the occasional outdated *New York Times*—even bagels were sometimes imported from Miami.

The film's international cast and crew (roughly 150 British, Australians, Canadians, Americans and local Belize residents) lived in rental homes and at the Villa and Fort George Hotels in and around Belize City. Following careful consideration, the actor determined that living anywhere within the confines of Belize would not be idyllic for his mental health.

"I had the feeling that if I didn't get away from it all, I would go quite mad after awhile," explained Ford.[55]

Leasing the *Mariner II*, a 126-foot air-conditioned yacht with an onboard gourmet cook and crew of five, the actor commuted to the mainland by speedboat when his services were required. Ford's wife Melissa remained on board the *Mariner* where she continued work on a teleplay concerning Gen. Custer, entitled *Son of the Morning Star*.

Dubbed "Dive Daddy" by the cast, crew and locals, Harrison would spend his down time occasionally scuba diving, powering the fully restored 1926 craft to the crystalline waters of Belize's Lighthouse Reef.

"I learned scuba in Hawaii; I'm a warm-water diver.... In Belize, the water is very clear. We went down 125 feet, as deep as I've ever gone."[56]

Additional location scenes were 20 miles off the Belize mainland in San Pedro, an area on the southernmost tip of Ambergris Caye. There, on its palm-tree-shrouded shoreline, stood the set of the "Junkpile," the makeshift community Fox built after the apocalyptic demise of his "Jeronimo."

Rigid round-the-clock security was enforced throughout the set. Endowed with special privileges, Ford was permitted to host his longtime friend, singer Jimmy Buffet who spent time in Belize fishing, as well as rehearsing dialogue and exchanging ideas concerning Allie Fox with Ford.

Returning the favor, Ford offered his songwriting talents for a song on Buffet's upcoming "Floridays" album, entitled "Nobody Speaks to the Captain No More." The musician respectfully credited the song by listing one of its three songwriters as Allie Fox. Furthermore, the tropical images of the album sleeve were actually taken by Buffett himself at various environs as Ford was busy filming.

This was not Ford's first foray into collaborating with Buffett. The two began their musical partnership the year prior on the Buffett album "The Last Mango in Paris." For the track "Desperation Samba," Ford provided all the background whip-cracking.

Just as unorthodox as the notion of relocating the Fox family to the jungle were the physical characteristics of Allie Fox.

"The image of Harrison as Allie Fox is the antithesis of the way [Ford]'s ever looked," said Producer Hellman. "He's been deromanticized; there's nothing heroic about him."[57]

Ford is solely responsible for the appearance of Fox. "The glasses and the whole physical thing was meant to indicate a character whose investment of ego was in another area," explained Ford. "This is a person who's unselfconscious about his appearance so the glasses I picked are too small for my face, the shirt that I wore we cut off the bottom of it, so as to change the proportions of my body and make me look more ungainly."[58]

Ford also made movement adjustments, further accenting Allie's peculiarity.

"If you watch, I think you'll see that [Allie] moves differently to how I move, that there's a kind of loose jointed, abstract — he's not in touch with his body as much as I normally am," said Ford. "It's either half a step behind him, or a half a step ahead of him."[59]

For Paul Theroux (who visited the set with great frequency), Ford proved to be the ideal selection.

"Harrison had it all," stated Theroux. "Even the quietly smoldering gaze and the serious grin. He was Allie to the fingertips."[60]

For the film's visual style, cinematographer John Seale used a unique approach.

"*Mosquito Coast* was lovely because one simple word came out — documentary. It's as though Allie Fox took off into the jungle and we had to tag along. Allie is such a powerful character. The camera is always behind him trying to keep up, just like his family. He's always turning his back to us. That was part of the initial thinking, 'What would a documentary cameraman do?'"[61]

In pre-production, Seale watched the 1985 film *The Emerald Forest* to assist him in his research for his new project. Envisioning the look of *The Mosquito Coast* as entirely different, Seale dismissed his research, considering *The Emerald Forest* as "a washout; it was too pretty."[62]

"With *The Mosquito Coast*," explained Seale, "we began with some lovely shots that will make the audience say, 'Wow! That's the tropics!'— but as we go deeper into the jungle, it becomes more nitty-gritty, more documentary-style. We're avoiding the perfectly lit Hollywood look. Our jungles are dark, creepy, and threatening."[63]

But Seale emphasizes that the film is not about the jungle; it is about human beings. By making the most of closeups of the actors with the jungle as background, he allowed the story to maintain its focus on the people.

In the movie, Fox purchases a dilapidated town called Jeronimo and turns it into a thriving village. Most of the action took place along the Sibun River in an area of Belize known as Gracey Rock. Construction crews built three versions of Jeronimo in various phases of development so they could be photographed in continuity for cost and time efficiency.

Creating jobs for nearly 300 locals, the production brought more than $3 million to the local economy, Belize's third largest industry for that year. (It trailed slightly behind sugar and marijuana.) Because of the remote location, the production created a network of roads, built a temporary medical treatment facility and constructed bridges.

Ford participated in the creation of the sets, including forming a congregation of local Belizeans armed with machetes to make a clearing. He also designed several of Allie's inventions, including the bicycle-washing machine.

While clearing a 100-foot area of field, the construction crew discovered significant archaeological find. Standing 20 feet high was what was believed to be the remnants of a minor Mayan temple or public building. Readjusting his production schedule, Weir and his team improvised. They dealt with the inconvenience by using the ruin as a camera platform. When Jeronimo photography was completed, the sets that were left were donated to the locals to be used as community centers and shelters for the homeless.

Following the last day of photography on location in Belize (and within its capital Belize City at the Manatee Bar) around April 26, the production moved north to its next location in Armuchee, Georgia, a town with a population of 3,000. The Carroll farmstead was selected for the Fox household. The farm scenes were originally slated to be filmed in Massachusetts to remain true to the novel. Producers reconsidered and chose the tiny Georgian community due to the predictability of its weather and because spring was coming early there, which coincided with their shooting schedule. Additional locations included downtown Rome, Georgia, and the port of Baltimore — the site chosen as the point of departure for the jungle-bound Fox family.

"*Mosquito Coast* was such a different experience from *Witness*," said Ford. "It was much more difficult. On *Mosquito Coast*, I wanted very much to be directed. I wanted not to have control of the situation. I wanted to be able to give in to the excesses of the character, to be pulled back from the brink by Peter when he thought it was necessary, or encouraged to go close to the edge when he thought I should. I've been a servant of the story and of the director on *Mosquito Coast* to a greater extent that I've ever been before. Allie Fox is a difficult person just to be with, even for an audience. We were aiming for a point where the audience could tolerate to be there and yet say what we wanted to say."[64]

Following months of editing at facilities in Belize, Australia and Berkeley, California, *The Mosquito Coast* was released on December 19, 1986. Ford felt the film was unjustly evaluated. "I don't think I've ever seen critical reaction to a serious film like this," said the actor. "So many critics have rejected the character out of hand."[65]

It was Ford's intent to create an uncomfortable character. He felt that if the audience understood Allie, than they misunderstood the point he was attempting to make.

"It's a movie that surprised me very much," admitted the actor. "I would have thought that this character would have been more admired because of his unusual characteristics and the fact that he is not a normal film hero. It seems to have created more confusion than admiration.

"I must say, however, that I find audiences have a different relationship to the film than many of the critics.... The emotional reaction to the film is very strong."[66]

For Ford, the underlying story of *The Mosquito Coast* simply told the story of a relationship between fathers and sons.

"I have been a son and I have been a father," said Ford. "I deeply understand the relationship between Allie Fox and his oldest son, Charlie. Allie is popular with his son, and I'm proud of the relationship I've had with my sons. But even though I haven't been nearly as tough on them as Allie is on Charlie, I know that I have been close to the loss of control that Allie exhibits. I've seen it in my father and I have seen it in other people, and they are not bad people. It's very common and it's a part of the movie that I think people are going to respond to. A lot of my friends have told me that they have been so deeply moved by this aspect of the film that they want their children to see it."[67]

Ford's two children, Willard and Benjamin, did see the film and were affected by it. "One thing that did amaze them, I think, is just how personal the process of being an actor is," said Ford. "I think they were surprised to see me use so much of myself on the screen ... I think what makes the film work is that it supplies a context for Allie's behavior. We see the enormous pressure of being a father. The film is saying, 'This is fathers and sons.'"[68]

Paul Theroux felt so strongly about the film's translation of his novel that he spoke out against the harsh negative reviews. His letter to *Time* magazine read: "In a welter of desperate commonplaces, your critic claims that Peter Weir has made a bad job of the movie *The Mosquito Coast*. As the author of the novel, I think I have greater authority than your reviewer for saying otherwise. The movie is triumphant, not only beautifully made but a great adventure, magnificently acted and directed."[69]

"My only argument with film critics," said director Weir, "is that they try to fit their personal reactions into a critical framework. But I've found that in filmmaking, you don't analyze — you just do. Films are magical; they are dreams. You can't analyze that. But if you're lucky, you can create the magic, make the film seem like a remembered dream."[70]

The magic that Weir spoke of was partially recreated on screen, bringing forth one of Ford's most compelling performances. Film critics were in agreement with Weir as well as one another, steadfastly praising Ford's powerful acting.

"It is a brilliant performance," declared Roger Ebert, "so effective, indeed, that we can hardly stand to spend two hours in the company of this consummate jerk."[71]

Los Angeles Times critic Sheila Benson claimed Ford's on-screen presence was the film's only strong point: "Harrison Ford's power — even with his back to the camera, even when we can't read his face — is terrifying."[72]

Despite its critical acclaim, *The Mosquito Coast* earned just over $14 million domestically — a figure that didn't even cover production costs. The final tally resulted in the least successful vehicle on Ford's resume.

Despite receiving what some critics considered a well-deserved Golden Globe nomination, Ford felt otherwise about his performance and about the film as a whole: "Yeah, I'm proud of it. I'm not particularly proud of it. I'm proud of the work that went into the making of the film. I'm pleased enough with the job that I did. I can see ways of improving it, and I'm never completely satisfied. But I think it was a worthy effort."[73]

Perhaps traces of Allie Fox were still in Ford's system while making that statement. Today, when looking back in retrospect, there is no hesitation when the actor claims that *The Mosquito Coast* stands as one of his proudest moments as an actor.

21

Pregnancy, Paris and Polanski

In 1987, filmgoers saw Ford's collaboration with the notorious director Roman Polanski: the thriller *Frantic*.

The acclaimed director of *Chinatown*, *Rosemary's Baby* and *Tess*, to name but a few, Polanski was born in France and raised in Poland. Despite his legendary status as an exceptional filmmaker, his past is riddled with misfortune. During Hitler's Auschwitz campaign, Polanski eluded the Germans but his parents did not. In 1969, Polanski's wife, actress Sharon Tate, and four of the couple's friends were murdered in the director's Bel Air home by Charles Manson and his followers. And on December 19, 1977, while photographing a 13-year-old model for the French fashion publication *Vogues Hommes* in friend Jack Nicholson's California home, Polanski had "a moment's unthinking lust" and was subsequently charged with statutory rape.

The director underwent 42 days of psychiatric counseling at the California Institution for Men at Chino. Soon after his release, he fled the States just prior to his scheduled trial and ultimately sought asylum in Paris.

"My career was ruined. It was a nightmare, like discovering you have cancer," claimed the director.[1]

At the time, Ford's wife was collaborating with Polanski on a screenplay for Steven Spielberg about the Belgian children's book hero Tin Tin. At the director's request, Mathison flew to Paris for a meeting.

Concerned that his wife—who was pregnant at the time—was flying to a country experiencing a period of international terrorism, Ford insisted that he escort her. Meeting Polanski for the first time, Ford—who had recently declined involvement in director Penny Marshall's enormous box office success *Big*—was approached by the director with the *Frantic* project. Reenacting the script during a two-hour period, Polanski convinced Ford.

However, Ford had one stipulation before he would commit to the film: "When it was over, I said, 'If that's what it's going to be like when it's written down, I'll do it.'"[2] The final shooting script was co-written by longtime film collaborator Gerard Brach (with additional script doctoring by famed producer/director Robert Towne of *Chinatown* fame, who chose to remain uncredited).

Then titled "Paris Project," it was ultimately changed to *Frantic*. It didn't take long for the new title to be targeted by Ford: "I always knew calling it *Frantic* was a mistake," said Ford. "The script never had a frantic pace. I told Roman Polanski we should call it 'Moderately Disturbed.' He was not amused."[3]

The movie is about Dr. Richard Walker, an American heart surgeon in Paris with his wife to attend a medical convention. Soon after their arrival, his wife mysteriously disappears from their hotel room while he is showering only a few feet away.

In the confusion in the baggage claim at Paris' Orly Airport, Mrs. Walker innocently picked up the wrong piece of luggage. Unbeknownst to her, the contents of the foreign suitcase contain an object coveted by Middle Eastern terrorists. She is held for ransom until the proper owners are reunited with the appropriate suitcases.

"It was terrific — a compelling story about a man who loved his wife," recalled Ford. "I was very receptive, because I'm always worried about [Mathison]. That pretty much defines my reality."[4]

For Polanski, the story held astounding personal relevance.

"It's interesting," said *Frantic* co-producer Thom Mount, "to see what Polanski does with a story about a man afraid of losing his wife, since few people we know have lost their wives in a more publicly hideous manner than Roman. It's safe to say that the subject matter means something special to him."[5]

The idea for the film came about while sitting in a Tunisian villa during the filming of Polanski and Mount's 1986 commercial and critical failure *Pirates*.

Mount recalled, "We were about two-thirds of the way through shooting *Pirates* when Roman and I said, 'Enough of this stuff. Let's make a movie in a civilized city.' So we decided on a thriller set in Paris."[6]

According to Polanski, the action takes place in Paris because he wanted to do a movie from home. "And, also, I wanted, by the same time, to do a film about Paris, the city in which I live and which I know, and I thought is quite misrepresented in many movies — particularly in American movies. America still has the concept of Paris from *Irma La Douce* and *Moulin Rouge* and I wanted to show the city of today, with its freeways and high-rises and nightlife and garbage trucks, etc."[7]

"What intrigued me, from the start," said Mount, "was a situation to which anyone who has ever traveled can relate. It's difficult enough to cope as a visitor [like Dr. Walker] when you don't speak the language, comprehend the culture, or know your way around. If you're plunged into an emotional crisis, it can be a nightmare."[8]

"I wanted to create this feeling of total disorientation, total exhaustion," explained Polanski. "Harrison doesn't get any real sleep during the two days and two nights of the film. He just takes catnaps. He starts out immaculate, and quickly he's unshaven with red, bulging eyes."[9]

Alongside Walker in his search for his wife is the character Michele. Described by Mount as a "subterranean Holly Golightly," Michele is a young Parisian nightclubber and part-time contraband smuggler who holds the key to the disappearance.

For the role of Michele, Polanski selected Emmanuelle Seigner, a 21-year-old French print fashion model. Granddaughter of legendary French stage and screen actor Louis Seigner, Emmanuelle was Polanski's companion at the time of filming.

Until then, she had only appeared (in a minuscule role) in Jean-Luc Godard's 1985 film *Detective*.*

"[The film is] about a man who loves his wife, and faced even with this beautiful French companion, he never falters from his faithfulness to his wife," explained Ford, who found that one particular element extremely appealing on a personal level.[10]

"I have a wife and children," stated the actor, "and if circumstances like that occurred in my life, I can't imagine feeling much different from Dr. Walker.

"I thought it was very interesting to see a happy relationship. It's nice to have a relationship with a woman that's not caustic, jokey or glib. Although I must say there's very little chance to establish that relationship before she's grabbed."[11]

Because the story revolves around the wife's absence, producers needed a charismatic performer in the role, someone would create an indelible mark on the audience.

"She had to project so much appealing warmth in a few short scenes as to remain a presence throughout the mystery," explained Mount. "We thought in terms of the theater ... someone accustomed to walking on stage and immediately winning an audience."[12]

Polanski enlisted stage actress and singer Betty Buckley. Establishing herself in stage productions like *1776* and *Promises, Promises*, Buckley was honored with a Tony Award for Best Actress for her portrayal of Grizabella in Andrew Lloyd Webber's musical *Cats*. She starred in such films as *Tender Mercies* and *Carrie*, but was perhaps best known for her portrayal of the stepmother in the 1970s television series *Eight Is Enough*.

Also in the cast were John Mahoney (*Suspect, Moonstruck, Frasier*) and Jimmie Ray Weeks (*One Life to Live, Another World* and *As the World Turns*) as U.S. Ambassadors to France who diplomatically assist Walker in his search for his wife, only to complicate matters with bureaucratic red tape. The director himself played two cameo roles (a cab driver and a traffic policeman).

Prior to casting, Walker's profession and reason for being in Paris were yet to be determined by director Polanski. Based on Ford's persona, Polanski decided that Richard Walker would be a surgeon.

Although Ford portrays a "doctor who does practically no doctoring on screen," the actor researched his first on-screen doctor role by meeting with various surgeons and heart surgeons.

"I learned there's a certain degree of authority they have in their world that they seem to want to take into the world outside," said the actor. "Heart surgeons, especially, I found, are among the elite of the doctor world. I also found a certain elegance or vanity of gesture that was common to these guys. Lots of hand movements. I already gesture enough with my hands, so that wasn't a challenge."[13]

The film was photographed entirely in Paris. At the Studios de Boulogne (once a World War II aircraft manufacturing facility), were an array of soundstages and production offices.

Polanski and Seigner's relationship remained strong after their marriage in September 1989. The director later cast her in his Bitter Moon *(1994) and* The Ninth Gate *(2000.)*

With the legendary Roman Polanski while filming *Frantic* (Warner Bros., 1987).

Previously used by directors Billy Wilder, William Wyler, John Huston, Jean Renoir and Arthur Penn, the studios were home to production designer Pierre Guffroy's recreations of several sets. From the American Embassy to a discotheque, Guffroy created sets for places where logistical difficulties existed for on-location shooting.

The soundstages were also home for the set of The Blue Parrot, the nightclub that provides Dr. Walker with his ticket to the city's underground. Inspired by the Parisian nightclub Bains Douches, the set was a twin of the original, from the tiles on the floor to the bolts in the door.

Polanski employed 120 elite members of Les Bains clientele as extras for the scene. The actors were not given any information regarding the specifics of the film.

"With the exception of four actors, everybody in the scene was a regular of the Bains," explains Tim Hampton. "You could never find people who dress like them or behave like them. We treated the scene as a party, which continued long after filming was completed."[14]

The second nightclub locale (where Walker and Michele rendezvous with the terrorists) took place within the fictional A Touch of Class. The Middle Eastern flair of the interior was inspired by the world-famous Regine's, located on Paris' Rue de Ponthieu.

For one scene, a barefoot Ford was photographed dangling precariously from an aerial television antenna. Nearly 50 feet above the floor of the studio and not secured with cables, Ford handled the action required for the scene during the week-long shoot.

"My insistence on doing this [rooftop] sequence myself wasn't because of an ego trip. Because I play a man who would think and move in a certain manner, a way that even the best stuntman couldn't match for realism, Roman Polanski opted to let me try it. Dr. Richard Walker is a complex character. He's not Indiana Jones with a medical degree, and I wanted to do him full justice."[15]

"We weren't shooting him out of a cannon or anything," recalled an anxious Mount, "but it was stuff that you and I would not be thrilled about doing. The whole crew held its breath for 12 hours at a time."[16]

The production also took to the streets of Paris for on-location photography.

The prestigious Grand Hotel was the setting for the disappearance of Sondra Walker. The lobby of the Grand and the cafe, an alleyway and a flower shop were just the setting the filmmakers envisioned.

Looming high above the banks of the River Seine in a section known as the Ile aux Cygnes (the Isle of the Swans) stands a 36-foot replica of Ellis Island's own Statue of Liberty. It was selected as the setting for the film's climax where Walker and Michele ultimately confront the abductors. The monument — a replica of the original — stands as a token of gratitude from the United States to France for their gift of the original.

Split up into districts known as arrondissements, Paris filming became a complex bureaucratic matter. Each arrondissement required its paperwork and branch of government, further complicating the logistics of filming.

Co-producer Tim Hampton recalled, "We dealt with the equivalent of nine different 'governments,' sometimes two or three on a single scene ... a chase, for instance, which crossed from one arrondissement to another."[17]

Ford's stay away from his home was made more bearable by the presence of both his wife Melissa and newborn son Malcolm; they spent the entire shooting schedule in Paris alongside Ford.

Filming wrapped in July 1987. When the actor initially read Polanski's and Brach's final draft of the screenplay, he was so absorbed by the story that he had not realized that his services were required for nearly every scene. Shooting *Frantic* was inarguably the most mentally and physically laborious he'd ever experienced until that point.

"To imagine how terrible someone would feel if his wife were kidnapped wasn't hard," claimed the actor. "The frustration and anxiety I had to create had a serious residual effect on me. I took it home with me every night in a way I never had before. I usually get that out of my system, but this one was unremitting, relentless.... My wife often found me in the same frustrated mood as my character, a mood I'd thought I'd been able to drop. It was more of a strain than I'd anticipated.

"There's no question that Roman is hard to work with," admitted Ford. "He pushes actors to the limit. He goes over a scene again and again, maybe 20 times, before deciding how he wants to shoot it. He's got so much energy, and he exhausts you very quickly.... Nobody could outlast him in any circumstance. He's tough, but the results he gets makes working with him worthwhile."[18]

Despite the physical and mental overload demanded by Polanski, Ford maintained that he never felt manipulated. "I felt like a partner, a part of the process," he added.[19]

"Often, when Harrison read a line, it was a different reading than I anticipated, but it worked," said Polanski. "Somehow, it was more inspiring or original than what I had in mind.

"You wait all your life to work with this kind of an actor," continued Polanski. "On a human level he is utterly straight and honest. He understands. He helps. He contributes. I have told him that someday he will be a fine director, and *I* will act in one of *his* pictures. He thought I was joking."[20]

Frantic's cinematographer Witold Sobocinski was overwhelmed by Ford's knowledge and contributions, "It's the first time in my life that I have experienced such a level of satisfaction, working with an actor so totally committed to the film. Extremely disciplined, punctual, communicative, Harrison was interested in all the aspects of production. I never knew an actor who would show so much willingness to help on the set. I owe him a lot. Working with Polanski requires full concentration. Sometimes, after 12 hours of shooting I felt quite drained of energy. Harrison understood it well. At the end of the day, when the last take was in the can, we would give each other a 'high five,' like basketball players after a game, before going to have a beer in the neighborhood bistro."[21]

"It's a very good relationship and a very odd one," observed Thom Mount. "Polanski's this mischievous little Polish devil and Harrison's a thoughtful American guy. And so you had a kind of creative and philosophical Mutt and Jeff."[22]

Made on a $20 million budget and 16-week shooting schedule, *Frantic* was released on February 26, 1988.

The film opened to mixed reviews. Most compared it to a Hitchcock film. It grossed a modest $4,359,424 on its opening three-day weekend on just 1,101 screens. The eventual domestic gross was under $18 million. While it received a poor reception in the United States, *Frantic* was extremely popular with Polanski's overseas viewers.

Generally all of the critics agreed that Ford provided an exceptional performance given the material at hand. Jack Kroll of *Newsweek* steadfastly praised his ability and his aura: "Ford makes you realize what a movie star really is—someone whose every on-screen move is totally enjoyable, an indefinable synthesis of his own personality and the role he's playing."[23]

Meanwhile critic John Simon of the *National Review* harshly claimed that Ford "takes dullness to heights even Charlton Heston and Gregory Peck would have found hard to scale."[24]

Although the box office reception and critiques were mediocre, the release was a personal milestone for its director: "Of course I'm pleased with the critics' response," said Polanski. "But I'm much more pleased to hear that there are lines around the block in New York. I make films to be seen by people."[25]

22

WORKING GUY

The year following the release of *Frantic*, Ford began a successful partnership with director Mike Nichols for two film projects: the 1988 comedy *Working Girl* and the 1991 drama *Regarding Henry*.

Decades earlier, a much younger Nichols rejected a much younger Ford while conducting casting calls for his 1967 classic *The Graduate*. The director simply failed to see the attributes of Benjamin Braddock in Ford, and instead the role went to a young Dustin Hoffman, who became wildly popular following the film's release.

After the long months of filming and post-production on *Frantic*, Ford was ready for a break. Instead, he decided to continue working—but at a much more relaxed pace. So he took on the secondary role of Jack Trainer in *Working Girl*.

For Ford, the idea of playing a secondary role (opposite stars Melanie Griffith and Sigourney Weaver) was appealing.

"It was nice to do a film where other people carry the load," said the actor. "I got a couple of days off a week, didn't have to work as hard!"[1]

The screenplay, written by Kevin Wade, was conjured up on the streets of Manhattan during rush hour. Walking alongside the film's eventual producer Douglas Wick in 1984, the two made observations of an everyday routine.

"Everywhere we looked," explained Wick, "Kevin and I noticed smart-looking, pretty young women rushing to work in tennis shoes and carrying high heels. We started talking about them and realized that they all must have a story."[2]

Following years of unsuccessful attempts to sell their story to 20th Century–Fox, the script eventually found a home with Mike Nichols. Besides introducing Dustin Hoffman in *The Graduate*, Nichols gave a shot at stardom to actors like Jack Nicholson, Meryl Streep, Cher, George C. Scott, Warren Beatty, Matthew Broderick, Alan Arkin and Ann-Margaret. His now-legendary films include *Carnal Knowledge, Catch-22, Silkwood* and *Who's Afraid of Virginia Woolf?*, among others.

"One of the things that's hardest for a director to find in the '80s," explained Nichols, "is a good story. There are so few good stories left, and this was a very strong contemporary story with a good and enjoyable plot. Kevin worked out a lot of details very carefully, and the characters' lines were very surprising. Kevin writes dialogue spoken by real people in the course of real lives, and it's funny, it's alive."[3]

Producer Wick found Ford and the character of Jack Trainer similar.

"We wanted a guy who looked like he could be a winner on Wall Street, but who also had the look of a burnout around the edges," said Wick. "Harrison has that funny warmth and softness that goes against the grain of his personality."[4]

For Ford, accepting the *Working Girl* script not only gave him the opportunity to work with Nichols, but also to return to a genre not visited since Robert Aldrich's 1979 *The Frisco Kid*.

"A lot of my films have been comedies in the sense that I play these bigger-than-life guys," said the actor. "Indiana Jones would be nothing without a sense of humor — but this is the only all-out comedy I've been offered that came with heart and soul.[5]

"I don't have a real focused idea what the difference is between comedy and drama," said Ford. "I think it's all communicating ideas. And there are comic ideas and there are straight dramatic ideas. When it's straight dramatic ideas, you're not supposed to move your face as much...."[6]

"Well, I'd always wanted to play a comedy. Plenty of scripts are offered, but I rarely find one as ambitious, as filled with complex relationships and interesting characters as this one. Most comedy scripts are real disposable. This film has a terrific dramatic structure, and I liked what it says about modern male-female relationships. There's a circumstantial equality here not often portrayed in film...."[7]

The working girl of the title is Tess McGill (Melanie Griffith). (Prior to Griffith's commitment — a factor that helped Ford decide to commit — actress Shelly Long from *Cheers* was scrutinized as a possible Tess.)

Tess is an ambitious secretary with a vision not unlike the countless others in her field — the dream of climbing the corporate ladder. Each morning, Tess commutes to her cubicle in Manhattan via the Staten Island Ferry. In the evenings she finds the time to trek to night school. Unfortunately, she finds herself forced into unemployment when the boundaries of sexual harassment are broken at the workplace.

She also has an unfaithful boyfriend (Alec Baldwin). Tess finds a new job at a brokerage house as secretary to Katharine Parker (Sigourney Weaver). Soon Tess discovers that her new boss is a cutthroat executive.

Tess forwards a business idea to Katharine, then learns that Katharine passed it along as her own to the higher-ups. Following a skiing accident, Katharine is hospitalized and Tess takes matters into her own hands by moving into her temporarily disabled boss' office, where she begins to develop her plan.

Tess enlists the services of investment broker Jack Trainer (Ford) to help her realize her dream. The plot thickens when she realizes that Trainer and Katharine are romantically involved.

"He's an investment banker who was very successful at a certain point in his career and appears to be in decline," explained Ford. " He's a divorced man. His girlfriend is Sigourney Weaver who is an ambitious and manipulative woman and seems to be running him through the hoops. And he finds— he develops a relationship with a girl he's first just attracted to physically — who turns out to be very bright, very sweet, and he falls in love with her.[8]

"...It's part of the irony that this guy," continued Ford, "relatively powerful in his world, is saved from ruin by a girl, a secretary."[9]

"We all like people who have to struggle a bit," explained Nichols, "and that's the main thing about Tess — she struggles. There's a very powerful, completely

With Griffith (left) and Weaver (right) in 1988's *Working Girl* (20th Century–Fox, 1988).

invisible barrier that she has to break: the barrier of class. Tess has high intelligence and great ability for the job she wants to do, but she doesn't have the sort of marks of class that are required of the person who gets this kind of work. She doesn't talk right, she doesn't look right, and in the upper reaches of Wall Street and industry, that's a huge drawback. Eighty percent of the battle is style. And Tess literally has to masquerade in order to demonstrate her ability and free herself."[10]

With Griffith and Weaver, Nichols approached the casting with a determination to present two individuals with contrasting backgrounds and goals: "Melanie is so specifically a working person. She doesn't come with any marks of snobbery or upper class. The character of Tess is always a down-to-earth person who connects with everyone and puts on no airs."[11]

Weaver's previous experience playing a wide variety of independent, serious and ruthless characters made the portrayal of Katharine quite simple. "What works against me in casting is that people tend to feel I'm very Bryn Mawr or something like that," explained Weaver. "But in this instance, it was exactly what Mike wanted. I had gone to all the 'right' schools. The character of Katharine comes from that world of privilege and feels entitled to screw with everyone else, because she's certain that the power's better off with someone like herself. She was brought up to believe that."[12]

The evolution of Jack Trainer went through several transformations, from a simple cameo in the early script stages to a full-fledged character.

"[The character is] a critical part of the story and no surprise that it became more complex. We spent two weeks in rehearsal, which is a rare treat for me. And the script did change during that period.... It's not a question of getting bigger, I think it's a question of it got better. It got more defined."[13]

One aspect of defining Ford's character was attempting to explain the real-life scar on his chin. "I think Mike told me at one point that he wanted to deal with the scar and have some story," recalled Ford. "I think it was my idea to say that I fell on the toilet. It was somebody else's idea about the earring."[14]

Describing his role as that of "the love interest," Ford noted that his character is virtually the lone male presence in a primarily female-dominated film.

"I was never worried about being overshadowed by what the women did because I saw the way the thing worked," said the actor.[15]

To provide a smoother transition between pre-shooting rehearsals and actual filming, the cast conducted independent research to better acquaint themselves with their characters.

Admitting he was completely green in the Wall Street world, Ford sat in on client meetings with various bankers and brokers. He observed their language and mannerisms, hoping to emulate the traits accurately.

In the course of Griffith's and Weaver's research came the realization that sexism did exist within the workplace.

"Women still have to fight to be equals with men," said Weaver. "They have to be aggressive but not too aggressive, feminine but not too feminine...."[16] A lot of the women I met were slightly quiet about what they were doing, even though they were very smart and capable. I think there was still a lot of concern about how they were being perceived, both by men and women, within the firm. They tend to downplay the reality of their successes."[17]

Filmed throughout New York City, *Working Girl* began shooting in mid–February 1988. Joining Nichols on the project was costume designer Ann Roth, who stitched the duds for *Silkwood* and *Heartburn*; film editor Sam O'Steen, who has been alongside Nichols since 1967's *Who's Afraid of Virginia Woolf?*; *Heartburn* musical collaborator Carly Simon; and cinematographer Michael Ballhaus (who worked with Martin Scorsese on *After Hours* and *The Color of Money* and was Oscar-nominated for James Brooks' *Broadcast News*). Ballhaus was described by the director as offering him the unique opportunity of "going to heaven without having to die first."[18]

For the interiors of Petty-Marsh, production designer Patrizia Von Brandenstein (*Silkwood*) used the vacant twenty-first floor of 1 State Street Plaza in lower Manhattan. Construction crews spent three weeks fabricating the brokerage house's secretarial pool, surrounded by private offices and prop elevators.

The set looked so realistic that Gene Shalit, who had just completed interviewing director Nichols for a segment of *The Today Show*, stepped into the elevator awaiting passage to the ground level.

Scenes set in the offices of the Trask Company — where Tess hopes to get her idea of a radio acquisition to the firm's owner, Owen Trask (Philip Bosco) — were photographed inside the landmark U.S. Customs House on Broadway. Katharine Parker's Manhattan townhouse was actually an Irving Place private residence leased to the production by its owner. For the site of the Trask wedding reception, the fictional "Union Club" was created from two separate — yet neighboring — Fifth Avenue mansions.

Additional locations included Pier 17 at the South Street Seaport; the Staten Island Ferry, which stipulated that filming take place only between rush hours and after 8 P.M.; the exterior of the St. Stanislaus Kotka R.C. Church in New Brighton (the wedding of Tess' sidekick Cyn [Joan Cusack]; Bay Street Landing in St. George (the exteriors of Tess' Staten Island apartment); and the raw, unpredictable streets of Manhattan.

The $20 million dollar production wrapped on April 27, 1988. It was released on December 21 that same year.

On the evening of Monday, December 19, 1988, guests at the Los Angeles premiere at 20th Century–Fox studios arrived to find an area of the lot transferred into the streets of New York awash with holiday spirit. Guests were entertained by a performance from the Rockettes and wandered among the faux Fifth Avenue storefronts that served as the backdrop for hot dog vendors, an ice sculpture of the Empire State Building, reconstructed miniatures of the Statue of Liberty and the Brooklyn Bridge, and a replica of the Rockefeller Plaza ice rink with a 500-skater capacity.

Guests included Ford and wife Melissa, Mike Nichols and wife Diane Sawyer, Tippi Hedren with daughter Melanie Griffith (accompanied by on-again-off-again husband Don Johnson), Sigourney Weaver, Tom Hanks and wife Rita Wilson, Debra Winger, Steve Martin, Patrick Swayze, Jane Fonda, producer Lawrence Mark, Penny Marshall, Goldie Hawn and Kurt Russell, Whoopi Goldberg and Patti D'Arbanville — to name a few of the 2,000 invited.

The film opened to an estimated $7 million (it would eventually make $62 million) in its first week and enthusiastic applause for Ford's low-key yet highly effective performance. The film went on to win four Golden Globe awards including Best Picture in the Musical or Comedy category. Melanie Griffith won for Best Actress in a Musical or Comedy. A Best Supporting Actress nod went to Sigourney Weaver, and Carly Simon won Best Original Song for "Let the River Run."

The film was also considered for Oscars for Best Picture, Best Director, Best Actress (Melanie Griffith), Best Supporting Actress (Sigourney Weaver and Joan

Cusack) and Best Original Song. Simon won her second Oscar for her songwriting.

On the reason for its success, director Nichols, stated, "I think it's in some ways reminiscent of certain romantic comedies of the '40s, and simultaneously it's like nothing that there's been.... The picture's about breaking through the class barrier — the invisible, unmentioned class barrier. And there's no fun if you try to break through this class barrier and you don't make it. That's not worth making a picture about."[19]

23

BONDING WITH CONNERY

"I wasn't happy with the second film at all," Steven Spielberg once said of *Indiana Jones and the Temple of Doom*. "It was too dark, too subterranean, and much too horrific. I thought it out-poltered *Poltergeist*. There's not an ounce of my own personal feeling in *Temple of Doom*."[1]

Employing counterpart Menno Meyjes (screenwriter of *The Color Purple*), George Lucas began to ponder the idea of personalizing his beloved Indiana. "The stories I had originally were just stories," said Lucas, "they didn't really involve too much of how his character developed."[2]

Attempts to produce an appropriate script dated as far back as 1985. It was then that Chris Columbus initially developed the third installment's first draft. Unsatisfied, Spielberg hired screenwriter Jeffrey Boam — with whom the director previously worked on *Innerspace*, the 1987 film he produced for director Joe Dante.

"Steven called me up in early 1987 and asked me how I would feel about working on the new *Indiana Jones* movie," recalled Boam. " I told him, 'I don't know why you didn't call me in on it a long time ago.' I felt this movie was right up my alley."[3]

Despite the enthusiasm for his new assignment, Boam recalled the pressure of confronting the project. "The biggest challenge was making something as exciting as the first two *Raiders* films," said Boam. "Writing sequels is generally easier than starting from scratch. But, when you've got these two enormously successful films in front of you that are considered classics, you don't want to be the one to drop the ball. Giving the audience something new was the real challenge."[4]

Boam's primary focus was to develop a screenplay that would create an intimate relationship between the audience and the characters. He answered questions that remained unanswered until then — confronting issues regarding the human side of Indiana Jones, such as the origins of his trademark hat, whip, scarred chin and fear of snakes. Boam delved even deeper into humanizing Jones by introducing his father into the storyline.

The story brings the estranged pair together. Indiana discovers that his father, who had devoted 40 years of his life to the discovery of the Holy Grail (the sacred cup that held the blood of Christ), has been abducted by Nazis. In search of his father, Indiana confronts the armies of darkness and rescues his father, and together the two continue their quest for the Grail. Pre-production for *Indiana Jones and the Last Crusade* began several months prior to the start of filming. Production offices were opened at Elstree Studios. There, logistic coordinators plotted and planned, while production artists, costume designers and construction crews worked fervently, preparing for the first day of principal photography.

Outside the studio, location scouts traveled the globe and casting agents scoured the worldwide pool of talent.

Living up to the verbal contract made when *Raiders* was filmed, Ford agreed to reprise the role if the script met his expectations (this time to the tune of $2.5 million up front as well as 5 percent of the final studio take). Similar commitments were made from John Rhys Davies (Sallah) and Denholm Elliot (Marcus Brody). With the bulk of the cast back from the original film, Lucas and Spielberg's relief was apparent. The next task would prove to be the most challenging — the casting of new characters, specifically that of Indiana Jones' father.

"Sean [Connery] was immediately my first choice. I never had to think about it," recalled Spielberg, "because the second I thought, 'Who is worthy enough and strong enough in the area of screen charisma to play Harrison Ford's dad?' I ruled out every character actor that the casting people gave me on a single slip of paper. And I immediately went right to Sean Connery, never thinking we could get him...."[5]

Following negotiations with agents and Paramount Pictures, Connery became the official new member of the Indiana Jones family.

Initially, Lucas and Boam envisioned Jones, Sr., to be somewhat crotchety, like Henry Fonda in *On Golden Pond*, but when Sean Connery was factored in, Boam decided to make him a tough Victorian schoolteacher. "You always turned in your papers on time to this man," said Boam.[6]

Aside from including Connery to help guarantee the film's financial success, Spielberg also wanted to give Ford the opportunity to act opposite a strong actor like Connery — a first for the *Indiana Jones* films.

"I think George saw the role played by an anonymous, English character actor," said Spielberg. "I wanted another star. He thought Sean was too powerful. I said that Harrison would wipe the floor with him, or that they'd wipe the floor with each other. And I loved the idea of this character back-seat driving throughout the film."[7]

For Ford, the concept of introducing Indiana's father is the idea that sealed the deal for him: "It wasn't that we planned this from the beginning, that we would explore the father-son relationship in the third movie," Ford said. "But we knew that if we made a third movie, we would have to dig deeper into the character.

"The reason we introduced the father," continued Ford, "was that the father-son experience is everybody's experience and when you're trying to communicate in a movie, you look for a common experience in the audience. Every person tries to please their father and every father feels obliged to discipline and instruct his child. I felt that way about my father and my children will feel that way about me. It's a natural thing."[8]

What is unnatural in this particular father-son relationship is that in real life, Jones, Sr., would had to have produced Indiana when he was 12 years old. Ford, who was 46 at the time of the filming, explained his early reservations: "My initial reaction when they proposed Sean was that he's not old enough; and I forgot that I was too old. I'm playing 12 years younger than I am, and Sean's 12 years older than I am."[9]

Connery — then 58 — avoided the age issue altogether and instead introduced the gender issue: "I never had any problems playing the father of Indiana Jones. What I really wanted to play, though, was his sister."[10]

Spielberg cringed at early accusations of directing "Indiana Jones Meets James Bond." Ford, too, dismissed any similarities between the two characters, hoping to eliminate any future Bond references: "James Bond is absolutely an unvarnished hero," claims the actor. "There is no wrinkle in his armor, he absolutely wins every time.

"One of the things that's interesting about Indiana Jones is he has doubts about himself. We see him fail. That's never allowed in James Bond."[11]

Supplementing the cast was Irish-born actress Alison Doody as Dr. Elsa Schneider, the Austrian art historian who would sacrifice anything to acquire the Holy Grail — including betraying her friends and her country.

"In a sense, I see her very much like Indiana Jones in that she wants to go out there and get what she wants, taking great risks to achieve it," said Doody. "She might be like a mirror image of him. She's also very well educated."[12]

No Lucas film would be complete without its share of love-to-hate henchmen. "A good villain can't be a buffoon or someone you see as an object of humor," explained Lucas. "He has to be somebody to fear and have the realistic motivations of a normal human being."[13]

To provide *The Last Crusade* with the necessary antagonist, actor Michael Byrne was cast as Vogel, a nasty Nazi. Alongside Vogel was Walter Donovan (portrayed by British actor Julian Glover), a wealthy Fifth Avenue industrialist and ancient artifacts collector concerned with acquiring the Grail at all costs. River Phoenix was cast as the boyhood Indiana Jones for the film's opening sequence, which dictates how Indiana Jones acquires his trademarks.

Behind-the-scenes contributors from previous *Indiana Jones* films included producer Robert Watts; cinematographer Douglas Slocombe; composer John Williams; editor Michael Kahn; production designer Elliot Scott; costume designer Anthony Powell; stunt coordinator Vic Armstrong; special effects supervisor George Gibbs of Industrial Light and Magic and sound designer Ben Burtt from Sprocket Systems, a division of Lucasfilm.

As producer Watts recalled: "The first day on the set was like one big family getting back together."[14]

Principal photography began on a dry riverbed in an arid coastal region of southern Spain known as Almeria on May 16, 1988. There, Indiana Jones confronts a Nazi cavalcade led by an enormous tank. The elaborate sequence lacked any and all details as it appeared on the daily call sheets.

"We had nothing written at all," recalled Spielberg. "I made the whole thing up in about three days, and it was fun. It was fun plotting it out ... it came very naturally, but at the time the chase began with no middle and no ending. I had no idea where it was going, so I started with Indy pursued by a tank and the tank is firing at him."[15]

Stunt coordinator Vic Armstrong's crew included wife Wendy Leach, who doubled for Alison Doody (and had doubled for Indy's two previous leading ladies). All

Father (Sean Connery) and son in *The Last Crusade* (Lucasfilm, Ltd., 1989).

told, the sequence cost the production an estimated $200,000 a day for 10 minutes of screen time.[16]

"With Steven and Harrison you've got to really be on your toes," said Armstrong, "because they are obviously very inventive people, and they can throw things at you at the last second. After lulling yourself into a false sense of security, suddenly it's, 'How are we going to get out of this one? What can we come up with to make this one work?' You can never afford to relax for a second."[17]

For the sequence, two replicas of an International Mark Seven tank were created. The first, an exact replica constructed with an all-steel shell surrounding two V8 engines, weighed in at nearly 25 tons. The second construct, the "float tank," was constructed on top of another vehicle with wheels, much like the design of a parade float — hence the nickname. For safety's sake the vehicle was manufactured with rubber treads which spun ceaselessly yet never made contact with the earth. In the event that an individual fell off of the top of the tank, an out-of-sight "people catcher" was constructed alongside the entire length of the tank to provide a safe landing area. It also had platforms that could accommodate the camera crew.

The most time-consuming and dangerous of all stunts involved a "transfer" (a stunt in which an actor or stuntman leaps from one moving object to another). In this instance, Indiana Jones (Armstrong standing in for Ford) leapt from his *horse* onto the moving tank 14 feet away and landed face down on top. (In his first of two attempts, Armstrong landed six feet shy of his target, barely missing the vehicle's treads.)

While the life-risking stunts were done by Armstrong and his crew, Ford found it integral to participate as much as he could without exposure to grave bodily harm.

"I am an actor and there are important opportunities for expression of character in those physical moments. That's why I think it's important to do the things I do in the movies. But it's also what distinguishes an *Indiana Jones* movie from another adventure film. You sit there in the theater and know I'm doing it."[18]

Ford's participation included the one-on-one fisticuffs, the horseback riding and the sequence in which he was required to hang precariously from the side-mounted cannon of the tank.

"The best moments in Indiana Jones' personality," explained Spielberg, "the best character moments, come within an action sequence. A look and expression after a punch.... It's all part of the same panache, so it's very, very important that Harrison does get involved in some of the fisticuffs."[19]

To invigorate his 46-year-old chassis, Ford (and Spielberg on occasion) maintained a strict regimen of exercise with Body by Jake Manhattan outfit owner Fran Horneff, who was on the scene for the workouts while filming was underway.

The workout, which began daily between 6 and 6:30 A.M., consisted of a concentration on skeletal strength. They would begin with entire body stretches followed by an upper body workout consisting of bench pressing 115 pounds at repetitions of 100; 200 reps with 15-to-25-pounds for the upper body, back and arms; 170-pound repetitions worth of leg extensions; 150-pound reps for leg curls; 100 squats with 100 pounds, and around 400 sit-ups before finally cooling down.[20]

Jake Steinfeld, Ford's personal trainer since 1979, said, "He's very strong. He has a lot of determination and doesn't quit. That's why he looks consistently good year-round."[21]

Aside from maintaining his physique during the filming of any given film, the actor admitted that he'd never participated in anything physically demanding for sheer entertainment value until he reached age 45.

Fully aware of his physical capabilities and limitations in front of the camera, Ford conferred with stunt coordinator Armstrong regarding every physical requirement. "He's a great personal friend of mine," said Armstrong, "so I always make a point of getting with him, talking through the action, talking through the fights to see if he's happy, see if it feels logical the way we're throwing the punches, the way the fight's going to go, the momentum. Because, it's like music. You have highs and lows in a fight ... you have to time it all out and try and get emphasis in different places, so it's not all over in one fell swoop."[22]

Dismounting from the tank, Armstrong once tripped and fell, tearing several ligaments in his knee. "That was the only significant injury I got," said Armstrong. "And it wasn't even in the shot! Fortunately I only had some horse scenes after that, so you couldn't see that one leg was hanging a bit dead. But I suppose it's like they always say: 'It's the little things that bite you.'"[23]

Relocating to Mojocar, Spain, the production filmed scenes involving Jones Sr. and Jr. escaping by foot and car from German fighter planes.

The scene in which one plane follows the vehicle driven by the Jones boys into a mountainside tunnel required that both its wings be ripped from its fuselage before continuing down the tunnel. This complex effect was later created in post-production at Elstree studios.

Using 14 parking spaces in the studio's lot, the filmmakers constructed a 210-foot miniature of the tunnel and applied optical effects.

In another scene (similarly fine-tuned at Elstree), a weaponless Connery uses his umbrella to startle a flock of seagulls, which in turn disable the remaining fighter craft, thus causing it to crash into a cliff wall. Artificial birds made of rolled up toilet paper were intermingled with real birds to produce the effect.

Moving on to the last of the locations in Spain, the production set up camp in Granada's Gaudix railway station. There construction crews transformed the present into the past, creating the Middle Eastern town of Iskenderun. The production used period artifacts, cars, camels, beggars — even a detailed mock-up of a mosque in the background.

Following the completion of three weeks of filming throughout Spain, the crew traveled to Elstree Studios. For ten weeks they filmed on the sound stages where construction crews months earlier had created the film's elaborate sets.

"The sets seem to be bigger and bigger these days," said director of photography Douglas Slocombe, "and particularly Steven Spielberg sets — they're absolutely enormous. I always felt that the fellow who built the Coliseum in Rome must have been an ancestor of Steven's."[24]

Other sets included Walter Donovan's Fifth Avenue penthouse apartment, the interiors of the Austrian castle Brunewald, the interior of the German zeppelin and the sewers of Venice.

For the sewer sequence in which Jones and Dr. Schneider discover an archeological find, thousands of rats were used to hamper their search. In what Spielberg considered to be "the biggest contract stable since the old days of MGM,"[25] 6,000 brown rats were bred in captivity for cleanliness and disease control for the sequence. In addition, 1,000 mechanical rats were created for the scenes involving fire.

Those crew members who couldn't cope with the scene were permitted to excuse themselves until photography was complete. For Ford, the rats were merely extras. It was the droppings, the discomfort of filming in knee-deep water and the chore of keeping the rats under control that grew bothersome. For the latter, "rat wranglers" stood by at the ready.

"First of all, I'm not frightened of snakes or rats," said Ford. "I used to raise rats when I was a kid. If I see a rat, I have the same immediate chemical response as most people, sure. But when a scene is about rats, and there are 7,000 of them, there's no reason to have an inappropriate fear. They're co-workers."[26]

Alison Doody was anxious around the rats — but not because she was afraid of them. Instead, she was fearful of crushing what she affectionately referred to as "little hamsters." Doody even took the time to dry the wet rodents under the set's lights between takes so they wouldn't become ill and was pleased to say that she never saw a dead or injured rat.

Producer Frank Marshall recalled that at the conclusion of filming, several of the crew members felt such admiration for the rats that several were taken home.

On Sunday, June 26, 1988, Ford, Spielberg and Connery took a well-deserved break from filming and traveled to Scotland's Gleneagles Hotel and Estate to participate in the fifth Rolex–Jackie Stewart Celebrity Challenge Shoot. The event, sponsored by Jackie Stewart's Shooting School, attracted both celebrities and members of royalty in the shooting of clay pigeons with proceeds benefiting the "Search '88 Cancer Trust."

The production utilized several of England's resources outside the studio. They traveled to the Royal Horticultural Hall in Victoria to shoot scenes for the Berlin air terminal where Ford and Connery travel on a zeppelin.

At the Stowe School in Buckinghamshire, filmmakers gathered a larger number of extras, assembling them in the school's courtyard for scenes involving the Berlin book-burning rally. Nazi banners were draped from the school's buildings hundreds of extras filmed from dusk till dawn.

At one point, Indy accidentally (and literally) bumps into Adolf Hitler (played by actor Michael Searle), who signs his grail diary.

"That's so stupid," claimed Ford, "it could only be Steven — nobody else could do something like that and get away with it. It works for him because there's a child-like glee in it that's part of the whole process. It's not just dumb, it's dumb and inspired and gleeful and — I don't know, but it does work for Steven most of the time."[27]

Searle accidentally signed the diary "Adolph" instead of "Adolf" and wrote with his left hand (history books tell us Hitler was right-handed), so closeups of the autographing were later shot in post-production. Lucasfilm Archives curator Don Bies stood in for Ford while visual effects supervisor Mike McAlister stood in for Hitler.

For the duration of filming in England, Ford, Melissa and Malcolm resided in a rented home at the luxurious Beaumont Gardens in Hampstead, North London. Despite its privacy and security (intensified with the presence of 24-hour guards posted at the walls surrounding the entire community), Ford's rental was burglarized.

Ford was downstairs when the thief — locally known as the "Suburb Climber"— reportedly climbed up to the upper level by the drainpipe. The thief entered through an office window and proceeded to steal an estimated $84,000 worth of jewelry from the bedroom cabinet. Spotting the burglar attempting to break into a neighboring home, Ford called the police and soon thereafter realized that he, too, had been robbed.

The conclusion of photography at Elstree Studios brought an end to an era: *Indiana Jones and the Last Crusade* entered the history books as the final Hollywood production to be filmed at the beloved compound.

(Studio head Andrew Mitchell called it "another nail in the coffin of the British film industry.") The 27-acre site was sold for $36 million in 1988 by the ailing Cannon Group, Inc., to Peter Earl, chief executive of the investment banking group Tranwood P.L.C.

In addition to lending public support with the Elstree S.O.S. (Save Our Studios) campaign, Spielberg met with the House of Commons. He joined 55 members of Parliament who collectively signed a motion calling for the preservation of the studio—

hoping to ultimately designate the site a historic landmark. It was Spielberg's "overseas Hollywood since 1979," and he offered to raise $20 million as a bid for the property, but was denied the sale. Despite repeated offers from both Warner Bros. and George Lucas, Mr. Earl was unflinching with his desire to destroy what Spielberg called "the finest production house in the world."[28]

Soon after its sale, the Star Wars Stage was packed and shipped to Shepperton Studios, while the rest was razed. In 1993, half of the acreage was sold to the Tesco supermarket chain.

On Monday, August 7, the production moved to Venice, Italy, where filming resumed along the Grand Canal at St. Mark's Square and the Doges Palace. The canal was used for the motorboat chase involving Indy, Dr. Schneider and their pursuers following their escape from the Venetian sewers.

Later that same week, the crew traveled to Jordan to photograph the exterior of the ancient city of Petra. The 3,000-year-old city carved in stone seemed ideal as the resting place of the Holy Grail and the film's conclusion.

With its European production schedule wrapped, *Last Crusade* returned to the United States for the opening and closing sequences.

Spielberg initially rejected the concept for an opening involving River Phoenix as a young Indiana Jones. Fearful of exhausting the use of a child's point of view based on his previous project *Empire of the Sun*, the director reevaluated the idea after reading the final draft of the script.

"I had written several openings," recalled Boam, "but the consensus was that all of them were basically empty exercises. The big problem was that the teasers in the first two films always told us something new about Indiana Jones, and what we were discovering was that we had nothing new to say. Finally, George came up with the idea of seeing Indiana Jones as a boy."[29]

Nothing traumatic happens in the sequence, explained Boam. Nor does it reveal any dark secrets in Indy's past. "What we see is that Indiana Jones, as a young teen, was always right on the verge of becoming the adult he ultimately became," said Boam. "What we show is that moment that he became Indiana Jones. All the elements, his style, his clothes, it all comes together in this sequence."[30]

The scene was originally slated for the Long House Ruin cliff dwelling at Mesa Verde National Park near Denver, Colorado. In the end, Spielberg withdrew his request to film there following an outcry from conservationists (led by actor Jon Voight) concerned that the production would damage the delicate 700-year-old mud and sandstone ruins, and also would be considered sacrilegious by the native Hopi Indians who still resided there.

Spielberg also nixed filming at Monument Valley: "Steven wanted the 'look' but he refused to go to Monument Valley," recalled producer Marshall. "He considers it too sacred. He says, 'It's John Ford's country.'"[31]

Finally selected was the Arches National Park in Moab, Utah. There the production filmed the opening scenes of the 1912 horse-mounted Boy Scout troop of which young Indiana Jones was a member.

The state of New Mexico also permitted the filmmakers to film the train sequence on board cars of the Cumbres and Toltec Scenic Railroad of New Mexico.

For Phoenix, researching the character of the teenage Indiana Jones (which in the script was generically described as "boy on the train") was easy, considering the head start he had been given: In addition to having spent several months in 1986 working alongside Ford filming *The Mosquito Coast*, the young actor accepted last-minute direction from Ford on Spielberg's suggestion.

"I would just look at him and not mimic, but interpret it younger," said Phoenix.[32]

On February 21, 1989, the production moved to a flat and barren expanse of land that served as the ideal setting for the closing scene in which Indiana, Henry, Sallah and Brody ride off into the sunset.

The scene was shot in the Texan panhandle region just south of Amarillo on the Christian family ranch, where the only preparation involved the removal of one square mile of mesquite growth.

Overcast skies threatened to halt photography, when — only moments before the scene was shot — the heavens opened up, revealing an idyllic sunset.

"We needed a great sunset with a flat horizon," said co-producer Frank Marshall. "You have to see 22 miles in the distance, and that's hard to do. It was raining all afternoon. Then, an hour before sunset, it cleared up. We've been blessed on this movie."[33]

In March 1989, merely two months prior to the film's release date, a last-minute decision found the filmmakers adding the Austrian motorcycle chase.

With the help of makeup artist Steve Anderson, who applied an artificial beard on the freshly shaven face of Sean Connery, the scenes of father and son tear-assing around in a sort of Nazi motocross were filmed in Fairfax, California. This scene would officially put an end to principal photography.

"Preparing for one of the *Indiana Jones* films is kind of like preparing to go on summer vacation," said Spielberg. "Despite all the hard work, all the physical labor, and all the thought that goes into assembling one of these puzzles, it's just so much fun to make because everything we do is for the audience. Very little of what we do is really for the esoteric sides of the artist in all of us. And not dealing with that is a relief. So it is a bit like going on vacation and having a good time at summer camp with old friends."[34]

For Alison Doody, in particular (who received a bouquet of flowers on her first day of filming with a note stating "Welcome to the family"), the experience — despite her anxiety at the onset — was one she would not soon forget. "It really was like a family, and I think it shows on the film how well everyone got on. There was no clash of personalities, which can happen very easily."[35]

Spielberg recalled his crew's sense of relief the moment his two leading men arrived on the set. "The two are like royalty," said the director. "Not the royalty you fear because they can tax you, but the royalty you love because they will make your lives better."[36]

Spielberg stated that watching Ford and Connery are like watching Redford and Newman in *Butch Cassidy and the Sundance Kid*. "There's a real cinema sparkle about them," he said. "You know, one day it's Indy playing Costello and Sean playing Abbott and the next day it's Sean playing Buster Keaton and Harrison playing Harold Lloyd — it just goes back and forth. Their relationship often reminds me of some of the silent movie characters because so many of their scenes are silent...."[37]

Because the focus was more on character, a photographic technique known as a "two-shot" was frequently used with Ford and Connery's scenes. In a "two-shot," both subjects are filmed within the same frame so that the audience is aware of the actions of both simultaneously. What Spielberg found most difficult during these sequences was maintaining a straight face.

"The biggest thrill was putting Harrison and Sean in a two-shot and calling 'Action!' and trying not to ruin the take by laughing."[38]

"A couple of those scenes were like vaudeville routines," recalled Ford. "It was great fun working on that stuff with him. It was something we fell into pretty easily. I was struck with my part. I knew what I was supposed to be doing and Sean found his place very rapidly. It was a question of just give and take, passing the ball at the right time, seeing who was open."[39]

"I enjoyed it enormously," Sean Connery on his collaboration with Spielberg, Lucas and Ford. "[Spielberg] immediately picks up on what you're attempting to do. I found him and Harrison Ford fun to work with once we got through the initial teething problems of not having worked together, Harrison having played this part for such a long time and not having somebody he had to really compete with and deal with in terms of being his father. And so we explored the fun side and the problem side and I could be as contrary and difficult as most fathers are and lacking of understanding in every direction. He was very encouraging to the improvisation."[40]

One such example of improvisation took place at Elstree while filming the father and son conversation aboard the zeppelin.

The temperature was nearly 110 degrees, difficult for any scene, but particularly difficult for Connery: "Everyone was having problems with the heat and I was wearing a three-piece tweed suit," recalled Connery. "And it seemed ridiculous that the bottom part of my body wasn't in the frame, so I took my trousers off. Harrison at first didn't quite appreciate it and then, with his face dripping with perspiration, realized that it was quite clever, so he did the same."[41]

During the classroom scene where the professor side of Indiana Jones is shown, Ford made one alteration to the script. He amended the original dialogue by explaining to the class that if it is truth they seek, "go down the hall to Dr. Tyree's philosophy class."

This reference was a personal tribute to Dr. William Tyree — Ford's former professor of philosophy at Ripon College, who became his close friend during Ford's four-year stay.

Recalling her nervousness just prior to her love scene in Venice with Ford, Alison Doody was grateful that Ford was purely professional — with the exception of when he told her just how her last name was translated in America.

"He used to joke around and ask me if I was okay," said the actress. "I was shaking a little before the love scene and was so nervous — he'd stand there behind Steven Spielberg and pucker up his lips and do these silly kisses and sing out, 'Alison, I'm ready!' All those little things he did made light of the difficult moments."[42]

Ford would even offer Doody his prefab reply to the inevitable questions regarding what kissing her leading man was like: "Tell them Harrison Ford is so famous he doesn't even use his own tongue!"[43]

Paramount's mega-million-dollar investment *Indiana Jones and the Last Crusade* was released on May 24, 1989 — Memorial Day weekend — on 2,327 screens nationwide; the studio insisted that owners raise admission prices by 50 cents per ticket. For the four-day period, the film earned a record-breaking $37 million, which remained undefeated until 1994's *The Flintstones*, which brought in $37.2 million.[44] (It is estimated that 40 percent of the annual box office total generally occurs between Memorial Day and Labor Day.)

Beating out the preceding six-day record holder *Indiana Jones and the Temple of Doom* with $42.3 million, *The Last Crusade* earned an impressive $46.9 million during the same time period. Continuing strong from $50.2 million in a full week to $77.1 million in 12 days,[45] *Last Crusade* went on to garner a grand total of more than $150 million domestically, and nearly $495 million worldwide.

Is there the possibility of another Indiana Jones outing in the future? "Well, it's a finality for me," confessed Spielberg. "I certainly don't control the destiny of the *Indiana Jones* movies—George could make as many as he'd like — but it was certainly my graduation gift to be able to work on something like this and, in the best way possible, say good-bye to all my old friends and move on."[46]

"Well," said Ford, "there comes a point when you start wearing those old jeans around and people say 'I don't care what the story is about those pants, get yourself something that isn't ripped open like that.' It's been very, very good to all of us — to George and Steven and I — and I think it's pretty much run its course with us. I'm not sentimental about it. I'm more interested in the opportunities that are just over the horizon than I am in the past."[47]

However, referring to the 1983 installment of the James Bond film featuring his co-star, Ford continued, "if there's anything I learned from Sean, it's to never say never again."[48]

On May 26, 1989, Ford handed down one of the many fedoras and leather jackets worn in the films* to the Smithsonian Institution's National Museum of American History. There, the costume joined Judy Garland's *The Wizard of Oz* slippers and bow ties worn by Frank Sinatra for a public exhibit honoring the entertainment industry.

In June, Ford presented one of the many bullwhips from the *Indiana Jones* films to Christie's auction house. It went on the auction block the following December to help raise an estimated $6.7 million for a new addition at the archaeology institute at London's University College.

Despite Spielberg's desire to say goodbye to the Indiana Jones character, he welcomes the opportunity to work again with Ford on future projects.

"He's more like Humphrey Bogart every day ... but better looking!" exclaimed Spielberg. "I think when Harrison moves into his late fifties, the way Sean has, he's going to really fall into the Clark Gable–Humphrey Bogart roles even in a more suitable fashion than he's assuming those roles today. I think the older he gets, the better he's going to get and he's never going to lose his popularity. I see Harrison being a real face on the Mt. Rushmore of Hollywood."[49]

---

*A total of 48 were handcrafted by the Wested Leather Company of London, England, for Ford, his stand-ins and the stuntmen.

24

HIS BAD HAIR DAY

Nine months before Scott Turow's novel *Presumed Innocent* was published, it was being optioned to Hollywood. Acclaimed film producer-director Sydney Pollack (*Tootsie, Out of Africa, The Firm, Sabrina*), Mark Rosenberg and their recently founded Mirage Productions purchased the rights for a reported $1 million.

On July 15, 1987, lawyer-writer Turow's sophomore novel — which took six years to complete — was published by Warner Books and stayed on *The New York Times* fiction bestseller list for 44 weeks. With more than one million copies sold in hardcover, and 40,000 copies in paperback, the novel was considered one of the best suspense thrillers of the 1980s.

Producer Pollack contacted acclaimed director Alan J. Pakula (*Klute, All the President's Men, Sophie's Choice, The Pelican Brief*) to direct. Pakula (who was killed in New York in a 1998 automobile accident) signed on to the project in January 1989. He said, "I was fascinated by the book. I thought it was a wonderful exploration of our system of justice.... It's also a crackling good suspense yarn."[1]

Rozat (Rusty) Sabich, a devoted husband and father and a dedicated prosecutor serving Kindle County, is selected to investigate the murder of colleague Carolyn Polhemus — a woman with whom he had an affair. In a twist, all the evidence points to Rusty as the prime murder suspect. With the aid of renowned defense attorney and adversary Sandy Stern, Rusty hopes that his family, career and life can be salvaged.

After Robert Redford was vetoed because of his age, Pakula visited Ford at his Jackson Hole ranch to discuss the character.

"The reason I cast Harrison is that Rusty is nice, decent, and everybody can relate to him," said Pakula. "He didn't shirk playing those kinds of Everyman things, whereas a lot of stars would have said, 'Well, I've got to be cooler than that.' Once he decided to do it — and he took his time deciding — he gave himself to the role."[2]

Ford — who signed on for $7 million — read the book after he read the script so as not to prejudice his opinion of the material. His initial concern was with the script's lack of material involving Rusty. "If there was anything I was worried about, it was that everybody else had a better part. That wasn't because I was jealous of their roles, but Rusty was such a repressed kind of guy, and the other characters were a little easier to find."[3]

Ford was also anxious to confront the complexities the translation from book to screen presented. "I was interested in the character and his dilemma," said the actor. "But the difficulty was that the novel had been written in a first-person narrative form. And that worked well in the book, but there was no way that could be made to work in a film. As well, we had the difficult job of disguising 'whodunit' in a dramatic way."[4]

Oscar-winning screenwriter Frank Pierson (*Dog Day Afternoon*) said, "We're doing a very straightforward story in which the audience at all times believes that they know what's going on, but they don't because the major character, through whose eyes they are seeing it, doesn't know it either. There are a lot of traps that you can fall into, leaving an audience feeling they've been lied to, manipulated or tricked in some way. I thought the book was shameless in the way it tricked the reader."[5]

"Scott dealt with the most grotesque, lurid material—infidelity, kinky sex, murder, and he conveyed it in this disciplined rational, one might say lawyerly way," explained Pakula. "I felt it was the tension between the cold, controlled prose and the heat of the events that made the book such a success.[6] ... You'd say the book was made to be a picture. But it's not that simple. When I read it, I saw right away that it was a tough one."[7]

The cast included Bonnie Bedelia (as Rusty's wife), Raul Julia, Brian Dennehy, and Paul Winfield.

Pre-production began in June 1989. Personally guided by Chief Assistant Prosecutor George Ward, Ford visited Detroit's Recorder's Court at the Frank Murphy Hall of Justice and Wayne County prosecutor's office. For two weeks he researched various prosecuting attorneys to help him pick up the characteristics and mannerisms to portray his role convincingly.

"I was not so anxious to see courtroom behavior, which I've seen before," explained the actor, "but to have a chance to observe the more banal aspects of lawyers' lives. To see the little details, like how they handle files, how they behave with their adversaries—not in the courtroom but at the coffee machine or in the judge's chambers.[8]

"I needed to ground it in some reality. To see what their offices looked like, how hot it was, how tired they were, what was in their briefcases, what it looked like, what it felt like. I hate it when people just give me a briefcase from props. You have to tell the prop person you want heavy stuff in it because they're liable to take pity on you and take all the stuff out of it. Feeling that case as heavy is something you shouldn't have to act."[9]

Immersed in his research, Ford returned to his hotel room each night accompanied by case files. Other cast members researched their roles by experiencing on-hand judicial proceedings.

Presumed Innocent was a reunion for Ford and Paul Winfield: They met and became friends during their years at Columbia Pictures during the '60s. "I was the token black," recalled Winfield, "and no one would even speak to me except Harrison, who took me under his wing."[10]

Winfield met with a New York Superior Court judge nicknamed "Turn 'em Loose Bruce." The judge enthusiastically offered to participate and insisted that Winfield don a judiciary robe and take his side at the bench to observe several cases.

"Thank Heaven I wasn't passing sentence," admitted Winfield. "I misjudged at least two-thirds of the cases. I guess I'm a real sucker for a convincing story."[11]

Director Pakula also observed criminal trials in Detroit. After a chilling yet mesmerizing murder trial, Pakula admitted, "I could very easily become a trial junkie."[12]

Ford visited Turow in his suburban Chicago home to get a sense of the point of view from which the book was written. At the same time, Ford dispelled any apprehension the author may have had regarding the film's casting.

"If you read the physical description of Rusty in the book, of course, Harrison's perfect," believed Turow. "Then when I saw *Frantic*, I was pretty much convinced he was right, and when I met him I knew he was right."[13]

Ford completed the second phase of preparation for the role by suggesting a buzz cut for Rusty. The actor "coerced" Pakula for nearly three weeks before the director submitted to the actor's proposal.

Pakula recalled, "I told him I wanted him to be recognized. I hired a movie star and, instead, I got this unknown character actor. But, after a couple of weeks, I couldn't imagine him looking any other way."[14]

"This is no minor detail," said Ford. "There are many things I found I could express with that short haircut. Simplest of all, I wanted to tell the audience to leave their baggage at home — not to expect the Harrison Ford they've seen before. Second of all, I wanted to create a character who is not vain, who has no personal vanity, because that indicates his problems — the infidelity, the involvement with the crime — are extraordinary things in his life. I wanted to create a character who is not as hip, not as fashionable as the woman with whom he has had the affair, to create a man who is conservative by nature and by choice. Something as simple as this plain old haircut can do all that."[15]

Entertainment Weekly (in their "Best and Worst for 1990") called Ford's haircut the worst of that year. Joining the ranks of Kevin Costner in *The Bodyguard* and others unofficially inducted into the "haircut hall-of-shame," the actor looked, according to the publication, like "a medieval monk who'd just stepped out of the shower."[16]

"Never in my life," claimed Ford, "not since carpentry became such a prominent part of my story, has one item been such a big deal. People have gone nuts about it. Completely, absolutely nuts."[17]

Informal rehearsals for *Presumed Innocent* took place three weeks prior to principal photography; it was a ritual Pakula was adamant about. During this phase, Pakula noted Ford's genuine enthusiasm and continuous offers of character-related contributions.

"It's absolutely essential for me and the actors to know their placement, emotional and chronological," explained the director. "You don't have time to go through the whole structure each time."[18] "I'll say, 'Let me see where you're going to go with it, and then we'll play with it.'"[19]

"As a director, you can orchestrate performances but you can't give 'em. You can make a good actor look bad but you can't make a bad actor look good. The trick is knowing when to say something, and when not to. Often you just say, 'Let's do another one,' and they'll see themselves what's needed. Harrison senses what you're thinking before you say it, because he's spent so much time discussing the film and the character."[20]

The setting for Turow's novel is a Midwestern city (presumably modeled after Detroit). Executive producer Susan Solt explained the ultimate decision of deciding where the story should unfold: "Kindle County, USA, had certain requirements. It was on a waterway so we needed a ferry, appropriate federal buildings, a city smaller than Chicago with suburban neighborhoods, somewhat blighted urban settings ... we had to come up with locations and designs that were real to the book and also truthful to the experience of living in this prototype community without saying where it was. We weren't looking for generic settings, but a universal feeling."[21]

The producer's final choices were Newark, New Jersey, and Detroit, Michigan. The filmmakers recreated the courtroom on a studio lot.

"From a logistics point of view," said Solt, "it's very hard to light and have holding areas for the extras, but also very difficult because it's a working courtroom. What was particularly important to Alan Pakula and [production designer] George Jenkins was finding the particularly American institutional governmental architecture which made a statement about our justice system and our government."[22]

"You see Newark and Detroit fighting for survival," said the director. "The courthouses are decaying and overcrowded. There are cartons of papers stacked in the corridors. Yet they're symbols of the rule of law, and they hang on to a certain kind of grandeur, even if you get the feeling the cities are tearing apart at the seams."[23]

The film's principal photography began with exterior filming in Detroit on July 31, 1989. Locations included the Renaissance Center's Westin Hotel, Hart Plaza, the Woodbridge Tavern, Eastern Market, Jackie's Bar and Restaurant, St. Aubin Marina and the International Plaza Garage rooftop.

The production ventured across the Detroit River, to Windsor, Ontario's, Reaume Park on August 3. The filmmakers wrapped the area's photography with a 13-hour day filming the scenes where Barbara Sabich drops off husband Rusty for his ferry commute to the city. Cast as a background extra, Windsor Mayor John Millson sported a trenchcoat in 88-degree heat, making his film debut as a commuter barely noticeable on the upper deck of the ferry.[24]

Newark was the next stop. The production utilized the North Reformed Church for two days as the setting for the funeral of Carolyn Polhemus. Near the church's main entrance is a plaque memorializing a pastor who died in 1857: Abraham Polhemus. A surprised Pakula found the unscheduled prop unsettling: "It's a bizarre coincidence that sent a chill right down my spine," said Pakula.[25]

On August 14 and 15, the filmmakers photographed scenes in Newark's City Hall, before venturing to Gil's Bar and Restaurant. The Essex County Courthouse was used for a brief courtroom sequence, and Newark's city morgue was used as the coroner's office of "Painless" Kumagai (Sab Shimono). A housing project scheduled for demolition was used for scenes involving Rusty and partner Lipranzer's (John Spencer) questioning of a suspect.

In late August, the crew relocated to East Orchard Street home in Allendale, New Jersey. Situated 30 minutes north of Manhattan, this ideal suburban setting was used for the exterior and interior scenes of the Sabich household.

As the wrongly accused Rusty Sabich in *Presumed Innocent* (Warner Bros., 1990) with Raul Julia as lawyer Alejandro "Sandy" Stern.

In the house's root cellar, the production filmed the pivotal sequence where Rusty's wife reveals her role in the murder of Carolyn Polhemus.

As the scene progresses, the conversation moves upstairs into the Sabich living room, where Bonnie Bedelia delivers her speech. During this scene, all that is required of Ford is to react—to simply take his mark, observe and listen.

"Listening is never nothing," said Ford. "Listening is an active activity. You may not move around, you may not swing from the trees or hit anybody, but you still have to be available to what happens, and you have to let it show."[26]

"As much as I think of myself as a technical actor, as much as I'm totally aware of the mechanics of acting, there are times when something mysterious happens. I don't know any more about it or understand it any more than you do. I just trust and have faith in it."[27]

While the verbal exchange that occurred between the two characters was in the script, the tears from Ford's eyes were not, according to an unsuspecting Pakula.

"The pain in him was so real, he totally gave himself to that character's feelings," said the director. "There's a lot of movie stars-actors who would feel that that's unmanly, showing that kind of vulnerability, that kind of pain. It's not manly to cry and I didn't ask him to cry. To not worry about his image, to just play it honestly as an actor, was a great gift to the film. It took a lot of courage to do and a lot of faith in being his own man."[28]

From there, the filming resumed on Stage 1 at Kaufman Astoria Studios in Queens, New York, for three weeks of courtroom scenes.

Practicing Manhattan attorney William Fordes served as technical advisor to the production. Despite huge contributions to the sets' authenticity, Fordes never lost sight of his position. Pakula remained steadfast at having the final word. "You're overruled on this, one, counselor," Pakula would say.[29]

A Cleveland, Ohio, courthouse was the model for the film's final courtroom scenes. "It captured the old-fashioned majesty of justice," said Pakula. "The belief in justice as some great ideal that represents the most rational part of man."[30]

George Jenkins, whose first assignment was William Wyler's 1946 *The Best Years of Our Lives*, reunited with long-time collaborator Pakula overseeing production design responsibilities. With help from the art department, every inch of the room was recorded and later recreated (including a 1910 mural) in painstaking detail at Kaufman Astoria Studios. Originally constructed by Paramount in 1920, the studio also accommodated the sets for Sandy Stern's office and other associates' cubicles.

For Pakula, the attention to detail — both on screen and off — enabled his actors and the audience to better acquaint themselves with the characters being portrayed and the environment around them.

An example of this can be found with a glance at Pakula's past. While filming *All the President's Men*, his production team recreated a 33,000-square-foot replica of the *Washington Post* newsroom on a Burbank Studios soundstage. Faithfully committed to realism, Pakula demanded truckloads of actual trash from *The Post* be sent in and strewn about the set for authenticity.

"There are clichés in film," explained Pakula. "Courtrooms are one of them, newspaper offices are another. Spending a few weeks or months in the real location protects me from falling back on theatrical archetypes I've seen in a thousand other films."[31]

Visiting the New York set, Scott Turow's wife Annette saw a rehearsal and applauded the director's efforts with a tearful tribute to a scene which, prior to that day, was merely typed words on a page. "I knew the dialogue by heart, but suddenly it got the better of me, to hear it spoken in such a realistic setting — and to realize that soon millions of other people would hear it too."[32]

Another set was the office of Carolyn Polhemus, where Ford and Italian-born actress Greta Scacchi acted out the erotic desktop lovemaking sequence, seen in the film via flashback. For Ford, it was his most sexually involved work.

"I don't do live sex shows," said Ford. "I'm an actor. It's a very different sort of thing. There's a kind of chemistry you have to have, but it's vastly overrated. You don't sit around with an actress trying to stir up chemistry."[33]

"To me a scene that involves making love is like any other scene, except you get to kiss a pretty girl. It's always acting. Alan Pakula let us stage it ourselves. He was especially sensitive to Greta and her privacy. I remember the details of that scene very well, not because it was a lovemaking scene but because it was a scene that was extremely technical."[34]

Pakula described it as "some of the most explicitly sensual [scenes] I've ever done." The director was insistent on filming its entirety seamlessly and without closeups.[35]

"I put the camera in this strange, objective, chilly way, in this half-light," explained Pakula. "Not making it seem romantic, but dangerous and chilling, and in some way frightening. It has an icy, voyeur look. Otherwise it would just be soft-core porn."[36]

Although he didn't condone the behavior, Ford understood his character's uncontrolled infidelity when propositioned by Carolyn. "Sexual obsession fuels a compulsive relationship that has Rusty behaving a way he never thought possible," said Ford. "Always in his life, he was a man in control — moral, hard working and loyal. But when he's weakened enough by the intimacy that occurs working with Carolyn, she seduces him — tells him how good it's going to be — and it was."[37]

"It's a graphic scene without being offensive," claimed Pakula, "and he worked with her very carefully, very closely, to make her as comfortable as possible. I give him the credit for that scene. He really staged it himself."[38]

And how did Ford the actor and faithful husband stay on the path of righteousness in a land of temptation?

"Temptation," he stated, "is a two-way street; it rarely crops up unless one seeks it. There's a stink people carry when they are looking for sexual adventure. It is not on me though...."[39]

And if that stink were to linger in his vicinity: "I just shut my eyes and think of Jesus," joked the actor.[40]

Filming at Astoria Studios was completed during the last week of September 1989. It had a scheduled release date of summer 1990, but executives were wary of competition from potential hits like *Die Hard 2* and *Ghost* (both of which went on to dominate the summer box office). The studio previewed *Presumed Innocent*, receiving unanimous approval from both men and women, young and old — statistics Ford was overwhelmed by.

"I hadn't expected it to do well with a younger audience," said Ford. "I think it's a film that people will think about for more than the time it takes them to get into their cars."[41]

Warner Bros. issued the usual press kits to theater owners and members of the media containing production information and cast and crew bios. But in the case of *Presumed Innocent*, they also included a formal request to keep the end of the film a secret so that it would truly be a mystery for all audiences. The press complied, leaving those who hadn't read the book aghast at the film's conclusion.

On its opening weekend, *Presumed Innocent* earned an impressive $11.7 million. Applauded for its craftsmanship, its performances and its faithfulness to the book, the film ultimately amassed approximately $86 million.

Ford noted his distaste for the public's general view of celebrities: "I get kind of bored with all the movie talk," conceded the actor. "I think it takes away some of the pleasure we should get from movies. We're so informed about how much people are making, who they're sleeping with, how angry they were at the director. All this gets in the way of people just looking at a movie and being entertained.

"The thing that makes me good at what I do, if I'm good at all, is not feeling special. Not feeling different than other people. What I have to sell as an actor is my sympathy and understanding of what real people's lives are like. I need to know what I have in common with all the people who are coming to the movies I make."[42]

"Harrison has been extremely involved in keeping it authentic," said executive producer Susan Solt. "He took the lead, and everyone followed suit in really immersing themselves in the characters they portray."[43]

"Harrison is bright as hell," said Pakula. "He also has enormous technical skill from having had to do those complicated films. I've said it and it's true, he'll make a wonderful director when he wants to. Cinematographer Gordon Willis was amazed how much he understood about the process.[44]

"Harrison would plan a scene. But I never knew what he was going to do next. He does not protect himself. He allows himself to feel something and lets himself go with it. When Brian Dennehy said to him, 'You're a good man, Rusty,' Harrison's face just collapsed and all the guilt in his character came out. I didn't know he was going to do that! He almost started to break down and then he pulled himself together."[45]

When Rusty tells his wife he will be tried for murder, he mentions that it will be financially ruinous for them. She responds by saying they'll have to mortgage the house. "When Bonnie Bedelia said that, Harrison just broke," explained the director. "This responsible man who prides himself in taking care of his family, realizes his behavior is destroying the family and bankrupting it. I left a tiny bit of that in, but what happened in the take is what happened to him. You can't fake that."[46]

Considering the moments working alongside Ford to be a monumentally rewarding experience, Dennehy commended Ford's talents: "It's a tremendous performance by Harrison. And not in an easy framework. Because he essentially plays catch. In other words, he's surrounded by actors; all of whom are bouncing off him. And you can't take your eyes off him. It's riveting and very moving, and tremendously effective. It's a terrific picture and a hell of a performance."[47]

Collaborating with Ford for the first time, actress Bonnie Bedelia recalled critics' reservations about Ford's ability to perform outside of his usual genre before they were ultimately convinced with the release of *Witness*.

"When I heard that, I couldn't believe it," said Bedelia. "What'd they think he'd been doing? Do you think that's easy, what he does? You'd have to be an idiot not to see that. I was really surprised at the business for thinking that way, as though acting in *Witness* were any more difficult than what he'd done before."[48]

Bedelia relished the comfort and ease of establishing a successful chemistry with Ford during filming.

"A lot of it became just Harrison and Bonnie," explained the actress, "which is the way it should be, but not always the way it is. All you really have on your relationship on-screen is the amount you're willing, as actors, to expose to each other. To look in someone's eyes and have them right there with you — I've worked with a lot of big stars, and I can't stress how often that's not the case."[49]

Professional theory aside, Bedelia as a woman, reevaluated her assessment of her leading man: "Who couldn't feel the chemistry with Harrison Ford? You'd have to be half kangaroo or something. He's like the ultimate man — as a human being, as just a male person. I'm completely in love with him. I haven't told him yet, but I think Melissa might know!"[50]

25

TIME TO REHABILITATE

When 23-year-old screenwriter Jeffrey Abrams threw producer Scott Rudin his "pitch" during a party, he never suspected that the conversation would eventually lead to a $450,000 check and a position in the annals of Hollywood history.

The screenplay for *Regarding Henry*—then entitled *Henry Forgets*—took Abrams a mere seven days to write. It told the story of Henry Turner, a powerful and ruthless lawyer whose family takes a back seat to his career. After suffering a brain injury from an assailant's bullet, Henry is given a rare second chance in life to atone and set his priorities straight.

"It was startling to discover that so young a writer could achieve a story of such emotional complexity, intimacy and detail," said producer Rudin.[1]

Rudin envisioned only one man to adapt the character to the screen: "The script had an incredible humanity to it, and Harrison was the first actor I thought of for the role," said Rudin. "He is one of the few guys I know who could pull it off, who could make you believe that he was both a shark lawyer and a diminished adult."[2]

Scripts come and go. In fact, on average, only one out of every 100 scripts is deemed worthy by Ford.

Initially hesitant to portray a lawyer in back-to-back films, Ford accepted the role of Henry Turner due to the intensity of the emotional content in the story and the opportunity to represent a film character unlike any he had encountered before.

"It's not what you see in a script that attracts you, but what you feel in it," said Ford. "I felt a very strong emotional response to the dilemma this guy goes through. It was a very positive emotional response to the character's struggle and to his success.... You can have a very clever, very interesting story, but without the emotional connection between the audience and what's happening on the screen, it's like witnessing an event that you don't really care about. I spend my whole life operating on the premise that if it moves me, it'll move them."[3]

The script was relayed directly from Ford to director Mike Nichols per Ford's request. Ford's interest in Nichols' involvement was twofold. Apart from his eagerness to reunite with the director, Ford believed Nichols had "the intellectual and dramatic skills to balance one against the other and come away with something that is greater than the sum of its parts."[4]

"Jeffrey's screenplay was about something I'd never seen dealt with," said Nichols, "something that happens in life that we rarely hear anyone talk about. For all the searching for happiness that we do, we tend not to notice that sometimes it's catastrophe which reorders our lives in wonderful ways. There's something about cutting loose everything and starting again after a catastrophe that somehow tells you the most about what life really is, especially family life. *Regarding Henry* is a movie about paring everything down to what is real life — love and family. Jeffrey told this story in a way that is surprisingly funny and very moving...."[5] It was one of the very few times in my life that I have read a script and the next day said, 'I want to do it.'"[6]

"The hardest thing about this movie was [that] basically the villain was Henry, at least during the first part of the film," said Abrams. "In plotting it, I had to figure out how to make it work dramatically for the villain to actually become the hero. But I love the thought that you can do something wrong and then years later you can go back and make it right, like Henry does. That's something I do believe: There is hope for even the smallest regrets. A lot of people feel that if something is done, it's done, but I think you can always go back and correct yourself, change things for the better."[7]

The material held tremendous personal relevance for Nichols. "I was sick for six months, about four or five years ago," acknowledged the director. "A doctor had innocently given me a sleeping pill that made me pre-psychotic. Nobody knew, but I got crazy for six months. I was in this depression. It turned out to be this sleeping pill and, when they weaned me off of it, I was back to normal in ten days.... It was six months of real hell. But it did bring wonderful things in its wake. It changed my life completely."[8]

Because Ford, Nichols, Rudin and Abrams were venturing into material that all were unfamiliar with, weeks of research were required.

Ford and actor Bill Nunn consulted with leading neurologist Bruce Volpe and neurosurgeon Dr. Richard Fraser and met with various physical therapists, occupational therapists, and speech therapists at the Burke Institute in White Plains, New York, and the Los Ranchos Clinic in Los Angeles. Ford (who claimed that not conducting research for any role "is like playing Jesus without reading the Bible"[9]) and Nunn attended rehabilitation sessions that gave them insight into the characteristics and care of patients with neurological disorders.

Nunn, whose previous work included *New Jack City* and the Spike Lee outings *Do the Right Thing* and *Mo' Better Blues*, portrayed Bradley, Henry's physical therapist and eventual best friend.

"Bradley and Henry are buddies," said Nunn. "They genuinely like each other. After talking to therapists, I've found that often does happen. They are loving and caring and their work at times requires a lot of patience."[10]

"From the research I did," said Ford, "it seemed that people in these situations are struggling to keep up all the time. So they fixate on what's really happening. They don't have time for thinking about telephone calls they have to make."[11]

Ford refused to create a character similar to Tom Hanks' *Big* (a project both he and Nichols previously rejected). Although there was a regression, he did not want Henry Turner to be a child. Ford imagined an individual whose mind and body had been "simplified."

"Behind the simplicity," claimed Ford, "there's confusion and anxiety and embarrassment. I saw embarrassment in all the neurological patients I observed during my research."[12]

The actor continued, "My research technique is to put as much in as possible and then let what comes out be the product of instinctive choice — or emotional choice. So everything you see on the screen is me. The bad Henry and the good Henry are both within me. It's a matter of degree and proportion, how much of each is in there."[13]

Ford and Nunn's research itinerary included conferring with actual patients and their families on the rehabilitation process. One patient, attorney Tom Frost, who was injured in an automobile accident, became a technical advisor to the film.

"He was a Princeton-educated lawyer whose priorities, according to him, before the accident were work, tennis and family," said Ford. "Now his priority is family. He went through a transformation that was amazing to his family and friends and very much consistent with what happens with Henry. I found it very helpful and very reassuring."[14]

The filmmakers were aware that — outside of Hollywood — not all treatments conclude with successful rehabilitation.

"We do not want to give false hope to those people whose outcome is not as successful as Henry's," said Ford. "We felt responsible about getting the details right, without being coy or untruthful."[15]

Ford continued: "Although Henry is disadvantaged by his accident, what he's been able to come away with balances out what he's suffered. He starts out as a guy whose family life is grim at best. Suddenly he's an appropriate, interested father and husband who needs his family."[16]

Annette Bening was chosen to portray Henry's wife Sarah — a woman who undergoes a similar transformation alongside Henry. Nominated for an Oscar for a previous role in *The Grifters* (and also for her later work in 1999's *American Beauty*), Bening had collaborated earlier with Nichols (a cameo appearance in *Postcards from the Edge*).

"I think Sarah and Henry had once been very much in love," said Bening. "In a quite unconscious way they've lost track of each other in establishing a comfortable lifestyle with a circle of friends, work, and taking care of their daughter; life is humming along. Ironically, it takes a disaster for them to find a purpose in their lives."[17]

"Because everything is threatened," said Nichols, "she is needed in a way she's never been needed by her husband. She finds ways to be useful — and a new identity. Like he does. She goes from society wife to something very different."[18]

Nichols held rehearsals and began filming in the early weeks of September 1990. Ford, Bening, and Nunn benefited from the rehearsals by strengthening the interrelationships between the characters and creating a comfortable working atmosphere among themselves.

Assembling the film's production team, Nichols mustered colleagues from previous collaborations, including editor Sam O'Steen, director of photography Giuseppe Rotunno and production designer Tony Walton.

"With the right colleagues," said Nichols, "I know that everything is being taken

Ford's second partnership with director Mike Nichols in *Regarding Henry*—which also starred Annette Bening (right) and Mikki Allen (Paramount, 1991).

care of perfectly. Everyone knows his job, and I trust everyone implicitly — any new idea I have, they'll be able to translate — so I can relax. No one person can make a movie. It's just not possible. You need all the 120 or so people involved. And surely they have to be interested enough and excited enough by the idea to make their contributions."[19]

Abrams recalled his overwhelming sense of enthusiasm as he saw his labor of love transform into a reality he never imagined possible.

"I couldn't have concocted a better cast and director for this, not even in my dreams."[20]

Principal photography for *Regarding Henry* began in New York on September 14, 1990. Locations were scattered throughout Manhattan, including the Upper East and West Side; Greenwich Village; the Metropolitan Museum of Art; the Edwardian Room; the New York Public Library; the Capri Cinema; the Manhattan Surrogate Court; the Ritz-Carlton Hotel; the law offices of Rogers and Wells in the Pan Am building; the Junior League; the Oak Room at the Plaza Hotel, and the Optimo Store on Lexington Ave (the site where Henry gets shot). On October 15, the production ventured 90 minutes north of the city to Millbrook for three days of filming Rachel Turner's (Mikki Allen) boarding school scenes at the Millbrook School. Ten years earlier, the campus was seen in *The World According to Garp*.

Continuing in Los Angeles at Paramount in mid–October, the crew filmed the Turner apartment and clinic scenes created by production designer Walton.

Occupying most of Stage 18, the enormous set took months to construct and decorate. Its interior was inspired by artist Stephen Sills and designer John Saladino. The majority of the apartment's furnishings were purchased in New York and shipped to California. The remaining furniture was constructed specifically for the set.

While most dwellings designed on sound stages do not include ceilings, the Turner apartment was an exception. Walton conferred with cinematographer Rotunno for the on-set lighting and both agreed that windows should provide the source of light, hoping for a more natural flow of illumination throughout the set.

Alongside Henry's physical rehabilitation is his emotional "rebirth." To coincide with Henry's emotional progression, the filmmakers made modifications involving set design, lighting and costumes.

The interiors of Henry's apartment advanced from a cold and dull aura (prior to the accident) to the softer, more lustrous ambiance following his release from the rehabilitation clinic. The gradual shift in lighting reflected the redevelopment of Henry's emotional perceptions.

"We wanted to reflect the rather cold and blinkered life that Henry had been leading," said Walton. "We tried to withhold a good deal of life and color from the early part of the film and use a cool, restrained palette. This part of the film is quite leanly decorated. When Henry goes to the rehab clinic, the look becomes more dreamlike and begins to gain visual vitality and energy."[21]

Another technical aspect that complemented Henry's change was the use of wider-angled shots of the Turner apartment and the inclusion of open doorways, revealing unlimited possibilities for Henry that may lie behind.

Costume designer Ann Roth also participated in Henry's evolution with the selection of clothing worn throughout his rehabilitation. Before the accident, Henry sports the standard courtroom attire of Savile Row, described by Roth as "pared-down, no-detail clothes that don't catch your eye. They make no comment; they are self-contained, all-in-one clothes."[22]

Following the accident, Henry begins to wear clothes that are casual and comfortable, selected with a lack of concern for criticism. To complement the easygoing attire, makeup–hair supervisor J. Roy Helland transformed Harrison from the slicked-back moderate-maintenance style of the old Henry, to the boyish, bangs-on-the-forehead look of the new Henry. Ford placed a stone in his sneaker to give himself a lethargic and awkward gait, a common characteristic of most rehabilitations.

Because his scenes would be shot out of order, Ford tracked Henry's physical progress on index cards and referred to them during filming. The cards had three separate categories: physical capacities, mental skills and speaking skills. Numbering the cards from zero to 10 to track the stages of Henry's rehabilitation, Ford knew precisely what would be required of his performance at any given time.

"When you shoot a film out of sequence," explained the actor, "it's easy to get confused on where the character should be, and we didn't want to make that mistake. Accuracy was everything to us."[23]

Ford also relied on the timely assemblage of footage by editor Sam O'Steen to keep abreast of Henry's progress.

"People have almost a superstitious resistance to looking at a film in the shooting process," said Ford. "But as I was going through a rehabilitation — an event that must show a clear progress — I wanted to see it that way. So we did."[24]

In November 1990, the infamous European publication *News of the World* published a written apology to Ford. This followed a court hearing concerning allegations stating that Ford acted in an unprofessional manner during the filming of *Indiana Jones and the Last Crusade*. This gossip — combined with other fraudulent incidents reported to have taken place in his hometown of Jackson Hole, Wyoming — appeared in his hometown newspapers, one article entitled "Indiana Jones? He's the Wyoming Wimp."

The complete text of the apology, entitled "We're Sorry Harrison Ford," read as follows:

> In the issues of *Sunday Magazine* dated 4th December 1988 and 7th May 1989 we published two articles concerning Harrison Ford, the world renowned and respected film actor. The articles caused Mr. Ford and his family considerable harm and distress. As a result Mr. Ford issued a writ for libel. The first article alleged that Mr. Ford had behaved in an inconsiderate and arrogant manner on the set of the latest Indiana Jones film, *Indiana Jones and the Last Crusade*, and that his cowardice on the set, in refusing to do stunts, was regarded with contempt by the stunt men. The second article concerned Mr. Ford's behavior in his home town, and portrayed him as arrogant and unpleasant. In addition, the article alleged that Mr. Ford had caused a serious accident, injuring people, and then attempted to cover it up. Other incidents were alleged which portrayed Mr. Ford as confused and obsessed with a tough screen image which he could not live up to. Both of these articles also suggested that Mr. Ford's marriage was in difficulties as a consequence. We now accept that the allegations contained in both of the articles were untrue and without foundation. We unreservedly withdraw them and apologize to Mr. Ford and his family. We have agreed to pay Mr. Ford a substantial sum by way of damages and legal fees in addition to undertaking not to repeat the articles or what was said in them. We will also apologize to Mr. Ford in open court. Mr. Ford did not embark on this litigation to make financial profit from it. Accordingly he will be making a payment to charity which, as a result of this settlement, will be substantial.[25]

Principal photography for *Regarding Henry* concluded as scheduled during the month of December of that year. Normally, the end of filming is the time for actors to clean out their trailers and bid adieu to colleagues and friends. But such was not the case for Harrison Ford.

"I go to dailies," said Ford, "I see various cuts of the film, I attend test screenings, I involve myself in post-production right up until they begin to strike the prints of the negative. Then the process is over, the case is closed, and I go on to another one."[26]

The film's premiere was held on the upper East Side of New York City on Monday, June 25, 1991. Following the screening, a benefit party for the National Head Injury Foundation was held in the Rainbow Room at Rockefeller Center. Guests included Ford and wife Melissa; Nichols and wife Diane Sawyer; and *Henry* co-stars Bill Nunn and Mikki Allen. Other attendees included Nichols' pal Carly Simon with husband Tim Hart, Glenn Close, Kenneth Branagh, Marlo Thomas, Robert F. Kennedy, Jr., and *Prime-Time* executive producer Rick Kaplan, among others.

The film, released on July 10, made $43 million — a failure considering Ford's presence. Thwarted by negative reviews (mostly stating that Mike Nichols had lost his touch), Ford was quick to defend his director and friend: "I was very surprised on the basis of which Mike Nichols was attacked. Mike was criticized because the Mike that critics knew to be sophisticated and flinty had made a movie that was emotional, and they just said 'That's not Mike. He's just trying to take advantage of the sentimentality of the '80s.' That just infuriated me. Mike is incapable of that kind of insincerity. To have his work dismissed that way I thought was completely unfair."[27]

Recalling a specific moment from the film, Ford acknowledged that there were elements of both Henrys that, to a certain extent, were present within him.

"There's a scene at the beginning, when Henry goes to his daughter's room and makes a so-called apology for yelling at her that just ends up starting things all over again," recalled the actor. "That's something I recognize from my own experience with my kids, and something my father did to me."[28]

In reflection of the phrase "live and learn," Ford looks back at the neglect of his previous marriage as an analogy to Henry Turner's avoidance of his family and the dangers inherent if the responsibilities and priorities of family man and working man are not clearly established: "That's one of the reasons I decided to do *Regarding Henry*.... It's the story of a man who cares more for his job than for his wife and children. It's only after he undergoes a trauma that he realizes what's really important in life: his family.[29]

"This second time around," he said, "I have no intention of blowing it. I'm still as dedicated an actor as I ever was, but now I know when to draw the line. While I'm on the set, nothing else matters but the role I'm in at that moment. But once shooting is over, I forget about it and head home, ready for my wife and kids. And I want things to be normal and calm. I don't appreciate excitement off the set."[30]

Although the negative effects his profession have had on his personal life are standard issue, Ford remains focused and passionate about his craft. "It's crucial to be happy with what you're doing," said Ford. "You can't have a high self-esteem and you can't love others if you don't like your job. I enjoy being an actor because it lets me control my own life and the pace at which I do things.

"I can take or leave a project," the actor continued. "I can pick and choose the movies I want to make. These things are important to me. As for the stardom, the money, the awards — they're all secondary. They don't mean a thing if a person isn't happy."[31]

26

AT WAR WITH IRISH TERRORISTS ...
AND TOM CLANCY

By August of 1991, Ford was ready for a break from the roles he referred to as "coat-and-tie jobs"—the kind that required him to carry a briefcase and play someone who was physically inactive. More than two years had passed since he finished work on *Indiana Jones and the Last Crusade*, and he had played two lawyers in a row.

He was offered the lead role as an executive whose daughter is kidnapped in Paramount's *Night Ride Down*—a Joel Silver project set during the 1935 Pullman porters strike—but turned it down on August 13, 1991.

"I thought if I didn't use my license to do action-adventure, then pretty soon it wouldn't be viable," he said. "I figured it was time to roll around in the mud."[1]

Meanwhile, Brandon Tartikoff, the new studio chief at Paramount, was eager to proceed with sequels to *The Hunt for Red October*—the 1990 box office hit based on Tom Clancy's best-selling novel. He saw them as a series of "tent-pole" films that would be sure fire moneymakers. Tartikoff not only increased the budget for the first sequel, *Patriot Games*, from $28 million to $35 million, but also wanted assurance that Alec Baldwin would reprise the role of CIA analyst Jack Ryan and sign to a three-picture contract at $4 million per film.[2]

Contract negotiations with Baldwin proved difficult. The main stumbling block seemed to be Baldwin's commitment to the Broadway revival of *A Streetcar Named Desire*, even though it later turned out that the scheduling conflict might have been resolved. In any case, Paramount was aware that Ford was seeking action-oriented material, after having previously rejected the lead role of Jim Garrison (ultimately played by Kevin Costner) in Oliver Stone's *JFK*. The studio approached him with the *Patriot Games* project and on August 23 offered him a $9 million contract to play Jack Ryan.[3]

Ford's acceptance brought "a great sense of relief," Phillip Noyce, director of *Patriot Games*, said. "Because the worst thing that can happen to a film is that it doesn't have a star and you can't find the right person. Usually in that case the film gets put on the shelf."[4]

Mace Neufeld, producer of *The Hunt for Red October* and *Patriot Games*, had worked with Ford in 1978 on Robert Aldrich's *The Frisco Kid*. He recalled trying unsuccessfully to get Ford to work on some projects, including *No Way Out* and *The*

Hunt for Red October. Neufeld had envisioned Ford as Jack Ryan from the beginning. The actor had admired the *Red October* script but turned down the role because the film centered on the Russian submarine commander Marko Ramius, ultimately played by Sean Connery. "But the biggest problem for me was the setting," Ford said. "I thought, 'Who the hell wants to go see a submarine movie?'" He added: "Not doing that film was one of the biggest mistakes of my career."[5]

The *Patriot Games* role offered him the opportunity to deal with ideas within the context of action — affording an excellent (and infrequent) opportunity to explore a character of some complexity against an action background. Ryan finds himself in morally complex circumstances, he said. "I find just that kind of complexity interesting. I'm not playing a hero; I'm playing a person in these circumstances. I'm trying to help describe how one might feel in these circumstances given this background, and I'm not asking anyone to set Jack Ryan up as a hero. I want you to feel, and that's all." Rather than play a hero, Ford said, "You play a human being who has a certain set of circumstances, who has a life, a job, a wardrobe. You don't play a 'hero.' What was interesting about Indiana Jones, for instance, was not that he was a hero but that he was indomitable."[6]

Ford was also intrigued by the irony of the situation in which Ryan is involved and that he has to return to the very career that nearly destroyed the wellbeing of his family. The story unfolds during a lecture-travel trip to London, accompanied by his wife Cathy (Anne Archer) and daughter, Sally (Thora Birch). Ryan, an ex–Marine and retired CIA analyst, witnesses an attempt by Irish terrorists to assassinate a relative of the royal family, Lord Holmes (James Fox). He intervenes by disarming terrorist Sean Miller (Sean Bean) and killing Miller's younger brother. This incident sets off a series of confrontations following Miller's escape from prison, and Ryan is thrust back into the line of duty to protect his family and himself from the avenging terrorist.

Of Ford's performance in *Patriot Games*, Neufeld said: "What you see in this movie is Harrison using all of the combinations of characters he's played in various films — the cop, Indiana Jones, Han Solo, the lawyer from *Presumed Innocent* — and he kind of rolls them all into one to give a very, very, very interesting Jack Ryan."[7]

Neufeld recalled finding a letter from Tom Clancy in his files that read: "I went to see *Witness* last night, and you're absolutely right. Harrison Ford is the perfect Jack Ryan. Wait 'til you read the first chapter of the new book I'm writing, *Patriot Games* and you'll see."[8] But Clancy reportedly had some early reservations about Ford, suggesting he was too old to play Ryan. Ford observed that Clancy was satisfied until other issues arose — with all the author's criticisms winding down to nothing more than a lack of understanding of the filmmaking process.

Clancy was initially displeased with liberties taken by screenwriters W. Peter Iliff and Donald Stewart in their transformation of his novel and repeatedly raised issues during the pre-production phase of *Patriot Games*. His objections were most notable during script meetings. Noyce recalled that the author would interrupt sessions with argumentative faxes and phone calls on a daily basis. "He sent me reams of faxed comments, all of which were appreciated. His almost anal-compulsive attention to detail saved me a lot of research," Noyce said.[9]

As the comments from the author continued, however, the task of pampering him by providing the most accurate translation of his novel became tiresome. Clancy, moreover, complained about discourteous treatment by Paramount and a lack of cooperation from the filmmaking team — which was in contrast, he said, with his experience with *Red October*. "My assumption was that because of the success of that movie, together we could generate a partnership in which both sides respected each other," he said. "That didn't happen in this case."[10] In contrast, Neufeld recalled he found Clancy's attitude distressing because he felt he'd treated him with the utmost respect. He explained: "We'd spent enormous amounts of time with Tom, and there were enormous numbers of changes made as a result of good suggestions that Tom made. But in the movie business nobody ever gets 100 percent of what he wants."[11]

Scott Turow, author of *Presumed Innocent*, understood of Clancy's concerns. "But you have to recognize that a lot of what's precious to you isn't precious to somebody else," Turow said. "When Sidney Pollack bought the rights to the book, he told me some idea he had and I made a face. He said, 'Look. It's your book, but it's my movie.'"[12]

Neufeld acknowledged that the filmmakers have to be concerned about offending the author and alienating fans of the book, but emphasized the difficulty in doing so when adapting pages to the screen. "The biggest one is getting the screenplay right," he said. "Once you get that right, the rest of it then seems to me to be much easier. But the first thing is the script. I love to work with books, although they are extraordinarily difficult to do, because you have to retain the spirit of the book, and as much of the detail as you can, while selecting just key scenes."[13]

The process of adapting a novel (especially one of more than 400 pages such as *Patriot Games*) is always difficult and controversial. Director Noyce readily affirmed that there would always be something that an author feels is important that is ultimately ignored or not implemented as it was originally envisioned: "I tried not to become too concerned about Tom's concerns and just to make the best adaptation and the best film we could possibly make."[14]

He also noted that Clancy had sold the rights to Paramount for $1 million, so he really could not end his relationship with the studio. In the end, the author was satisfied with the results achieved by Neufeld and crew, so much so that he ultimately agreed to sell them the rights to his novels *Clear and Present Danger* and *The Sum of All Fears*.

The four-month pre-production schedule for *Patriot Games* required an immense amount of research into territory unfamiliar to the filmmakers. They conferred with people in Naval Intelligence, the CIA and anti-terrorism organizations in the United States and England. George Churchill Coleman, commander of SO-13 (Special Operation 13), Scotland Yard's anti-terrorism branch, was an invaluable advisor both before and during pre-production. During production, Wilf Knight, a retired veteran of 26 years with the Metropolitan Police, acted as a special consultant regarding British law enforcement and terrorist activity.

In order to familiarize themselves with their characters as terrorists, actors Patrick Bergin (Kevin O'Donnell) and Polly Walker (Annette) spent a weekend in an anti-terrorism training program with the British Special Air Service (SAS). While there, they received weapons instruction and took part in a mock kidnapping of an individual whom they delivered to a ship off the English coast. Bergin and Walker had to stay in character all the time. "I was not an actress doing research for a role but a terrorist preparing for a mission," Walker said. Bergin recalled that everyday objects took on a new significance. "It's another world you step into which is fascinating," he said, "but also quite frightening."[15]

For Noyce, the task of translating the story to film centered on conveying the frightening nature of that world of action and violence, rather than merely emphasizing action and violence.

Because the first version of the script "was mainly an action film that relied on the biggest explosion, the goriest death, and so on," he declined the offer to direct the project. ("Well," he admitted, "it wasn't really a *no* no. I'm not brain-damaged.") After signing on, Noyce worked on rewriting to try "to make it scary, but avoid making the action scenes about the action as opposed to about the audience's fear of things."[16]

That effort worked. Neufeld noted that the film's "threatening" tone earned it an R rating, not the PG-13 he had hoped to get by avoiding graphic violence and sex. "We consciously, from the beginning, tried to tone our violence down, but we have to have it," Neufeld said. "That's part of the story."[17]

Although integral to the story, violence is not exalted, as Ford pointed out. "It is not a football game to Jack Ryan. This is an important idea, one that was not so clear in the book, and one that is a worthy addition to the story."[18]

Actor and director were in accord on that central point. Explaining his feelings about film violence, Noyce did not permit audiences to feel that human life is meaningless or to view the bloody mangling of bodies and tearing of limbs as merely entertaining episodes without implications. The characters must feel the implications of violent actions as well, he said. "In this film, it's very important that Jack Ryan has remorse. Because it gives value to loss of life, even the loss of the life of the man whom you would most like to see dead in the world, and who would most like to kill you."[19]

Ford noted that *Patriot Games* is about the human cost of violence; when certain circumstances compel Ryan to defend his family take action, he feels conflicted about it. These observations exemplify his notion of dealing with ideas within the context of action and exploring a character of some complexity set against an action-oriented background. Ryan, he said, is a reluctant participant in the action, but the mystery of the situation in which he finds himself and his instincts and training ultimately pull him in. Furthermore, rage also plays a part, he added. "I think it's a fairly complex answer, and I try to give it complex expression. He was a little embarrassed by the fact that he really would just get pissed off.

"But," Ford continued, "I think there's much more to that. He is an expert in combat training. He did see these two guys.... There's a moment there when instinct and bile combine to cause him to wade into the middle—besides, if we didn't do that, we wouldn't have a story. So I had to find the best possible way to give expression to a nature that might do that kind of thing, and I believe it works."[20]

Ford admitted to a degree of sympathy for the goals of the IRA. He revealed a story told in his family that his grandmother had removed the gold fillings out of her teeth and sent them to the IRA for funding. (Ford emphasized that her story was not about the IRA directly, but only peripherally.) His sympathy does not, however, extend to the methods of the IRA or anyone else who practices acts of terrorism. Although terrorism has worked in previous endeavors throughout history, he does consider it to be an unacceptable form of behavior.

In the film, Noyce attempted to bring out an edge in the terrorists, who represent a fictitious renegade IRA faction, intending that audiences would not find their activities acceptable. But there is an element of truth in the story, he said, noting that Irish extremist groups have in fact perpetrated terrorist acts in the past, but that his film was not a sensationalizing of the truth.

But the story of *Patriot Games* is more about personal conflict than political acts, however, as Sean Bean pointed out: "From the moment Ryan kills his brother, Miller's focus becomes entirely Jack Ryan. Kevin and Annette maintain a political agenda throughout, while Sean Miller replaces political action with a personal vendetta."[21] The conflict centers on family: Miller consumed by the need to avenge his brother's death, and Ryan fixated on protecting his family from further harm. As one of the teasers for *Patriot Games* put it: "Not for honor. Not for country. For his wife and child."

Anne Archer credited Ford with the effort needed to create an emotional tie between the audience and the Ryans. The movie works better, she said, "because you get behind these people; there's a kind of humanity there and you care about them. You're worried about what's going to happen to them so it makes the action more 'Oh, my God!' You get more emotionally involved.

"Their marriage had been in trouble, their lives had been too separated because of Jack's relationship with the CIA, and it was hard on Cathy. But they turn over a new leaf in the beginning of *Patriot Games*. Jack's not with the CIA any more; he's become a professor. They take this wonderful trip to Europe to try and have a child — it's like a fresh start in life. Then, of course, everything starts to unravel."[22]

She continued, "I think whatever problems they were dealing with were exacerbated by Jack's 'classified' work with the CIA. But when it becomes a question of 'real' survival for her family, she wants Jack to go back to the CIA because she knows his skills as an analyst are unmatched by anyone. She's also operating from the most basic instincts as a wife and mother which is to do whatever it takes to protect her family."[23]

Archer, who received both Academy Award and Golden Globe nominations for her work in *Fatal Attraction*, said she had one reservation about the role: that she would be portraying a wife and a mother yet again. "On the positive side, it had Harrison Ford, so everyone was going to see this movie — no one has an audience like Harrison Ford. It's based on a novel by Tom Clancy, one of the most popular novelists in the world, so this movie was going to get a lot of attention." It being a Paramount film and one directed by Phillip Noyce with the potential for sequels were a few of the other reasons she considered the role. "There were so many reasons why I should do it for my career that I put aside the fact that she was a wife and mother."[24]

Principal photography for *Patriot Games* began in England on Saturday, November 2, 1991; cast and crew shot for about a month throughout London and on the

Flanked by director Noyce and Samuel L. Jackson at Annapolis Naval Academy (Nimitz Library Special Collections, 1992).

sound stages of Pinewood Studios. The filmmakers had to take extra precautions (including requiring the use of security badges) while filming in London because of recent IRA activity in and around the city.

The Royal Navy College at Greenwich substituted for Buckingham Palace, the location in the novel of the initial terrorist incident. Special effects supervisor George Gibbs—whose work in both *Indiana Jones and the Temple of Doom* and *Who Framed Roger Rabbit?* were rewarded with Academy Awards—took extreme caution with the special effect explosions so as not to damage the historic architecture at the location.

Back in the United States, Noyce, Neufeld and Ford toured CIA headquarters in Langley, Virginia, an activity the agency had not permitted previously. Ford's involvement helped to open certain closed doors. "They greeted him like a movie star," Noyce said, "and it meant that we saw a lot more of the CIA than most people have seen before. Because we had Harrison doing research, they let us into the satellite analysis room."[25]

Ford said the "rather extraordinary access" they were granted—because he asked—meant "we saw things that added to our sense of reality and aided in the replication of that reality."[26] These observations included not only the physical details but also "the energy of the environment—the way people dress, behave and relate to their fellow workers."[27]

Although the hosts were extremely generous and cooperative, they did set specific limitations, including permitting photography only in the main entrance and lobby. Production designer Joseph Nemec III (*Terminator 2: Judgment Day*) was able to make rough sketches of inner offices—which Paramount later recreated in detail on Stage 5 at the studio lot in Burbank. Members of the production crew had to sign confidentiality releases and were not at liberty to discuss the classified areas they observed.

The CIA set in Burbank took about eight weeks to construct and occupied 3,500 square feet. It consisted of a satellite analysis room, analysts' work cubicles, the data analysis room and Room 4337—an operations room that surveyed satellite imagery. Video Image created special video graphics for the terminals on the set. In September during pre-production, Nemec, associate producer Lis Kern and Video Image visual effects supervisor John Wash discussed interior specifics. Nemec recalled that the CIA would not allow them access to certain computer graphics information like the formatting or blocking of information. "So in our initial meeting, we covered everything from the type of generic news footage that would play on television monitors to the size and color of the font images appearing on the 23 computer screens."[28]

The shooting of the scene in Room 4337—in which CIA personnel are monitoring a raid on a terrorist training camp in North Africa via satellite—provided perhaps the one best example of Noyce and Ford's method of doing a scene. Noyce described the scene as disturbing, but was fully prepared for audiences to view it as pure entertainment.

Ryan's reaction to the technologically cold slaughter depicted like a video game on large wall screens registers primarily as incomprehensibility and disbelief at the lack of humanity involved. "The dilemma Jack faces is a crisis of confidence," Ford said. "I think he also feels dehumanized by the distance and the sanitary nature of their elimination."[29]

He explained, "I prepared for that sequence by not preparing myself for it. Phillip said, 'Come on, let's go see the set of the satellite analysis room. Do you want to see the tapes?' I said, 'No. Set the camera up, have the room set up and fill it with the people, and invite me in like it said in the script, to a place I've never been before, and let's shoot it.' I knew that it should be a complex moment for the character, but I had no very clear plan about what I was going to do under those circumstances."[30]

That was typical of him, Noyce said. "Harrison is never concerned with technique. He always hones in on the emotional focus of a scene. He makes Jack a most believable agent. He plays Jack as Everyman, which allows us to be in his place."[31]

Noyce had nothing but praise for his leading man's talent and contributions. "Working with someone like Harrison was just the opposite of intimidating—it was liberating," he said, citing Ford's realism, research and thoughtful, analytical approach. "When I first met Harrison and we flew to Washington to shoot interiors at the CIA, if he wasn't already Jack Ryan, he certainly was when he hopped off the plane. Some actors metamorphose into the character, and then the separation between the character and themselves becomes impossible to define."[32]

Ford required no direction, said Noyce, who believed the best direction is always the least amount possible. He explained: "I always wait for the actor to deliver what he or she has to offer. If it doesn't work, then say something. But before you know what they have to deliver, why fill them up with a lot of bullshit? The least said the better. The most important thing is that the actor is prepared before the film starts, that the choices that they will make will come out of something that's very deep, as opposed to 'Can you smile just a bit more?' or 'Cock your eye' or something which is only on the surface."[33]

Neufeld cited Ford's insight into the collaborative nature of filmmaking, claiming that it's that kind of smart dramaturgy that the actor has that is beneficial to any project and any director who ignores those contributions does so at their own peril.

Noyce agreed. "He's worked in so many different styles for so many different directors — he's a walking encyclopedia of film knowledge. He's a man who in prepping a scene gives detailed thoughts to each sequence — he'll help the writer, the cinematographer, the director — yet in the execution of the scene, he becomes an actor again, completely cooperative."[34] Compared to Mel Gibson ("too perfect") and Arnold Schwarzenegger ("too well endowed"), "Harrison Ford is the way we would be, if we could be our most heroic selves."[35]

Questions about the purpose and usefulness of the CIA caused Ford some concern. "Obviously, to do this I had to come to terms with how I felt about the CIA and the intelligence community, with its history of political manipulation from within and from without," he explained. "Like every imperfect machine, one tries to control it and make it work as best as it can. And if the question is, 'Did I find anyone at the CIA to admire?' The answer is yes, I did. I found people of considerable intelligence and sophistication who honestly felt that our form of government was the last best hope for mankind and dedicated their lives in service to this operation.

"And Jack Ryan is not without his own sensitivity to the issues of whether or not the work he's doing under the auspices of the CIA is good or not. This isn't 'Let's kick ass for the old red, white and blue.' I wouldn't be happy playing a character that was so unthinking."[36]

Although he said he considered whether his taking the role would add to the CIA's credibility, he also thought, "Let's not take yourself too seriously, kid." Besides, he said, his responsibility is not dealing with the issues surrounding the CIA. "I am not a politician. I am a craftsperson who sells stories. I'm an assistant storyteller."[37]

Filming resumed for two days in the Mojave Desert in an area near El Centro, California, that doubled for the North African terrorist training camp. In addition to filming the ground shots, the production used special satellite and video photography for playback in Room 4337. Video Image worked for months manipulating the photographed images to create the impression of a satellite image capturing a covert military operation in progress on the Earth far below.

Lis Kern declared, "I think just the impersonal nature of not seeing an actual, live-action attack, but seeing it actually through the infrared photography creates a sort of an icy quality."[38]

The simulation of thermal image photography was necessary for the effect. It was produced by determining that any object producing heat must be black, and any cool object must be the color of the surrounding environment — desert, in this case. Dark materials, such as peat moss, cork and fuller's dirt, were added to the ground explosions because normal flame and smoke would not have registered properly. In addition to the use of these materials to match the color scheme needed for the infrared vision, the ground personnel of the operation were outfitted with special gray body stockings and black makeup.

What was once a whale-watching pond at Marineland Park in Palos Verdes, California, became the location for exterior scenes of the Ryan residence overlooking Chesapeake Bay in Maryland. The six-week conversion required the installation of a duck pond, boathouse, apple orchards and the construction of the house — a 1920s era Maryland colonial — on the 5,000-square-foot area. Seventeen palm trees were uprooted, safely stored and later replanted at the site following filming.

On Stage 18 at Paramount, Nemec designed the interior of the home around "a modern approach in a classically constructed interior," he said. "Phillip wanted the house to reflect the solidity of the family. The Ryans are a contemporary family with a strong sense of security in their lives and their professions."[39]

Ford also insisted that the home have a traditional look. "I wanted not to have to play Jack Ryan as a person who had bought into American values. I wanted it to be understood, to be felt," he said.[40]

Relocating to Annapolis, Maryland, for the week of November 30–December 6, the cast and crew received permission to film in one of the U.S. Naval Academy's classrooms in Sampson Hall — where scenes of Ryan instructing a group of midshipmen were shot as well as an office scene involving Ford and his Academy colleague, portrayed by Samuel L. Jackson.

Prof. Craig Symonds, chairman of the History Department, made these locations readily available for the production.

As a memento, Symonds added Ford's framed photo to an area of Sampson Hall that honors individuals who have had an impact on the lives of Academy midshipmen. Ford's photo remains there with the caption "J Ryan: Associate Professor."

The Academy also granted permission for exterior filming at Gate 3 — located, ironically, at the intersection of Hanover Street and Maryland Avenue — for the scenes in which Ryan thwarts an assassination attempt against his own life.

Elsewhere, U.S. special effects coordinator Dale Martin (*RoboCop*) visited Navy wave tank facilities, where he conducted research into the techniques of wave creation and control. This insight was used in the last moments of the film for the final confrontation between Ryan and Sean Miller on Chesapeake Bay. The scene required a high-speed boat chase amidst turbulent waves, torrential rain and high winds. Rear-screen projection on locations including the open sea and the B-tank at Paramount provided the final footage. The six-minute sequence, which Noyce considered to be a small though very important part of the total production schedule, proved to be by far the most technically challenging and innovative task of the entire production.

Based on his experience of filming on water for *Red October*, Neufeld was certainly not anxious to film within the element again. By opting to film within a controlled environment such as the B-tank, considerable guesswork was eliminated and shots were matched more effectively.

For the filming of those scenes, Noyce recalled, "they told me to go up and have a look in the carpark — 'That's where you can film.' I thought they were crazy. I didn't know that Cecil B. DeMille had already built an ocean there for his film *The Ten Commandments* and parted the waters of the Red Sea right there in the carpark at Paramount Pictures. So I went out and, sure enough, there was my car parked in a big swimming pool."[41] (This location was also used for filming of the whale scenes in *Star Trek IV: The Voyage Home.*)

Encircled by eight-foot-high walls, the half-acre lot contained one million gallons of water at a depth of four feet for the water scenes. Atop a dozen 110-foot telephone poles (imported from Oregon) that surrounded the tank, sprinkler systems emitted the appropriate amount of rainfall. Stretched high above, three 60 × 100' silk tarps diffused lights rigged above the water. Powered by aircraft and Chevrolet engines, three wave making machines were installed. Fire hoses and five enormous wind machines were added to further simulate the stormy weather conditions. Dump tanks containing 7,500 gallons of water provided the enormous waves that would torment Ford and Bean inside their 20-foot hydraulically mounted Wellcraft speedboats.

With all of the elements in place and ready for shooting, Neufeld recalled, the production swiftly became a logistical nightmare. "I thought this was my Waterloo. The wind machines broke. The lighting was shooting in the wrong directions. The special effects guys in the water got hypothermia," he said. "And Harrison bumped his head."[42]

Ford complained that the press had overblown the incident: All he got was a rash from his cold, damp clothes, he stated, "Whatever discomfort I went through was nothing next to what other people went through. The stunt men spent 29 days at sea, all night, in all kinds of dangerous conditions, and the tabloids reported that I had been grievously injured and had to be pulled from the bottom of the tank. What I did was bump my head and get a tiny little gash that didn't even require a Band-Aid."[43]

Stunt co-coordinator Steve Boyum described the experience of collaborating with Ford: "Sophisticated movie audiences demand to see the real actor in action. That's difficult unless you're working with an actor like Harrison Ford. He's in incredible physical condition and has great ideas on how to play the scene. He's probably done more action than most of the stuntmen in the business."[44]

Second unit director and stunt coordinator Dave Ellis concurred with Boyum's statement, recalling that he once told the actor that if his acting career amounted to nothing and if he was seeking a new line of employment, he would be welcomed as a stuntman with open arms.

Ford insisted on giving credit where it was due: "I do physical activity, I do not do stunts. I am not a stunt man. I would never undertake to endanger a production by risking myself. I've developed skills in thinking about the physical requirements of action. I'm good at expressing the mental state of someone entering into a dangerous situation. In that direction I contrive as much as possible. But when it comes to the actual stunt itself, there are plenty of pros around for that. Stunts are always done by stunt men."[45]

With the fight sequence between the two principals shot and printed and the

75-day shooting schedule completed, Ford returned to his Wyoming ranch. Following poor audience test screenings, the filmmakers were recalled to the B-tank for re-shooting just five weeks before the proposed release of the film, bringing the production's final budget to $42.5 million.

Of reports that the production was "in trouble," Neufeld asserted, "All of that was blown up way out of proportion. It was about 50 seconds of screen time. And we had an opportunity, after seeing it three or four ways, of spending two days to make it better. And we did, and that's hardly earthshaking news. That happens a lot, particularly on major films."[46]

Ford explained, "We made a mistake. We shot the ultimate moment between Sean Bean and myself underwater, which rendered it in slow motion. The necessary energy of that event was lost. It was all very balletic, and it was an attempt to make a humanistic ending. We knew it had failed when we saw it because it was too soft to express the consequences of the story that had gone before, so we filmed it again."[47]

Days after the Rodney King riots in Los Angeles, Paramount was asked to remove all billboards advertising the film in the South Central Los Angeles area. The billboards read "6-5-92, The Games Begin" and were thought by some to be capable of aggravating the current situation. The advertisement depicted a disgruntled Ford thrusting a handgun point-blank at the observer — and could have easily been considered inappropriate overlooking any community. Furthermore, the film's opening date, June 5, created an unintentional reference to the 1965 Watts Riots.

On the afternoon of Wednesday, June 3, *Patriot Games* had its premiere screening at Mann's Chinese Theater in Hollywood. Prior to the screening, Ford became the 176th screen personality (and more than likely the first in mismatched Converse All-Stars) to place his handprints and footprints into cement, alongside the squares of George Lucas and Steven Spielberg.

Typically not attracted to such Hollywood rituals (especially those scheduled on his wife's birthday), Ford admitted that it was an event he declined to partake in on more than one occasion. In the end, he succumbed only to promote *Patriot Games*.

Two days prior to the world premiere, *Variety* carried a review of the film that caused an uproar among Paramount executives. Irish-American critic Joseph McBride called the film "a right-wing cartoon of the current British-Irish political situation."[48] In an apology to Paramount, *Variety* editor and former motion picture executive Peter Bart claimed that the review "was, to put it in a word, unprofessional." In retaliation, Paramount indefinitely withdrew all of its future advertising from the magazine.

Upon its opening weekend, *Patriot Games* grossed an impressive $18.5 million. The film continued strong throughout the summer season and earned an estimated $83 million ($178 million worldwide), classifying Ford as the uncontested new and improved Jack Ryan. It wasn't long before the character was likened as the "James Bond of the '90s."

In the fall of 1991, Warner Bros. re-released 1982's *Blade Runner* to audiences on the West Coast for a four-week run, resulting in record-breaking attendance. Part of what drew the public back to the theaters to relive the "cult classic" was the chance to view it the way Ridley Scott had intended. Barry Reardon, president of Warner

Bros. Distributing Corporation, discovered a 70mm print of the film and ascertained that it was Ridley's original cut. *The Director's Cut* was the new subtitle, and the differences were drastic — to a technophobe.

In addition to having a fine-tuned audio track, the new version omitted scenes of Deckard (Ford) firing his weapon and being raised agonizingly above the ground by his nostrils. It included a previously filmed and unreleased "dream sequence" involving a beautiful slow-motion shot of a unicorn, suggesting the possibility that Deckard himself was a Replicant. (In the summer of 2000, during an on-line interview with Amazon.com, Ford said, "It was a question of some discussion and I argued against it. My point to Ridley was that the audience deserved, even required, to have someone on-screen that they felt they could emotionally invest in."[49]) In addition, the original bleak and abrupt conclusion was reinstated, leaving audiences of the 90s with the option of inventing the conclusion they may find appropriate. Yet, what was most significant — and apparently much appreciated — was the removal of Ford's widely panned voice-over narration — a classic example of "better late than never."

The film was re-released on September of 1992 to a limited number of screens and earned an estimated $4 million-plus in box office sales. Shortly thereafter, it was placed on the Library of Congress list of protected films.

Meanwhile, Ford received a number of offers, including leads in *The Shawshank Redemption*, Paul Verhoeven's *Mistress of the Seas* (later re-credited and re-titled as Reny Harlin's *Cutthroat Island*), *I Love Trouble* (with Julia Roberts) and *Crisis in the Hot Zone*—a project that evolved into *Outbreak*, starring Dustin Hoffman.

The Fugitive, coincidentally another role that had been offered to Alec Baldwin, came Ford's way when Baldwin declined after Warner Bros. rejected the concept developed by Walter Hill and David Giler. Ford actually had been interested in the property three years earlier when Stephen Frears (*Dangerous Liaisons*, *The Grifters*) was being optioned as the film's director. Following Frears' withdrawal from the project, Ford lost interest — but only temporarily.

27

ON THE RUN FOR THE MONEY

The Fugitive told the story of Dr. Richard Kimble. Accused of murdering his wife, Kimble is on the run from the law in an attempt to prove his innocence.

The original television series, which formed the basis of the film, premiered in September 1963 and lasted four years on ABC. On August 29, 1967, 72 percent of television viewers watched *The Fugitive*'s final episode "Judgment"—the moment when the doctor's innocence was finally proven. It was the most widely seen television episode ever, and maintained that record until the 1980 final episode of *Dallas* in which J.R.'s assassin was revealed.[1]

The idea of making the television series into a film was cooked up in the early 1970s. P.A. Arnold Kopelson, who represented the original television series' executive producer Quinn Martin, became interested in purchasing the rights (owned by Keith Barish of Taft/Barish Productions). Kopelson was unable to negotiate. Ten years later, when their partnership was severed, he made the purchase.

"It has always been my dream to produce a major motion picture based upon the series," said Kopelson. "The story is one we can all relate to. We sympathize with Dr. Richard Kimble, falsely accused of killing his wife. We know he's innocent and root for him to find the real killer."[2]

Ford added, "He's well-off, has control over his life and circumstances, he's in love with his wife and doing something he loves to do … then he gets caught in a shitstorm."[3]

Ford was hesitant to accept the project when Kopelson first approached him with the script. It was the third revision of the draft that ultimately attracted him.

The producer recalled his jubilation when Ford finally signed on to the project. "This guy is as big as they come. Harrison's name on a marquee opens a movie anywhere in America. His name on a marquee opens a movie in Bangkok. That's the definition of a movie star."[4]

With a leading man committed, Kopelson began the search for the appropriate director.

"Right around the time we were looking for a director, I saw *Under Siege*. My immediate response was 'I want [Andrew] Davis to direct *The Fugitive* and I immediately began discussing that with Warner Bros."[5]

Ford agreed with Kopelson's selection: "It seemed we'd found a director who could bring the kind of energy and excitement that this project deserved."[6]

Known for directing political thrillers, Davis' credits also included *The Package*, *Code of Silence* and *Above the Law*. Unfamiliar with the original television series, Davis explained his fresh approach to the film: "The movie is a modern version of a classic thriller. The challenge for me was to make it seem fresh and alive in ways that people wouldn't expect and still satisfy all of the strengths of the TV series. The main difference is that this film has a much more in-depth view of Richard Kimble and what caused him to be a man on the run," said Davis.[7]

The director continued, "What *The Fugitive* has is a very strong dramatic spine. If you start off with a good spine, you can't go wrong. Of course you've seen it before; it's a classic 'hunted man' story, told with a little twist. It's almost a myth."[8]

Davis said he deliberately stayed away from watching lots of episodes. "We knew we wanted to make a thriller that could stand alone as a complete story without referring back to the series," he explained.[9]

"It had to be more than a chase film, the story of a bungled burglary," said Davis. "And since neither Harrison nor Tommy Lee nor I were familiar with the show, it made it easier to look at with a fresh eye."[10]

Ford explained that the film had the basics of the story from the series, but contained more scope and breadth. "There's an overlay — a medical mystery, not in the original — which gives a great canvas to work on, and I think that's appropriate," said Ford.[11]

One element that remained faithful to the original was the obsessive pursuit of Kimble by U.S. Deputy Marshall Samuel Gerard.

Having directed Tommy Lee Jones in two previous films (*The Package* and *Under Siege*), Davis chose the acclaimed actor to portray Gerard. Jones (whose other acting credits include *Love Story*, *Coal Miner's Daughter*, *The Client*, *Heaven and Earth*, *Natural Born Killers*, *Blown Away*, *Cobb*, *Men in Black* and *Double Jeopardy*) was rewarded with a Best Supporting Actor nomination for his performance in Oliver Stone's *JFK*.

For Jones, accepting the role was a sure thing: "I've worked with Arnold before, I've worked with Andy before, and I've never had the opportunity to work with Harrison Ford. Those are reasons enough for going to work."[12]

Davis regarded Jones as an indisputable asset to any project, and was enthused to reunite with him for *The Fugitive*. "I think he brings a critical balance to the film in terms of his and Harrison's strengths; the dynamics of their relationship are explosive."[13]

Davis continued, "The drama is in the bad guys. Stanley Kubrick has made a career out of loving villains, and I tend to lean that way myself. I started my career in journalism. I always wanted to be a muckraker, so I'm drawn to people to stir things up.

"With *The Fugitive*, the interesting thing is that Tommy is the pursuer, but not the bad guy. He has to carry the mantle of the antagonist for much of the story, and the power of the film comes from his evolution from an adversary to an ally of Harrison's."[14]

Ford viewed Kimble's on-screen relationship with Gerard as somewhat justifiable, while seemingly on the brink of obsession. "Gerard is just doing his job," stated Ford. "Ultimately, Kimble doesn't care whether or not Gerard believes in his innocence or not. Kimble's sole intent is to find the real bad guy, the person behind the murder."[15]

Jones concurred: "I think the character is meant to be chasing just another fugitive. He has no other motive than to do his job and do it well."[16]

The role of the one-armed man Sykes was portrayed by Andrew Katsulas (*The Sicilian, Someone to Watch Over Me*). "I know I saw an episode or two when I was a kid, but it doesn't really stand out in my mind," the actor said. "Besides, I would have been much too afraid of the one-armed man. He was a scary guy."[17]

Sela Ward was chosen to portray Kimble's slain wife Helen, who appears in the film in flashbacks. "I only had a teeny window of opportunity to say a whole lot about how much these two people love one another so you'll care about the loss," said Ward.[18]

To spice up the film, the filmmakers introduced Anne Eastman (Julianne Moore), the ruthless doctor who betrays Kimble as he roams the hospital corridors in search of evidence. Originally, Ford and Moore were supposed to be romantically involved, but that idea was vetoed when Davis deemed it inconsistent with Kimble's unwavering love of his wife.

Prior to filming, Ford and Davis felt that Kimble's lifestyle and personality were essential elements that would emotionally bond the audience with the characters throughout the film. "Kimble is a very urbane and sophisticated person but not pretentious," explained Ford. "For example, he loves to collect art and display it casually, but he's not a guy who is buying art for vanity or to be known as a collector.

"One evening, Andy and I were discussing doctors in a restaurant," said Ford. "A baby was playing at our table and I asked the maitre d' if it was his child. He said it belonged to a doctor from Northwestern and his wife who were sitting just around the corner. We invited them over for a drink, and we learned that they were longtime friends of Andy's assistant. He appeared the way I already looked. His beard and long hair substantiated my characterization. The doctor, who happened to be an art collector, invited us back to his house to view his collection. The house not only had the art I had been trying to describe, but the architecture that would best articulate the murder. I asked them if we could have our art department see their home. It subsequently became the model for the Kimble house."[19]

The filmmakers disagreed with Ford on the subject of excessive facial hair.

Ford recalled, "The studio was not happy with the beard. They figured they'd paid for the face they wanted to see, so they were very concerned about that.

"My idea for the beard was that I had very little time between the escape and the end of the movie to meet the dramatic obligation of disguise. I could do it as though it were a Peter Sellers movie, with funny noses and glasses, but I wanted a simpler approach. Shaving off the beard changed my appearance."[20]

But there was another reason for wanting the beard, said Ford. "It establishes the guy as slightly idiosyncratic. That, his flowered vest, and the particular kind of art on his walls describes him as a character who is a bit outside of the medical establishment, which comes into play later on in the story."[21]

Davis enthusiastically accepted Ford's fine-tuning of Kimble's physical characteristics. "The idea of being able to have something to change his look was great because you were going to be able to see his bohemian, irreverent, doctorish side. Then he would become a chameleon and change."[22]

The decision to grow the beard became useful when George Lucas called upon Ford to portray a older Indiana Jones in hopes of goosing the slumping ratings of *The Young Indiana Jones Chronicles*. Agreeing under the condition that the filming take place in his hometown of Jackson Hole, Ford arrived on the set on his snowmobile and filmed the required scenes in one day. The episode, entitled "The Mystery of the Blues," aired on ABC on March 13, 1993—a failed attempt to revive the program.

"I really am pleased with *The Young Indiana Jones Chronicles*," Ford said of his friend's efforts. "So I was happy to be a part of it."[23]

During pre-production, the crew visited the University of Chicago Hospitals located on the 184-acre campus in the Hyde Park–South Kenwood section of Illinois. The production used an actual morgue and various other surgical rooms for filming.

Dressed in the appropriate garb, a disguised Ford mingled with a group of unsuspecting medical students to prepare for his role as Dr. Richard Kimble. He met with several doctors and observed various surgical procedures.

Ford said, "I scrubbed up and was able to assist as far as the law allows in a couple of operations. Bits of reality help an audience to believe in what they're seeing."[24]

Ford was given permission to attend an actual heart bypass and arterial unblocking surgery. Surgeon Jim McKinsey recalled, "That man does his research! He wanted to know everything. One scene involves pathology, and he spent time there learning the terminology. He was professional and asked questions constantly."[25]

While in the City Hall area, Ford visited Mayor Richard Daley's office to help promote the city's "Give Graffiti the Brush" program. The charity provided volunteers with thousands of gallons of paint to cover up the areas of the city in need of a makeover. The mayor's administrative assistant, Amy Anzevino, recalled, "Suddenly a lot of secretaries came to see the mayor on pressing business."[26]

Although the script called for the hospital interiors to take place at Cook County Hospital, the crew deemed it impractical to use the facility.

Scouting for the appropriate location, the crew found the now-vacant Shakespeare School in Woodlawn, Illinois. There, nearly a dozen sets were constructed including a full-scale hospital corridor to accommodate the myoelectric labs and various other rooms. "At first we laid out a corridor with rooms on both sides, but we needed to do something to open up the place. We took one of the walls, with rooms located behind it, and broke through to create a nurses' station. This was no easy task, because with these old buildings, the walls are at least 20 inches thick. It definitely gave my team a tough time," recalled production designer Dennis Washington.[27]

Additionally, the production also constructed Kimble's initial confinement quarters, a police squad room and an interrogation area.

The Fugitive was shot over a 15-week period beginning January 25 on location in North Carolina, Chicago and its suburbs.

Alongside co-producer Peter Macgregor-Scott, special effects supervisor Roy Arbogast and stunt coordinator Terry Leonard, Davis and his crew created what was undoubtedly the most brutally realistic bus-train crash sequence in film history.

Macgregor-Scott said, "You wake up in the morning, and you say, 'What am I going to do today? I'm going to wreck a train!' It's like, it's a wonderful way to start the day!"[28]

The production team insisted on the use of full-scale props rather than relying upon miniatures and/or special effects to ensure a realistic and dramatic effect.

"Both Andy and I feel if you can do things full-size, you're much better off, because you can see the results right away," explained Macgregor-Scott.[29]

"Not to degrade Steven Spielberg," said director Davis, "but he shoots storyboards. There's not a frenetic, accidental, anything-can-happen quality. Basically, my concept is, shoot the shit out of it and use the best pieces. And the rest is fate."[30]

One of the most difficult aspects of this sequence was locating a private railroad that would permit them to film a crash of the necessary magnitude. The Great Smoky Mountains Railway in Dillsboro, North Carolina, was chosen as the site of the choreographed calamity.

Aside from overseeing the film's stunts, *Indiana Jones* veteran Terry Leonard also worked as second unit director. He explained: "The problem with derailing a seven-car, 250,000-pound train is the risk to crew and equipment. So in anticipation of trying to outsmart what the train was going to do, I contacted a number of insurance investigators and told them what we wanted to accomplish. Because they investigate accidental derailments all the time, they were able to tell us what we could reasonably expect to happen once the train hit the bus. We were then able to position the cameras accordingly."[31]

Roughly one dozen cameras were placed in steel-shielded boxes used for combat photography. They were strategically placed alongside the track and installed in the bus and locomotive to capture what producers hoped would be accomplished in the first and only take.

With the cameras in place, the train was set back approximately one mile and pushed toward its collision (it was planned that the train would not exceed 32 m.p.h. Macgregor-Scott recalled, "The trainman pointed the speed gun and said, '32, 36 ... Christ, it's going 42 miles an hour!' It could have been a disaster.... Bang! ... and it was over. And we got what we got. There was no take two on that."[32]

Armed with an explosive charge designed to detonate on impact, the lead locomotive pushed the Department of Corrections bus more than 300 yards in a fiery trail of shattered glass, steel and plastic. To create the illusion of the second locomotive derailing, the production constructed a rail system concealed beneath the topsoil so that it could ride along the tracks yet provide the impression that it had truly derailed.

Through the use of special effects created during post-production, shots of Ford were superimposed over the images of the actual wreck. This helped to provide the sequence that called for his character to outrun the train as it closed in upon him.

Sold to the railway for one dollar, the remnants of the demolished bus, lead engine and train car teetering over the edge of an embankment remain as a tourist attraction.

Although the $1 million event was filmed with near-flawless results, a disaster of a smaller scale but of larger significance to the production occurred.

As man on-the-run Richard Kimble in 1993's *The Fugitive* (Warner Bros., 1993).

While filming a running sequence through dense foliage for the film's trailer, Ford fell and tore a ligament in his right knee.

"When we rehearsed it," recalled Ford, "there had been a hole next to the camera I could run through; when we shot it somebody set a century stand in that hole and I put all my weight on my right leg to cut left to avoid it."[33]

Despite the injury and the complications it could have caused the project, Ford insisted that filming resume. Pressing on, the actor benefited from a genuine limp to offer a more credible fugitive from justice. (In June later that year, he underwent orthoscopic knee surgery in Jackson Hole to remedy the injury.)

The actor also thrust his head into the side of the bus during its chaotic spiral following the train crash. Referring to the actor's penchant for "physical acting" to enhance realism, Macgregor-Scott recalled, "He wanted that crash into the window. I mean, the guy's unreal."[34]

"It's a reality," claimed Ford regarding his responsibility to the audience, "if the audience sees a movie with my face in it and they don't have a good time, they don't put the blame on Andy Davis, they put the blame on me."[35]

Elsewhere, the crew filmed Ford swimming in the bone-chilling 41-degree waters of the Tuckeseigee River to escape capture. To avoid hypothermia between takes, the actor would jump into a portable tub of hot water.

Filming resumed along the Tennessee border at the Cheoah Dam, located on a Cherokee Indian reservation. The tunnel set, in which Kimble is pursued by Gerard and his men, was constructed in Chicago and transported to an area above the dam. Dennis Washington designed a network of tunnels constructed of corrugated metal and concrete with detachable wall segments that would facilitate camera positioning. Dressed in foul weather gear, the crew worked in tight quarters with a live running-water recovery system to provide a dark, dank environment.

To provide adequate lighting while maintaining the set's disturbing atmosphere, grills and grates were added that would appear to be sources of natural light flowing into the drainpipe.

For nearly two days and at an expense of $2 million, the crew and actors filmed the scene that required Ford to dangle over the edge of the pipe. Protected only by a safety harness, the actor swayed precariously high above the raging waters below.

"I don't like heights very much," admitted Ford. "It takes me a minute or two to steel myself for heights, but then I get used to it real quick.... There are a lot of people around to assure the safety of the things I do. I don't worry about it, I have great confidence in them."[36]

The production used six dummies in place of Kimble when he was forced to jump into the raging water below.

Davis was skeptical about filming in his hometown of Chicago; it was Ford who persuaded him to bring the filmmakers to the Windy City.

"Originally, I wasn't even going to try and come to Chicago," said Davis. "I thought that the weather would be too cold and difficult for shooting. But Harrison, having seen several of my prior films shot in Chicago, suggested doing it here. This town has a lot of character, and furthermore, we knew we would have the cooperation of the city, good crews, a rich pool of talent, great sets, and endless resources."[37]

"Chicago," continued Davis, "is definitely a major character in the movie. Harrison and I are both from Chicago, so it was kind of a homecoming. In Kimble's case, the fabric of the city — the jails, the hospital, the Saint Patrick's Day parade, the El — they all become the fabric of his survival."[38]

"Chicago's a familiar milieu for Andy to work in," said Ford. "He knew the town, he knew the locations he might be able to use here…. All the elements which we needed were here, the exciting architecture of the city and the Polish neighborhoods, the Maxwell Street area. There's just so much texture in a city like Chicago."[39]

For the city lockup where Kimble searches for the one-armed man, the production utilized Chicago's City Hall. There, Kimble partakes in a high-speed foot chase with Lt. Gerard and his men. It has an on-screen time of approximately 60 seconds, but the scene took several days to film.

"A scene like this will finally be made up of 20 or 25 cuts," said Ford. "You have to think about how to do it in an efficient way, so you're not busting your ass to get something that will never play all in one shot."[40]

Ford damaged his previously injured right knee cartilage in a scene that required him to run, rather than fall, down the steps to avoid capture. The pain he suffered was not enough to prevent him from continuing. He packed his knee in ice for a brief 15 minutes before he was back in front of the camera.

"You feel terrible," said Davis. "The show must go on, but at the same time, he's in real pain. He's a trouper. He hung in there."[41]

Ford explained the key to his ability to withstand the daily physical abuse endured: "I administer a little Scotch at the end of the day, for medicinal purposes only."[42]

Kimble flees from the lockup by way of Daley Plaza and melts into the annual St. Patrick's Day Parade to evade his pursuers. Photographed earlier, on March 17, the annual event draws thousands of spectators from all over Illinois and neighboring states.

Davis said, "We thought it would provide a wonderful texture to the story for Kimble to get lost within the very fabric of the city. The irony is in the contrast of the celebration of the parade versus the tension of the chase of the fugitive."[43]

With the camera crew in position and the principles on their marks, the scene had to be filmed in one take. Macgregor-Scott recalled, "We just decided to go with it and whatever happened, happened. The people in the parade were doing double takes and saying things like 'Wow, it's Indiana Jones. What's he doing in the pipefitters' union?'"[44]

Filming in that type of situation takes a great deal of concentration and an even greater amount of patience, said Ford. "It's not that much different, except, well, we're working with real people instead of actors. So you do it often enough to get some good moments without people looking into the camera or staring at me."[45]

Taking further advantage of the locations the city had to offer, the production used the Loop section of the El train for the scene in which Kimble confronts Sykes the one-armed-man. The crew filmed the scenes in three consecutive nights during off-hours and finished before rush hour the following morning.

Gerard's offices were located on the twenty-seventh floor of a high-rise building next door to the famous Wrigley Building. Washington explained that they made a conscious effort to create an authoritative and official ambiance. "What Andy and I wanted to do was to give Gerard a commanding sense of authority and one way to do that is to give him height," explained Washington. "Subconsciously, the audience will sense he is above everyone else, particularly Kimble."[46]

Having grown up in the vicinity, director Davis filmed a sequence in a predominantly Mexican-Serbian neighborhood known as the Tenth Ward. Decades earlier, in 1966, the area had become infamous when serial killer Richard Speck murdered eight student nurses there. On South Houston Street (which Davis likens to "an area gasping for breath"), the production filmed the scenes of Kimble's apartment, situated on the city's southeast side near the U.S. Steel plant; the director quipped, "No one would expect a highfalutin doctor to be there."[47]

Scenes set in Sykes' home were filmed in historic Pullman, Illinois, on South St. Lawrence Street. Annexed to Chicago in 1890, Pullman was designed to provide a community of superior living to encourage greater productivity in the workplace due to the better health and spirit of the employees.

Davis said, "The row houses give the town a unique architectural quality, and it seemed a fitting place for Sykes to live. Moreover, there is very little through-traffic, which made it easier for shooting purposes, almost like a backlot."[48]

Additional locations included the Four Seasons Hotel and the Chicago Hilton. There, the medical convention and rooftop scenes were filmed. The shooting of a helicopter pursuit scene was at one point interrupted when Vice-President Al Gore was nearby. The Secret Service determined that the filming made protection too difficult and requested that the helicopter scenes be postponed until the visit was concluded.

The most significant relationship on a set is between the actor and his director. Apart from this collaboration, Ford claimed that there are two other individuals who provide the professional and emotional assistance essential for his daily on-the-set welfare. "Probably the second-most important relationship on a film set is between the actor and the dolly grip. He's the one who has to anticipate an actor's movements and sense when he wants to do something. These guys are down to you. They are like nobody else," said the actor.[49]

While these individuals are responsible for Ford's day-to-day professional success, having his family within arm's reach supersedes all other needs. "It's the only way you can keep a marriage together," said Ford. "If you're on your own on film locations it can be lonely and depressing — that's when trouble can start.

"I have a beautiful wife, and I want to be with her. You can't say: 'I'm off on location, see you in three months!'"[50]

"Being away so much did not help my marriage. When I first started, I wasn't paid enough to be able to bring my family with me. That's no longer the case.[51]

"When Melissa works on something, I try to go with her. When I'm working she goes with me. We hire a nanny to look after the children and they spend time with a tutor each morning to keep up with their school work."[52]

Criticized for not offering his children a more traditional education (such as a boarding school), the actor stated that travel is the best form of education. "It broadens the mind, and the kids have already visited more countries than most adults will do their entire lives."[53]

Producer Kopelson remembered: "Warner Bros. came to us with an August 6 release date, and we had no screenplay in a finished state. While we were shooting, we would get together at every waking moment to work on the script. Harrison came to the first meeting, and I started realizing he brought so much, he became part of the team."[54]

"It's not like he's meddling," said Kopelson. "He became part of the process because we respected what he had to say. In casting sessions, production meetings, looking at architectural drawings for the construction of sets, costume design, going to locations—it became obvious to us that Harrison's talents went way beyond his screen image. This man was not just an actor. He was a director, an actor, a producer. And I welcomed that involvement."[55]

Screenwriter Jeb Stuart was on hand throughout the entire production. He praised the value of Ford's contributions: "He becomes the soul of the whole project. After four months of working 16- to 17-hour days under a tremendous amount of pressure, when you're looking at parts of the script and have to make a decision to do it or not to do it, it's important to be able to say, 'No, this isn't right' as opposed to 'Well, let's go with what's here.' Those are tough decisions, but Harrison kept us on the right course through the whole thing.

"He constantly makes you play at a better level," continued Stuart. "You work real hard, and you think you've got something really good. And Harrison—as a coach almost—would say, 'That's great. But what if we did this?' Harrison is able to handle many balls up in the air at one time, to say, 'I see where all the dead ends are, but let's move in this direction.' And that's pushing you at a pretty high level."[56]

Davis concurred: "He's wonderful to work with because he's into process, into how things work. He started off as a woodworker, and he likes design, style, making things really refined that were raw. He basically just wants to be an element of the storytelling; he wants to service the story as best he can. He makes it a lot easier for the director, because he brings a lot to the party in terms of a point of view and ideas, which is much better than having somebody with an empty head who says, 'Tell me how to hold the apple.'"[57]

The best example of this involvement is the scene in which Kimble is interrogated by the police for the murder of his wife. Having insisted that the questions remain undisclosed to him until the scene was photographed, Ford's reaction to the other actors' dialogue was more spontaneous and sincere. "When the policeman asked me, 'Did anyone else have a key to your apartment?,' I used my own experience and thought, 'Yeah, the maid.' It's not real complicated."[58]

Apart from incorporating his instincts into the characters he's portraying, Ford used another proven method to get him through particular scenes: "They used to have this thing that they called telephone logic that they were teaching people at MGM," said the actor. "Mike Nichols told me this: 'If you're gonna get bad news, go with a smile on your face, otherwise they're not gonna know when you get bad news. If you're gonna get good news, you go with a frown on your face, so that you can make a change of statement.'"[59]

"It's about all you need to know—about movies. There are certainly more complicated schools of thought about what we do, but telephone logic will see you through many, many situations," he claimed.[60]

Davis opined. "Harrison had a difficult part since he had no one to interact with for so much of the film. But just look what he does with his face and body...."[61] He's almost a silent movie actor. He has the body language and the ability to exaggerate things."[62]

"Harrison is everybody's next door neighbor," said Kopelson. "He's very much like David Janssen [the original Kimble from the TV series], in that you feel for him, you empathize with him. He's very quiet and brings an introspective power to the role."[63]

On May 16, 1993, the filming of *The Fugitive* concluded. Seven editors and their 21 assistants frantically prepared for the release deadline.

Finally, with more than 1,500 guests in attendance (including Sylvester Stallone, Liam Neeson and Christian Slater and cast members Sela Ward and Joe Pantoliano), *The Fugitive* premiered in Los Angeles on August 5, 1993.

Sela Ward recalled the overwhelming excitement at the premiere. "It's so great to be involved in a project where the buzz is good and everybody's jazzed about it.... I don't know what it is about Harrison. He's such a good person. Tonight I was in there rooting for him the whole time — and I'm in the movie!"[64]

Film producer Lauren Shuler-Donner also expressed her enthusiasm. "Usually I hate industry screenings because the audience acts like it's dead," said Donner. "But here, people went crazy."[65]

Opening wide on August 6, the film celebrated a record-breaking opening weekend for the month of August with $23.8 million domestically. The film got positive reviews, including the rare A+ grade from audiences polled by Cinema Score.[66] It ran for months, gathering a domestic total of more than $183 million, plus an additional estimated $176 million overseas.

Ford earned himself another Best Actor Golden Globe nomination for his portrayal of Dr. Kimble. Oscar-wise there was a total of seven nominations including Best Picture, Best Supporting Actor, Best Cinematography, Best Film Editing, Best Original Score, Best Sound and Best Sound Effects Editing. The uncontested winner in the majority of its 11 nominations, Steven Spielberg's World War II Holocaust drama *Schindler's List* nearly shut out the competition.

For Spielberg, the Oscar ceremony marked the occasion of his first win for Best Director and Best Picture, despite having been nominated for each several times before. When Ford was asked if he would present the Oscar for Best Picture of the year, he didn't hesitate, believing with certainty that he would be handing over the award to a good friend. (For the 1998 Oscar ceremony, Ford was again asked if he would present Best Picture — this time with Spielberg's *Saving Private Ryan* as a nominee. Ford accepted, convinced that his friend would win yet again. The evening of the awards, Ford was visibly shaken when he opened the envelope and revealed to the countless millions that *Shakespeare in Love* had won instead.)

The Fugitive did not walk away entirely empty-handed. On March 21, 1994, Tommy Lee Jones received an award from the Academy of Motion Picture Arts and Sciences as Best Supporting Actor for his portrayal of Gerard. He outperformed then-newcomer Ralph Fiennes for *Schindler's List*, Pete Postlethwaite for *In the Name of the Father*, Leonardo DiCaprio for *What's Eating Gilbert Grape?* and veteran Oscar nominee John Malkovich for *In the Line of Fire*.

During his acceptance speech, Jones thanked several executives, Arnold Kopelson,

Andy Davis, Peter MacGregor-Scott, friends and family, and, "Above all, I thank a man who needs no support at all, Harrison Ford."[67]

Based on the overwhelming box office popularity of *The Fugitive*, a sequel seemed logical, and the notion was considered during the post-production period. Producer Arnold Kopelson recalled: "While we were shooting, there was some thought that 'Hey, we can't do this, it could be detrimental to a sequel.' But we decided to make the best movie we could, and that meant locking up the story tightly. I don't know if we can open it again, but it would have to be an intelligent storyline to consider it."[68]

When this was brought to Ford's attention, he said, "I can't imagine it. I can't conceive how they could come up with a script that would work. It's in their best interest to try, but I can't conceive it."[69]

Fugitive co-writer Jeb Stuart was rehired by Kopelson to bring Richard Kimble back to the screen. He wrote several drafts—none of which caught Ford's interest.

For co-star Joe Pantoliano, the executive decision to progress forward with a sequel was clearly one involving a "quantity, not quality" preface. The actor said, "They'll just get another guy who wants to make $10 million to run around in the woods."[70]

That "other guy" turned out to be Wesley Snipes, who starred as another wrongly accused fugitive with Tommy Lee Jones and his posse in pursuit in the 1998 film *U.S. Marshals*.

Ford was able to thoroughly immerse himself into his work yet maintain the distinction between fiction and reality at the close of each filming day. The issue of the misuse and abuse of the nation's legal system raised.

"It's a serious problem in any country," said the actor. "The law has no mind of its own. The law is an instrument that is used by people, and it is as effective as the people who use it. And, of course, mistakes are made. What was interesting to me in this case is that I wasn't playing a black or Hispanic that was being charged with the crime, but I was playing a privileged white man, who is charged with a crime. And in my investigation, in my research, it seemed to me that I came upon many situations in which, when the cops get their hands on a person like that, they want to demonstrate their evenhandedness, because they're forever putting away disadvantaged, poor minority people. When they get their hands on a white person who is rich, and who they think 'done it,' they are all the more resolved to put this guy away, so as to demonstrate how color blind they are."[71]

Has the actor ever had the experience of being wrongly accused of something?

"Never," claimed Ford. "I was always correctly accused. I have almost always been caught for things I did wrong."[72]

28

Jack's Back

"Jack Ryan has become kind of the '90s thinking man's James Bond," said returning *Clear and Present Danger* producer Mace Neufeld. "We may not have the bizarre villains who live underwater or the beautiful women who throw themselves at Bond. Our stories come right out of the headlines and are very real."[1]

In contrast to James Bond and Indiana Jones, Tom Clancy's CIA analyst Jack Ryan functions very much in a recognizable context. He is a reluctant hero whom the audiences would again identify with yet again in his next cinematic outing.

Danger reunited Ford with Philip Noyce, Anne Archer as Cathy Ryan, Thora Birch as Sally Ryan, James Earl Jones as Admiral James Greer and various other familiar behind-the-scenes personnel. It welcomed new members Donald Moffatt (who portrayed Henry Turner's employer in *Regarding Henry*) as the president; Canadian newcomer Henry Czerny as Robert Ritter; Harris Yulin (*The Believers*) as the president's National Security Advisor James Cutter; Portuguese-born actor Joaquim deAlmeida as the former Cuban intelligence officer newly employed by the Colombian drug cartels; and Willem Dafoe (*Platoon*, *The Last Temptation of Christ*) as Mr. Clark, the newly acquisitioned gun-for-hire at the helm of a covert operation.

The story unfolds as Ryan becomes Deputy Director of Intelligence at the CIA in place of the ailing James Greer. Swept into an unfamiliar world of politics and deceit, Ryan heeds the words of caution from Greer: "You want to know about politics in Washington? I can explain it in four words: Watch your back, Jack."

While investigating the murder of a political supporter and acquaintance of the U.S. President, Ryan discovers that the friend maintains ties to a Colombian drug cartel, representing "a clear and present danger to the national security of the United States."

Ryan suddenly becomes involved when, unbeknownst to him, the CIA vengefully orders covert operations against the cartels. Caught in the crossfire, he is confronted with the most important moral decision of his life—to plead ignorance of the government's actions, or to turn his back on the politicians and disclose the truth to the American people.

"Ryan finds himself drawn into this situation that finally only he can resolve," explained Ford. "We all have moral decisions to make in our lives and the nature of them depends on the exact detail of the circumstances. I think Ryan behaves well and admirable, not out of super patriotism or out of national zeal, but out of regard for his fellow human beings, out of compassion and intelligence and sense of responsibility."[2]

The film addressed some of the most pressing questions of appropriateness and morals affecting the United States' place in today's modern political climate. It juxtaposes the strength of America as a worldwide power against the elite leadership of South American cocaine cartels.

Within the story lay difficult questions—whether the greatest evil lies with the drug cartels, the soldiers-for-hire (who prove themselves ready to sell themselves to the highest bidder) or the powerful men within the U.S. government who have convinced themselves that they answer to no one. Throughout the course of the film, Ryan finds his own answers to these questions.

Noyce recalled his reservations toward pursuing a second Jack Ryan excursion. "After *Patriot Games*, I swore I didn't want to be a part of the series any more ... mainly because of all the shit we had to put up with from Tom Clancy.... But when I read the book, I thought it was complex, exciting, and relevant."[3]

The novel, first published in 1989, was a *New York Times* No. 1 bestseller, and had sold more than 8 million copies worldwide.

In March 1992, Noyce hired writer-director John Milius. As a director, Milius was responsible for *Red Dawn* and *Conan the Barbarian*. As a screenwriter, he received an Academy Award nomination (1979) for his work on *Apocalypse Now*.

Milius's first challenge was to condense material that Clancy had described in infinite detail, so that it could be translated to the big screen, and yet retain its rich texture and multi-faceted nature.

Although Milius' first draft impressed friend and author Clancy, one important and unavoidable flaw was present: "There was no place for Harrison Ford in that film," exclaimed Noyce. The novel posed a problem. Ford's character, Jack Ryan, does not appear at all within the first 300 pages of the novel. Backtracking, Noyce said, "There was a place, but the audience would have rioted."[4]

Red October and *Patriot Games* scribe Donald Stewart was summoned to produce the character of Ryan in order to provide what the ticket buyer wanted to see: Ford.

Clancy dismissed Stewart's version of the novel, calling the attempt "really awful." Elaborating, Clancy asserted, "First things first, *Clear and Present Danger* was the No. 1 best-selling novel of the 1980s. One might conclude that the novel's basic story line had some quality to it. Why, then, has nearly every aspect of the book been tossed away?"[5]

Furthermore, the author lashed out at the production with continuous faxed statements, including, "If a camel is a horse designed by a committee, then this 'script' must have been crafted by a panel of maniacs," and even took steps to ridicule Noyce's resume: "If you shoot this script, *Sliver* [Noyce's botched follow-up to *Patriot Games*] will look like *Citizen Kane*."[6]

"I've gotten quite used to Mr. Clancy's lack of sympathy for our efforts," said Ford.[7] "You do things when you're typing that you would never do if you had to fucking stand there and deliver [the lines]."[8]

Putting Clancy's comments out of their minds, the team hired a third and final writer to help resolve the remaining script issues once and for all. Steve Zaillian (who wrote and directed *Searching for Bobby Fischer* and won the Best Adapted Screenplay Academy Award for *Schindler's List*) was there to make the screenplay more like the novel while also strengthening the character of Jack Ryan.

Noyce recalled the issues involved in having three writers condense a nearly 700-page book to a 126-page screenplay: "All three worked on the final script. Usually the second writer throws out the first guy's work, and the third throws out the other two. It's unfortunate for the forests of the world, but it's also a pity for the sum total of human endeavor."[9]

Location scouting for *Clear and Present Danger* began six months prior to filming. Due to the unstable military and political climate of Colombia and its neighboring locales, the production considered utilizing Puerto Rico as a substitute for the South American scenes but rejected the idea because of tax complications. Finally, the filmmakers agreed to film in Mexico.

Apart from Noyce's recollection of guard dogs, soldiers and barbed wire surrounding the hotel embassy in Cali, Colombia, Neufeld also recalled perils. Although Mexico was an ideal location offering seaside, mountains and jungle forests, it was a dangerous locale. The crew worried on more than one occasion that the film could well be their last — but they persevered for the sake of the film.

Further scouting was done in Los Angeles, the Orange and Santa Clarita counties of California, the Pacific Ocean, Washington, D.C., Xalapa, Coatepec, Mexico City, Cuernavaca, Xico and La Concepcion, Mexico.

During pre-production, returning production designer Terrence Marsh decided upon locations such as a Hancock Park residence for the Ryan home; John Wayne, Van Nuys and Los Angeles airports; The Westwood V.A. hospital; downtown's Water Grill, which doubled for the Washington, D.C., restaurant in which Cathy Ryan chats with Moira Wolfson (Ann Magnuson) and catches a brief glimpse of the "Latin Jack Ryan" (Cortez); and the Chase Building, which provided the interior sets for the FBI conference room and the DEA field office in Colombia.

Before production began, Neufeld and Noyce sent the Pentagon a copy of the script hoping to receive cooperation. Despite the healthy relationship nurtured during the filming of *Patriot Games*, the CIA was displeased with the depiction of various agencies and chose not to participate.

"The CIA, of course, withheld their cooperation this time," said Ford, "though they cooperated on *Patriot Games*, because the CIA didn't feel comfortable with this film. But it is interesting that one branch of the government cooperated and another did not."[10]

Neufeld believed the refusal was simply the result of poor timing. At the time of their request for cooperation, hearings were being held on Capital Hill concerning covert operations — and there was a newly appointed director (R. James Woolsey) in office.

Meeting with Pentagon representatives one week after filming began, Neufeld, Noyce and Donald Stewart hoped to negotiate with the government and make the desired alterations. (Neufeld ascertained that the Pentagon was cooperating because of the positive portrayal of the military in the film; the movie was practically free advertising.)

In addition to an assigned on-set military advisor, the newly acquired cooperation from the Department of Defense allowed the moviemakers to film various military installations such as Los Alamitos Reserve Center and the U.S. Coast Guard station at San Pedro. They were also permitted to film in the skies above Nellis Air Force base and on board the aircraft carrier USS *Kitty Hawk*.

"I could have used carrier shots that we took for *Flight of the Intruder* and used models," said Neufeld, "but there's a difference between using, say, a Blackhawk service pilot than something that's painted to look like a Blackhawk and flown by a civilian pilot."[11]

"Each branch of the Defense Department has a rate card, just like Hertz or Avis," said Neufeld. The Blackhawk helicopter hourly rental rate: $1,500; F/A18 90-minute rental — $5,000; USS *Kitty Hawk* daily rental: $26,000.[12]

In addition to the hardware provided by the American government, the production was also granted permission to meet with individuals of various agencies during both filming and pre-production. Ford, who had met with members of the CIA for *Patriot Games*, furthered his research by convening with personnel from the DEA, FBI and the State Department. Harris Yulin, who portrays National Security Advisor James Cutter, met with the former National Security Advisor to three presidents, Brent Scowcroft. At Camp Pendleton, California, the United States Marines (under the direction of technical advisor Jared Chandler) trained actors Willem Dafoe, Raymond Cruz and others in the technique of jungle stealth maneuvers.

The 17-week filming schedule commenced on November 8, 1993, in and around the suburbs of Los Angeles. The most elaborate sets designs for the film were the interiors of the CIA headquarters, constructed and filmed at Sony Studios in Culver City. Two stages were used. The first contained the interiors for the offices of Ryan, Ritter, Cutter and the White House's press briefing room, while the other stage housed the CIA "Large Room."

To lend authenticity to the "Large Room," state-of-the-art information retrieval and analysis equipment was required. Placed among several video monitors and other hi-tech audio and video resolution equipment were the Storagetek data storage unit and the Integraph computer. The Storagetek was capable of storing more than 50,000 years of *The Wall Street Journal*, while the Integraph computer was used to produce images for cartography and architectural purposes.

On December 2, 1993, while filming the scene in which Ryan and a CIA voice-print analyst (actor-director Vondie Curtis-Hall) attempt to identify Felix Cortez through the use of a sonograph (a voice analysis computer utilizing the same comparison techniques used to identify individuals through fingerprinting), an eerie correlation to current events occurred: Colombian drug cartel leader Pablo Escobar was apprehended and murdered in Medellin, Colombia, through the same process.

"I was stunned when life imitated art in that way," said Ford. "It was confirmation that what we were doing had some substance.

"I think that's one of the things that people find engaging about Clancy. He gives them the feeling that they are in on the secret stuff, that he has access to information that the ordinary person doesn't, and he tells it like it is."[13]

At nearby Paramount Studios, scenes were filmed involving President Bennett

(Moffatt) in the Oval Office. Careful not to cast similarities, Noyce clarified: "We certainly didn't want to be specific. It was a composite of presidents."[14]

Because of certain themes throughout the film, the production was wary that the situations involved in *Clear and Present Danger* might be considered regurgitations of past historic political incidents.

"We can find historical precedence for this kind of abuse of power throughout American history. No sense pinning it all on Reagan and Bush or Ollie North," said Ford. "We're talking about a general problem that's inherent in the system: the potential for the abuse of power. This film is not a political statement."[15]

In the early weeks of January 1994, the production moved to the Washington, D.C., area to film exteriors at Andrews Air Force Base, the White House and Arlington National Cemetery.

One scene required the camera to follow Ryan's vehicle as it leaves the guard gate and proceeds onto the White House grounds. But the production was denied all access to the compound due to strict security provisions. Using a computer-generated optical transition, technicians filmed a panning shot of the White House with a pause at the main gate where Ryan's vehicle would eventually exist. Back at Video Image's parking lot in Venice, California, a full-scale, elaborately detailed reproduction of the main gate was filmed with Ford approaching it in his vehicle. When the two elements were fused together, Ryan's Taurus appeared to be driving from the checkpoint to the compound in one shot.

At Arlington National Cemetery, the production filmed the funeral of Admiral Greer. Filming in mid–January, the production experienced record-breaking temperatures — the lowest D.C. had seen in more than a century. From an actor's perspective, Ford claimed that the weather provided "a certain mood and texture to the scene"[16] — creating a somber ambiance appropriate for the sequence.

The Military Honor Guard assisted in the authentic reproduction of the folding of the American flag and the stance of various military personnel. "It adds to the reality of our story," Neufeld said. "There is something to using the people who do these things everyday that cannot be substituted."[17]

On January 17, 1994, an earthquake destroyed part of the Los Angeles area. Hearing the news while waiting to depart for Mexico at Dulles International Airport, the crew's fears heightened as the production attempted unsuccessfully to contact friends and colleagues in California. After arriving in Mexico, it took nearly two days to establish communication stateside. To intensify problems, five reels of footage filmed in Washington, D.C., were destroyed in a film lab during the disaster.

The production encountered bureaucratic stumbling blocks with the denial of permits to import weapons and explosives required for filming due to recent fighting between rebels and Mexican soldiers. In retrospect, Neufeld considered the situation "an exquisitely wrong sense of timing."[18]

The production had been assured its permits weeks earlier, recalled Neufeld. "But after the revolt, no Mexican politician or military person was willing to sign off on it because they thought the press there would turn it into a big political scandal, saying 'the Americans are now here.' Our truck was just sitting on the Texas-Mexican border for two weeks."[19]

Threatened with bad publicity, the Mexican government surrendered to Neufeld's proposition and issued the permits.

Protecting their investment, *Clear and Present Danger*'s producers strategically held off on filming the intense pyrotechnic and stunt scenes until the final moments of the project. The decision was made partly because Ford needed additional time to fully recuperate from the knee injury sustained on the set of *The Fugitive*.

"The worry about physical danger was compounded by the increasing fatigue everybody was feeling," said Noyce. "Certainly compared to *Patriot Games*, it was more stressful. It was harder to reach agreement on things."[20]

Ford recalled the increasing tension. "We had less of a script this time," said the actor, "so we had more to argue about — I mean argue in a responsible way, not bicker. The first time you work with a person, the debate tends to be polite. Then the marriage continues and maybe the second time you know each other better, so you conduct the argument more like a husband and wife than business associates."[21]

For nearly eight weeks, the production constructed the set of "The Kill Zone"— the film's most involved action sequence. There, Ryan and members of the American entourage are ambushed by a Colombian murder squad assigned by Felix Cortez. The scene was awash with logistically complex elements including rockets, gunfire, exploding vehicles and scrambling victims.

Since it was impractical to use the streets of Bogota, Colombia, producers enlisted craftsmen to create a faux setting. Nearly 200 yards long, the stretch of imitation residences and storefronts provided an authentic looking street scene where the ambush would occur.

For safety's sake, "dummy" rockets launched from rooftops were guided by wires to ensure contact with the intended targets— the procession of Chevy Suburbans far below.

To provide the explosive effect, the vehicles were strategically dismantled and partially welded back together (creating fault lines) and packed with gasoline mortars rigged to detonate when the guided rockets struck.

"That was the most difficult by far, because of the proximity of the actors," said veteran special effects supervisor Paul Lombardi. "You've got Harrison Ford in there. They'd hate it if you blew him up."[22]

The film's stunt coordinator, Dick Ziker, confessed that despite what the daily call sheet requested of Ford, the actual time a double was actually used was much less significant than originally planned. "Harrison does the stunt. I pay the double."[23]

Noyce recalled as more vehicles got destroyed, the amount of smoke produced began to limit everyone's visibility. Consequently, the sequence went several days over schedule. As Ford recalled, the sequence lasted "two days more than forever."[24]

Alongside father and son team Paul and Joe Lombardi, a crew of ten worked for nearly three days preparing the pyrotechnic effects for the spectacular explosion of a Colombian drug-smuggling plane.

Rigged with weakened wings, a twin-engine Aero Commander enclosed by a specially built hangar was loaded with several hundred gallons of gasoline and explosives. Photographed by several cameras, the $40,000 set was instantly destroyed in a mere ten seconds of screen time. Although medics and firefighters stood at the ready during the explosion, the real danger loomed after the smoke had cleared. With debris scattered more than 150 feet away from the initial blast, the production took great care to inspect the wreckage for undetonated devices.

The production team created a villa for drug lord Ernesto Escobedo. Within a 30-minute radius of Cuernavaca, Mexico, were the villas of Posada Tepoztlan, Vista Hermosa and San Gabriel de las Palmas. They were photographed individually and later integrated on screen to create the hacienda. The lavish Posada Tepoztlan offered a breathtaking view of the Mexican countryside. Vista Hermosa, originally constructed in the sixteenth century, became a popular vacationing resort for celebrities and other affluent Americans visiting the country during the 1940s and '50s. Also established in the 1500s, San Gabriel de las Palmas was built by (the real) Cortez and was used during the Mexican Revolution as a headquarters for Pancho Villa.

For the film's final confrontation between Ryan and Cortez (Joaquim DeAlmeida), the production used the water-powered Murietta Coffee Factory. In operation for more than a century, the location was transformed into "Cafe Lindo" by Terence Marsh and construction coordinator Sebastian Molitto. In addition to the various props, including coffee sacks with Colombian markings, a specially built helipad was created for the sequence.

On March 14, 1994, the *Clear and Present Danger* production celebrated its last day of filming with fireworks reminiscent of Independence Day.

For the massive explosion caused by an American "smart" bomb attack on a drug cartel member's hilltop hacienda, the filmmakers opted to destroy an actual home, providing a suitable location was found. Constructed of reinforced stone and concrete, the home of a couple going through a divorce was purchased.

For weeks the Lombardis and other associates prepared the house by planting dynamite packs throughout the structure and underneath the half-dozen vehicles in the driveway. With a security perimeter surrounding the house and with local residents expecting the blast, nine cameras recorded the cataclysmic event.

"After shooting two films in a series, you would think the third would be easier," said Noyce. "But it hasn't. *Danger* has been the hardest. Harder than *Red October*. Harder than *Patriot Games*."[25]

Difficulties stemmed from corporate decisions governing cost and time, which created skepticism among the filmmakers regarding the effect of those limitations on the final product. The producers were forced to shorten the film to comply with budget restrictions—and, in doing so, compromised their vision of the film.

Noyce fought to balance the film's ending with its dramatic mid-picture action sequence. His hope was for added chase scenes, for the cartel's army to invade the surrounding town and for Ryan to be pursued by hundreds of men—but this was deemed unacceptable by the picture's financiers.

Paramount imposed a fee of $176,000 to the production for each day over schedule. Because of this pressure, it was routine for the filmmakers to continuously write and rewrite the script on a daily basis, often done in the hours before the start of photography.

One example of this in *Clear and Present Danger*, explained Ford, was an ambush scene. "Probably on the day of shooting I realized there was no emotion in the sequence. The audiences have only to look at their watches to know that I'm not going to get killed at this stage of the film. So I proposed that we kill the FBI agent [Dan Murray, portrayed by actor Tim Grimm] who is in the car with me. But to make the audience care, we had to build up my relationship with him, just with tiny fragments of dialogue dropped in here and there—casual conversations about coffee and food and stuff. Without that the sequence would have just been blowing stuff up."[26]

"The big action sequences have always been there, but I think what audiences appreciate is the mature way in which they're presented," said Neufeld. "People are not just shot and car chases aren't just thrown in for no logical reason. In fact, logic is this film's strongest point. The action grows out of the plot."[27]

Other daily revisions were brought on by Ford's desire to humanize Ryan, such as his difficulty selecting a tie for a White House conference (and having a back-up tie in his coat pocket). Ford also introduced a humorous note during the sequence in which Ryan is illegally signed on to Ritter's computer and is frantically attempting to copy certain files as Ritter is simultaneously deleting the data from another computer. It was Ford's notion to conclude the confrontation with an even higher degree of adrenaline-pumping frenzy, insisting that the machine be out of paper.

Unlike the novel, the film ends with Ryan publicly testifying against the President's scandalous actions. It was Ford's suggestion to further justify Ryan's decision. The choice becomes a moral one, concerned not with his politics, but with his fear for the welfare of innocent people and the integrity of his government. Ford felt the viewers deserved—and needed—to know that Ryan would testify.

Tom Clancy and John Milius protested the new ending. The latter deemed it unrealistic while voicing his own thoughts on the American government: "To go before Congress, which as we well know is a nest of snakes, is ridiculous," he said. "Anyone in this day and age who thinks that Congress is an honorable organization is a fool."[28]

Noyce was weary of the public's opinion of a "hero" who turns his back on his own government. "I don't know how audiences will react," he said. "I truly don't. No doubt, some people will go in saying, 'Yeah, blow up the bad guys.' But then the film moves into gray areas, and I think smart audiences will appreciate that. This movie is really about a man fighting institutions.... We may be asking too much from the audience. But this is not a simple film."[29]

Four million dollars over its intended $55.5 million budget and 13 days over schedule, *Danger* was ready for post-production dollars.

Willem Dafoe, who was initially nervous about working with Ford, ultimately found the entire experience inspirational and said that Ford possessed an "uncanny ability to know what's being conveyed to the audience."[30]

Screenwriter Donald Stewart said, "He puts up with absolutely no bull as far as logic is concerned. And that's a hard master. He simply will not say or do something that doesn't make sense to him or ring true—which a lot of actors are only too glad to do. So in a story meeting, he just gives you a better solution, a better gesture and, nine times out of ten, a better line. After 20-odd years in this business, he's the only actor that I really take notes on."[31]

"I like it because it's an intellectual challenge. It's an opportunity to work with a group of people on an idea and to try to bring it to the fullest expression that you can," said Ford. "I like the fact that there's a kind of front-line feeling to it, that it's dangerous, that the potential for screwing up and making mistakes is there, so that it becomes important to get it right."[32]

Four days following the completion of principal photography for *Clear and Present Danger*, the thirty-first annual Publicist Guild of America awarded Producers Mace Neufeld and Robert Rehme the Motion Picture Showmanship Award during a mid day ceremony held at the Beverly Hilton Hotel. Awards committee chairman Henri Bollinger honored the producers for their "extraordinary showmanship as successful filmmakers in Hollywood."[33] The previous year Neufeld and Rehme were deemed "Producers of the Year" during the annual NATO/ShoWest convention. While the recognition noted by peers and friends is both honorable and gratifying, the co-producers admit that sharing the duties with a partner is a double-edged sword.

"One of the best things about having a partner is that you have two minds, two bodies, two 16-to-18-hour days to devote to projects," said Rehme.[34]

"The downside," Neufeld acknowledged, "is that you have to split every cent you make."[35]

On Wednesday March 9, 1994, George Lucas stood nervously behind a podium at Bally's Hotel in Las Vegas. On behalf of the National Association of Theater Owners, the director proudly presented Harrison Ford with an award of a unique nature.

Nato/ShoWest assembles annually with limo-loads of celebrities who participate in trade shows exhibiting the latest in hi-tech projection equipment, and plug their projects to the nearly 7,500 exhibitors. That year, the organization awarded Ford with its first-ever title of "Star of the Century," following a presentation of clips highlighting the actor's career.

"Over the past two decades," said the convention's general chairman Tim Warner, "Ford's talents have firmly established him as the most prominent and successful actor ever to work within the motion picture industry. His movies, which continue to break box office records all over the world, now account for more than $2 billion in

Bringing Tom Clancy's Jack Ryan to life in the film version of *Clear and Present Danger* (Paramount, 1994).

domestic theatrical grosses, an achievement unparalleled in the 100-year history of exhibition."[36]

"I just saw my whole life flash in front of me," joked Ford of the highlights. "Am I dead? It's my worst fear: Heaven's just like Las Vegas."[37]

Accepting the award, a charmed and slightly embarrassed Ford replied, "I figured out why you're giving me this award six years early. If you waited any longer, you'd have to give it to Macaulay Culkin."[38]

Although grateful, Ford recognized that it was the success of his films that had earned him the honor—not the quality of his acting or respect for him as an actor.

Negotiating with theater owners on this premise, the actor disclosed the conditions of his acceptance: "I'll make you a deal. I'll try to keep making films that put people in your theater seats, and you try to keep their shoes from sticking to the floor."[39]

Philip Noyce and legions of other colleagues past and present disagreed with Ford's candor, stating that the title "Star of the Century" was a well-deserved achievement and true testament to the actor's talent and contributions.

"Harrison has, through a combination of experience and intelligence, an enormous amount to offer on any movie he works on," said Noyce. "He has worked not only on a series of the most successful films ever made but also with the most successful directors. It has all rubbed off on him. And yet, with this encyclopedia of knowledge, as a director you never feel that he's intruding upon your autonomy. Rather it's a partnership—and a very valuable one...."[40] He has such an analytical mind that he's more of a collaborator than simply an actor. He's thinking way down deep into the situation. I'm trying to look at the table. He's looking at a crumb."[41]

Neufeld said, "Much of what he is personally comes through in his roles. To me, and I think a lot of his audiences, he appears to be the kind of guy you might want to be friends with. He's not movie-actorish and yet he's a very skilled actor who makes it seem effortless—in some ways like Clint Eastwood, although Harrison's range, his personality, is a little broader. He's good looking without being a pretty boy. He lets the scars show, along with a little vulnerability."[42]

"He has his insecurities, he admits to them, but he also understands everybody else's insecurities," said co-star Henry Czerny (Robert Ritter). "He's not a guy that comes on-set and expects people to support him without having done his homework.... He would allow people the chance to laugh at him so he wouldn't feel so reverent."[43]

James Earl Jones, who portrayed Admiral James Greer in both Jack Ryan films, admired the actor for his non-egotistical attitude. "He is also as generous as he is demanding, which is the way it should be. He is totally available to his fellow actors, and he demands availability from you as well. If he's going to be off camera to give you what you need, he wants you off camera giving him what he needs too. It's not just a ritual; something really has to happen."[44]

Ford has always been quick to dispel the notion that his success in the motion picture industry is based on talent: "I have had scientifically provable luck from time to time," he alleged. "Being in the right place at the right time and then doing the right thing. You cannot get where I got without luck. Bags of it. Fucking bags of it.

You can be as good as I am or better. You can be incredibly more attractive and charming and capable and still be shit out of luck. The only thing that I have done that is not mitigated by luck, diminished by good fortune, is that I persisted. And other people gave up."[45]

* * *

"Frankly, I'd rather be home milking the cow. But I'm pleased to be able to bring people's attention to the movie," said a publicity-weary Ford at the August 2 Los Angeles premiere of *Clear and Present Danger*.[46] Taking place on the Paramount lot, the $300-per-ticket screening was followed by a soiree to benefit the Stop Cancer Fund. Approximately $300,000 was raised by attendees and co-stars Joaquim deAlmeida and Ann Magnuson and Henry Czerny, screenwriter John Milius, director Noyce and producer Neufeld. Others present were Tom Arnold, Buzz and Lois Aldrin, director William Friedkin, Alan Ladd, Jr., Ron Meyer, Sid Ganis, Rob Friedman and Paramount executives Sherry Lansing, Barry London and Jonathan Dolgen.

One week earlier, on July 26, *Danger* was shown at a $150-per-ticket benefit screening for the American Film Institute at Washington, D.C.'s, Kennedy Center. The screening was the first of its kind since the 1983 premiere of *The Right Stuff*. Complete with vegetation, a waterfall and simulated bird chirps, a Colombian rain forest-themed pre- and post-screening party was held on the Roof Terrace. Guests included retired General Colin Powell, Treasury Secretary Lloyd Bentsen, Supreme Court Justice Ruth Bader Ginsburg, Republican Party Representative Michael Huffington, Democrat Representative Pat Schroeder, Republican Senator John Warner, Democratic Senator Charles Robb, Senator Ted Kennedy and his nephew, Democratic Representative Joseph P. Kennedy II, Housing and Urban Development Secretary Federico Pena and Librarian of Congress James Billington, to name a few.

"It's the hottest crowd we're going to play this to," he said, "unless we held a screening in Cali, Colombia."[47]

Pentagon entertainment liaison office head Phil Strub said that the film "depicted the military in a very good light."[48]

In fact, the film provided such an accurate portrayal of what government agencies really do with taxpayer money that several branches requested the use of footage to be used as training films.

The Drug Enforcement Agency (DEA) applauded the validity of the sequence involving the interception of dialogue through the use of cellular phone transmissions. Similar enthusiasm came from other government organizations.

The Air Force and Army Special Operations School was particularly impressed by the scene in which the FBI Director became trapped during the ambush sequence, *so* much that they requested to use the piece in a training film — a true reversal of roles and an unforeseen honor for the movie.

Clear and Present Danger opened wide on August 5, 1994. It was ranked No. 1 in its opening weekend in both the United States and Canada with $20,348,017. Surpassing the $100 million mark in 37 days, it ultimately accumulated a grand total of $121,981,248 in box office receipts (Ford had 11.5 percent of the total gross income and an $11 million salary).[49] In addition to receiving Academy Award nominations for Best Sound and Sound Effects Editing, the film was the sixth most successful film of 1994 in North America, outpacing the totals of both its predecessors, *The Hunt for Red October* and *Patriot Games*. Combined, the three films have exceeded 500 million in U.S. dollars worldwide.

"It's a rare occasion in the film industry when the third film in a trilogy surpasses the box office gross of its predecessors," said a proud Mace Neufeld. "This is a testament to the talent that worked on the film, the tremendous talent and worldwide appeal of Harrison Ford, and the superb marketing and distribution expertise of Paramount. We're extremely pleased with the results and acknowledge the contributions of everyone involved."[50]

Jack Ryan's cinematic future was uncertain. Due to Paramount's unstable relationship with author Tom Clancy, one option that Neufeld considered was the creation of an original direct-to-screen Jack Ryan script, specifically tailored with Ford in mind.

"It was never my intention to do that," Neufeld stated on the possibility of eliminating Clancy's involvement. "But if we have no choice … that's the direction we'll go."[51]

Partly the cause of this was Clancy's apparent $2.5 million sale of the rights to 1993's *Without Remorse* to Savoy Pictures for screen adaptation, and his refusal of Paramount's offer to purchase his 1994 novel *Debt of Honor*. Stubbornly opposed to any future collaboration with Paramount, the author stated, "A lot of things have to happen before Paramount is able to purchase the book from me. A few people over there have thoroughly poisoned the well."[52]

Neufeld, however, remained optimistic: "If Rabin and Arafat could shake hands, Clancy and Neufeld could."[53]

29

SOMETHING WILDER

In the early 1980s, critics officially began to liken Harrison Ford to a contemporary Humphrey Bogart. Ironically, come winter of 1995, Ford found himself in the hot seat bombarded with questions concerning his feelings toward remaking a Bogart classic.

In 1993, screenwriter Barbara Benedek (*The Big Chill*) submitted a screenplay to producer Scott Rudin (*Regarding Henry*). Recognizing a script unintentionally similar to a 1954 film entitled *Sabrina*, Rudin brought forth the similarities to the attention of Benedek.

Following Rudin's suggestion, Benedek took time to view the film and decided to dismantle the original film and fashion it into a contemporary story.

The 1954 film (based upon Samuel Beckett's play *Sabrina Fair*) was directed by Billy Wilder and starred Bogart and screen gem Audrey Hepburn.

Benedek began remaking the six-time Academy Award–nominated film after receiving blessings from both Rudin and Paramount Pictures Chairwoman Sherry Lansing.

While rewriting the script, Benedek's focus gradually changed as she discovered that Rudin had submitted it to a colleague he'd worked with during the making of 1989's *Regarding Henry*: Harrison Ford.

Ford was immediately attracted to the property, noticing a particularly significant similarity between Linus and himself: "At first, I thought, this is not something I know a lot about. This guy makes jillions of dollars, and he has an incredible amount of power and authority. Then I thought, wait a second. That's what I do."[1]

Despite the similarity, Ford vowed that there was one undeniable difference between the two: "I'm not as big an S.O.B. as Linus."[2]

In an attempt to lure him into the project, Ford personally approached Oscar-winning actor-producer-director Sydney Pollack. Ford persistently placed phone calls to the director for a period of nearly two weeks.

"I probably called him three or four times," recalled Ford. "I was talking to him about the script I had read, Barbara Benedek's script, and about he and I working together, and how much I wanted that to happen. I just kept telling him how great he was."[3]

Ford was convinced that Pollack was best-suited for the material at hand. The actor also maintained that he would refrain from all-out involvement and settle with living up to his job description — to act, and only to act.

"I wanted to be directed," said Ford, "because I'd had my fill of doing it the other way. I'm usually involved in story conferences and production details, and I just didn't want that this time. If we end up with a good movie, that's all I care about."[4]

"I didn't want to do a remake of Billy Wilder," said Pollack. "People are very unforgiving about remakes, particularly of something like *Sabrina*. So many people were so charmed by it. I said no two or three times...."[5]

"The kicker was when I got a call from Harrison Ford," recalled the director. "I love him as tough guys, but I really love him in romantic roles like *Witness*. I thought about him and this idea of a hard-edged fairy tale. Because of Harrison, I got real interested in Linus. So I said, 'What the hell?'"[6]

Having finally committed to the project, Pollack enlisted the services of Billy Wilder as a special consultant during its screenwriting stage. Pollack also hired frequent collaborator David Rayfiel (*The Firm*, *Havana*, *Three Days of the Condor*) to assist Benedek with the task of modernizing the classic tale.

"The question I asked myself going into this project was 'Can you mix the economic attitudes of the '90s with a romantic fairy tale of the '50s?'" recalled Pollack. "I was lucky enough to get Billy Wilder to talk about ways to contemporize the script. I stole as many of the highlights from the old movie as I could. But I felt that this version could be much more an examination of Linus as a character, and that intrigued me."[7]

To coincide with the changing culture of the 1990s, the character of Linus Larrabee was significantly altered. "All work and no play," jokingly referred to as "the world's only living heart donor" by Sabrina, Linus is a true businessman — ruthless to the core in every sense.

The critical difference between Linus and his colleagues is never more evident than in his "anything for a buck" attitude. While they are all caught up in the world of corporate finance, Linus has long since worn away the line separating business from pleasure. Business had become the end-all be-all for Linus.

Excited at the prospect of his younger brother David's forthcoming marriage to the daughter of a rival businessman — the owner of Tyson Electronics — Linus anticipates that the marriage will guarantee a proposed merger between the two companies. While his hopes for the couple's good fortune appear honorable, they are ultimately misguided.

When the chauffeur's daughter Sabrina is suddenly thrown into the mix, the lives of both of the Larrabee men are irrevocably changed.

Forever the playboy, David's love for Elizabeth Tyson (Lauren Holly) begins to falter as he finds himself unexpectedly falling in love with Sabrina. Afraid that breaking off David's engagement will mean an end to the firm's merger, Linus takes matters into his own hands. He executes an elaborate plan to coax Sabrina into falling in love with him rather than David.

Linus reveals to her his cruel intent just as she begins to fall for him. His plan backfires, though, when he realizes that the unexpected and unthinkable has occurred — he has fallen in love with Sabrina.

The screenplay for *Sabrina* was nearly complete and yet there was no leading lady to portray the title role.

Having interviewed nearly 40 actresses for the title role — most of whom were virtual unknowns — Pollack narrowed the selection down to a handful of candidates. The short list included the likes of Julia Roberts and Robin Wright-Penn. Thoughts of casting Winona Ryder reportedly caused quite a ruckus in the Ford household, with Ford's wife vehemently responding to the consideration with a firm "No."

"It's bullshit," claimed Ford. "One of the interesting things about Winona Ryder, something I admire, is that she doesn't seem to have an age. She's ageless. I don't know where they came up with the story. Even if my wife had said it, and she didn't, it's not good thinking. This is after all, an inter-generational love story. But I do think there is something about Winona Ryder that's a little too close to Audrey Hepburn. What was difficult was finding an established actress who was willing to bear that comparison."[8]

Nixing the American selections altogether, Pollack favored a trio of European actresses for the role, and ultimately chose British actress Julia Ormond (*Legends of the Fall*, *First Knight*) over British ballerina Darcy Bussell and French screen star Juliette Binoche. Paramount Pictures Chairman Sherry Lansing offered her enthusiastic support, vowing that the actress was "the most beautiful thing I had ever seen in my life. She's just breathtaking. She's magnificently beautiful. I think she's breathtakingly beautiful."[9]

Ford wholeheartedly concurred that his newly chosen 29-year-old co-star was the ideal Sabrina. "Julia has a lot of classical training, classical discipline," said the actor. "She has a good head on her shoulders, a very good sense of herself and the world around her. It's not her star quality that distinguishes her so much as the capacity of her mind. Of course, it doesn't hurt that she's so damn easy to look at."[10]

The next step was to complete the love triangle by casting the appropriate actor for the role of Linus' playboy brother David (portrayed in the original film by actor William Holden).

Great difficulties arose for casting agent David Rubin: "No big star would consider the part," noted an industry observer. "Not only does Ford get the girl, but since it's a Cinderella story, it's basically a girl's movie."[11]

Due in part to the preconceptions about the film, the role passed from Tom Cruise, Alec Baldwin and even John F. Kennedy, Jr., into the hands of Greg Kinnear, a relative newcomer to the silver screen. (Kinnear, whose only screen appearance was a cameo in *Blankman*, additionally acted as writer-anchor for E! Entertainment Television's *Talk Soup* and hosted the short-lived NBC early morning talk show *Later with Greg Kinnear*.)

Based on his résumé, one would not expect Kinnear to make his first cinematic foray in the company of Sydney Pollack and Harrison Ford. In fact, when Pollack interviewed him at the suggestion of a friend, the director admitted to Kinnear that his chance of landing the role was a "long shot."[12]

"It was one of those bizarre, once-in-a-lifetime phone calls I got," said Kinnear. "My agent said Sydney Pollack wants to meet with you. And I thought it was a gag. I'm still convinced it was some sort of horrible mix-up — some sort of bureaucratic mistake in paperwork."[13]

Although Pollack initially considered it a gamble to cast Kinnear, he would later state that "he's exceptional in the film. Anyone who has their doubts better hold off till they see the guy's work."[14]

Ironically, those cynics were enthralled three years later when Kinnear earned himself a Best Supporting Actor nomination for his work opposite Jack Nicholson in James Brooks' *As Good As It Gets*.

Production designer Brian Morris and location manager Joseph E. Iberti spent much of the summer of 1994 scouring the eastern seaboard of the United States to find a location for the Larrabee estate. The filmmakers at last chose an estate named Salutation, situated in the town of Glen Cove, New York, overlooking Long Island Sound.

The 20-acre estate, located on Dosoris Lane — which coincidentally was the original street on which Billy Wilder filmed his *Sabrina*—was built by Junius Spencer Morgan, grandson of noteworthy financier J. Pierpont Morgan. Completed in 1929, the estate was occupied by his wife Louise C. Morgan following his death in 1960. She remained there until her death in 1974, after which the entire estate and its contents were auctioned off.

The home was well-suited for the script both structurally and geographically, but the production made several alterations to the interior and the exterior of the house, which the crew affectionately nicknamed "Camp Larrabee."

Vacant for many years, its parquet floors and wainscoting were thoroughly cleaned and restored to a lustrous finish. While furniture was being specially designed and constructed, Brian Morris oversaw the interior application of a custom paint color — a variation of vanilla that he christened "magnolia." The existing kitchen was reconfigured and furnished to better suit the needs of the script.

The moviemakers also made several drastic changes to the mansion's grounds. Above the existing garage they built a two-story wing which would serve as the quarters for Sabrina and her father Fairchild (John Wood). In addition, they installed a decorative pond, nestled between the garage and house and accented with stepping stones and mock lily pads. Complete with reproduction statuary and a faux flagstone surface, the West Lawn's outdoor ballroom dance floor and bandstand area would serve as the setting for the Larrabees' parties. The production would further set-dress the scenery by incorporating artificial plants including dogwood and wisteria blossoms, dispersing them throughout the compound's grounds. Local residents offered their private sailboats, mooring them along the nearby docks in the background.

To complement the elegant surroundings of the Larrabee estate, costume designers Ann Roth and the director's brother Bernie Pollack outfitted Julia Ormond and Harrison Ford, respectively.

Although Roth was assigned to be the overall costume designer for the film, Pollack felt special attention was necessary for Ford. Having first collaborated on *Clear and Present Danger*, this was the second project for Bernie and Harrison.

Fashion designer Nino Cerruti created the impeccably tailored garments traditional of the East Coast — the old-money look of suit and bow tie — which Ford would don for the bulk of the film.

"The clothes are very beautifully fitted and sewn," attested Cerruti. "This creates the impression of a man of considerable means who's not vain, but is used to everything being just so. Remember, we are creating a character who's very set in his ways."[15]

"Clothes are terrifically important," believed Ford, "because people appropriate visual information much more quickly than spoken information. It's critical not to give them a false clue."[16]

On the other hand, Ford was careful to point out that the clothes were an aid to filmmaking: "It's not about clothes. It's about precision storytelling, about not being a few degrees off in any area. That's my job — I'm an assistant storyteller.[17]

"You move in a different way in different kinds of clothing. Shoes affect the way you walk; shirt cuffs affect the way you hold your arms," the actor added.[18]

Sometimes what he does not wear is most important. During the filming of a sequence that required him to sit behind his executive suite's desk, Ford did not need to wear Cerruti's entire outfit. Because his waist and everything below it were out of camera range, Ford settled for his own denim and loafers.

"Then I realized it was affecting my performance," noted the actor. "I kicked myself for not taking the time to put on the entire suit."[19]

Aside from his genuine concern for the craft, the actor is not forgetful of the perks: "And if I happen to end up with a lot of nice suits, there's nothing wrong with that."[20]

Just a short time before *Sabrina* began principal photography, Ford appeared in a French film entitled *Les Cent et Une Nuits* (*A Hundred and One Nights*). The scene, which depicted a startled and unkempt Ford in an unscripted and obvious stolen shot, played out when he was introduced as himself

With Julia Ormond in Sydney Pollack's *Sabrina* (Paramount, 1995).

to a famed director of the French cinema. The film told of "Monsieur Cinema," a legendary 100-year-old director who hires a young woman to remind him of how important film was to his life by recalling memories and introducing him to celebrities at both his villa and on the streets of Hollywood.

Calling Ford's involvement a "cameo" in the film would have been too generous. He was on-screen less than ten seconds when it finally opened in French theaters in January 1995.

Elsewhere and only days later in the United States, Paramount's *Sabrina* began principal photography on January 30, 1995, in and around the Larrabee estate.

After several weeks on location at the estate, the production ventured into New York City to film the sequences involving the offices of Larrabee Communications. The Park Avenue address of the America's Society building was photographed for exterior entranceway shots. The interiors of Linus' offices were filmed on a sound stage at Kaufman Astoria Studios elsewhere in the city.

Additionally, the production filmed on various streets throughout Manhattan, at Elmhurst Hospital, the East 60th Street heliport and the entrance of the Vivolo Italian restaurant, which was transformed into a Moroccan eatery where Linus and Sabrina enjoy a finger-fed meal. The interior sequence was photographed on a set on a Kaufman Astoria sound stage.

Next on the schedule was the city of Paris, France. There, the cast and crew spent three weeks filming Sabrina's life abroad, against the backdrop of the beautiful landmarks of the City of Lights. Among the highlights were the Eiffel Tower, the Alexandre III Bridge, the Seine, Monmarte, Place du Trocadero and the Louvre Pyramid.

In Paris, the production mainly filmed sequences involving Julia Ormond and her colleagues from *Vogue* magazine — portrayed by French film stars Fanny Ardant (Irene) and Patrick Bruel (Louis). Ford's services were required for just one day. Filmed on a bridge along the Pont des Arts, a lengthy kiss-and-embrace scene between the principals (utilized in the final moment of the film) was photographed without a hitch — until infamous European "gutter press" got involved.

Proving that "a picture is worth a thousand words," the tabloids speculated about an affair between Ford and Ormond. Their story was made more believable by accompanying photos meticulously edited to eliminate all traces of the movie set.

Ford completely ignored the incident. He and his wife Melissa went on with their life together. They were amused by the reports that she rushed to the Parisian locale as "the avenging wife"— a trip she simply couldn't recall taking.

"Harrison doesn't attract that kind of innuendo much. He's lucky," claimed his wife.[21]

In an effort to clear her name and to draw attention to the absurdity of the rumors, Ormond stated: "Now, you tell me, if Harrison Ford was having an affair with someone, would he take them to a very public bridge in Paris and suck face with them? I mean, get real."[22]

It was suggested by the production that the two actors make a conscious effort from that point forward not to appear in public close to one another. The two appearing within the same photograph could easily have been manipulated and circulated, thus adding more fuel to the fire of rumors.

On April 23, 1995, Paramount relocated its production to an island location 270 miles east of New York City, where, coincidentally, President Clinton and the First Family frequently vacationed. Situated off the Massachusetts coast, Martha's Vineyard (winter population 14,000, summer population 100,000) served as the setting for Linus and Sabrina's getaway, substituting for the afternoon sail Bogart and Hepburn took in the original film.

For two days, scenes of the Larrabee cottage were photographed at the summertime residence of musician Billy Joel, located on Menemsha Harbor in the town of Chilmark. Joel's cottage — on loan for the three-day shoot — was given cosmetic changes to accommodate the seasonal look demanded in the script. To create the image of springtime on an island whose blooming season is late, silk leaves and flowers were affixed to tree branches.

On the third and final day of island photography, the production ventured onto Main Street in the town of Vineyard Haven to film the couple's bicycle ride. They wrapped with scenes of Linus' jet arriving at and departing from the Vineyard's airport.

While the island made a great impression upon the crew members, many were too busy to enjoy it. Nearly everyone, including Ford, expressed an interest in returning there soon — for pleasure rather than business.

The production then returned to the Long Island estate to photograph two key party sequences. The nighttime exterior scenes required an array of outdoor light riggings. The production built its own miniature power plant to provide sufficient energy to the ten-kilowatt lights affixed to the Condor cranes high above the set. So bright were the lights that disoriented birds chirped incessantly, thinking that dawn had arrived. Similarly, the compound's tree frog community did likewise, yet with a more irritating effect.

"I was joking about fires, floods, pestilence — and then the frogs hit," recalled director Pollack.[23]

The sequence where David courts his guests, and Linus entraps Sabrina, were filmed in the greenhouse at the Planting Fields Arboretum in nearby Oyster Bay. The miracle of editing created the illusion that the solarium was on the mansion grounds.

The forces of nature plagued the production, delaying shooting and resulting in a return trip to Paris for additional photography. As a result, Paramount's planned summer release of its $50-million-plus investment was postponed to a December 15, 1995 release date.

Just prior to its release, Sydney Pollack met with Billy Wilder to preview his contemporary version of the old classic.

"The hardest thing I will ever do in my life was when I sat in a dark screening room and showed it to him," acknowledged the director. "He made it clear that we were remaking his baby. He's the only guy who can call you a son of a bitch and be encouraging at the same time."[24]

Pollack survived the ordeal, claiming that Wilder was "unsentimental" about his efforts.

"You have to realize," explained Pollack, "this is very hard for a filmmaker. I'll know what it's like some day when they remake *The Way We Were*."[25]

Despite hearsay that Ford and Pollack clashed during the filming (which the two vehemently denied), the filming of Sabrina was a largely enjoyable shoot for everyone involved.

Greg Kinnear claimed that as for intimidation, working with Ford on his first assignment ranked "about 101 on a scale of 100."[26]

"It seems to me that the bigger they are, the more powerful they are, you get a sense that they can be any way they want," claimed Kinnear. "Sometimes that can be very dark and negative — I mean, you hear those stories and you read about them. But Harrison is the exact opposite. This is a guy who can be any way he wants, and what's remarkable is that he's unbelievably gracious, nice and down-to-earth. He didn't have to go out of his way to make this an easy experience for me, but he did, from the very first day. I was standing around and it seemed to me that everybody knew everybody else, except for me. I don't come from this world, you know, so I was the guy standing over in the corner eating a bran muffin. I felt very awkward. All of a sudden, up walked Harrison and he said, So you're my brother, huh? Goddamn good-looking, isn't he?' And everyone started laughing. I will be eternally grateful to him for that."[27]

That same day, Ford reportedly pulled a joke on Kinnear, helping to alleviate the day's stress and reinforce their relationship.

Just before shooting was to commence, Kinnear asked the experienced Ford whether chewing gum was permitted during photography. Ford gave him the go-ahead. Moments into the first scene, Ford reacted with a whiny outburst: "Are you chewing *gum*? Sydney, I can't work with this guy!"[28]

"Yeah, he's quite the jokester," asserted Kinnear. "He's always had a pretty good time at my expense, I don't mind telling you."[29]

Relative screen newcomer Lauren Holly — who portrayed Kinnear's other love interest — was similarly impressed by Ford.

"I now have a crush on someone for the rest of my life," professed the actress. "He's just a great example for all up-and-coming stars because he's such a hard worker, a completely dedicated family man, so proud of his children and wife — just an all-around gentleman."[30]

Holly's screen mother, Angie Dickinson — who plays wife to Richard Crenna's Patrick Tyson — found working with Ford to be both an enlightening and therapeutic experience.

"Harrison was charming every minute he was on the set," said the famed actress. "He's about the only man on the screen these days who gets my heart pounding."[31]

Predictably, New York City was the setting for the world premiere of Sabrina. On Monday, December 4th, hundreds gathered to attend the special screening held at Sony Lincoln Plaza and the after-party held at Tavern on the Green.* The exclusive New York premiere's guest list included Ford, accompanied by his wife (whose screenplay adaptation of The Indian in the Cupboard was just released as well), Julia

---

*On the opposite coast, the film's December 8 L.A. premiere was organized as a fund-raiser to benefit "Stop Cancer."

Ormond, director Pollack, Stephen Bogart (author-son of Humphrey and Lauren Bacall) and Ford's previous *Fugitive* co-star Joe Pantoliano.

The Paris-based Cerruti offered each attendee a personal-sized bottle of his "1881" body fragrance. Additionally, as a gesture in silent tribute to Linus Larrabee, polka-dotted ties that Ford wore in the film were also distributed as gifts to all.

Unfortunately, the film received a mixed critical reception and was not warmly received at the box office. Following the film's $5,560,000 opening weekend, it performed sluggishly. In the end, it totaled only $53.7 million in domestic ticket sales—barely recouping the initial investment made to put it on the big screen.

The Academy of Motion Picture Arts and Sciences was charitable to the film. It was nominated for two Academy Awards: the first for John Williams' score and the second for the Best Original Song "In the Moonlight" (written by Williams and Alan and Marilyn Bergman and sung by ex–Police vocalist Sting).

In addition Harrison Ford got his fourth Golden Globe nomination.

While some critics enjoyed Pollack's update, others inanely looking for a Xerox were left unsatisfied. Ford explained that the 1995 version was intended to stand on its own rather than rest on its similarities to Billy Wilder's earlier classic. Before committing to the project, the actor decided not to view the original. "I don't think it's important for me to see it. If people know I've seen it, then I'll have to talk about that. So if I've never seen it, I'm much cleaner...."[32]

During the film's pre-production period, the actor made the decision to view the film, solely to ensure that he could participate in knowledgeable conversations with his director.

"Obviously, it's a film that was made 40 years ago. It's in and of that time. And this movie is in and of its time. Obviously, there are some differences in the Linus character. Which made it more interesting for me to play."[33]

Comparisons were made between the portrayals of the film's central characters. Julia Ormond (who would be given the honor of "Female Star of Tomorrow" by Nato/ShoWest in March of that year) was initially reluctant and later considered "a very brave" actress to have considered taking on the role of Sabrina Fairchild. Ford himself was not the least concerned about portraying Larrabee after Bogie. "I didn't give a damn. I didn't care at all. I figured it was 40 years ago and I'd never seen the movie...."[34]

"I didn't put myself in a position to judge his performance," exhorted the actor. "It was no part of what I was about, when I saw the film. I don't worry about imitation because I don't have his box to work out of. I don't have his experiences. I don't have his personality. I have mine. So we're necessarily different.

"I was freed of any apprehension because I didn't allow the notion that we would be compared. It would spoil my pleasure. I found the movie pleasurable. I did not assess his role in that pleasure, because I knew that we were going to reconstitute the recipe."[35]

The actor was quick to respond to critics' negative feedback. "It's funny. Nobody would be asking this question if we'd done *Hamlet*. Stories are always being retold, particularly stories as good as *Sabrina*."[36]

30

A DEVIL OF A TIME

Throughout Harrison Ford's career, the terms "high-profile" and "big-budget" were commonplace when used to describe the projects in which he was involved. To coincide with the nation's economy and the ever-changing demands of Hollywood, those terms would be radically redefined by Ford's next project *The Devil's Own*.

When word began to circulate that Ford would share top billing with the highly publicized 32-year-old actor Brad Pitt, the project instantly became one of the most anticipated films of 1996.

The production should have had all the elements required to ensure an uneventful shooting process. Yet, by the release date of March 26, 1997, it was at the center of controversies reminiscent of Kevin Costner's 1994 film *Waterworld*.

With its grossly over-inflated budget (reportedly in excess of $75–$85 million) and rumors of feuding among the films central cast members, the production of the film proved Murphy's Law: "Anything that can go wrong, will go wrong."

Producer Lawrence Gordon — whose impressive credits included *48 HRS*, *Die Hard*, *Predator* and *Field of Dreams* — personally asked that the script be further developed. It told of an IRA soldier who flees to America to escape a life of violence, but is involuntarily thrust back into it. Screenwriter Kevin Jarre (*Rambo: First Blood Part II*, *Glory*, *Tombstone*) was hired and initially produced an acceptable draft nearly ten years earlier. As the producer recalled, Jarre disappeared for several years, only to return with an acceptable screenplay.

In 1991, Gordon's casting brought him in contact with the then relatively unknown Brad Pitt. Until then, Pitt had appeared in a slew of forgettable feature films and television movies. With Pitt enthusiastically accepting the script — which Gordon recalled "was supposed to be a gritty, low-budget thriller with Brad as the only star"[1] — the project seemed to be moving forward toward the pre-production phase.

However, the project was soon left at a standstill due to concerns over the questionable investment in an actor whose credits were none too impressive. Furthermore, the producers faced resistance to the politically controversial subject matter on which the story was based.

Although its life force waned during the ensuing years, interest in the project was later renewed. This stemmed primarily from Pitt's Golden Globe–nominated performance in *Legends of the Fall* and his second Golden Globe and Oscar nomination for Best Supporting Actor in *12 Monkeys*. With his now impressive résumé (which also boasted the box office sensations *Se7en, Thelma and Louise, A River Runs Through It* and *Interview with the Vampire*), Pitt catapulted to international stardom, both as a critically acclaimed actor and as a male icon who frequently dominated the world's "Sexiest Man Alive" lists.

Rights to *The Devil's Own* were originally offered to Universal, but representatives there didn't see the project's potential. The proposal was then sent to Columbia, where optimistic eyes saw the very success Gordon and Pitt envisioned when they first received Jarre's script. The studio agreed to invest the estimated $60 million required to bring the project to fruition. It commenced by expending $1.5 million for Gordon's producing services and $9 million for Pitt's talent and good looks — no small amount considering his prior role in *Se7en* had netted him just $4 million.

Since their leading man's presence alone was enough to guarantee that the final product would be hugely successful, Columbia then had to decide whose name should be placed below his as co-star. Both Gene Hackman and Sean Connery were considered, but, in the end, each was overruled due to his advanced age.

It was Pitt's suggestion that Harrison Ford be cast as Tom O'Meara, the 23-year veteran NYPD cop who considers Rory (Pitt) to be the son he never had.

"I wanted Harrison because, well, I've always loved Harrison," said Pitt. "You get this sense of integrity."[2]

While Gordon was tantalized by the idea of attaching two of the biggest names in film to his project, there were immediate obstacles.

Initially, the studio balked at the suggestion that Ford be included. After all, they were convinced that Pitt alone guaranteed a hit. Luckily, one man — Mark Canton, the studio's then ill-fated chairman — embraced the idea.

Ford was approached with the offer and signed on. In doing so, he commanded the industry's maximum price tag of $20 million in addition to points (equal to an estimated 15 percent of the films final financial take).

Barry Josephson, Columbia's production head, recalled the reaction to the decision: "We presented the studio with the option of making the movie with just Brad. At the end of the day we were happy with the direction it was headed. Those two guys together was a coup. People called to tell us, 'I can't believe that you pulled that cast off.'"[3]

For Gordon, Ford's decision was the icing on the cake. "I'd been sending Harrison every script I'd had for 20 years," revealed the producer, "so it was to my great pleasure and surprise when he said 'yes' to this one."[4]

The script Ford read and approved told the story of an Irish-American New York City policeman, O'Meara, who opens his home to Irish immigrant Rory Devaney. Regarded by family man O'Meara as the son he never had, Rory (a.k.a. Frankie "The Angel" McGuire) reveals his true identity as an IRA member sent to the United States to acquire weapons. O'Meara discovers the disturbing truth that his guest is not who he claims to be, but is in fact a criminal. O'Meara must choose either to sympathize with Rory and turn a blind eye to the moral consequences, or to remain faithful to his job as an officer of the law and allow those ethics to dictate his actions.

Ford chose the role not only out of a liking for the O'Meara character, but more so for the complexities that lie beneath the surface. He claimed that neither his character nor Pitt's character could have been classified as a hero. He saw the film simply about two decent men who become friends and, as the story pans out, must turn against each other.

"In American film there is a good guy and a bad guy," said the film's director Alan Pakula, explaining the unique qualities that attracted him to the project. "It's the first thing my grandson always asks: Who's the good guy and who's the bad guy? When I say Harrison Ford and Brad Pitt are both good guys, that throws him.

"What's interesting to me," continued the director, "is what happens when people with two different senses of what is right and what is wrong meet. What's interesting is the fact that these two men can love and respect each other. It makes it more complicated. Much more interesting and much more human."[5]

To round out the cast, the producers selected Margaret Colin as Ford's wife Sheila; Ruben Blades as Ford's partner in crime fighting Sgt. Edwin Diaz; George Hearn as the IRA-sympathizing judge Peter Fitzsimmons; and Treat Williams as Irish-American arms dealer Billy Burke.

Ford had befriended Williams at England's Elstree Studios during the 1979 production of *The Empire Strikes Back*— where Treat had managed to make his way onto the exclusive set, and was in tan fatigues to portray a rebel officer.

The daughter of a retired Irish-American New York police officer, Margaret Colin found that portraying the role of the Irish-American wife of an Irish-American New York police officer came instinctively. The actress had previously appeared in *Three Men and a Baby*, *Amos and Andrew*, *Terminal Velocity* and the phenomenally successful *Independence Day*, among others.

Alternately, Ruben Blades' role as a Big Apple cop could not have been further removed from his own background. With a feature film history including *The Milagro Beanfield War*, *Predator 2*, *Mo' Better Blues* and *The Two Jakes*, the actor was a graduate of Harvard Law School. Blades was also an advocate for international human rights causes and had sought election for the Presidency of his native Panama, garnering nearly 25 percent of the popular vote. Noteworthy for his efforts to popularize Salsa music throughout North America, Blades had been awarded multiple Grammy awards. Actively involved in both careers, the actor could on occasion be found performing to New York City audiences immediately following the completion of his scenes.

While Pitt was initially interested in the involvement of director Bryan Singer — whose *Usual Suspects* had won him the respect of many in Hollywood — the list of proposed directors was narrowed down to the aforementioned Alan Pakula, pending availability.

Having reviewed the script, cast and offer laid before him, Pakula enthusiastically signed on to the project. Offering the multi–Oscar-nominated director-screenwriter a $5 million salary, the studio further negotiated to provide him with a percentage of the film's final cut — a benefit that producer Gordon willingly sacrificed in exchange for Pakula's commitment.

It seemed that the project was a dream-come-true for the director. Yet, despite all of its appealing qualities, amendments were necessary before filming could commence.

On the New York streets filming Alan Pakula's *The Devil's Own* (Columbia, 1997).

In Jarre's script, Ford's O'Meara was a secondary character. It was Ford and the studio's joint decision to beef up the character. With Columbia's hefty financial investment in their cast, the studio sought a balance between getting their money's worth from their actors while respecting Jarre's talent. As screenwriter David Aaron Cohen put it: "Take it from Columbia's perspective—'Twenty million, and you want Harrison to be the *supporting* actor?'"[6]

With that, two additional script doctors were hired to expand Ford's role. Despite his admiration for the story, Ford thought that if he were to accept the role, it would have to go through a certain transformation in order to be acceptable.

In November 1995, that transformation began. Unsatisfied with Jarre's rewrite and facing time restrictions, Gordon and Pakula sought outside assistance. With that, Vincent Patrick (*The Pope of Greenwich Village*, *Family Business*) and Cohen (*V.I. Warshawski*) were sent in for rewrites.

"Once Ford got in there," recalled Patrick, "there was no way they were going to shoot [the original] script. It had to become a two-hero piece with equal action heroes. Supporting two stars is what this was about."[7]

While Pitt was completing principal photography on Barry Levinson's *Sleepers*, a mustachioed Ford (unsuccessfully attempting to persuade director Pakula to consider a different look for the role; this resulted in his appearance on *Movieline*'s list of "The 100 Dumbest Things Hollywood's Done Lately"[8]) met almost daily with Patrick and Cohen during the months prior to production to discuss the development of the script. Much to Pitt's chagrin, it appeared that major modifications to his character were evolving without his consent.

"He came in and panicked and said, 'This is not the film I wanted to make,'" recalled Director Pakula.[9]

Patrick sympathized with the young, Missouri-raised actor: "Alan is faced with a situation where you have Brad Pitt in love with this script for four years and suddenly it's being changed. Nobody can like that."[10]

As the on-paper dynamics of the relationship between Ford and Pitt's characters changed, it was only natural that his screen time did likewise. Rumors spread that Ford did not like the idea of being upstaged by a rookie. Several enhancements were made involving O'Meara's character, thereby stretching out his screen time and inadvertently altering the storyline.

"It was never a question of the quality of the parts or of the amount of time on screen," explained Ford. "What was a factor was how the character was described and how he behaved."[11]

Segments of Jarre's original script were drastically altered or completely deleted. Changes involving Pitt's character included the film's new introduction that depicted a childhood Rory witnessing the murder of his father, subsequently providing him with the reason for enlisting in the IRA. Rory was likened by screenwriter Vincent Patrick as a kind of "existential anti-hero."[12] The script's earlier incarnation portrayed him as a member of New York's seedy underworld who partook in the excessive consumption of alcohol and cocaine and who resorted to violence with regularity.

One moment which displayed Rory's violent demeanor as originally intended was seen during the scene in which Burke's henchmen conduct a home invasion and assault on a cowering O'Meara and his wife.[13] As it was originally written, Rory suddenly appears, reacting vehemently — with a swinging sledgehammer.

Patrick recalled the sequence as it was originally written in the early draft, and was pleased and proud of the rewrite: "What you have is a fight in which these two guys together do the fighting. And one puts his arm around the other guy's shoulders, and, you know, quote, 'male bonding' is occurring here."[14]

O'Meara got a younger and more attractive family. Also, the disheveled character that the script described was replaced by a well-mannered, job-devoted, family-oriented man. Additionally, a sequence in which Ford's character fumbles with his firearm was omitted, considering the character's flawlessly professional attributes. Also added was an incident where his partner Diaz shoots an unarmed robbery suspect in the back, testing the limits of O'Meara's morality as he reflects upon what action to take, helping to further define his character.

"It was important to me," said Ford, "that there was some moral compromise of my character so that we didn't have one character with a black hat and one character with a white hat."[15]

In the meantime, and on multiple occasions thereafter, Pitt journeyed to Belfast, Ireland, to help him prepare for his role. "I did all the research I could. Unfortunately, the troubles in Ireland have gone on for 300 years and I don't think there's any way to completely understand them if you haven't grown up in them...."[16] Pitt convened with Brendan Gunn, a Belfast native who tutored the actor on the history of the conflict and served as his dialogue coach.

"When we first started, I went to meet Harrison," recalled an amused Pitt. "We'd only met a couple of times. And he said, 'What have you been doing?' I said, 'Ah, I've bean warking on the ah-ccent. It's bean coming alon' vary good.' And he says, 'Yeah? Let me hear some.' He's good that way."[17]

Ford researched his role by meeting members of the New York City Police Department. He joined them nearly one dozen times on routine patrol throughout various areas including the Washington Heights section to get a feel for a patrolman's daily lifestyle in addition to getting a better sense of the neighborhoods.

On March 14, 1996, 33-year-old Kevin Gillespie, the New York City policeman who served as the actor's technical consultant, was shot and killed in the line of duty — the first in a long list of unforeseen tribulations for the production.

Everyone appeared to be in agreement about the Patrick-Cohen rewrites, but Pitt was still unsatisfied. He believed that his character was beginning to evolve into a stereotypical nasty. Pakula saw that his actor's prime concern lay with the lack of respect being paid to the current Irish situation: "He got anxious that what we wanted to do was 'Patriot Games II,'" the director explained delicately, careful to avoid insult to Ford's 1992 film. "Brad didn't want to come out playing the straight heavy. I told him no way was that going to happen."[18]

To calm the frustrated Pitt, the producers hired yet another screenwriter — Terry George (*In the Name of the Father*) — roughly one week before principal photography commenced. George's primary purpose was to concentrate on fixing what the actor thought was a superficial outlook on the IRA situation.

"The first draft we had was full of leprechaun jokes and green beer," recalled Pitt. "I had this responsibility to represent somewhat these people whose lives have been shattered. It would have been an injustice to Hollywoodize it. It was coming very close to shooting time. It made me very uneasy.[19] ... I know how it gets on a set. It costs $150,000 a day to shoot and we have to shoot something the next day and if we don't have it written down things get sloppy."[20]

Pitt's discomfort grew more apparent. With the clock ticking away and only one week remaining before the rigidly enforced February 5 commencement date of principal photography, the actor threatened to walk away from the project. Fueling his disgust was Mark Canton. The studio head insisted that the cameras roll with or without any filmable material available.

Pitt had threatened to leave the ailing production behind. But a threatened $63 million fine (a figure calculated from the estimated foreign and domestic earning of the film if it were to be released) caused him to rethink his position.

According to a spokesman for Sony, "Everyone was willing to gracefully walk away from the movie and the studio held it together. Mark would have been much too embarrassed. Even if it was good business."[21] Lawyers for the film claimed that, "It was Mark Canton's way of buying the continuation of his job."[22]

Pitt was then faced with a predicament: either he remain to fulfill his contract or he abandon the project that had once enthralled him and surrender to the lawsuit.

"My feeling," recalled Pakula, "was then let's see if we can find some gifted young Irish actor, get Harrison to stay, and go ahead with the film."[23]

Low morale and mental fatigue afflicted everyone involved. Even Ford, despite having dealt with such complications in the past, was dismayed by Pitt's reaction.

"I felt exactly the same way as he did, at times," acknowledged Ford. "What the hell are we doing here? Why the hell should we go ahead at great risk to ourselves and our reputations to try and pull this thing out? There was no one piece polished enough to [place] it in the setting and say, 'Oh, doesn't that look nice.' So there was a lot of work to be done and that happens from time to time. The same thing happened to me on *The Fugitive* and I'm not surprised by it."[24]

Although Ford's feelings mirrored Pitt's own, he noted, "I didn't for a minute think that anybody was going to let us walk away ... I regret it when it happens and then you soldier on, get to work and try to make it better."[25]

After careful consideration, Ford's co-star retracted his threat. Prompted, no doubt, by the outrageous thought of signing his name to a $63 million check, the actor agreed to live up to his contract despite the unresolved issues still at hand — and was rewarded with an additional $3 million insisted upon by his CAA (Creative Artist's Agency) agent, Kevin Huvane.

When filming in such a vastly complex environment as New York City, the planning stage is overwhelming: hotels are booked; permits are secured; space is rented; schedules are made.

And so the cast and crew readied themselves, confident in their ability to overcome the troubles they knew must be looming ahead. Notwithstanding their fruitless attempts to secure ready-to-shoot script, Gordon, Pakula and crew were held at executive gunpoint and given an ultimatum: "It's now or never."

Five weeks into filming through one of the most agonizing winters recorded in New York history, the production added yet another employee to their ever-expanding payroll. Robert Mark Kamen (*A Walk in the Clouds*) became the fifth screenwriter hired to work on the screenplay. Kamen was immediately given what was called a compilation script. The screenwriter worked for 16 weeks and earned $1 million for his efforts, but remained uncredited despite a Writers Guild arbitration. Patrick and Cohen took first and second billing while Jarre followed — having applied what fellow scripter Patrick downplayed merely as a "polish."[26]

"They were running out of script to shoot," recalled Kamen. "They had a script that wasn't acceptable to either actor. Alan didn't start with a script that everyone had signed off on. We were flying blind. You can't say, 'This is what we're shooting today, here are the pages,' because we didn't have any pages. It was scary."[27]

Members of the Sony brass (including Mark Canton) personally visited the production almost daily, fearing further delays. Their visits were further prompted by rumors of on-set tension that were difficult to ignore given the media attention it got. The Sony elite meanwhile discovered that the already hefty budget was being mismanaged. The crew reportedly began playing basketball when there was no material to be filmed, resulting in overtime pay and unhappy investors.

The inevitable rumors began to circulate regarding ill will between the film's leading men. Tabloids reported that the two were at odds. They claimed each would begrudgingly retire to his own dressing room trailer to avoid dealing with the issues at hand.

Kamen contended that the relationship between Ford and Pitt was one of healthy professional interaction: "It wasn't the tension between them that made things tense," he explained. "It was the tension each had with his own part."[28]

"Whatever disagreements we had on this film, and we had our disagreements," said Pakula, "at least these are passionate men who have passionate feelings about what is right and what is wrong, as I did myself."[29]

"If truth be told, Brad and I got along just fine," revealed Ford. "There was never any conflict between the two of us. There was never a personal acrimony between us. There was often a question about how best to resolve a problem but I never felt a lack of respect or sympathy between us."[30]

"People weren't hiding in their trailers," stressed Brad Pitt. "I'm so against that. I don't admire it, I don't respect it, I have no time for it. It kind of bothered me...."[31]

"What's funny to me is that the tabloids started all the problems," continued the bewildered actor. "People ran with it from the tabloids. The movie was going along normally, like a normal movie. I mean, we'd get there at night — it was a 24-hour kind of thing — because after the shooting day was done, they'd want to get together: 'We're going to shoot this tomorrow. We're shooting this stuff this week,' keep constantly working scenes. It was a night-and-day thing...."[32]

Columbia production head Barry Josephson recalled, "Alan was changing the screenplay. Therefore he opened it up for consultation with the actors. They never argued. It was clear in every meeting what Brad wanted to hold onto, and what was important to Harrison. In the end there was agreement."[33]

Pitt traveled to Los Angeles to attend the Academy Awards; he had received a Best Supporting Actor Oscar nomination for *12 Monkeys*, but the award went to Ed Harris for his performance in *Apollo 13*. While there, Pitt reportedly considered not returning to the New York production. During Pitt's two-day trip, the production found itself at a complete standstill with Ford sidelined by an abscessed tooth.

As before, the actor reconsidered his plan to walk, stating, "It's a work in progress. There are too many good people involved to give up."[34]

Among the various locations photographed throughout the Metropolitan New York City area were Central Park's Wollman Ice Skating Rink; the 1889 Bar and Grill; the Waverly Coffee Shop; the Cloisters Museum at Fort Tryon Park; Baruch College and the Brookdale Campus of Hunter College (whose combined interiors provided the locales of the NYPD); Isham Park; the Staten Island Ferry; a shipyard at 1 Beard Street in Red Hook, New York; the historic Old Town Bar; the Bronx's Piper's Kilt II bar; a Gramercy Park residence (see as the home of New York City District Attorney John Fitzsimmons [George Hearn]); and various New York streets.

Producer Robert F. Colesberry (*Mississippi Burning*) — who shared the producing credit with Lawrence Gordon — considered the inevitable complications an asset to the production.

"A lot of logistical planning goes on subsequent to starting any film," said Colesberry. "But New York is unique. You shoot in the city and you have to work not only with the police but with the people who live there. New Yorkers are not like people in a small town who look upon the inconvenience of filmmaking as a novelty. However, I've lived and worked in New York most of my life and I find that New Yorkers are still the most tolerant people anywhere. They're used to something different happening all the time. That's what gives the city its energy."[35]

Ford, who both lives and works in New York, shared Colesberry's viewpoint:

"You can't replicate New York. It's unlike any place in the world. The combination of the architecture and the people who live here is so distinctive as to be un-reproducable anywhere else."[36]

Several film studios were also used, including Chelsea Piers and Kaufman Astoria Studios in Queens (which was familiar ground for Pakula and Ford, who had filmed portions of *Presumed Innocent* there). Filming also took place outside the city limits at the St. Barnabus Episcopal Church in Irvington, where scenes involving the confirmation of O'Meara's daughter played out. A private dwelling in Montclair, New Jersey, was used for the exterior of the O'Meara residence. The Greenport Long Island waterfront was used for the scenes in which Rory's boat is docked.

Following the completion of United States principal photography in July 1996, the production relocated to war-ravaged Ireland. There, the film's violent 1972 prologue was shot among the streets of the Inchicore neighborhood and the picturesque hillsides of Dublin. During Pitt's stay in Ireland, the actor began to wither both physically and mentally.

At one point, the tabloids cooked up an extraordinarily convoluted "conspiracy theory" involving Ford and his wife. Mathison had written the screenplay for Martin Scorsese's Dalai Lama drama *Kundun. Kundun* was considered to be in competition with Pitt's upcoming film *Seven Years in Tibet*, another Dalai Lama film. It was reported that Ford intentionally caused the delays in *Devil*'s shooting so that Mathison's project would be released without competition.

In response, Ford simply stated, "It was just plain bullshit. I was very insulted."[37]

Pitt received flack for his frequent unwillingness to sign autographs. He was known to cover his head with his coat, or enlist the services of production assistants to shroud him with umbrellas. He regularly harassed the press during filming — most memorably when he recklessly pointed a prop pistol towards some persistent shutterbugs.

"Brad Pitt is the hardest person — harder than Robert De Niro, harder than Marlon Brando—to get pictures of in the history of New York," said celebrity photojournalist Mitch Gerber.[38]

"Harrison was a supreme pro throughout the filming," asserted celebrity photojournalist Alex Oliveira. "He could have cared less if we were there."[39]

Ford could often be seen greeting his fans with handshakes and autographs. On a day in early May, en route to the Gramercy Park shoot, Ford and his longtime driver-assistant Pat King assisted an individual who was having an epileptic seizure on a curbside. The two remained with the ailing man, preventing him from hitting his head on the concrete, while they awaited the arrival of EMS.

The Hogs and Heifers saloon in Manhattan's meat packing district was one of Ford's regular hangouts. The bar was notorious for its female employees and patrons who danced upon the bar, wearing their brassieres atop their heads.

The late Alan Dell, proprietor of Hogs and Heifers, said of Ford, "He's really a regular guy, the best of all the stars I've met. He likes to shoot pool, listen to country music and drink Bass Ale and straight bourbon. He really likes the place and has been coming in about once a week."[40]

On one occasion during the chaotic earlier stages of filming, Ford was reported to have participated in the saloon's brassiere ritual—garnering headlines in several local and national tabs. Matters worsened when the actor was reportedly sighted there with an individual whom *The National Enquirer* described as merely the "mystery blonde."[41] Together the "couple" became inebriated and took to the beer-soaked floor as their private bed on which to roll around. *Star* magazine's headline for the week of May 28, 1996, read "Married Harrison Ford and Sexy Galpal Get Down and Dirty in Biker Bar."[42]

Ford later dismissed the rumors, insisting that the only way to remedy the damage caused by the accusations was to not react at all. "That's just another page in the story," said Ford. "So I just don't do that. I just ignore it."[43]

During the months that passed following the completion of principal photography, the cast and crew assembled to view the film's rough cut. The footage assembled, as a whole, impressed everyone. One exception was the film's final conflict between Rory and O'Meara, which was considered inadequate.

With less than two months before the film's scheduled March 26, 1996 release date, director Pakula reassembled Ford, Pitt and a reduced crew on a Los Angeles soundstage, where the rewritten scene was filmed over a period of two days.

Pakula indicated that only slight alterations were made to the scene. All were in agreement that Ford's O'Meara needed to be more vulnerable—that the audience could see and feel him in danger.

Just weeks before the film's conclusion was re-shot, Brad Pitt sat with a *Newsweek* magazine reporter to discuss the current lensing of his *Seven Years in Tibet*—but *The Devil's Own* also came up:

> Maybe you know the story. We had no script. Well, we had a great script but it got tossed for various reasons. To have to make something up as you go along—Jesus, what pressure! It was ridiculous. It was the most irresponsible bit of filmmaking—if you can call it that—that I've ever seen. I couldn't believe it. I don't know why anyone would want to continue making that movie. We had nothing. The movie was the complete victim of this drowning studio head who said, "I don't care. We're making it. I don't care what you have. Shoot something."[44]

Ford was disappointed by Pitt's remarks: "I think Brad forgot for a minute that he was talking to someone who is paid to write this shit down," noted the actor.[45]

"Brad called that night," recalled director Pakula, "and said, 'Alan, you must be feeling terrible.' I said, 'I'm stunned, Brad, because you told me you were relieved and thrilled with the film.' He said, 'It came out wrong. It's not the way I meant it. That's all I can tell you.'"[46]

"Listen," admitted the actor, "I'm not [back-pedaling]. I've got to be honest with what I said even though it didn't do anyone any good."[47]

Pitt attempted to rationalize the situation in a public apology he wrote (likely prompted by Sony) and had published in *Newsweek* the following week. He wrote:

> It seems I unwittingly fired up a shitstorm. Let me clarify. My discussion with Jeff Giles regarding *The Devil's Own* had nothing to do with my experience shooting the film or the film as a final product. I was referring to my dilemma before

filming began. To me, it was irresponsible that a studio would want to continue with a project without a completed script. You wouldn't start building a house without blueprints. But it wasn't the threat of a lawsuit that kept me in (lawsuits can be fought). It was the belief held by Pakula and Harrison Ford, myself and others that we could pull off a compelling and personal story. And that's just what we did. It's a good movie. I understand how the media made its presumptions, and I understand why my original comments made great copy. I am completely at fault. What will be interesting to see now is if the media will run with the positive the way it ran with the negative.[48]

It is impossible to determine whether his original comments hurt the box office. One thing that was certain, though: Of all those involved in the painstaking production, none were disappointed with the final product.

From director Pakuka—who dislikes directing actors "who don't give me a hard time that way, because it's not very inspiring"[49]—the challenges confronted during the production were to be anticipated when capturing such an involved story. Pakula claimed the greatest challenge for him as a director was to intertwine the personalities of two of the biggest actors in the industry, to ensure that their contributions merged soundly together.

"They are two quite remarkable actors," said Pakula of his leading men, "possibly the two greatest stars of their generations. People ask me what a star is and I say a star is someone who holds an audience's attention on the screen, someone who involves the viewer to such an extent that he or she becomes part of the story in a way that is beyond acting. It's a factor of personality.

"This is the kind of problem every director would love to have: how to weave two riveting personalities into a story. It's a suspense story which I love doing. And each of these actors is capable of keeping an audience wide-eyed and holding its collective breath as his character moves the mystery along."[50]

Although stating without hesitation that the making of the film was the most taxing of his career, Ford also found the experience to be professionally rewarding. The actor considered Pitt's performance to be "very compelling,"[51] and pointed out that he would most certainly act alongside Pitt again, given the respect they had for one another.

"Brad has had enormous success in a relatively short time," said the actor. "That's definitely not what happened to me. He has made some really wise career choices. I admire Brad's work because he takes his work seriously. If, anything, that's one quality we share."[52] Pitt called Ford "completely cool."[53]

"Harrison Ford has this extraordinary decency in the characters he plays," said Pakula. "He is a moral man in an immoral time. He has the ability to convey a high standard of integrity into any part...."[54]

"Whatever problems we had along the way," said Pakula, "in the end Harrison and Brad, two sympathetic, complex actors who themselves have heroic qualities, delivered the depth of acting I needed."[55]

The Devil's Own was released nearly five months after its originally planned November 1, 1996, release date. It was not well received as a whole, but was unanimously praised for its principals' champion performances.

The New York Times' Janet Maslin wrote, "*The Devil's Own* delivers two traffic-stopping star turns for the price of one."[56] *The Chicago Tribune* praised Pitt's performance and claimed, "Ford radiates strength."[57] Mike Clark's *USA Today* review emphasized Ford's integrity, stating that its presence in the film is "automatically credible."[58] *Siskel and Ebert* offered a pair of thumbs up, elaborating, "It's a real treat to watch! Ford and Pitt are in top form!"[59]

Todd McCarthy's review (published in *Variety*'s March 24 issue) applauded the film, yet was pessimistic as to its potential for mass appeal: "*The Devil's Own* is neither the best nor the worst $90 million–$100 million-area budgeted picture ever made, but it must be the one in which the cost is least evident on the screen. A reasonably engrossing, well-crafted suspenser that bears no signs of the much reported on-set difficulties, Alan J. Pakula's latest is much more interested in the moral stature and culpability of the main characters than in heavy action and thrills. Presence of two of the biggest names on the screen today will ensure muscular initial biz domestically and perhaps even more overseas, but grim nature of the yarn and lack of visual fireworks will likely hold this back from the blockbuster status that was certainly hoped for from this combo of stars, making financial break-even a longshot."[60]

A New York City premiere party was held at Manhattan's Four Seasons restaurant on Thursday, March 13, 1997. There, Ford and Pitt did their best to promote the film and dispel the myths of rivalry by courteously posing together for photographs. Following the official opening, its domestic and foreign tallies seemed in line with McCarthy's predictions. Despite a Wednesday opening date, the film garnered a moderate $14.3 million by the end of its opening weekend and amassed approximately $43 million by the end of its box office run.

The year 1996 proved to be a most trying one for Harrison Ford. Between the bad publicity he got during the filming of *The Devil's Own* and its subsequent "poor" reception at the box office, Ford's status as king of the box office seemed to be in jeopardy. After the relatively poor results of *Sabrina*, followed by *The Devil's Own*, Ford chose a project that would end his current losing streak.

31

"America's Kick-Ass President"

Until the 1960s, Presidents of the United States of America traveled by air in such planes as Franklin D. Roosevelt's "The Flying Hotel" and "The Sacred Cow," Eisenhower's "Columbine" and Harry S Truman's "Independence."

During his 1961 administration, President John F. Kennedy officially inaugurated a new institution — the latest in the line of presidential aircraft.

In September of that year, "Air Force One" (originally a Lockheed C-118, but later converted to a Boeing 707) entered the upper atmosphere with its sole purpose to provide a high-altitude limousine service. High above the Earth, the craft chauffeured the world's most important individual in comfort, ease and security.

An American icon, Air Force One would come to represent the soaring symbol of freedom through democracy.

It was thanks to actor Kevin Costner and director Ivan Reitman that Harrison Ford was able to participate in Columbia Pictures' *Air Force One*.

At the suggestion of Costner — who regretfully had to turn down the project due to scheduling conflicts — the screenplay made its way to Ford, then filming *The Devil's Own*.

"Actors hoard good scripts, so it was gracious of Kevin to step aside," claimed an inside source as reported by *Daily Variety*. "He's friends with Harrison, and he wanted the film in good hands."[1]

The film's producer (a long-time friend of Costner), Armyan Bernstein officially cast Ford under the strict provision that shooting commence in 1996. Having long before signed to star in director Ivan Reitman's *Six Days, Seven Nights*, Ford was faced with a difficult decision — as both projects were to begin production concurrently.

Reitman and the film's distributor, Caravan Pictures, deliberated and graciously agreed to delay their production by nearly six months to accommodate Ford's abrupt schedule change.

Ford attached himself to *Air Force One* on the basis of the unique qualities of the material before him (and the now-expected $20 million paycheck).

A recipient of the Nicholl Fellowship in Screenwriting from the Academy of Motion Picture Arts and Sciences for a script written in 1992, Andrew W. Marlowe was elated when his latest project, *Air Force One*, attracted producers throughout Hollywood. It quickly became his first produced screenplay.

Described by Bernstein as "more *Fail-Safe* than *Die Hard*,"[2] Marlowe's script told the tale of the hijacking of an airborne vessel by radical Russian terrorists. What set this story apart from the handful of similar stories that dealt with mid-air terrorism was that the confrontation played out on our Commander in Chief's own Air Force One.

"The challenge," John Shestack, one of the film's producers, claimed, "was to come up with an action movie that was unique and where was there left to go? Effects had gotten as big as they possible can get; body counts had gotten as high as they can go. There really wasn't anything left except to make the action hero be the most powerful man in the world."[3]

Ford's two previous films having been flops, the actor was anxious to star in a winner. When director Wolfgang Petersen's name came into consideration as director, it quickly became the conclusive selling point to secure the actor's final commitment before officially signing on in August 1996.

Ford noted that he was attracted to the role by "the incredible responsibility that the President has—how there is no one moment in his life when he's not beholden to the country's welfare ahead of his own or his family's. As I reflected on it, I was most impressed with the enormous burden of the Presidency. I also thought it was a compelling story with a satisfying sense of triumph at its conclusion. And the prospect of a collaboration with Wolfgang delighted me."[4]

"As you can tell from my films like *In the Line of Fire* and *Das Boot*, I'm always interested in stories that have to do with a political reality," said Petersen. "I like that sense of 'this could happen,' instead of some totally outrageous plot that comes out of nowhere. So when I looked at the idea of Harrison Ford playing an American president who becomes involved in a very dramatic situation that deals with Russian hijackers in the late '90s, it immediately appealed to me."[5]

German director Petersen was taken aback when Ford requested a face-to-face meeting in New York to discuss the project.

"In Europe we don't have these kind of super-superstars," claimed Petersen, "who control the world and say, 'You will be the director.' Normally, I as the director say, 'You will play the part.' And the actors are happy and they fall around my neck!"[6]

At the end of Ford's "interview" with Petersen, the director recalled with amusement, "We had a great time together and he said, 'You have the job.'"[7]

Delighted with their agreement, Petersen confirmed that, given the film's premise, he would not have signed had it not been for the opportunity to work with Ford.

"You're not going to see Harrison Ford sitting behind a desk in the Oval Office in this movie," promised the director. "This President is a man of action and there is no other actor who can match Harrison's combination of strength and intelligence in this kind of role."[8]

To portray the passionate leader of the terrorist group (for a salary of $3 million), the producers selected British actor Gary Oldman, whose intensity and talent was displayed in the films *Sid and Nancy*, *J.F.K.*, *Immortal Beloved*, *The Professional* and *The Fifth Element.* Those qualities were precisely what was required to bring his character Ivan Korshunov to cinematic life.

"[Ford and Oldman] are both highly intelligent actors," explained co-producer Gail Katz, "and they're playing highly intelligent characters, each representing completely opposing points of view. They are sparring intellectually on the one hand and physically on the other. That combination of forceful individuals stepping into roles that allow them to exhibit their strengths really makes the movie take off."[9]

Ford described Oldman as a "very powerful" actor, whose on-screen menace "comes with a disturbing ease."[10] In time, he would refer to his co-star as "Scary Gary."

Actress Wendy Crewson (whose previous film credits included *To Gillian on Her 37th Birthday*, *Corrina, Corrina*, *The Good Son* and *The Doctor*) was chosen to fill the shoes of First Lady Grace Marshall.

Twelve-year-old Liesel Matthews would portray the President's daughter Alice; it was her second film following her motion picture debut in *The Little Princess*.

Nominated for an Academy Award for Best Supporting Actor in *Married to the Mob* (1988), Dean Stockwell (widely known for his role in David Lynch's disturbing yet short-lived television series *Blue Velvet*) was selected to portray White House Secretary of Defense Stanton Dean.

The remaining terrorists would be portrayed by Russian actors: Elya Baskin (*2010*, *Moscow on the Hudson*) as Andrei Kolchak and Levani Outchaneichvili, four-time winner of the NIKA (the Russian equivalent of the Oscar) as Sergei Lenski. The producers selected actor and former amateur boxing champion David Vadim (*G.I. Jane*) as terrorist Igor Nevsky. For the non-speaking role of Gen. Radek, Petersen cast a friend and fellow German, Jurgen Prochnow. Prochnow had previously portrayed the director's German U-boat commander in *Das Boot*. *Air Force One* marked the pair's sixth collaboration.

Rounding out the cast of United States government officials were Tony Award Winner and Oscar nominee William H. Macy (*Fargo*) as Major Caldwell, Paul Guilfoyle (*Ransom*, *Mrs. Doubtfire*) as Lloyd Shepard, Donna Bullock in her motion picture debut as Melanie Mitchell, Xander Berkeley (*The Rock*, *Apollo 13*) as the traitorous Secret Service agent Gibbs and internationally acclaimed actress Glenn Close (*Fatal Attraction*, *Reversal of Fortune*, *101 Dalmatians*) as the Vice-President.

In August 1996, Close was attending a birthday celebration for the vacationing President Bill Clinton in Harrison Ford's hometown of Jackson Hole, Wyoming, at the home of James Wolfenshohn, President of the World Bank. The five-time Oscar nominee happened to be seated immediately to the right of the President, and it was there that Close was offered the role of Vice-President Kathryn Bennett in a rather peculiar manner.

Mid way through the main course, Ford reportedly table-hopped and knelt down to confer with the actress. Bewildered at the sudden offer — and the unorthodox manner in which it was presented — the actress agreed to give the script a once-over.

"With Clinton there egging Harrison on, what *could* I say?" recalled the actress.[11]

Amused by the unusual negotiation, President Clinton proudly stated, "I'm probably the only president who got to pick two vice-presidents."[12]

"I don't base the character on President Clinton in any way, shape or form," stated Ford. "I spent a short but sufficient period of time [alongside the President] to get a sense of the flavor of the air around him. I'm much more interested in the

The "Ass-Kicking President" gets some pointers from director Wolfgang Peterson (Columbia, 1997).

relationships between him and those people who can fill his needs and how that feels."[13]

Ford also observed the mannerisms of the White House staff. "The way people around the President reacted was very special. I do think that's what creates the feeling of presidential behavior."[14]

Although determined to maintain an independent approach to his character, Ford made one exception. Aware of the impact the film's title would have, and knowing that the audience would react as intended only if convinced by the realism of the film sets, the actor sought permission from Clinton to tour the real Air Force One.

Ford, with director Petersen, cinematographer Michael Ballhaus (who had previously photographed Ford in Mike Nichols' *Working Girl*) and production designer William Sandell, toured the plane the following day as it stood in wait at a nearby airport in Wyoming.

"It looked like a big, wonderful hotel room," recalled Petersen, who was surprised to discover that there were two fully functional planes on call at all times. "But I always had the feeling they weren't showing us everything. I think AFO [Air Force One] has a good portion of top-secret stuff that only a few people know about, and they're definitely not film people."[15]

Writer Andrew W. Marlowe shared Petersen's pessimism: "It's very difficult to call the Secret Service and say, 'If you're a terrorist and you want to get on board Air Force One, what's the best way to go about it?'"[16]

Understanding the barriers preventing the U.S. government's full cooperation, the production made the best of what was available to them. Initially, the production had even been denied permission to use *Air Force One* as the film's title and had considered using *AFO* instead. In the end, though, the government reconsidered.

As they had been forbidden to photograph the interior of Air Force One, the group was forced to rely on memory, supplemented by detailed research. They painstakingly viewed hours of CNN footage to provide insight into what director Petersen considered "the most classified flying document in the world."[17]

The moviemakers also viewed newspaper clippings, official photos and the World Wide Web. "We were on the Internet hunting down the guy who'd been the steward on it, or the guy whose brother-in-law was the mechanic. We eventually got quite a lot of corporate cooperation, showing us exactly what the cabin looks like. But no one would really talk to us very much about what the underbelly of the plane looks like, which is a big part of our movie, or what the mission control center looks like."[18] Ford noted that the plane's design was not one of science-fiction, but more within the boundaries of reason and reality. "There were none of those only-the-President-may-push-this buttons," joked the actor.[19]

While the presence of an escape pod (an idea popularized in the 1981 John Carpenter film *Escape from New York*) was crucial to the plot, it became the focus of much criticism from government officials. Their claim was that no such device existed aboard the real aircraft. Petersen had it from "a very reliable source"[20] that such a device did in fact exist.

"It just makes too much sense," he said. "And when we were touring the plane, the cargo hold was one area that was off-limits to us. I left thinking, 'There's a pod down there, there's a pod down there!'"[21]

Whether fact or fiction, the pod was incorporated into their version of Air Force One along with other examples of creative license. Other "extras" included the existence of the tail-cone that facilitates mid-air emergency departures via parachute and the exaggerated size of the plane's conference room (which in actuality seats only eight).

When all was said and done, Petersen was thrilled with the results of the transition from blueprints to reality on Stage 15 (the nation's largest) at Culver City Studios in Los Angeles, California.

"From a pure entertainment point of view," explained Petersen, "a movie that looks real gives you more chills than a movie that doesn't. And we're damn close to reality here."[22]

Recreated in full scale, the interior of Air Force One was built atop enormous hydraulic gimbals that could tilt at an angle of up to 30 degrees to believably simulate turbulence.

Constructing three complete levels, Sandell intended that the interiors "reflect the mood of the script: cold and austere blues and grays for the upper level, which is the nerve center of the plane,* and warm grays and beiges for the middle level, where the business of the Presidency takes place. The mysterious lower level was

---

The cockpit was taken out of Warner Bros. storage following its use in the film Executive Decision.

designed to be very dark and foreboding, an almost spooky place, with a nod to *Das Boot*."[23] (While filming, cast and crew would occasionally refer to the film as "Das Plane.")

Heralded by many critics as the most convincing war movie ever made, Petersen's 1981 film *Das Boot* earned six Academy Award nominations including Best Director and Screenwriter. The film — which so realistically told the tale of a World War II German U-boat captain and his crew, involved in the War in the Pacific — eventually became the then–highest grossing foreign film released in the United States.

Having filmed in a claustrophobic location for *Das Boot*, Petersen was able to successfully tackle filming within the similarly tight quarters of Air Force One.

"They're both metal cigars filled with people who have no way out," said the director. "So I could easily relate to *Air Force One*."[24]

"One of the problems about working in a confined space is reinventing the visual components so they don't become too repetitive," Ford later said. "Thanks to Wolfgang and Michael Ballhaus, I think that was very well accomplished. I had the good fortune to have recently seen Wolfgang's re-cut of *Das Boot* [on April 2 at the Academy of Motion Picture Arts and Sciences, accompanied by Petersen and actress, Rene Russo] and what he's able to do is manipulate the tension in new and interesting ways that always turn it back to human behavior. He also always brings a moral context to the stories he tells. I find that fascinating."[25]

Not wishing to be entirely dependent upon computer graphics and miniature work to provide the many aerial shots of the plane, the producers opted for an actual Boeing 747 in flight.

Renting a 747 passenger plane from a charter company, Sandell's team applied the necessary exterior details to transform the plane into a believable version of Air Force One.

Principal photography for *Air Force One* began on September 16, 1996, at Rickenbacher Air National Guard Base in Columbus, Ohio. Standing in for Germany's Ramstein Air Field, Rickenbacher played host to the moviemakers' Air Force One, six fighter planes, dozens of helicopters, ground vehicles and troops. In this scene, the aircraft briefly touches down on "Ramstein's" tarmac before being commandeered by the Russians. Taxiing at dangerous speeds, the plane continues goes off the runway until the terrorists regain control and proceed skyward.

Live-action, miniatures and CGI (computer generated imagery) were used in the scene. The production was lucky to secure the participation of a commercial airliner "kamikaze" pilot to recklessly steer the plane about the runway. Petersen was also accorded the unusual privilege of nearly complete military cooperation.

"On this one," claimed Air Force General Ron Sconyers, "we actually called the producers to see if they would be interested in having some Air Force support. Because this picture was officially sanctioned, we've let them use Air Force bases and equipment not normally made available to Hollywood."[26]

Among the equipment lent from military facilities all over the country were six F-15 fighters, one C-5A Galaxy transport plane, a C-141 Starlifter, two UH69 Blackhawk helicopters and two C-130 cargo planes. The production employed nearly 250 personnel to operate and maintain the nearly 20 vehicles necessary for the sequence.

Assistance was provided by both Ohio and California National Guard units, as well as all four branches of the United States Armed Forces. Ex–Air Force One personnel, political consultants and hostage negotiators lent their insight into the events.

William Sandell's production design team turned the deserted Mansfield Reformatory in Mansfield, Ohio (where *The Shawshank Redemption* was filmed), into the dilapidated Russian prison where Gen. Radek is incarcerated.

Doubling for yet another Russian locale was Severance Hall in Cleveland — home of the city's Philharmonic Orchestra. There, the second unit filmmakers and their six cameras (headed by Ballhaus' brother, Sebastian) photographed a group of stuntmen portraying a paramilitary outfit.

Establishing shots were photographed at Red Square in Moscow. Los Angeles' Wilshire Abel Theater acted as the banquet hall where Ford's character informs the world of his new policies towards international terrorism. (Former Democratic and West Wing speechwriter Pat Cadell assisted with the text for Ford's speech.) Los Angeles International Airport (LAX) substituted for the Moscow airport. The remaining interior filming was done at Sony Studios in Los Angeles.

"Air Force Fun," we called it," remembered Ford. "And it was, each day. We had no weather problems. We had no sets that weren't ready. We had no problems whatsoever. It was 20 minutes from my Los Angeles house [via his motorcycle, which made the film's producers understandably concerned], and we got every day's work done easily and comfortably, and it was great fun. I loved working with Gary [Oldman], loved working with the other actors involved.[27]

"[Oldman] has such energy, and he made you totally understand that individual. I could never have done that," continued the actor. "I don't have the mindset to play anti-hero. It's not in my makeup. I know my craft, and when you know your craft, you not only know what you can do, you also know what you can't do."[28]

"With an action thriller," claimed Oldman, "the energy has to be maintained at such a high level that it can be quite exhausting. It helps tremendously when you have someone like Wolfgang up there steering the ship who seems to have boundless energy, never looks tired and can crack a few jokes."[29]

Oldman's conscience would surface when the time came to fight a fellow actor whom he naturally admired. Yet on the Los Angeles soundstages, he would overcome his instincts and become the violent terrorist required by the script.

Oldman would at times find himself at times staring unavoidably into the eyes of his six-foot-one antagonist and exclaiming with astonishment, "You're Indiana Jones."[30]

Despite his experience in films of all genres, Oldman was not accustomed to his co-star's penchant for participation in what he considered to be basic "running, jumping, falling down" scenes.

"I think the fact that my face is [in the scene] adds a veracity to the experience and an emotional component that's missing when it's being done by a stunt guy," claimed Ford. "Over the years I have developed a certain capacity to do stunts safely...."[31]

"It's all choreographed, it's all plotted out. The fun of it, for me, is that it's like an athletic endeavor. You choreograph it, you set your mind on what it is. You don't want to hurt somebody, you want to be very sure of your moves, and so it's a pleasure to perform those things for me. I enjoy it. It's like playing tennis, or ballet dancing or something like that."[32]

Insisting on realism, the actor demanded that Oldman attack him with passionate and angry blows. "Normally, when people get beaten up in a scene," remarked Michael Ballhaus, "they're always scared. They say, 'Don't hit me too hard.' Harrison was the opposite."[33]

Elya Baskin, who played Oldman's right hand man, was amazed how much physical pain Ford endured during the filming. Ford's insistence on receiving actual physical blows made the shocked reactions of his co-stars effortless and all the more genuine.

As evidence of his dedication, Ford could be seen walking about the set between takes in one of the 20 specially tailored, $3,000 Cerruti 1881 suits (modeled after his own personally owned garment), applying pressure from an ice pack to his various bruised or battered body parts.

"Oh, man, Harrison is fearless," asserted Ford's co-star, William H. Macy. "He got a fat lip. He gave himself a black eye. These guys—the terrorists led by Gary Oldman—were just pounding the hell out of him. He did it day after day and I saw him. We were going, 'Harrison, chill out, it's O.K.' 'No, no, I can do it.'"[34]

Wendy Crewson claimed he "makes everything easy because he whirls you along with him. Harrison has no inhibitions at all as an actor. None. He just flings himself straight into the middle of the action—flat on the floor, slammed against the wall—whatever...."[35]

Ford believed that the mental and physical labor he invested in *Air Force One* produced some of the best fight scenes of his career.

Although Ford was ready and able to participate, he did appreciate any relief offered to him: "Some days, they didn't get around to me," recalled the actor. "They were beating the shit out of each other on those days."[36]

Ford did sustain damage to his right shoulder's rotator cuff. This injury was an unexpected result of his body weight having been powerfully thrown down against the plane's deck during a fight sequence.

"They're frequently accidents," admitted the actor, "not the result of trying to do something courageous."[37]

The actor (now in his sixties) divulged his secret for staying in good form, declaring the sport of tennis to be his exclusive form of exercise.

"I don't play social tennis," said the actor. "It gets into bizarre competitiveness and socializing. Competition doesn't interest me. I don't care if I beat someone or someone beats me. I'm interested in playing points well, not in winning. Beating someone is not the measure of oneself.[38]

"...I haven't worked out for years. I used to work out, but I got bored with it. Also, I'm pretty careful about what I eat—but I'm not obsessed. And I'm lucky genetically, I guess."[39]

With nearly 30 films under his belt, the experience Ford has acquired through the decades has become invaluable to not only himself, but to all those around him.

As Michael Ballhaus explained: "That is extremely helpful because an assistant can say to him, 'Harrison, when you do this scene, please don't come any closer than this mark. The focus ends here.' He would hit his mark exactly and know what they meant. If you said the same thing to DeNiro, he would look at you and say, 'What are you talking about?'"[40]

"Harrison knows how making a movie works, inside and out," said co-producer John Shestack. "He knows how to block a fight scene. He gets down alongside the cinematographer and discusses camera angles. And when the day is over, he is the first one to pop a beer and kick back with the rest of the crew."[41]

By late January 1997, the mock-up Air Force One interior photography was finally completed and the production moved into the post-production phase. It was then that the creation and integration of the film's special effects supervised by Richard Edlund was completed. This included the filming of the cargo ramp sequence in which 400-cubic-inch airplane-engine-powered fans hurled the wire-harnessed Ford to and fro. It was also then that the computer-generated image of Air Force One's catastrophic ocean crash landing was designed (rather neglectfully, due to unfortunate time and money constraints).

During his much-deserved break following the exhausting three month-long portrayal of America's "kick-ass President"[42] (the film's initially proposed slogan, which—for obvious reasons—was later rejected), Ford and others gathered to pay tribute to the 40-year career of his former co-star and friend Sean Connery. At the podium of New York City's Avery Fisher Hall on the evening of May 5, 1997, Ford paid his respects before hundreds of Connery's friends and fellow actors at the black-tie gala presented by the Film Society of Lincoln Center.

"We come from the same school of acting," said Ford: "Get there on time, do it and go home. It ain't brain surgery.

"There's one essential difference," continued Ford: "Sean does everything from Arab sheiks to dragons with a Scots accent. As an actor, he honors his homeland every time he opens his mouth."[43]

Ford rendezvoused with Connery during the post-ceremony party to share fond memories and to discuss the possibility of yet another adventure with the involvement of Steven Spielberg and George Lucas.

Despite incessant inquiries from hopeful members of the press regarding another sequel, Ford maintained that the project was one that was far from ever becoming reality. In fact, *Indiana Jones* had become so dated to the actor that even the whereabouts of the memorabilia he had in his possession were not known.

"It's somewhere in a closet," admitted the actor, referring to the famed hat, whip and jacket combo, "behind lots of stuff. I'm not even sure what closet."[44]

To promote *Air Force One*, Ford exhausted both the late night and early morning talk-show circuit (including Oprah Winfrey, where the actor testified that Raisin Bran was his favorite breakfast cereal) and gave many print media interviews. His photo made the covers of a multitude of magazines, including *People*, *Entertainment Weekly* and *Movieline*.

For John F. Kennedy, Jr.'s, publication *George*, the actor agreed to wear a face other than his own for the first time since his days as a youth on stage. Revealing his mischievous side, Ford allowed makeup artists to work their magic atop his cherished "Everyman" facial features. Coloring his eyebrows, lids and hair, they transformed the world's biggest box office attraction into his own childhood hero with the final application of an Amish-style beard, a historically accurate costume and a dimple upon his right cheek. Ford's astonishing likeness to our nation's sixteenth President Abraham Lincoln graced the magazine's August 1997 cover and exposed yet another side of the so-called "reticent" actor.

At approximately the same time, *Air Force One* was made available for exhibitor screenings (at the first showing, a teary-eyed Ford embraced his director following its conclusion).

Meanwhile, the rumor mill was churning with the news that the film would face serious competition from two other high profile and widely anticipated films to be released on the same date (July 25). Employing his industry clout, the actor telephoned the other parties involved (the companies releasing *Conspiracy Theory* and *Titanic* simultaneously with *Air Force One*) with the hopes of working out a mutually beneficial arrangement.

He personally appealed to Jonathan Dolgen, the chairman of Viacom Entertainment Group and owner of Paramount Pictures, the studio that was soon to be releasing James Cameron's epic *Titanic*.

"Harrison was definitely irritated," recalled his agent Pat McQueeney. "He didn't make any threats. He was not huffing and puffing. It was a friendly phone call. But Harrison did say, 'Jonathan, what the hell are you doing?'"[45]

"There is too much product out there being released much too quickly on the heels of the other," voiced Ford. "And none of us do the business or ourselves any honor by stepping on each other's toes."[46]*

Ford had a similar conversation with Warner Bros. chairman Bob Daly, hoping for the postponement of the Mel Gibson–Julia Roberts starrer *Conspiracy Theory*. Daly respectfully pushed the release back to August 8.

With a little help from Ford's friends, *Air Force One* was officially set to be the lone release for July 25, 1997.

On July 21, the film's world premiere was held at the Cineplex Odeon in Century City, California, benefiting CAN (the Cure Autism Now Foundation). Attendees included Ford, Petersen, Wendy Crewson, Dean Stockwell, Paul Guilfoyle, Gail Katz, Armyan Bernstein, the film's composer Jerry Goldsmith, Rene Russo and Arnold Schwarzennegger and wife Maria Shriver.

Encouraged by the film's, highly-charged trailers, audiences were once again enthused and eager to experience the Harrison Ford to whom they had grown accustomed. They flocked to movie theaters, where up to three screens per complex were reserved for the film.

Air Force One's $37.1 million earnings became the biggest opening weekend of all of Ford's films, just ahead of the supplementary $31.5 million the re-release of *Star Wars* had recently earned. The opening weekend also proved to be the biggest

---

*Titanic was ultimately slated for release in December 1997, posing no threat to the box office stability of Air Force One.

ever opening for an R-rated film, out-performing the previous $36.3 million record holder, 1994's *Interview with the Vampire*.

Two weeks later, the film had amassed nearly $81 million — nearly twice the amount Ford's prior picture, *The Devil's Own*, had earned throughout its entire duration.

Concerns that business would suffer with the opening of *Conspiracy Theory* were put to rest when that film was finally released.

Although it knocked Ford's new film off the number one slot after two weeks there, *Theory* proved to be no match for *Air Force One*. Earning $19.3 million its opening weekend, Gibson's film edged only slightly ahead of Ford's film — which in its third weekend had earned yet another $17.8 million, bringing its three-week tally to over $110 million.

After its first week, *Theory*'s receipts fell 36 percent. *Air Force One*'s popularity remained consistent, with a 24-day total of $130.6 million. By the time it had dropped from the 60 top-ranking films (as reported by *Variety* during the first week of February 1998), the film had earned an estimated total of $172 million in the United States alone (and a combined worldwide total of over $311 million). It became the fourth biggest moneymaker of 1997 — trailing behind Jim Carrey's *Liar, Liar*, Steven Spielberg's *The Lost World* and the reigning king of 1997, *Men in Black*.

"I'm enjoying making relatively big movies for big audiences," explained Ford. "I have employed the metaphor of being a fireman. If I'm going to leave my life and go out, uproot my family and leave home, I want to go to a big fire. I don't want to go to a false alarm, or put out a fire in a dumpster. I want to go to a three-alarm fire — and climb the big ladder."[47]

In the film, said Ford, "the pressure starts building very early and you think it's going to let off soon, but it doesn't. But that's only part of what I think makes this particular story cook.... And the character's moral path is consistent with a larger moral story as well. That's what really dignifies the process and creates a relationship between the audience and characters on screen, and that's rare in a film of this genre."[48]

Despite the film's few inaccuracies, President Bill Clinton thoroughly enjoyed it, attending two screenings. Enthralled with its success, Clinton joked, "I was present at part of the creation of it ... so I think I should have gotten some kind of cut out of the movie."[49]

Ford was given a $20 million salary for three months of work — approximately 20 times the amount that Clinton earned in one year. The operating cost of the real Air Force One is estimated to be between $35,000 and $40,000 per hour, whereas Petersen's version cost a dizzying average of $72,000 per hour.[50]

Asked whether he might entertain the notion of ever trading jobs with Clinton, Ford replied: "I don't think I have any of the appropriate traits to be President. I'm not considerate enough, I'm not careful enough, I'm not educated enough. I don't have the service and the grace that's probably necessary for the President."[51]

Ford's manager Pat McQueeney disagreed: "I can't think of anyone in the industry who would make a better *real* President than Harrison. He's very stern."[52]

Throughout the relationship the actor had so successfully maintained with

McQueeney, he has given no indication of his political preference. It has never been clear whether Ford is a Republican, Democrat or Independent (although it is known he admired the message of presidential candidate Bill Bradley during the 1999 debates, nixed the 2003 Iraqi War and rejected Arnold Schwarzenegger's campaign for office). Ford's political participation extends only to his continuous exercise of his right to vote.

"Those kinds of loose lips I have no respect for," said the actor, "in myself or anybody else. I'd prefer to see the debate over important issues conducted by experts rather than celebrities. I also don't want to attract attention to myself."[53]

Admiring him for the same, simple reasons as the rest of his audience, Ford's co-star William H. Macy hit the nail on the head, articulately stating: "He's the cat's pajamas. I mean he's such a movie star. He's got movie star hair, and a movie star voice, and a movie star face, and movie star cars. And he's just complete movie star. And so cool...."[54]

Further evidence that both *Air Force One* and its star were two of the summer's (if not the year's) biggest cinematic attractions, Ford was awarded the People's Choice Award for being America's favorite motion picture actor. Having outshined both Tom Cruise and Will Smith, Ford was given the honor based on a poll of the one reliable critic — the common man.

By the end of 1997, Ford had appeared in a total of five films. In addition to the fresh material in *Air Force One* and *The Devil's Own*, the first of the three films in the original *Star Wars* trilogy were re-released to audiences earlier that year (January 31). The re-releases marked the second time that the three films appeared in theaters since their original release dates (spanning the six year period of 1977 to 1983) More importantly, it marked the first time they were presented to the world in their "new and improved" versions.

Audio tracks had been fine-tuned and various scenes, considered flawed by creator George Lucas, were digitally enhanced. Furthermore, deleted scenes (including a lengthy dialogue between Ford's Han Solo and Jabba the Hutt) were reinstated and all new sequences were photographed and inserted into the new cut.

Labeling each a "Special Edition," 20th Century–Fox was delighted to officially release the trilogy to the public starting with the first film, *Star Wars*. The following weeks would see the releases of *The Empire Strikes Back* (on February 21) and *Return of the Jedi* (on March 7).

Ford claimed that he was "delighted that it happened, and pleased that it continues to appeal to a new generation of kids," but insisted that his wife take his own children to see it.[55]

"I'm embarrassed," admitted the actor. "I don't personally want to see 20-year-old acting of my own.... I did the best I could under the circumstances of the time. But I don't personally have any interest in seeing it."[56]

32

Trouble Overseas

In 1997, the big question among Ford fans was who would play his romantic partner in the upcoming $70 million–budgeted *Six Days, Seven Nights*.

More than 100 actresses were considered for the leading part, including Julia Roberts, Kristin Scott Thomas, Juliette Binoche, Andie McDowell, Sandra Bullock and Nicole Kidman. The dilemma was further complicated by Ford's insistence that his would-be leading lady actually audition for the role. Anne Heche agreed to submit to that old-time tradition.

Heche — then 28 — was a hot commodity and much sought-after by directors due to her performances in *Volcano* with Tommy Lee Jones and *Wag the Dog* alongside Dustin Hoffman and Robert DeNiro. She admitted that *Star Wars* was the first movie she'd ever seen. If Harrison Ford was to be her co-star, she claimed that she would eagerly accept any script offered to her, regardless of the content or quality. She endured a weeklong period of screen tests and read-throughs with Ford, after which she was offered the part. There was an unmistakable chemistry between the two — resulting in the belief that their pairing was a sure thing.

Just days following the decision, however, the actress publicly declared her sexual orientation. Heche openly declared that she was in love with comedienne Ellen DeGeneres, whom she had met weeks earlier at a post–Oscar ceremony party. The film's distributor, Touchstone Pictures, was suddenly faced with an unexpected complication: Would the public accept all–American leading man Harrison Ford in an on-screen courtship with a high profile lesbian?

Many insiders claimed that the knowledge of Anne's personal preference would destroy any sparks between a man and a woman falling in love. No one was more determined to prove them wrong than Ford and his producer-director, Ivan Reitman: "I was nervous about all the attention, but not about Anne," remembered Reitman, the director of *Stripes, Ghostbusters, Twins* and *Dave*, to name but a few. "The most important thing for me was to find someone who could play opposite Harrison Ford and hold the screen equally. Right away, I saw she had this way of getting under his skin. He was better with her."[1]

The actor telephoned Heche to dispel rumors that he was distressed by her sexuality, and to assure her of his confidence in her abilities. "It was Anne: the intelligence and the fire and the wit, and the 'I don't give a shit what you think.' All of that was appropriate and interesting for this character."[2]

Reportedly, Ford later offered both Heche and DeGeneres sanctuary at his Wyoming compound until the controversy dissipated.

"The core of the story," explained Reitman, "is the relationship of a completely mismatched and hopelessly incompatible man and woman: Quinn Harris [Ford] and Robin Monroe [Heche], who crash land on this tropical island in the middle of nowhere. All of us probably have had the fantasy of being lost on a desert island, dreaming about all that freedom.

"For this film, I took the fantasy a step further," continued the producer-director. "I thought it would be fun to take two very opposite people, put them into a difficult but humorous situation together and see how they survive — and what happens to them."[3]

The opposites attracted to one another in the film as noted are Harris and Monroe. Heche's character Monroe is the somewhat condescending and uptight assistant editor of a New York fashion magazine. Together with her new fiancé Frank (portrayed by David Schwimmer of television's *Friends*), she is en route to the fictional South Pacific island of Makatea for a romantic getaway. Hired to transport them to their final destination is Quinn Harris — a gruff, carefree cargo pilot-for-hire trying to make a living completely disassociated from the responsible world. He's a character who Ford felt had experienced "some serious disappointments in his life."[4] With a girlfriend of convenience at his side in the form of a beautiful dancer named Angelica (played by relative newcomer Jacqueline Obradors), Harris' life becomes complicated when his plane crashes on a deserted island with his passenger Monroe, whom he is flying to Tahiti to tend to emergency business. The two reluctantly come face to face with their differences and work to survive amid the threat of modern-day pirates.

"The reason I thought Harrison would be perfect for the part," claimed Roger Birnbaum (who shared producing responsibilities with Reitman and Wallis Nicita), "is that he conveys all the qualities the part required: wit, manliness and confidence. When he's on screen, even though there's trouble around, you feel somehow safe because he's there. That's a very rare quality. In the film, the main characters are stranded on a desert island and we needed the type of guy who, no matter what happens, is going to make things okay."[5]

The comedic adventure was rich with exotic locales. This appealed to Ford, especially since his two previous films lacked both humor and colorful landscapes. Tired of acting with a "grim and determined"[6] look on his face, Ford jumped at the opportunity to play Harris.

For Reitman, taking on the project meant more than just a return to the genre that had earned him acclaim. "I've always wanted to work with Harrison Ford. He's one of the great film actors of all time. Harrison is one of a very few legendary stars who can do action, and great dramatic work equally well. You believe him in whatever part he plays — action, drama or comedy. And, like earlier film legends, Harrison has a certain grace and strength that makes us want to watch him. The opportunity to work with Harrison was something I certainly didn't take lightly. I thought the chance to be able to do a combination of adventure, comedy, action and romance with him was a wonderful opportunity."[7]

Even after his very first foray into comedy, Ford had admitted that being intentionally funny was no easy task. Yet, Reitman acknowledged that Ford possessed a trait rarely seen in comedic actors.

"I think it comes from doing so many action films," contemplated Reitman. "He knows how to sell a moment with a look, with a glance, with an eyebrow shift, with something he does with his chin ... and because he works so well non-verbally it really gets into the comedic area, because so much of comedy is not just how you say a line but it's the little movement of the face or the shoulder that accents the line just the right way that either results in comedy or not."[8]

Ford's prior commitment to *Air Force One* set the production back nearly one full year. *Six Days, Seven Nights* finally commenced on July 7, 1997. Having initially scouted Fiji, Samoa and the islands of French Polynesia, production designer J. Michael Riva finally settled upon the Hawaiian island of Kauai. "There wasn't a spot on this lush island that ultimately wasn't utilized to give the film its beauty, texture, grandeur and richness."[9]

For nearly three months, the production filmed along the shores and into the mainland of Kauai — the very same island where ILM's dinosaurs wreaked havoc in Steven Spielberg's *Jurassic Park* and its sequel. The production imported hundreds of palm trees and planted them to better simulate a tropical region that more closely resembled the French regions of Tahiti.

The island proved to be quite trying for the filmmakers. Certain areas selected for filming were so remote and difficult to access that it seemed impractical to continue. The cast and crew were regularly transported to the day's shoot via airplane, helicopter, boat and even the occasional hiking boot.

"When I first read the script," noted producer-director Reitman, "I said, 'This'll be easy: It's just two people on an island.' But it's the hardest movie I've ever made."[10]

For Ford, shooting *Six Days, Seven Nights* meant a return to familiar territory — both literally and figuratively. Literally speaking, filming on the island meant a return to the very same location where he and Spielberg had shot the opening sequence to *Raiders of the Lost Ark*. Figuratively, the script at hand meant a somewhat milder return to the action-adventure genre. Despite the comedic and romantic angles of the story, filming presented the actors with a fair share of bumps and bruises.

"They were constantly getting kicked about," said Reitman, "dropping and falling and rolling, in water, on sand, on hard rocks, or forced to run in dangerous places. There were a lot of scrapes, but fortunately, nothing really serious...."[11]

One scene required Ford to guide a pontoon taken from a World War II Japanese Float Plane down a river and over a small waterfall. During filming, the actor's legs sustained a series of lengthy scratches following his less than graceful descent down the falls.

Out of concern for his leading man's well-being, Reitman asked whether Ford was all right, to which he replied, "Kinda. Do you want another take? It comes for the same price."[12]

From the onset, Heche swore she did not want to be treated like a prototypical cinematic damsel in distress. Neither the male-dominated crew, nor Mother Nature herself, cut the actress any slack.

Heche and Ford in Ivan Reitman's comedy-adventure *Six Days, Seven Nights* (Touchstone, 1998).

Even her hour-long daily Yoga regimen could not save the limber Heche from breaking her ankle at the start of her second week of photography. Yet, with Ford at her side as the seasoned vet experienced with such bodily hazards, Heche managed to survive her first physically demanding role: "He told me how to keep safe. He was always taking care of me, helping me know about the explosives *before* we had to jump off the boat...."[13]

"Beyond that, I just love Harrison's sense of humor. He's hilarious and charming and more real than I think he's ever been on screen. And I've kind of fallen in love with working with him. And, I have to admit, there are moments when I stood back during filming and would think to myself, 'Oh, my God, it's Harrison Ford — the biggest movie star in the world!' But I have to tell you, he doesn't bring that onto the set."[14]

Many of those working with Ford for the first time were pleasantly surprised to discover how he had earned his reputation as low-key, genuine and considerate: "He's done enough of these to sit back and relax," said Heche. "But he shows up on the set before everybody else, making sure everything's ready to go. He defuses any idea that he's any different from anybody else. He's happy to go help and be the gaffer, he's happy to go help build the set — he's involved with everything."[15]

"He's very interested in specific details of logic," said Reitman. "He'd want to know, 'Can a plane do this sort of thing? Is it possible to land this way?' And it forced a kind of logic that often filmmakers ignore because it's easier."[16]

Most serious amongst the films many hazards was the risk involved with the decision to allow Ford to pilot the film's airplane himself. Ford insisted that, for the sake of believability, the audience actually see him behind the windshield in total control of the aircraft — to put "the audience up in the cockpit with us."[17]

Normally, insurance companies discourage film stars from piloting themselves during the making of a film. In the event of an unforeseen accident, the project would be left with nowhere to go but in a downward spiral without its star.

"It's very complicated to fly a plane in a movie without a commercial license and credentials that are very substantial, but through long and arduous consultations with our insurance company, we managed to persuade them of my capacity to fly the plane in the picture," said Ford. "We've had to take certain measures to insure that we met minimal conditions for the insurance company such as having a safety pilot in the airplane — though he's hidden — and we've gotten wonderful material on film."[18]

Ford pulled double-duty as actor and pilot, marking the first time that any actor had been photographed piloting an airplane for the purpose of making of a motion picture. A camera was mounted on the side of a helicopter flying nearby as well as remote cameras affixed to the plane's wing structure.

"Harrison is totally aware of what everybody's doing and what the camera's focusing on," claimed his friend and aerial unit director, Steve Stafford. "And it's the same thing in his flying. He's very focused when he flies, and very safety conscious, and he spends a tremendous about of time in the training phase of flying which most other people don't. They just buy the airplane, go off and fly it.

"Harrison treats it like a professional pilot, so he's always into the training mode. If you walk into his trailer, he'll be reading an aviation magazine or studying up for his next rating. He's moving up through the ratings. It was Harrison's idea to put the audience up in the airplane with him, give them perspective as if they're flying with him. To his great credit, Ivan Reitman wholeheartedly agreed...."[19]

The plane specified in Michael Browning's shooting script was a Stinson Reliant four-passenger airplane. Ford, Reitman and Stafford reconsidered the selection, based on their opinion that it was not the brand of aircraft Quinn Harris would have considered his own. The Stinson four-passenger airplane was just that — a passenger airplane. Harris was a self-employed cargo pilot. Moreover, the Stinson was a tidy and pristine high-performance flying machine. To accent Harris's gruff personality, a junk-with-wings seemed appropriate — and after conducting some research, the team came up with the idea to give Harris a deHavilland Beaver.

Out of production for nearly three decades, the Canadian-made Beaver made such an impression upon Ford as a pilot that he chose the plane to be his co-star (three were used in total), and elected to purchase one which he had specially fabricated to suit his own specifications.

A private estate on Kauai's north shore was another island location. There, in Papaa Bay, scenes showcasing the legendary blues musician Taj Mahal and his "Hula Blue Band" were filmed amid the fictional Noa Noa Bar, at the equally fictional Tohotua restaurant. The production created a 1,250-foot airstrip that Ford's character flew in and out of himself, while the pontooned plane's takeoff and escape scenes were filmed on a Kipu Kai beach.

All told, *Six Days* generated jobs for roughly 250 crew members and 300 extras, and pumped $9.3 million into the local Hawaiian economy.

Come autumn, the *Six Days, Seven Nights* team packed its bags and headed to the beaches of Southern California for additional photography. Aside from soundstage work — where a living-breathing scorpion bit Heche — a hangar at Van Nuys Airport was reserved for the production. There the bulk of the time was spent photographing close-ups of Ford and Heche inside the cockpit of the Beaver. Propped 15 feet above the hangar floor was the Beaver, rigged to hydraulics so the effect of turbulence could be accomplished safely.

Following successful test screenings, executives at Touchstone decided to boost the film's release August date two months forward to June 12, 1998.

Dick Cook, chairman of the Walt Disney Motion Pictures Group, stated the news in a February 1998 press release: "This film is perfect for the summer and is ideally suited for a June release. With its unique blend of romance, adventure and comedy, it is an extremely entertaining motion picture experience which audiences are going to love. One of the things that makes this film so special is the incredible chemistry between the two stars. We are confident that this will emerge as one of the season's most popular offerings."[20]

Six Days, Seven Nights emerged on the box office scene with an enthusiastic $16.5 million opening weekend. Eventually garnering just over $72 million nationwide, the film's appeal remained durable overseas as it went on to earn another estimated $80 million.

Much of its success may be attributed to the public's curiosity surrounding the chemistry between Ford and Heche. The film's financial success testified to her ability to play a worthy love interest for Ford's character.

Richard Schickel confirmed in the opening line of his critique in *Time* magazine that the actress was "a completely persuasive object for Harrison Ford's attentions."[21] While most critics complained that Browning's script lacked originality and a consistent pace, or that the element of the modern-day pirates was simply a ploy to kill screen time, the film's stars were the highlight according to many reviewers.

"Ms. Heche and Mr. Ford make an appealing, wisecracking team, and they look comfortable with the rugged demands of their roles," wrote Janet Maslin of *The New York Times*.[22] *Los Angeles Times* critic Kenneth Turan opined, "The appealing professionalism and chemistry of both stars makes what's happening on screen more satisfying than it has a right to be."[23]

Producer-director Reitman said, "I loved working with Harrison and Anne. I think their chemistry is very strong together. That's what movies are about — how people react together; what happens to them? Because typically I do comedy, I'm always looking for those magical on-screen combinations — and Harrison and Anne have certainly got it."[24]

On Ford, Reitman stated, "I think that as long as you're a really fine actor, you can be humorous in the right situation as well — it's one of the great things about *Six Days, Seven Nights*. Harrison Ford's got all of this great charm and humor about him, but he doesn't often show that part of his personality in his films. The film really shows this lighter, very amusing side of Harrison."[25]

Although the tropical island filming of *Six Days, Seven Nights* was paradise compared to the physical rigors of *Air Force One* and the frustration-frenzied *The Devil's Own*, the heat and extended period of time away from his home(s) took its toll on Ford.

With a vacation finally booked for he and his family on (and sailing around) the island of Capri off the southern coast of Italy, Ford would do nothing career-wise other than keep in communication with a few key contacts.

As far back as April 1997, the actor had agreed to star in producer-writer-director Phil Alden Robinson's (*Sneakers, Field of Dreams*) *Age of Aquarius* for Steven Spielberg's Dreamworks production company at Universal.

Age would have starred Ford as an American relief worker who falls in love with a Bosnian woman (to have been portrayed by British actress Kristin Scott Thomas) and been photographed in Bosnia and Sarajevo for authenticity.

Ceaseless political unrest forced the filmmakers to reconsider their plans due to outrageous budget-inflating insurance costs in response to the high level of unpredictable violence across the region.

By September 1997, the long-pondered question of whether to pursue the $85 million (and growing) *Age* was finally put to rest when the producers threw in the towel.

The news of the Ford–Scott Thomas pairing excited executives, if only for a moment. Soon after the project was scrapped, their excitement was revitalized by the announcement that the two would remain cinematic lovers for their next project—a romantic journey guided by director Sydney Pollack.

33

THE END OF AN ERA

In the spring of 1998, Ford signed on to star in Columbia's film adaptation of author Warren Adler's 1984 novel *Random Hearts*.* For *Hearts*, Adler (a Wyoming neighbor and friend of Ford's) recalled the 1983 news story of an airliner that ran off the runway and into the winter-chilled waters of Washington D.C.'s Potomac River. He recalled the emotional impact it had on him at the time and used the event as the basis for his novel.

The author introduced into his story a Washington D.C. internal affairs detective and a New Hampshire Republican congresswoman. They soon discover that their spouses were on the doomed flight and were in fact having an extra-marital affair. Under those circumstances, the two surviving spouses struggle through their loss, attempt to understand and cope with the betrayal, and eventually find love for one another.

Almost immediately after its publication, *Hearts* was considered for development as a CBS movie-of-the-week with Dustin Hoffman attached. The actor noted his concerns with the quality of the script and labored to improve the material. More than a dozen years later, an acceptable script was produced and director Sydney Pollack expressed interest in it. Pollack hired his frequent collaborators David Rayfiel (*Sabrina*) and Kurt Luedtke (*Absence of Malice* and *Out of Africa*) to fine-tune the script. Following his approval, Pollack signed on as director and producer of the film and, not surprisingly, cast himself as an actor in it. (The director had previously appeared in his own *Tootsie*, Robert Altman's *The Player*, Woody Allen's *Husbands and Wives* and Stanley Kubrick's *Eyes Wide Shut*. Having originally discussed the project with Pollack during the 1994 filming of *Sabrina*, Ford signed on to play Dutch Van Den Broeck (originally known as Edward Davis in Adler's novel) in May 1998.†

"I thought it was a very compelling emotional tale," the 56-year-old actor said of the *Hearts* script. "I related to the character's loss, to his sense of bewilderment at this happening to him, to his sense of betrayal. I liked the expressions that were given of his grief.... I thought it was all pretty unusual."[1]

---

*The novelist received his first taste of fame with the release of his 1981 novel The War of the Roses. That novel was later translated to the big screen in a film of the same name starring Michael Douglas and Kathleen Turner.

†At around the same time, there was talk of his involvement in director Jan Debont's (Speed, Twister) sci-fi thriller Minority Report. Ford declined. In 2001, Steven Spielberg and Tom Cruise took on the challenge.

Shortly afterwards, *The English Patient*'s Oscar-nominated actress Kristin Scott Thomas signed on to portray Ford's female interest Kay Chandler. The film would not only mark a reunion for Ford and Pollack, but it finally allowed Ford and Thomas to work together.

"I didn't want 'Mr. and Mrs. North Solve a Mystery,'" explained director Pollack on his casting decision. "I thought it would be more interesting to have this high-born, sophisticated, elegant, privileged, cool woman thrown into a locked room emotionally with this tough-minded Washington, D.C. street cop.

"It was the most unlikely pairing I could think of. Harrison is the Everyman, and she is the aristocrat."[2]

Other actors cast in the film were Peter Coyote as Kay Chandler's unfaithful husband, Charles Dutton as Ford's I.A. partner and Pollack as Kay's media consultant.

A plane crash being the script's focal point meant for some participants a more intimate relationship with the project. In 1993, Pollack's son had been killed in a plane crash, while Thomas had lost both her father and her stepfather to the same unfortunate fate.

Filming began for *Hearts* on September 10 in and around the District of Columbia, and continued over the next several months. Neighboring Alexandria, Virginia (where Ford requested and received special permission to commute to the set via his Bell helicopter), was also gracious to the filmmakers. In October, the production moved to Maryland, where they filmed at the Patuxent River Naval Air Station. A portion of the airstrip was photographed, as was an enormous storage hangar dressed to serve as a makeshift morgue where crash victims were on display for identification. An area of the Potapsco River just beside the Francis Scott Key Bridge in Maryland was used as the site of the plane crash itself. There, a reproduction airplane tail section and pieces of debris were tossed onto the water's surface to simulate the aftermath. They created such an authentic-looking accident scene that over 40 nearby residents and passersby dialed Emergency 911 to report what they thought to be an actual accident.

Additional locations filmed in the D.C. area were the Department of Commerce Building, the Lincoln Memorial, Dupont Circle, Ronald Reagan–Washington International Airport and a remote region within the Patuxet Research Refuge where Dutch's getaway cabin was built.

After shooting footage in New York City in November and December (including an abandoned courtroom that was used as a location for *Presumed Innocent*), the crew moved to Miami's South Beach area and photographed one of its key locations — the Tides Hotel. A car scene was filmed involving a rather lurid sexual encounter in which rage between Ford and Thomas erupts into passion. Although the actor claimed that the exchange was not as emotionally charged as his love scenes with Lesley-Anne Down in 1978's *Hanover Street*, it was by contrast a great deal more challenging. Although no nudity was required, the emotions felt by each character at that juncture promoted an uncontrollable and forceful exchange.

As Pollack recalled, "It was a difficult scene, risky. It had to be unconventional, or you're going to dislike these people. They just buried their spouses. It has to come out of hurt and need and rage, and be angry and messy and awful and still erotic."[3]

Medical personnel stood by during the two-day shoot to tend to any cuts or scrapes caused by the passionate choreography of the scene.

After filming various club scenes in Orlando, the production returned again to New York where it filmed several scenes at Saks Fifth Avenue in midtown Manhattan. Principal photography came to a conclusion on February 3, 1999.

The story of *Random Hearts* is—in the context of the traditional Hollywood romantic drama—unconventional. This cinematic couple bonds through a tragedy.

"There's an artificial closeness that comes from sharing a tragedy and sharing a tragedy that's predicated on betrayal—absolute betrayal," explained Pollack. "I was obsessed by the obsession of Harrison's and sort of obsessed by wanting these two good people to get better and to find some sort of happiness together. Help each other heal, in a way.

"They're both emotionally very raw and open and in that context in those kinds of circumstances they become friends."[4]

Due to the unusual circumstances under which the two meet, the performances required to convincingly portray their relationship were not come by easily. For the director and his lead actors—despite their combined experience—this was a unique task: "Every day on the picture was a real challenge," continued Pollack, "particularly to the three of us—Harrison, Kristin and I—to try to find behavior that moved the story forward. Everything is dependent on temperature changes, if you will, between the character's, so it was a real acting challenge."[5]

"He knows what works, what buttons to push," said Thomas on her co-star's method of confronting acting issues at the front line. "One day, we were doing a scene, and I couldn't get it right—I was being really pathetic. I was kicking up a fuss, and Harrison was eating peanuts. And he cracked one open and he pushed it toward me, these two little nuts. That's what he was really pleased about, the fact that these two nuts just sat in their shells. It was like, you know, 'Look, the world doesn't come to an end. There are peanuts—peanuts—that are designed perfectly."[6]

With Ford's performance, his director claimed that what they received was a winning combination of strength and vulnerability unlike anything else he had ever delivered to a role: "It's a role with enormous complexity and enormous demands and he just gives a marvelous performance. I couldn't ask for anything more."[7]

Slipping into the difficult character of Dutch and "figuring out how to give him honest expression"[8] came relatively easy to Ford, due in large part to a personal relationship with his director. As both a mentor and friend, Pollack's understanding of Ford's personality and acting ability merged with his knowledge of Dutch's character, creating what he called "a Harrison Ford nobody's ever seen before."[9]

"Sydney is a remarkable filmsmith," insisted the actor. "He understands acting. He understands editing. He understands all of the aspects of filmmaking and I found him incredibly precise and detailed about what it was that he wants from each scene. And it was a pure pleasure for me to give him what it was that he wanted. He's got great courage, I think, to do a very unconventional relationship, with very unconventional characters."[10]

On February 10, 1999, just days after wrapping photography, Ford's father Christopher passed away having suffered from a blood ailment for several years.

With Kristen Scott Thomas in the film version of author Warren Adler's *Random Hearts* (Paramount, 1999).

Although always conscious of maintaining his privacy, the actor was unable to keep his private loss from entering his public life. The subject matter of the film, combined with the events of his personal life, made for a trying period.

"Emotionally, it really took a toll on me," admitted the actor. "It was a very difficult time in my life, and I'm a very private man. I had to tell my co-stars what was happening, which was hard for me. But many days I was happy to be on the set. Work has always been a comfort to me."[11]

The final closing credit of the film is a personal dedication to Christopher Ford. He was 92 years old.

Random Hearts' star power could not save it from becoming a cinematic "flop."

Variety magazine critic Todd McCarthy, although impressed with the overall picture, foresaw what was to become of the film and made note of it following the September 23 press screening at Sony Studios in Culver City: "An ideal rainy-day matinee attraction for well-to-do ladies of a certain age, Sydney Pollack's immaculately crafted anachronism hearkens back, in its relative restraint and civility, to the likes of *Brief*

Encounter. Harrison Ford's drawing power will no doubt generate a measure of initial B.O., but pic's somber sobriety and deliberate pace, combined with an utter lack of allure for anyone under about 40, spells a short theatrical visit for such a major star-director vehicle."[12]

The novel's author himself dismissed the treatment of his work, citing that he could see "the glaring errors that took away the impact of the original blueprint."[13]

At the end of its October 8, 1999, opening week, the $70 million *Random Hearts* fell several million dollars short of even paying Ford's salary, with a mere $13.5 million. Unanimously hailed for its performances (among others, Janet Maslin believed Ford gave "one of his best and most intense recent performances"[14]) while simultaneously chastised for its droning pace (one journalist's headline read that "*Hearts* needs a Pacemaker"[15]), the film's earnings continued to plummet from that point forth. Its theatrical release lasted hardly one month before finally exiting the theaters with a domestic tally of roughly $32 million.

The film's only award of any type was given on the evening of January 9, 2000, when Ford was presented with another People's Choice Award for the Favorite Actor of that year. Considering the poor reception of *Random Hearts*, it was evident that Ford was, as always, admired despite the failure of his most current project. Later that month, he stood front and center at the most anxiously awaited moment of the Golden Globes to present the award for Best Dramatic Film to the makers of *American Beauty*.

Twenty-two years after directing the original *Star Wars* film, director George Lucas stepped behind the camera and filmed a new entry for the beloved saga. Entitled *Star Wars Episode I: The Phantom Menace*, this prequel picked up prior to where the original *Star Wars Episode IV: A New Hope* had taken place.

The production and eventual release of the prequel was one of the most anticipated film events in cinematic history. Released theatrically in North America on May 19, 1999, *The Phantom Menace* opened to record crowds and the box office receipts expected of the continuation of the most successful movie trilogy in the history of motion pictures.

Although attendance was high, critics lambasted the film.

To pay his respects to George Lucas and to satisfy his own curiosity, Harrison Ford attended the film's initial theatric release.

During the 2000 Deauville Film Festival, he was asked to offer his opinion of the film: "It's a very different type of movie to the films we made," answered Ford diplomatically, "which depended on the relationship between the three characters or four characters. I see it as groundwork for the other films George is doing now, and understand and appreciate the efforts involved. I also think the actors are very good."[16]

34

THE NEW MODEL FORD

At the 2000 Deauville Film Festival, 58-year-old Harrison Ford was asked whether he believed in ghosts. On any other occasion, the question would have seemed an odd choice. But while promoting *What Lies Beneath*, it seemed nothing less than oddly relevant.

"No, I don't believe in ghosts," said the actor, "but I believe in the power of the subconscious mind and I do think that the human mind has the capacity to overwhelm the other senses of the organism to produce manifestations that a person can think are ghosts. I do think people believe they see ghosts."[1]

By the time those words were spoken at the September 8 press conference, *Beneath* had already been released in North America (on July 21) and had been readily established as a box office hit. After the dismal reception of *Random Hearts*, the financial success of this latest outing was a welcome relief for the actor.

The elements attributable for the film's success included the cinematic choreography of Oscar-winning *Forrest Gump* director Robert Zemeckis, the pairing of Ford with Michelle Pfeiffer and the subject matter of the film itself.

In 1998, Zemeckis and his producers Steve Starkey and Jack Rapke united to create their own film production company. During their first meetings, the founders of Image Movers discussed the genres they wished to tackle. Zemeckis was resolute in his intent to pursue his passion for suspense films.

"I think suspense and cinema are really made for each other," explained the director. "I mean, there are certainly very suspenseful books and stage plays, but I don't think anything can manipulate time and place and storytelling techniques the way a movie can. So I've always wanted to try my hand at directing something really terrifying and mysterious."[2]

The story behind *Beneath* stemmed from a simple premise brought forth by Steven Spielberg. An executive at the director's own production company (Dreamworks SKG) offered screenwriter Clark Gregg a sentence-long plot synopsis and requested that he elaborate upon it.

After spending nearly three months on an outline, Gregg eventually produced a first draft.

Gregg worked in collaboration with director Zemeckis for an additional two months of exhaustive rewrites to complete a second draft.

Immediately after hearing of the project, Ford—who claimed to have never been frightfully affected by Hitchcock's films—agreed to the role of Dr. Norman Spencer in June 1998 (after turning down offers to star in *The Patriot*, *Proof of Life* and *The Perfect Storm*, among others). "Ordinarily, I respond to a character and his dilemma. In this case, I responded to the idea of the film itself. It was so immediate, so contemporary. I loved the construction of the script and the surprises built into it, as well as the character."[3]

Zemeckis decided early on that, "It was essential to have someone of Harrison's stature and reputation in the role of the husband if the film was to have its maximum impact."[4]

Gregg was a Boston-bred director-writer who had received accolades for his stage performances as well as appearances in such films as *Magnolia*, *State and Main* and *The Spanish Prisoner*. He was well prepared for what Ford's sudden involvement would mean. The three collaborators continued to polish the script as the countdown continued toward the pre-determined starting date of principal photography.

"By the end of it," remembered Gregg, "I felt, 'God, if I ever have to collaborate with this many people again, I'm going to kill myself.' But I also thought, 'If I ever direct something myself, I hope I have people who question every single beat of the movie this tightly.'"[5]

This constant tinkering evolved into the tale of Dr. Norman and Claire Spencer, a couple whose seemingly normal life is disrupted when their home plays host to a supernatural presence.

The casting process played out like every director's dream when leading lady Michelle Pfeiffer committed to the project. Conveniently, Ford and Pfeiffer were just who the producers had envisioned as their leading man and lady.

"Usually you have to do a more elaborate dance to cast stars," claimed Zemeckis, "but with these two it was, 'Bam, bam!'"[6]

As Gregg wrote his screenplay, he envisioned the ideal setting for the story's paranormal activities. He was immediately reminded of the picturesque New England town of Burlington, Vermont; he'd spent several summer seasons acting in the Atlantic Theater Company, which he had co-founded with writer-director David Mamet.

After several scouting trips throughout the Carolinas and New England during the later months of 1998, Starkey was fortunate enough to almost zero in on the settings of Gregg's imagination in the State of Vermont. It was there where the producers happily discovered much of what they required within the confines of the Daughters of the American Revolution State Park in the town of Addison.

Zemeckis was in the process of filming *Cast Away* on the Fijian island of Manuniki during pre-production for *What Lies Beneath*. While his two-time Academy Award–winning leading man Tom Hanks was in the process of losing nearly 50 pounds and growing a beard for his starring role in the film, Zemeckis and his crew left the tropical island set and reunited stateside to film his supernatural thriller.

Days before Ford was required to begin shooting, he flew himself to the Vermont set to get a sense of how Norman Spencer would conduct himself in his own surroundings.

"He didn't want to walk into his house as the character on the first day without

In the rare role of an unsavory character in Robert Zemeckis' *What Lies Beneath* (Dreamworks, 2000).

having gotten a sense of it beforehand. He spent hours making sure everything felt right," remembered Zemeckis.[7]

In August 1999, *Beneath* photography began amidst the turning leaves of New England .

Production was facilitated by logistic and security controls; nevertheless, both houses (as well as the dock over the lake) were replicated on soundstages at Sony Studios in California, allowing greater control over the evening lighting conditions. Additionally, the California set's Spencer home was constructed with removable walls for greater flexibility and control of camera movements. Notably, six separate bathroom sets were built, attesting to the bathtub's importance in the film.

The film was shot in the brightness of the summer months, with a natural segue into the darkening colors of fall complementing the story's progression into its darkening turn of events.

The artist's haven of Charlotte, Vermont, posed as the fictional town of Adamant. Other locations included the University of Vermont and the scenic backdrop of Otter Creek Falls in Middlebury.

Following several additional weeks of soundstage photography on the West Coast, the crew returned to Vermont and filmed for another three weeks before finally wrapping photography in early November. The crew dismantled the Spencer home and returned the park grounds to their original state.

What Lies Beneath opened wide on July 21, 2000, and earned $29.7 million in its first weekend. Its ticket sales continued sold strongly throughout the summer, eventually accumulating over $275.4 million worldwide. Overall, it ranked in as the ninth highest grossing film of that year and was considered Ford's first box office hit since 1997's *Air Force One*.

The pleasure of watching the on-screen relationship between Ford and Pfeiffer was a certain drawing point for the public. Critics and fans saw them as a believable couple.

Entertainment Weekly's Lisa Schwartzbaum noted that, "After his corpse-on-corpse chemistry with [Thomas] in *Random Hearts* and [Ormond] in *Sabrina*, Ford's star-on-star alliance with Pfeiffer is a relief, the two Hollywood A-listers a pleasing love match of dignity and sex appeal."[8]

Humor was all it took for Pfeiffer to get through her uncomfortable love scenes with Ford.

"That was really rough," recalled the actress. "But you know it was my job and I was happy I was getting paid for it. I was so *bad*. All I did was giggle. I was completely annoying, but that was my defense mechanism, and Harrison put up with it...."[9]

What the public didn't foresee was the direction in which they were led by Dr. Norman Spencer.

"I'm not worried about whether or not people will accept me in this role," Ford claimed during its promotional tour, "because I think that the construction is so solid and successful, they'll have to. I'm not playing villainous from the beginning of this film so I think people are drawn into the story and as they discover what the truth of the story is, they've been lured into it in a way they haven't expected."[10]

Gone were the days of Ford as a cinematic "hero." For the first time in his career, he consciously elected to play an unsavory character. (*The Mosquito Coast*'s Allie Fox was merely misguided and misunderstood.)

For better or worse, the November 2000 issue of *Movieline* magazine listed him as the year's "Most Unexpectedly Believable Psychopath."[11] *The Wall Street Journal* claimed that the film was "as flat as a Ouija Board" and said that Ford had "returned, more or less intact, from the suspended animation of his recent roles."[12]

Other critics—most of whom noted a Hitchcockian feel to the picture—admired the film as a whole: *New York* magazine's Peter Rainer considered the project "a feat of horror engineering."[13] Michael Janusonis of *The Providence Journal-Bulletin* described *What Lies Beneath* as a "thrilling, chilling, terrifying ride."[14] (His movie companion had left him her own impression of the film in the form of several black and blue marks left on his arm.) Referencing a Hitchcock film was Lou Lumenick of *The New York Post*, who stated that the film "does for bathtubs what *Psycho* did for showers."[15]

In the early months of 2000—just prior to the North American opening of *What Lies Beneath*—Ford became attached to director Stephen Soderbergh's (*Sex, Lies, and Videotape*; *Out of Sight*; *Erin Brockovich*) documentary-like film chronicling the drug situation in the United States, *Traffic*. Ford was so impressed with Stephen Gaghan's script that he elected to participate in the $30–$40 million budgeted film with a sacrificial pay cut of half his usual $20 million salary (although he would retain a back-end take of ten percent). Even before Ford was officially attached to the project, he and Soderbergh met frequently to work out the script kinks and further develop its characters.

"I had great interactions with him," said the director to *Movieline* magazine's Stephen Rebello. "I liked him enormously. The irony is that his notes turned around that role. The part wasn't there. He and I had lengthy, detailed meetings with line-by-line discussions. He had really good ideas, all of which we incorporated and all of which worked...."[16]

But come February of that year, Ford's agent Patricia McQueeney pulled him from the project and left the filmmakers scrambling to fill his shoes. Ford agreed to the sacrifice: "I thought, 'Well, y'know, the audience deserves to have a better time with me. From time to time.'"[17]

Veteran actor Michael Douglas accepted the role that had been tailored for Ford and won a Golden Globe nomination for Best Actor. The screenplay (enhanced by Ford's contributions) earned Gaghan a Golden Globe Award and an Oscar nomination. Similarly, the finished film and its director were given Best Picture and Director nomination by voting members of both the Golden Globe and the Academy Awards for that year.

At the same time, negotiations became further solidified for Ford to reacquaint himself with the world of CIA analyst Jack Ryan in *The Sum of All Fears*.

"I haven't seen a script," said the 57-year-old actor. "If I do and like it, I'll definitely be in the movie. And no, it won't have to have less action than the others did. No one wants to see a hero have to pick up a cane to hit someone, but I'm still quite fit enough to fake it. It's all smoke and mirrors anyway."[18]

Not long after that statement, Ford officially backed out of the project. The actor was not only displeased with the script (which he claimed "didn't have the dramatic potential" or "opportunities that I thought we had taken advantage of in the first two films"[19]), but he'd also grown tired of the ever-cynical attitude of author Tom Clancy. As a result, both he and director Phillip Noyce decided against any further involvement in the Jack Ryan series.

In an act of casting that bewildered many, 28-year-old actor Ben Affleck signed on and became the third actor (including Alec Baldwin from *October*) to portray the beloved CIA analyst, Naval Professor and father of two.

"They produced a script," said Ford, "and ... I didn't care for it, so they went on to somebody else. Clancy was always complaining about how old I was. So I think at least he'll be gratified."[20]

Following his casting, Affleck telephoned Ford to seek his blessing. "Ben Affleck's a really interesting actor and seems to be a very nice person, so I wish him nothing but the best of luck."[21]

35

HARRISON FORD'S RUSSIAN PERSPECTIVE

On July 4, 1961, the Soviet Juliett class nuclear ballistic submarine K-19 was pushed into service before it was seaworthy, and—as a result—experienced a reactor leak within its nuclear coolant system. The crew's inability to contain the deadly leak could have resulted in an onboard explosion that might have been misconstrued as a first strike for a third world war between the Russian Motherland and its Cold War nemesis, the United States of America.

Due to the crew's heroics, the damage was contained and war was avoided—but not without a price. Over 20 sailors of the Russian Navy directly involved in the repair of the damaged reactor died from radiation exposure. Because the incident occurred during "peacetime," the Russian government refused to honor those involved. They were not to be deemed "heroes" and were forbidden to discuss the tragic events that befell them and their fallen comrades.

In December 2000, actors Harrison Ford, Liam Neeson and director Kathryn Bigelow traveled to Russia to hear the tragic story of K-19 told firsthand by those unsung heroes who, now free of Soviet rule, were finally able to tell their tale. The trip had a two-fold purpose: to fine-tune an existing script with accurate details of the disaster and to pay tribute to the survivors.

Since 1995, the K-19 project had been foremost in the mind and heart of director Bigelow. Her screen credits prior to production of the $80 million film included *Near Dark*, *Point Break*, *Strange Days* and *The Weight of the Water* (which was released after *K-19*).

For the 42-year-old director (and former wife of *Titanic* director James Cameron), the story of the *K-19* was precious because it told the tale of a great adventure, with a "ticking clock" suspense factor—coupled with a moving dramatic element. What Bigelow envisioned would make the story-to-screen translation all the more striking—because the tale she had to tell was true. Its events had personally touched the lives of dozens of men, yet very few people outside of the Russian Navy knew it had ever occurred.

"Our film examines the heroism, courage and prowess of the Soviet submarine force in ways never seen before," said the director. "It is a fascinating tale of ordinary people who became heroes when faced with a tragic situation. Capturing the nobility of their sacrifice has been the primary motivation involved in making this film."[1]

She remembered that on more than one occasion during those meetings she had found herself "embraced by them with tear-stained faces saying, 'You must tell our story.'"[2]

Cast as the steadfast Capt. Alexei Vostrikov (the name having been changed from the original Capt. Nikolai Zatayev), Ford was offered the role by Bigelow, to the tune of $25 million plus 20 percent of the gross after the break-even point. He was immediately attracted to the complexity of the role and his character's relationships with the other crew members. "There are the good guys, but there are no bad guys," he explained. "There's simply the technological problems that they face, and the moral issues that confront them."[3]

Apart from his role as actor in the film, Ford assumed the position of executive producer for the first time in a career spanning nearly 40 years. Having been involved in the creative process of many of his films without screen credit for his efforts, the actor felt it was time for a change.

"That's the unexpected challenge of the leading man," explained Ford. "I am going to get fucking blamed for this, so I might as well take the responsibility, in concert with the director.... We had too many goddamned producers. I wanted to make it clear to them up front that I would be among them, that whole creative group, and there was a lot of work to be done."[4]

During his Russian visit, the survivors voiced their objections to the script, which they claimed depicted them as undisciplined alcoholics. Their complaint was duly noted and the filmmakers quickly dispelled their fears by telling them that they had seen an early draft of the script. (The Christopher Kyle script, was later refined by legendary screenwriter Tom Stoppard, who was uncredited.)

"All that was eliminated from the original script," insisted the actor. "I never would have done the movie if it portrayed that point of view. We came to an agreement early on that we must maintain the Russian point of view at all costs."[5]

Ford adopted a Russian accent for his role, despite objections from the film's investors.

"I was convinced, against every opinion to the contrary, that using accents was absolutely necessary. We have English actors, an Irish co-star, several Russian actors and an American actor, and the Russian accent is to remind you that this is a Russian movie, not told with American jingoism. It disabuses the audience fairly early on that this is not a so-called Harrison Ford movie. This is a Russian movie about Russians, and the audience has to recognize the difference so they don't expect me to rip off my uniform and be revealed as an American spy or something."[6]

Because the original K-19 lay contaminated in a Russian scrap yard, the producers relied on their creative license to produce a believable replica. They discovered an inoperable diesel-powered Julliett-class submarine available for lease from a firm in St. Petersburg, Florida. Because the newly acquired submarine was of a different class and an altogether different size than the actual K class K-19, John Smith and his production design team had considerable work to do when it arrived in Halifax, Nova Scotia, 13 days later.

Ford confers with director Kathryn Bigelow on the set of *K-19* (Paramount, 2002).

With help from the blueprints of the original, the team retrofitted the aft section of the sub with a 100-foot-plus tail section and a larger tower to bring it closer to the actual 374-foot long, four-story-high specifications.

To accustom themselves to a submariner's life, the cast and crew members underwent various training exercises involving control of water leaks and on-board fires. Ford prepared for almost nothing. After viewing Russian stock footage from the early 1960s, he decided not to work out, thus allowing him to portray Vostrikov as sluggish and with a slightly altered gait.

The shooting schedule brought together a cast of nearly 50 actors—a truly international ensemble from Canada, Iceland, England, Russia, Ireland and the United States.

Partially funded by Intermedia and National Geographic Films, filming for *K-19* began in various government buildings and public locales in the city of Moscow during February 2001. While there, they filmed at Kievsky Station and withstood 20 degree temperatures to film at the Vvendenskoye Cemetery where the surviving crew members reunite to honor of their fallen comrades. Over two hours of prosthetic makeup application transformed Ford into a man 30 years older.

The frozen surface of Lake Winnepeg was used to simulate the Arctic Ocean ice cap. A faux sub tower was constructed atop the four-foot-thick ice, to hover above the submariners playing soccer below. A soundstage in Toronto, Canada, was then used for the interior of the sub. Ten sections were recreated in painstaking detail and photographed for a period of ten weeks. To stay true to actual environments, Bigelow and her production team built the sets at full scale, hoping that it would innately produce appropriate behavior by the actors in response to their surroundings. This made it difficult for Jeff Cronenweth (son of *Blade Runner* cinematographer Jordan) to position his camera and lighting equipment effectively, and made for a greater challenge for the actors. The bevy of pipes, lights and levers protruding from the ceiling inflicted more than its fair share of unwanted injuries upon cast and crew struggling to avoid them.

In early April, the production relocated to Halifax, where the frozen Halifax Shipyards stood in for the Soviet naval base at Murmansk. From there it was back to Toronto for additional interior work and then back to Halifax to film in the open and icy waters of the North Atlantic, before finally wrapping principal photography in June 2001. After exteriors of the sub were filmed, it was returned to its original state and purchased by the city of Providence, Rhode Island — where it is now offered to the public as a tourist attraction.

Ford's Capt. Vostrikov is a relatively unlikable hero — and the polar opposite of his traditional "hero" portrayal. Vostrikov, however, is understandable within the context of the story. He is a man whose life and career fall under the rule of the Communist party. While Neeson's Polenin likens the submarine crew to a family, Ford's Vostrikov views them as tools in the service of the Motherland. Only as the story progresses — and tragedies befall its crew — does Vostrikov begin to follow the example of Neeson's character, and disregard his sense of duty in favor of his belief in humanity.

"It's not that the film conceals the elements of my character. It's that my character does not reveal himself, because a captain who explains himself is no captain at all. This guy had the unenviable task of serving the high command, understanding that the whole theory of the military is that men are expendable."[7]

Vostrikov, Ford continued, "seems hardened to that reality in a way that makes him somewhat unsympathetic. But he learns, to the point where his command forces him to accept his responsibility to a higher moral authority."[8]

Perhaps it was the claustrophobic setting of the film, the unfamiliar story, Ford's Russian accent or the public's inability to accept him in a role outside the arena of such well-worn heroes as Indiana Jones, Han Solo or Jack Ryan: *K-19: The Widowmaker* did poor business. When the film was released on July 15, 2002, at over 3,000 theaters (after a Conservation International fundraising screening in New York), it was met with mixed reviews (most noting Ford's on-again, off-again accent and incessantly gruff tone).

The Hollywood Reporter said the film could "be favorably compared to *Das Boot*," with "brilliant film craftsmanship in every frame."[9] *The New York Times* wrote, "Mr. Ford is poised and compact, his mouth as thin and expressionless as the scar across his chin."[10] Associated Press movie writer David Germain wrote, "In one of his best performances, Ford personifies the steely demeanor expected of a Soviet naval commander, though the Russian accent he adopts fades in and out and borders on caricature at times."[11]

When the totals came in, the film had earned an estimated $34 million in worldwide box office receipts (denying Ford his 20 percent post-profit points).

"I do not consider the box office to be the true measure of the film," said Ford. "I think it's very wrong to characterize this as a failure."[12]

Despite *K-19*'s commercial failure, director Bigelow claimed that the project was one of the most rewarding experiences of her career, due in part to her collaboration with her leading men—citing them as "nothing short of inspirational."[13]

"Harrison is selfless and generous and fabulous when it comes to understanding the process of filmmaking. He also brings an intensity to the set that is ultimately rewarding."[14]

That intensity was even more evident to actor Peter Sarsgaard, who starred previously in *Boys Don't Cry* and in this film portrayed the sub's reactor officer, Vadim Radtchenko.

"It can be very intimidating at first," said the actor. "But it was right in this movie for it to be that way. I tried to preserve that feeling for as long as possible.... Just the feeling of it being Harrison ... and the amount of raw energy that he gets inside of him when he turns and focuses it on you ... he really got me going."[15]

Ford readily acknowledged the film's inability to grab the public's interest, stating philosophically that: "It is my job. That is why I am here, to take advantage of the opportunity of reaching people. I do take the responsibility for the product. I do whatever I can to support the film and reach its audience. Making movies is about communicating with an audience, and if we fail to communicate with an audience I am disappointed."[16]

36

THE BUDDY-COP FLICK FLOP

"I'm over it."[1]

The failure of *K-19*, though disappointing, did not deter the seasoned actor from looking forward to future projects. The actor next chose to share top billing in a "buddy-cop" comedy with 23-year-old Josh Hartnett, long before the script was even committed to paper.

"There was no script," said Ford of his atypical acceptance of *Hollywood Homicide*, "but there was a really strong concept and a willingness to be collaborative as the script was developed, so I took a shot."[2]

With Hartnett the hottest actor of his generation in Hollywood at that time (courtesy of 2001's *Pearl Harbor* and *Black Hawk Down* later that same year), Ford's decision to align his own audience with Hartnett's younger legion of followers would, he hoped, result in the kind of box office success to which he was accustomed.

Homicide was based on the real-life accounts of Robert Souza, a 20-plus-year veteran of the Los Angeles Police Department Hollywood division and former licensed real estate broker.

Souza's revealing and often entertaining recollections intrigued the film's producer, Lou Pitt: "It was the personal stuff they have to deal with while they're trying to solve crimes that I found really compelling," said Pitt. "I wanted to know more about who these guys are and to make a film that showed their personal lives in a way we've never seen before. Like too many of us, they have to find a way to juggle the demands of their work and their lives."[3]

Soon after meeting Souza and realizing that there was a story to be told, Pitt introduced him to writer-director Ron Shelton (*Bull Durham*, *White Men Can't Jump*, *Tin Cup*), who was then shooting the L.A. police drama *Dark Blue*. Director Shelton's idea was a movie "about a world you knew, but maybe from a different angle."[4] He and Souza took what they knew from their own worlds and created a hybrid story: one part drama, another part comedy.

Homicide (originally entitled *Two Cops*) depicts the investigation of the murder of a hip-hop group at a Hollywood nightclub. The task of finding the killers is delegated to L.A.P.D. cops Joe Gavilan (Ford), a veteran of the job, and his new rookie partner, K.C. Calden (Hartnett). Gavilan and Calden are polar opposites.

Because of budget restrictions in the city of Los Angeles, policemen — while not entitled to receive overtime pay — are allowed to accrue 90 minutes of vacation time for every hour of overtime worked. As a result, many lead second lives with second incomes—providing fuel for the film's comic relief.

While writing the script, Shelton relished the idea of casting Ford as Gavilan not only because his name spelled success, but also because he wished to present a Ford never before seen on the big screen.

"Harrison's a big dog," stated Shelton. "Usually, Harrison is so stoic, he's almost like a cowboy actor in an age where we don't make Westerns. But occasionally there's also been a twinkle in his eye. I wondered, 'How much is behind that twinkle?' I said to him, 'Harrison, what about the part of you that, with a couple of drinks and a cigar, is a different guy?'"[5]

Ford (a self-proclaimed admirer of television's The Simpsons and Jim Carrey's Dumb and Dumber, and someone who would embrace the opportunity to work with Steve Martin) described Hollywood Homicide as "the most antic"[6] kind of comedy he'd done thus far. "I was looking for something where I had a chance to push it a little more. I didn't want to be the straight man again in a comedy."[7]

Of Shelton — one of the primary reasons he had accepted the script — Ford stated: "Ron Shelton is a good observer of men and the world they live in, which is not necessarily the natural world. Ron knows what the pressures are, and pressure is the fount of all comic opportunity."[8]

Ford's Gavilan is a gruff, carefree, down-on-his-luck real estate broker with three ex-wives and two kids. Although committed to his duties as an officer of the law, he harbors a penchant for doing things his own way.

His young partner Calden is a part-time yoga instructor with aspirations of becoming an actor. Calden has joined the force only to carry on a family tradition. Unlike Gavilan, he treats his detective career merely as a means to an end.

Ford and Hartnett visited the Los Angeles Police Academy firing range and met with members of the L.A.P.D Hollywood division in an attempt to better understand the procedural intricacies of police work, and to find out more about the lives of individual police officers. Ford hoped to acquire knowledge beyond the typical details of police work; he wanted to learn more about the workings of an Internal Affairs investigation and to discover what was "singular and distinctive about the L.A.P.D."[9]

What he discovered was that the department had a "real sense of themselves as a very professional police department. They're very concerned about their image. They have rules about whether or not you can open your collar, not pull your tie down. You're supposed to keep a jacket on over your weapon at all times. They're very professional. They look real sharp. There's obvious differences between a New York street cop and an L.A.P.D. policeman and it's purposeful."[10]

Central to the film is the old school-new school chemistry between the experienced Gavilan and the novice Calden. They simply cannot see eye to eye. Ford and Hartnett mirrored this behavior. When filming began in October 2002, the on-paper dynamics between the two characters became easy to convey due, in part, to the real-life relationship between the two actors.

"These two characters are not buddies, said Ford. "They're guys who work together, who don't understand each other at all. I thought, that pretty much was reflected in our relationship, and I didn't try to disturb it."[11]

Hartnett was admittedly star-struck before he signed on to the project and met Ford for the first time. By the time filming had begun, however, those feelings had changed. Much of the fault for the widely publicized friction between them stemmed from their distinct differences in age, experience, taste and individual approaches to the craft of acting.

"He gave me a lot of shit about the choices that I made," claimed Hartnett. "'That's not a cop haircut.' Things like that. Other than Brad Pitt in *The Devil's Own*, I think I'm really only the second young guy he's worked with in his career, so when I kind of came into his territory, that's when he started to throw his elbows out."[12]

Ford was less eager to speak poorly of his cavalier co-star. He commented in his usual, diplomatic manner: "He's a very ... uh, he approaches the work in a very different way than I do. But he's a talented kid and he's got a lot of appeal," said Ford.[13]

The discord between them would later be exacerbated by a much publicized and near-fatal incident. During a stunt sequence involving a high-speed chase down an alleyway, Hartnett reportedly miscalculated, slamming the vehicle he was driving into a police cruiser that missed its own cue. As a result of the incident, Ford suffered a minor groin injury and Hartnett a concussion.

"Harrison still blames me," said Hartnett, "but he's wrong. I think that he's just doing it for effect."[14]

Ford painted a somewhat different picture. When asked by the BBC during the film's promotional tour whether Hartnett did, in fact, cause the accident, Ford insisted: "Yes, he did and he wasn't even sorry! Well, I guess he was a little sorry. It was an accident. We were doing a driving shot where we had the cameras mounted on the trunk and we were supposed to be cut off by a police car at the end of the alley. We were driving through and somehow, somehow, we hit the police car!"[15]

Ford attributed it to his young co-star's lack of experience, stating: "He just got a little too excited behind the wheel. But, you know, that's why I'd rather drive than ride any time."[16]

Filming began in October 2002 and took place exclusively in Los Angeles, a convenient location for Ford, a resident of nearby Brentwood. Although an uneventful shoot overall, there were the occasional interruptions, as when an actual murder suspect was chased through the set by real L.A.P.D. cops — forcing the cast to hide in their trailers until the danger passed. Many of the locations are recognizable landmarks, including several streets throughout the city of Hollywood (most notably Hollywood Boulevard), Rodeo Drive, Graumann's Chinese Theater and the Venice Canals. The exterior of the Freeway Club, where the murders occur, was also used in 2001's *Ocean's 11*. The parking lot of the L.A.P.D. Hollywood station (on North Wilcox Avenue) appears in several scenes — most memorably in the scene involving a handcuffed criminal, who commandeers an officer's gun and begins shooting before being tackled by Calden. Later, Gavilan and Calden drive the murder witness "K-Ro" (played by real-life rapper Kurupt) to the police station. They pass the same gritty marine area that was filmed for Lucy Liu's flame-thrower scene in 2003's *Charlie's Angels: Full Throttle*. One might also recognize the subway station in which Gavilan slides down a banister; in 2003's remake of *The Italian Job*, a Mini Cooper rumbles down those same steps and into the subway.

On location with director Shelton (center) and Josh Hartnett (Columbia, 2003).

After completion, extensive test screenings gauged audiences' reaction. Poor results forced the production to re-shoot a number of scenes.

To promote the film, Paramount and Revolution Studios set Ford and Hartnett out on an aggressive promotional campaign. Their efforts included participation in the usual talk show circuit and an appearance with the L.A. Lakers dance team sporting T-shirts featuring the film's title. Ford and Hartnett even appeared at the 2003 MTV Movie Awards (an event Hartnett recalled being persuaded by Ford to attend). On September 5, 2003, Ford — accompanied by girlfriend Calista Flockhart (of TV's *Ally McBeal*) — attended the Deauville Film Festival in France for a European screening of the film. Also in attendance there was director Roman Polanski, who had collaborated with Ford on *Frantic*. Ford presented him with the 2003 Academy Award for Best Director, which had been awarded to Polanski in March for his work on *The Pianist*. Polanski had been unable to accept the award at the Oscar ceremony in Los Angeles, having fled to Paris in 1978 to avoid serving time for a conviction on the charge of unlawful sex with a minor.

On June 13, 2003 (two weeks after Ford received his star on Hollywood's Walk of Fame just in front of the Kodak Theater), *Hollywood Homicide* opened on 2840 screens across North America. Commenting on the film's dissimilarity to other movies release around that time, director Shelton stated: "In the summer, you need some hook. We've got a movie that is not a sequel and has no special effects. If you want the loudest, most special effects–driven movie of the summer, we're not the one.

But if you want to hang out with some wonderful, oddball characters for an hour and 52 minutes, this is the one."[17]

That summer, the public was not looking for character-driven films. The 2003 season saw the boom of big-budget action and science-fiction movies, including *Terminator 3: Rise of the Machines*, *The Matrix: Reloaded*, *The Hulk*, *2 Fast, 2 Furious*, *Charlie's Angels: Full Throttle* and the wildly successful *Pirates of the Caribbean: Curse of the Black Pearl*. These films commanded the public's attention, leaving little room for the easy-going *Homicide*.

During its opening weekend, *Homicide* earned a mere $11 million. After a few months in release, the film had amassed a total box office of only $30 million. While not the lowest earning large-scale release of the summer (*Dumb and Dumberer: When Harry Met Lloyd* earned a lowly total of $26 million, and *From Justin to Kelly* took in a measly $5 million), its financial shortcoming was a devastating blow to a film that had been made on a budget of $75 million and had a $30 million marketing campaign.

Despite *Homicide*'s poor showing, reviews were not entirely negative. Mick LaSalle of *The San Francisco Chronicle* stated, "Like all Shelton's movies, *Hollywood Homicide* rambles and shambles, and like most of them, it ultimately settles into its own appealing rhythm...."[18]

The Boston Globe's Ty Burr rewarded Shelton with a backhanded compliment when he wrote that the film was "one of the most lazily scripted, poorly structured, smugly stereotypical star vehicles in recent memory. Bizarrely, this seems to be the point. Conceived as a shaggy-dog midsummer lark, the film sets up the action-comedy genre conventions as if they were traffic cones on the Santa Monica Freeway, then lets Ford and co-star Josh Hartnett drive all over them."[19] *Premiere* magazine's critic wrote, "*Hollywood Homicide* has the impact of a TV movie of the week: It neither packs a punch nor belongs in the same league as many of the other summer films vying for the top spot at the box office."[20]

Not even the film's widely varied cast, including Lena Olin, Martin Landau, Lolita Davidovitch, Dwight Yoakam, Lou Diamond Philips, Isaiah Washington and Bruce Greenwood, could deter attention from Ford's role. *The New York Daily News*' assessment of Ford's performance was harsh: "It's a humiliating comedown for Ford, and he looks creaky and grumpy, obviously aware that he is miscast and dreading every scene."[21]

More frequently, however, Ford's performance was lauded for being a departure from his many serious, rigid characters of previous films. Consistently, Ford and Hartnett's characters were commended for their quirky behavior and lively discourse. Roger Ebert of *The Chicago Sun Times* observed: "One of the pleasures of [the film] is that it's more interested in its two goofy cops than in the murder plot...."[22]

Although noting that the picture would unlikely result in "the career boost Ford needs," *The Boston Globe*'s Ty Burr summarized Ford's performance most succinctly, stating: "it's nice to see Old Grumpy having fun for a change...."[23]

As usual, his co-workers offered nothing but praise for his energy and work ethic. Lena Olin, who portrays Ruby, his 40-something love interest, was pleasantly surprised upon meeting Ford that he had not been ruined by fame. "I felt like I worked with my best buddy.... He just helps people out on the set, because we're all there to make the movie and I think that's adorable that somebody of that magnitude can keep the awareness up that we're all here for the movie. No one is here for Harrison Ford ... he's so eager still ... he's still struggling just to get it right, as we all do."[24]

Director Shelton agreed: "Not giving 100 percent to a job is something Ford just doesn't relate to. I don't want to say I was surprised, but I was delighted to see that after being the world's biggest movie star for 30 years, he cares so much about the details in his latest movie. I don't think he's capable of phoning in a performance. You expect that when you've been on top for 30 years you might relax a bit, but he doesn't."[25]

Shelton was further impressed by the number of stunts Ford chose to do himself. *Homicide* included no special effects or computer graphics, instead relying entirely upon old-fashioned stunt work. Ford's stunt double, however, saw little action. Shelton observed that Ford "did so many stunts it was frightening ... when you see him jumping over the railing and crashing on a roof fan, when you see him jumping out of a moving car, it's all him."[26]

For co-star Isaiah Washington, who plays Antoine Sartaine, a suave music executive, working with Ford was a singular kind of experience. Like Shelton, he was equally impressed by Ford's willingness—insistence, actually—on carrying out perilous stunts. The two shared a number of challenging scenes, and whenever Ford managed his stunts, Washington, did as well—albeit reluctantly: "I told Harrison ...'I really don't think we should be doing this. This is dangerous. We could die.' He said to me, 'I'll see you on the other side.'"[27]

Physical prowess aside, Ford has acknowledged the generation gap between himself and Hartnett, describing his young co-star as "a very different kind of beast. Ron [Shelton] is sure that we're from different planets. I don't know what planet Josh is from, but he is a very different guy, grew up in a very different world than I...."[28]

Harrison Ford has finally had to concede to Harnett's appeal for younger audiences, with the understanding that all things evolve: "My 12-year-old daughter and her girlfriends refer to him as Josh 'Hotnett.' He's huge. I used to be huge."[29]

37

ALL CAMERAS ASIDE

Today, Harrison Ford can reflect on his past and enjoy the personal and professional happiness that those years have earned him. His contentment results from the life he chose and built with his family and newfound love, Calista Flockhart. It is also a reflection of a fulfilling career, and with his years of giving back to the community a bit of his good fortune through charitable works and his support of deserving causes.

For nearly 20 years, Ford and wife Melissa Mathison were busy establishing an ideal home life for themselves and their children. However, as can happen with even the best of marriages, the two announced their separation in October 2000 after reportedly living apart for a month. Despite attempts to reconcile, Mathison filed for legal separation in August 2001 and moved with their children out of their New York City apartment and into a home in Los Angeles. In 2003, divorce negotiations ensued — and everything was settled amicably between the two.

When the press received word of Ford's newfound single status, there were immediate rumors of relationships between the actor and well-known actresses Lara Flynn Boyle and Minnie Driver. Such rumors were put aside, though, when — on the evening he was presented with the Cecil B. DeMille Award — Ford met actress Calista Flockhart at a January 2002 Golden Globes after-party. Romance soon followed.

Best known for her lead role in the popular TV series *Ally McBeal* (1997–2002), Flockhart — 22 years Ford's junior — forbids her boyfriend from viewing any episodic repeats. In addition, she's appeared in smaller roles in such films as *Quiz Show*, *The Birdcage*, *A Midsummer Night's Dream* and *The Last Shot*. However, Flockhart's focus since 2001 has been on her adopted son Liam, now nearly three. Since early 2003, they have lived as a family with Ford in his five-bedroom New England–style home in Brentwood, California. Additionally, when in New York, they reside with Ford in his newly renovated 5,700-square-foot penthouse in the Chelsea neighborhood of New York City. (Ford's Central Park West apartment — which he shared with Melissa and his children — sold for an estimated $16 million.)

Although Flockhart admits admiring Ford in his role as Allie Fox in *The Mosquito Coast*, their relationship now is based entirely on a personal respect and admiration for one another.

"Romantic love is one of the most exciting and fulfilling kinds of love, and I think there's potential for it at any stage of your life," said Ford of his new relationship. "I was not surprised that I was able to fall in love, and I wasn't surprised that I did. But I'm very grateful."[1]

As is his way, Ford has not divulged whether this new relationship may result in a third marriage. For the time being, he appears to be enjoying this new development in his life. He continues as well to have a strong relationship with his older children Benjamin and Williard from his first marriage — who both have professional careers and families of their own — and Malcolm and Georgia from his second.

Following permanent injuries to both his knees during his junior year at the University of Southern California, Benjamin Ford's dreams of becoming a professional baseball player were shattered. Choosing a career as a chef, Ford attended and graduated from the California Culinary Academy in San Francisco. His passion for the culinary arts stemmed from helping his mother prepare meals while growing up — using many ingredients from her garden. His father provided additional parental influence: "I got my [push] from my dad," said the younger Ford. "I feel a lot of pressure to be successful on my own terms."[2]

Floating from one posh restaurant to another in and around Los Angeles, Ben finally settled in as the proprietor of Chadwick's in Beverly Hills. The restaurant — which opened its doors to the public in August 2000 — was named by Ben in honor of Alan Chadwick, the man considered the godfather of organic gardening. Despite its popularity, Ben sold Chadwick's but retained its name for his own catering company: Chadwick's Fine Food and Special Events.

Pressure or no pressure, Benjamin — who shares his life with a television news producer and a son born in October 2000 — is well-liked and respected in his line of work. Although his patrons and co-workers may feel this way as a misguided tribute to his famous father, Benjamin's talents are quite simply the result of similar genealogical traits: "Ben's always been very self-critical," said the father. "That's what led him to perfect his skills."[3]

A graduate of the University of California at Santa Cruz, Willard Ford has become a substitute teacher in the Oakland, California, school system — and at one point was an organizer of bicycle tours of Vietnam as well as a Kung Fu instructor. He and his wife Aisha have a son, Eliel, who was born in 1994. Willard is responsible for managing all of his father's finances, which includes maintaining the family foundation.

"We've enjoyed extraordinary good fortune," said the senior Ford. "It's been a constant ambition of mine to help people who are in dire straits.... The work the foundation does is a private family matter. We don't call it the Harrison Ford Foundation because we don't want it to be connected with me. When we solicit proposals for funding, my name isn't attached. We do it through a third party."[4]

Of his sons, Harrison believes they foster in him "occasions of great pride and real joy in what they've become and how happy they are in their lives."[5]

Ford has admitted to having neglected the rearing of the children from his first marriage, describing that time as "babies raising babies"[6] — and has since assured himself that he would not make similar mistakes with his third son, Malcolm, born in 1987.

During an insightful 1992 interview following the birth of his daughter Georgia, he willingly delved into his rarely discussed personal life, admitting his pleasure in being allowed "the opportunity of being a father all over again — and the opportunity to try to get it right this time!

"A family is the most important thing in the world. But we all wish we could devote more time to it. I certainly do. I feel, like many, that I made mistakes in my own youth I would rather not admit. The way I've brought up two families has changed enormously over the years. I've changed too. I'm now more mature and can see the value of certain things that I was unable to see before."[7]

Accustomed to the inclement weather of his Midwest upbringing, Ford and Mathison intended to find a locale with four seasons— three of them winter. Initially, the couple scouted Sun Valley, Idaho, but eventually their search ended further west. The mountain valley of Jackson Hole, Wyoming (an area approximately 80 miles long and 15 miles wide), was their chosen site. Ford called the area as being "an antidotal atmosphere. It balances my working world real well...."[8] When I was growing up, I always had this picture in my head of an idyllic place with woods, open water and wildlife. There came a point when I realized I didn't have to be in Los Angeles all this time. My older kids went off to college and got stuck into their lives more, so I had the opportunity to live somewhere else. Melissa and I kept looking for something that matched our fantasy, and we found this place. It's helped me become more calm and peaceful."[9]

Situated seven miles from "downtown" Jackson Hole, the property — an enormous area of land naturally reserved for pasturage — was in such an unspoiled state upon the actor's first arrival in September 1984 that it required a septic system, as well as water and electricity.

Past the "Private Property: Please No Trespassing" sign is a seemingly endless driveway — at the end of which is a simple, white clapboard, four-bedroom, two-story, colonial-style structure — designed and built by Ford himself.

As part of a compound, the house serves as the centerpiece with a number of other structures surrounding it, making up a three-acre living area. There is an enormous barn for the Holstein cows and horses. There are two smaller homes, each serving as a getaway for sons Benjamin and Willard and their families. An office for Ford to conduct his business is situated beside the woodshop. The nearby garage facilitates his farm equipment, passenger vehicles, snowmobiles and his collection of motorcycles. There is also a tennis court and for the long-term visitors to his 768 acres, there is yet another road wandering away from the main compound leading to furnished guest homes. From family to friends, actors to actresses, from directors to producers, from American Presidents to the Dalai Lama himself, the accommodations were, according to Mace Neufeld, the most elaborately insulated and detailed log cabins he'd ever seen.

Novelist Jim Harrison was overwhelmed when presented with the craftsmanship and attention to detail. "I was a carpenter and a contractor for a while, and I'd hate to work for him," Harrison said. "He'd be incredibly demanding. I think he has an exquisite gift for carpentry. That Wyoming house is just a marvel. In terms of details, people don't build houses like that, for obvious reasons."[10]

Ford's vision of his home was very precise, with it possessing "a kind of simplicity and order and rhythm in the lines of the building."[11]

While in Jackson Hole, the actor remains in contact with Hollywood from his office, where all the latest communications technology surround his script-covered desk — dispelling any suggestion that he is hiding from his responsibilities behind the 13,770-foot-high slopes of the Grand Teton.

"It's just a family home," explained the actor. "It's a place for us to live. Don't think of it as anti-anything. We love it there. It is not a revulsion to the things that go on in Hollywood. I know that I am very much a part of what we think of as Hollywood. It is just a nicer place to live. When I look out my window there are elk grazing in the meadow. There are eagles overhead. The kids can run outside without danger of being run over or running into bad guys. This is a community that we are well knit into. I think to the people that live there, I will always be a little strange. I think the people in town are agreeable to letting us lead a normal life."[12]

In a relatively short amount of time, the sight of Ford among the estimated 4,500 other inhabitants of Jackson Hole became a common and — much to the actor's pleasure — uneventful sight. Demonstrating his admiration and respect for the land, he donated various parcels amounting to nearly 1,000 acres as a conservation easement to the Jackson Hole Land Trust between 1985 and 1989. With that, the actor has been promised by the non-profit and private organization that the area of land willingly forfeited will remain undeveloped in perpetuity. Years later, in December 1993, the actor donated yet another 379 acres of his land to the trust.

Ford said, "I believe in what the land trust does. On the property I hold, in my own small way I have tried to preserve the natural splendor and wildlife resources. The land trust has been an effective partner in helping me ensure that this land will remain relatively undisturbed forever."[13]

"We feel [Ford's property] is one of the most significant private parcels in Jackson Hole to be kept intact," explained the trust's president, Tom Rossetter. "Harrison Ford and Melissa Mathison have made this gift not only to the land trust but to future generations."[14]

"I have more of a sense of stewardship about it than ownership," claimed the actor, who in 1989 became a member of the land trust's Board of Directors. "I really want to preserve it for my kids — to let them know this is what's dear to me rather than a big pile of money in the middle of the floor."[15]

While the contribution to his community on behalf of the Land Trust in general relates to him and his property alone, the actor lends his support to other local causes. He has narrated segments of a local music festival and had been involved in the Jackson Hole Wildlife Film Festival — where he serves as an Honorary Board Member on the Board of Trustees. He also sponsors a kid's ski team each winter, is a member of the Jackson Land Trust Board of Directors, serves as a deputy sheriff for the town, and has organized benefit screenings of his films at the town's local cinema. (One such event — the 1993 premiere of *The Fugitive* the evening before its official nationwide release — generated nearly $12,000 for the Teton County Library fund.)

In 1999 he narrated a documentary entitled *Mardy Murie: Arctic Dance* on Jackson resident Mardy Murie. Murie was a 97-year-old woman considered by many the "Mother of the Conservation Movement." With her late husband Olaus, Mardy was partially responsible for founding the 1964 Wilderness Act, the Teton Wilderness and the Bridger Wilderness Act — all non-profit organizations that deal with the conservation of land and wildlife. As a result of her efforts, Murie was a candidate for the Wyoming Citizen of the Century Award. In 1998, she was awarded the Medal of Freedom.

In 2004, Ford appeared in a "documentary" film about a group of Extreme snowboarders entitled *Water to Wine*. Presumably done as a favor to his son Malcolm (who also appears in the film) and his friends, Ford portrays Jethro, the van driver. Complete with a beard and full Wyoming winter garb, it will undoubtedly remain as the only occasion anyone will ever hear a character of his ask, "What up, bi-atch?"

While there is nowhere he would rather be than his Wyoming home, the actor does own abodes in the Los Angeles suburb of Brentwood, California, and an apartment in New York City. The actor has also claimed to be the owner of an undisclosed amount of acreage on the surface of the Moon. Ford (alongside other celebrities who were humored by their "realtor" at Lunar Embassy in Rio Vista, California) paid $16 per acre (plus a lunar tax of $1.16) and now reportedly possesses a deed to at least one acre of the moon — "earth view guaranteed."[16]

Despite his reluctance to reside within a major city, both his California and New York homes were purchased and are currently maintained solely out of necessity. His Brentwood home exists primarily due to its proximity to his oldest sons and his mother, who resides in Orange County. Furthermore, the four-bedroom home serves as a convenient locale while filming at nearby Hollywood studios.

In the spring of 1990 he purchased a three-bedroom Central Park West apartment from actress Debra Winger for $2 million. "I never liked cities," admitted Ford. "Now I find I like New York, which I used to hate. Maybe just having the country there, knowing I can go there, lets me indulge my taste for other things. It's a safe haven for me. I like the idea of figuring out how to work in a place like New York, how to live a reasonable life in a place like that.... It's a funny thing, but you can have more privacy there. You go up in that elevator and you lock the door and you're in a cocoon. You go out into the street and it's like stepping into a river. Knowing you're not required to be there, knowing it's your option, makes it palatable."[17]

Ford has learned to accept the multitude of activities New York City and its suburbs offer. He participates in a multitude of fundraising events and concerts, including benefit performances for the Rainforest Foundation (founded in 1989 by musician Sting and his wife Trudie Styler) and Free Tibet.

Much to the chagrin of their father, New York fascinates the children. "They love it," said Ford in 1995. "They go deeper into Central Park than they do into their own woods. We have an elk herd on our property that numbers 300, 400 animals, and they come and stand in the front yard. You say to the kids, 'Look at the elk.' They say, 'Oh, yeah.' But they'll go to the basement of the Museum of Natural History and stand with their noses pressed to the glass looking at a stuffed elk."[18]

According to the actor, there is a time and a place for everything. "I don't feel good about taking the platform merely on account of my celebrity," said the actor. "I do believe in supporting things I believe in, and I believe that the people I support are in a position to make a better argument for the cause, based on facts and their expertise, than I am on the authority of my celebrity."[19]

He continued, "I don't believe that a complex issue should be decided on the basis of what celebrity is endorsing it. Yes, you can help bring attention to issues, but the quality of the argument often suffers."[20]

The actor has lent his (less visible) services for public service announcements for organizations like the Will Rogers Institute, the American Cancer Society, the National Organization of Disability (N.O.D.), the Environmental Media Association and Save the Children. In 1994, he narrated *Mustang: The Hidden Kingdom*, a Discovery Channel documentary telling of a Tibetan enclave that had remained undisturbed from outside influences for decades. In 1997, he narrated a PBS Frontline documentary about a humanitarian aid expert, *Fred Cuny: The Lost American*. Cuny disappeared amidst the war-torn nation of Chechnya in 1995—and in early 2002, negotiations fell apart for Ford to star in a biopic of the renowned activist. In October 1999, PBS aired *Jane Goodall: Reason for Hope*, a project he proudly narrated considering his belief that her work on behalf of the environment seemingly inspired a whole new generation.

In Fort Worth, Texas, on October 29, 2000, Ford narrated another program: *The Flight Line: The Army Helicopters of Vietnam*. This project—apart from its educational benefit—was intended to raise money for a proposed National Vietnam War Museum. In February 2001, he narrated a documentary about another topic close to his heart, *Lost Worlds: Life in the Balance*—a program about the diversity of life on Earth and the unassuming link the common man has to the natural world. In March 2002, the actor's voice was heard in *The Search for Life: Are We Alone?* for audiences at the American Museum of Natural History.

In July of that year, television and print viewers caught a glimpse of the actor holding a "Will Work for Food" sign for City Harvest. In April 2003, the New York–based organization honored the actor and the ad's director, famed photographer Timothy White, with the Heart of the City Award for their work to help feed the hungry.

The organization's Executive Director Julia Erickson called him "a true champion for New York's hungry."[21]

For all of the public service announcements and documentaries, he contributed his time without pay. The simple act of being involved was rewarding enough.

Ford is also one of the many contributing founders as well as a trustee for the Artists Rights Foundation, an organization whose mission "is to educate the public about the importance of protecting and preserving film art; to defend an artist's work threatened with modification or distortion; and to promote public debate about their issues to help safeguard our intellectual and cultural heritage."[22] He also holds a position as a board member with the Washington, D.C.–based environmental group Conservation International (CI), whose purpose is to identify ecological issues and to promote solutions for them. He has also spoken on behalf of the Archaeology Advisory Groups of Colorado, Alaska, Mississippi, Arizona, North Carolina and New

Mexico. He is a member of the Forest Stewardship Council, an organization that oversees that wood utilized for the construction of homes has "been independently certified to meet the highest standards for environmentally and socially responsible forestry." In February 1999, he facilitated an agreement between Conservation International and the Surinam government to save a 6,000-square-mile portion of the Amazon rain forest from being eradicated by Asian logging companies. The logging would have threatened the existence of native wildlife including the giant armadillo, the black spider monkey, the giant otter and the harpy eagle, to name but a few. On the final decision, Ford said, "It seems that when we hear about rain forests, it's always bad news. Humanity will have access to a piece of the planet that is as it always was."[23]

While filming *The Mosquito Coast*, the actor paid a visit to the Belize Zoo. Both its facility and unique inhabitants so impressed him that he paid tribute to the organizers' efforts by contributing funds for the construction of the Gerald Durrell Visitor Center, which opened its doors in 1991.

In the foyer, a photograph of Ford with a parrot and a toucan atop his shoulders taken during the 1986 filming is accompanied by a letter written by the actor. Its text — written on June 18, 1998 — conveys his appreciation for the efforts of the zoo as well as his encouragement for all the "Friends of the Belize Zoo" to continue their support.

During the summer of 1999, proposals to construct a toxic waste incinerator just 100 miles from Yellowstone National Park were put on hold because of opposition from several environmental groups. Alongside other concerned residents, Ford helped to form the organization Keep Yellowstone Nuclear Free. He donated $50,000 in the hopes of coercing the Federal government to consider other methods of disposing the harmful waste.

On Earth Day 2001, the actor attended a fundraising event in Washington, D.C., with other celebrities and political luminaries in support of the Yellowstone Park Foundation, to raise awareness of the park, as well as appropriate funding for a proposed $15 million Old Faithful Visitor Education Center.

For Riverkeepers — an organization the actor has been a part of for several years, dedicated to keeping the Hudson River clean and free from personal and industrial polluters — Ford offers his time and piloting skills in providing surveillance flights over the river courtesy of his Bell 407 helicopter.

For the actor, helping his fellow man is something he takes great pleasure in, but his true passion remains with the preservation of Mother Earth.

Conservation International (CI) chairman Peter Seligmann is grateful for the presence of such a good ally: "Harrison has a very precise, strategic mind. He can analyze an issue rapidly, understand it, and see the logic. I don't know where that ability came from, but I'm sure it has a lot to do with his success in the movie business. He's one of the smartest people I've ever dealt with."[24]

Feeling so strongly about CI's vital message and cognizant of the organization's capability to shape the future, the actor reportedly donated $5 million during the fall of 1999.

"The Earth we live on is facing a threat unlike anything it has ever encountered,"[25] said the actor to *Good Housekeeping* magazine in its October 1999 issue.

There are more of us packed into the same amount of space, and we are using up resources that can never be replaced. The way we are living is causing an animal extinction rate second only to the loss of the dinosaurs.... The very air that we breathe, the climate that we live in, is either benign or wrathful according to how we treat it. What's more, somewhere in this incredibly intricate interconnectedness between all living things, there are many undiscovered medicines, many undiscovered products. We're talking about new, more powerful anesthetics and possible cures for childhood leukemia coming out of the rain forest. And that's what people fail to understand. If it's not right in front of their faces—if the tree in their front yard isn't dying—people tend to ignore it. The final reality is that we have to live here, all of us, together on this Earth. We have no other place to live, and we damn well better take care of it. Or it will not suffer us.[26]

Of all the issues he supports, however, nothing holds a tighter grasp on his conscience than the occupation of Tibet.

In 1992, director Martin Scorsese (*Taxi Driver*, *Raging Bull*, *Goodfellas*) hired Ford's wife to develop a screenplay based on the Tibetan leader and his China-occupied nation of Tibet. Assisting her with her research in the Himalayan nation in April of that year, Ford found himself enraptured by their culture and beliefs.

Ford met with Tibet's leader and presented him with his wife's script. "I read the first rough script to him, I didn't try to perform. It took a few weeks. Each day took about three sessions of an hour and a half apiece. We would stop and discuss things. I would rarely make it through a day without having an emotional reaction to what I was reading and the situation I found myself in."[27]

Although Richard Gere (a devout Buddhist) is perhaps the most outspoken and well-known activist, Ford has also become a prominent figure in publicizing the situation and the radical need for change. On September 7, 1995, Ford testified before the Senate Foreign Relations Committee and the Subcommittee on East Asian and Pacific Affairs, hoping to attract attention to the issue.

As a result, he joined the ever-growing list of celebrities blacklisted by the Chinese government that includes Gere, Steven Segal, Goldie Hawn, composer Philip Glass, Tim Robbins, Susan Sarandon, Beastie Boys singer Adam Yauch, Brad Pitt, Spike Lee and Sting. China has denied travel permits indefinitely for both Ford and Mathison, who also spoke before the subcommittee that day.

"I'm sure I did a number of things to annoy the Chinese," admitted the actor. "I was nervous about public speaking, but it was a small panel. They sought our input. The ambition at the time was to prevent the Chinese from gaining Most Favored Nation status without redressing some of the problems they've created in Tibet."[28]

Since that incident, the actor has maintained his desire to see an independent Tibet. He actively chaired fundraising events with Mathison for the Tibet Fund and the American Himalayan Foundation.

During his lean years as a student at Ripon College, a teenaged Harrison Ford took a few flying lessons. But the $15 per week required was tough for him to come by in his position in the 1960s, so he never completed the training.

"The desire to fly never left me, and I promised myself that it was something I would take the time to do, sooner or later,"[29] said Ford in a June 1998 article he wrote and submitted for publication in *AOPA (Aircraft Owners and Pilot's Association) Pilot Magazine*. His interest was significantly re-invigorated as an adult during the countless flights he spent as a passenger in the front jump seat of his own Gulfstream jet.

Due to time constraints, the actor was never able to continue his training until 1995, when he began taking lessons high above the Wyoming landscape and from Teterboro Airport in New Jersey. Although failing his eye exam (which requires him to wear glasses while piloting). Ford passed both the written and hands-on testing and earned his pilot's license on September 19, 1996.

To earn his helicopter pilot's license, Ford attended training in Fort Lauderdale, Florida, during the winter of 1997 and at Bell School in Fort Worth, Texas, the following spring. After a year of training he earned his chopper license on January 30, 1998. He put his skills to the test with the purchase of his own Bell 206-L4 Long-Ranger.

In addition to owning a Beech B36TC Bonanza and an Aviat, the actor reportedly has also invested nearly $30 million on a custom-built Gulfstream G-IV jet for his traveling needs. The details include wall-to-wall carpeting, leather seating, an on-board office with a glass-top desk, a marble wet bar, a big-screen television and a Nordic Track cross-country ski machine. Aside from living quarters complete with computers for his two youngest children, a specially designed cargo area was included to safely stow the motorcycle of his choice.

Despite a virtually flawless history of piloting, the actor did come to terms with his own mortality one October morning in 1999. While sharing the controls with his helicopter flight instructor Toby Wilson, Ford's 1,600-pound five-seat chopper touched down rather ungracefully onto its side into a dry riverbed 45 miles north of Los Angeles. Ironically, the two were practicing an emergency procedure that prepares the pilot to cope with the event of an all-out engine failure known as an autorotation. Ford walked away unscathed, but his $750,000 piece of flying hardware sustained heavy damage.

"From 800 feet, you're on the ground in a matter of seconds," said Wilson. "It's a black-and-white issue. Either you live or you die. And I think Harrison likes the clarity of that."[30]

In July 2000, the actor offered both his piloting services and equipment to the state of Wyoming to rescue a hiker who suffered from dehydration and altitude sickness atop the 11,000-foot-plus Table Mountain in Teton County. In a similar event one year later, he was in the sky above Yellowstone National Park (accompanied by another plane from the Wyoming Air Patrol) searching for a 13-year-old Boy Scout who had strayed from his pack. After nearly two hours behind the stick, Ford found the boy. Needless to say, the word "hero" appeared in virtually all the news stories. Ford was disconcerted with the reference: "When a rescue helicopter is needed, I put mine at the disposal of the community. That was no heroic deed but just a medical evacuation. The sheriff called me and asked me if I was available."[31]

Much like his passion for acting and his woodworking, it is evident from overhearing a conversation with him that flying aircraft is something that he is not only passionate about, but that he passionately loves.

I love going into new airports. I love crosswind landings. I love short-field takeoffs and landings. I love landing on grass, or a dry lakebed, or dirt road. I love slipping an airplane and all it takes to finesse a good landing. I just love handling an airplane. I like flying alone, and it's not unusual for me to take four to five hours and do a round robin of ten airports, just for the pleasure of flying. Still, I also like having someone along to share the experience ... and admire my landings. Flying with pros is great because I always learn something from them and increase my knowledge and skill level. I probably fly about 250 hours a year. That's a lot of flying just for fun.

I like most the change in visual environment, the places that I visit and see, and the great people I meet in the world of aviation. I also appreciate the circumstances under which I meet these people. They accept me simply as a pilot who shares their love of flying and they seem to respect my genuine interest in aviation. The fraternity of aviators cares little for other trappings; they welcome you because of a shared interest and judge you on your flying skills. My only regret is that I waited so long.[32]

In March 2004, Ford assumed the role of Chairman of the America's Young Eagles program. Alongside other aviation enthusiasts, Ford encouraged children to appreciate aviation by allowing them to spend time in his cockpit flying among the clouds.

The results of Ford's first paying job in the film business can now be considered loose change compared with his present income. During his days as a contract player in the mid–1960s, Ford was cashing $150 paychecks. Today, he earns a trifle more.

By agreeing to star in *The Devil's Own* in 1996, Ford and a small crowd of others (including funny man Jim Carrey, heartthrob Tom Cruise and mega-man Arnold Schwarzennegger) became the first high-profile actors to earn $20 million per picture.

"Nobody is worth $20 million," admitted the actor to syndicated talk show host Larry King during the 1997 promotional tour of *Air Force One*. "It's raw material. You take raw material and you make something out of it and you sell it. And you get a certain price for what you sell. Now you go back and you have to pay for the raw material. I wasn't the first one to ask, but if other people were going to take that kind of money, I sure as hell was going to take it as well.... It's crazy."[33]

Looks: From handsome and boyish, to rugged and all–American; the one adjective used to describe Ford that he is most comfortable with is "Everyman." What is not Everyman, however, is the history of events Ford has survived during his acting career. Throughout the years, physical pain has complemented mental anguish. From his early years, beginning as a high school gymnast when his back was forever injured, to the present, it is evident that acting has taken its physical toll on the actor. His body houses an assortment of wounds few have experienced, while his mouth tells the interesting history that explains their origin.

On numerous unfortunate occasions, the actor's nose has been broken — an incident that is more or less considered standard procedure in his physically demanding line of work. In May 1997, Ford stated that he would like just one opportunity to give his nose "one more chance to find a normal position"[34] on his face.

Both of his knees have undergone operations after sustaining permanent damage from film work. As a result of a car accident during his commute to his job as a stage actor of the 1960s, the actor's chin was forever altered. He's had several emergency operations on his back to remove problem discs, which helps to explain his consistently unflinching and upright posture. (The actor reportedly arrived on the set of *Return of the Jedi* in a wheelchair.) Yet, a scrutiny of his body in search of his telltale wounds would reveal little. All are virtually undetectable with the exception of his scarred chin — and one other. He reported the amusing anecdote on Jay Leno's *Tonight Show* in 1994 to promote *Clear and Present Danger*.

The year was 1973. The project was the "Whelan's Men" episode of *Gunsmoke*. The experience marked the first occasion Ford would succumb to an on-the-job injury. "Well, I was a bad guy. I was playing a bad guy, and I was shooting out of the window at the sheriff and his posse, and the good guy came down the stairs, and I rolled around. I shot at him and he shot at me, and I was supposed to slump against the window and crumple to the floor. And the first time I did it, I separated my shoulder."[35]

Because of the tremendous pain, Ford was not able to sit still for very long immediately upon his "fall." As a result, the filmmakers couldn't depict his character as being dead and required that he recover and return for a re-shoot. Arriving on the set for his second attempt, Ford followed the instructions to safely perform the feat again. But on the first attempt, his prop pistol abruptly bounced off the floor and into his face, causing six teeth to pop out.

Being under contract to the studio at the time meant that they would pay for the dental work. But the actor was able to smile for only a short period of time. Six months later, the teeth began to fall out. Soon after, Ford discovered that the dentist who had performed the procedure was fired for a variety of other improperly handled tasks.

While filming *Random Hearts* in Washington, D.C., he was named by *People* magazine as the "Sexiest Man Alive 1998." Ford — ever weary of the spotlight — was baffled at this honor. He was quick to set it aside and neglected to make mention of it to his wife. When he arrived home from work that evening, his family had already heard the news from the television and greeted him a barrage of friendly laughs.

"Why this sudden outpouring for geezers?" he questioned. "I never feel sexy. I have a distant relationship with the mirror ... I've got a completely imbalanced, irregular face and a nose that's been broken three or four times. One eye is higher than the other. When people photograph me, they have to kind of twist the lights around to make me look like a movie actor."[36]

After peer pressure from his cohorts Jimmy Buffett and *60 Minutes*' Ed Bradley, the actor got his ear pierced in a shopping mall alongside Mathison — and it became the most talked-about subject in every interview with him since his buzz-cut in *Presumed Innocent*. Was it the earring that earned him the title of Sexiest Man?

"I don't think in and of themselves that earrings are sexy," he said. "If I did, I'd have six of them."[37]

Apart from his philanthropic contributions, Ford has also lent his services to other interested parties. He did a television commercial promoting the European automotive company, Lancia. The actor also participated in both print and television campaigns for the Honda Motor Company, Sony and Japan's Kirin Beer. For Kirin, print advertising executives shot the actor in a variety of poses. He participated with the understanding that they be seen only in Japan.

For U.S. consumers, Ford did voice-overs for Oldsmobile and posed for Ebel watches. Nearly a dozen ads went to print in various fashion magazines depicting his watch-clad hand in various poses—with none offering the consumer a glimpse beyond his forearm.

He also extended his narrative services for such documentary projects as 1992's *Behind the Scenes: A Portrait of Pierre Guffroy*, 1993's *Earth and the American Dream*, 1995's *American Cinema* and 1996's *Sex and the Silver Screen*.

In October 1998, Harcourt Brace and Co. released *The Emperor's New Clothes: An All-Star Illustrated Retelling of the Classic Fairy Tale*. Developed to benefit Steven Spielberg's Starbright Foundation for seriously ill children, the book and companion compact disc contained single-page chapters of Hans Christian Andersen's classic, written and read by a bevy of celebrities. Others involved in the good cause included Liam Neeson, Nathan Lane, Madonna, Carrie Fisher, Robin Williams, Dan Aykroyd, Rosie O'Donnell and Spielberg. Ford was joined by Mathison in the telling of *The Weaver Thieves*.

In 1994, the National Association of Theater Owners (NATO) presented Ford with an award in honor of the incredible success he has brought theaters around the world.

"Over the past two decades," said NATO/ShoWest general chairman Tim Warner, "Ford's talents have firmly established him as the most prominent and successful actor ever to work within the motion picture industry. His movies, which continue to break box office records all over the world now account for [considerably] more than $2 billion in domestic theatrical grosses, an achievement unparalleled in the 100-year history of exhibition."[38]

Despite the numerous accolades and nominations bestowed upon Ford for his artistic abilities (especially the more commonly recognized Oscar and Golden Globes), the actor has also received several lesser-known awards based solely on his popularity with the general public. A partial list includes the Germany's 1982 Jupiter Award for *Raiders* and the 1994 Spencer Tracy Award (developed by the late screen legend's daughter Susie and bestowed by UCLA's Campus Events Commission) for the best actor of that year. On June 25, 1996, he received the Lifetime Achievement award from the Academy of Science Fiction, Fantasy and Horror Films.

From being depicted on countless magazine covers, to having his handprints and footprints forever immortalized on the Hollywood Walk of Fame at Mann's Chinese Theater, Ford has remained atop the list of the most desirable celebrities for nearly two decades.

Taking time out of his on-location shooting schedule for *The Devil's Own* in New York City, Ford decided it was time to pay his dues to the American public yet again for their unfaltering support of his film career. With that, he participated in a rather unflattering ritual organized by Harvard University's Hasty Pudding Theatricals.

Named after a mixture of cornmeal, milk and molasses, the meetings were originally geared toward the mocking of members of the club, historical and imaginary subjects and the college government. The club's members soon evolved into devoting time parodying contemporary musicals; after the first production (1844), it soon became a campus favorite and a nationwide conversation piece.

As an integral component of the ceremony's composition, individuals who have made a lasting and impressive contribution to the entertainment world were dubbed as the Hasty Pudding Men and Women of the Year. Henceforth, they have been invited to attend and are required to submit to the organization's mayhem, which today remains "a synthesis of fantasy and humor, of class and crass, and of professionalism and bawdy camaraderie."[39]

The celebrities chosen have traditionally been required to wear selected articles of women's clothing and willingly degrade themselves by submitting to the imagination of the event organizers while on stage. Previous recipients have included Bob Hope, Paul Newman, Robert Redford, Dustin Hoffman, Warren Beatty, Robert DeNiro, James Cagney, Steven Spielberg, Robin Williams, Clint Eastwood, Tom Hanks and Mel Gibson.

Acknowledging the "deep-seated desire among our staff to see him in drag,"[40] Hasty Pudding Producer Matthew Colangelo—after several failed attempts—was finally able to lure Ford.

Wary of what lay ahead, Ford arrived in Cambridge on February 20, 1996, and was chauffeured to the rain-soaked campus. Just prior to a student-performed production of *Morocco 'Round the Clock*, he reluctantly took to the stage. There, the audience and members of the press watched as he took part in the university's traditional roasting.

The impeccably dressed actor hesitantly donned a feather-laden brassiere over his tuxedo. Further complemented by a wig of rubber snakes, the actor failed to fulfill a request by the program's hosts to translate the Wookie rumblings of his former *Star Wars* co-star Chewbacca from the overhead speakers. Finally, before the evening's ceremonies concluded, Ford placed himself in an undersized go-cart and pedaled it across the stage as requested by the hosts to relive the memories of playing Bob Falfa in *American Graffiti*.

The most unconventional tribute to the actor came from Norman Platnick, who worked at the Smithsonian Institution's Museum of Natural History. In 1957, a previously undocumented species of arachnid was discovered at Stevens Creek in Santa Clara County, California. Until 1993, the eight-eyed species was considered extremely rare for the North American region and remained undesignated.

In recognition of the fact that Ford had provided the narration for a short film describing some of the museum's research activities and expeditions, the species was named after him. On June 10, 1993, that eight-eyed spider was officially designated *Calponia harrisonfordi Platnick*.

Nine years later, a newly discovered species of Central American ant was christened *Peidole harrisonfordi* in honor of his conservation work. That same year, he was given the honor of naming of a newly discovered Tanzanian butterfly after his daughter, Georgia.

In honor of his body of work as a whole, the American Film Institute gave Ford the Lifetime Achievement Award. "It's a mystery to me how I happened to get invited to join that list," said the twenty-eighth recipient of the honor. "But I'm very flattered by it."[41]

The list of previous recipients includes the likes of James Cagney, Fred Astaire,

James Stewart, Dustin Hoffman, Steven Spielberg, Alfred Hitchcock, Clint Eastwood, Jack Nicholson, Sidney Poitier and Elizabeth Taylor.

On the evening of February 17, 2000, during a ceremony held at the Beverly Hilton in L.A., the actor sat amidst 1,200 attendees, including family and friends. Ford graciously accepted praise (both professional and personal) from Brad Pitt, Daryl Hannah, Mike Nichols, Sharon Stone, Anne Archer, David Schwimmer, Carrie Fisher and even Chewbacca before ultimately confronting his biggest fear — taking center stage.

"It's very, very painful for him," said director and friend Mike Nichols. "You can't see it from the outside, but if you're his friend, you know that for him, this is his version of walking through fire. He's never completely conquered it. It costs him every time."[42]

Ford accepted the award from Steven Spielberg and George Lucas, and then — with a tremor in his voice — nervously claimed, "You made me laugh. Now I'm going to get the hell out of here before you make me cry."[43]

Ford continues to be in demand. Indeed, the public's reluctance to bid farewell to Ford was evidenced by the hard work and relentless planning of a fourth installment in the Indiana Jones series.

During his *Hollywood Homicide* promotional tour, it seemed as though more questions concerned the return of the world's most beloved swashbuckler than his latest offering. The future viability of the action adventurer had yet to be determined, however — Ford, after all, was not getting any younger (although he claims to be "still quite fit enough to fake it."[44]) Moreover, schedule availability and script problems have complicated matters. Returning as executive producer, George Lucas would likely be unavailable to begin production until 2005, after finally completing work on the third and final *Star Wars* prequel. Director Steven Spielberg accepted a completed script by director-screenwriter Frank Darabont (*The Shawshank Redemption*, *The Green Mile*), but Lucas later rejected it. As of this writing, plans are for Lucas to assume the task of writing himself, in search of the perfect story to bring closure to this much-loved character. All involved vowed they would not participate in another film unless it could surpass the three previous films in every way.

As for Indiana Jones himself, Ford looks forward to rekindling his Indy roots, even as an older hero. "It's important to show that he's aged, he's suffered some wear and tear over the years. That's going to make this character that much more interesting. I can't wait to address issues like whether his strength is based on his youth or on other aspects of human nature, like his wisdom, his toughness, his resourcefulness, his integrity. In creating Indy, we gave him a certain history and identity, and I think it will be extremely fascinating to expand on that. It's something that I think the public would enjoy watching."[45]

In addition to *Indiana Jones* waiting just over the horizon, the actor signed on to *The Wrong Element*— a thriller directed by Richard Loncraine (*Richard III*, *Wimbledon*), telling of a corporate bank's security expert (Ford) who is forced to steal money from his own company in order to secure the release of his family that is being held ransom. It costars Paul Bettany (*Beautiful Mind*, *Wimbledon*) as the kidnapper.

Also announced is *Godspeed*— a sci-fi thriller with James Cameron as its producer.

Due to *Wrong Element* set for a spring 2005 commencement of principal photography, Ford put the James Cameron–produced sci-fi thriller *Godspeed* tentatively on hold.

Despite all of the accolades, the money, the stamps in his passport, the position of power and prestige within his profession, the insects named after him and the wax figure eerily depicting his likeness at Madame Tussaud's, Harrison Ford is insistent upon leading us to believe that his life is ordinary.

He doesn't use his clout to forge to the front of the line at Disneyland. He does not enter restaurant lobbies unannounced and demand a table.

What the majority of us know of him is from theater and television screens. He is a movie actor, with full-time employment in the town that is still the foremost provider of entertainment throughout the world. He insists that his face is one of the most recognizable throughout the world as the result of pure luck.

He emphasizes to those who look upon him as otherworldly that acting is merely a profession. It is a job that requires long hours, most of which are spent sidelined in tedium. The result is a paycheck — whose benefits provide both materialistic and intrinsic rewards. His income, like any other individual, has provided the things that make his life possible and those that make it enjoyable.

To Ford, the attention of pesky admirers is a minuscule price to pay for the good fortune that has been bestowed upon him. He musters patience and understanding for those who seek an autograph or a handshake because those same people are those that are responsible for his success.

Profession aside, his life in general is much like every other human beings. From being wary of darkened alleys to crossing the street, he has lived and he has learned. The unintended distancing from his family while he focused on his work had ended two marriages. Rediscovering his priorities, he's vowed to never allow anything to ever take precedence over his family. His family is his most sacred possession. He is content with the decisions he has made and looks anxiously ahead toward those he must confront.

And with the modesty that his worldwide audience so admires and relishes, he stresses the one underlying aspect of his existence: "I'm ordinary. Average. That's my point. No matter how much I accomplish, the collar around my neck will always be blue."[46]

Filmography

Television Appearances

The Virginian—"The Modoc Kid"
First broadcast on February 1, 1967, on NBC. *Starring:* James Drury, Doug McClure. Guest: John Saxon.

Ironside—"The Past Is Prologue"
First broadcast on December 7, 1967, on NBC. *Starring:* Raymond Burr, Don Galloway, Barbara Anderson, Johnny Seven. *Guests:* Victor Jory, Jill Donahue, Jean Inness.

My Friend Tony—"The Hazing"
First broadcast on February 16, 1969, on NBC. *Starring:* James Whitmore, Enzo Cerusico. *Guests:* Steve Franken, Tom Fielding.

Love, American Style—"Love and the Former Marriage"
First broadcast on November 24, 1969, on ABC. *Starring:* Carl Betz, Dana Wynter, Elliott Reid, Jenny Sullivan.

Dan August—"The Manufactured Man"
First broadcast on March 11, 1971, on ABC. *Starring:* Burt Reynolds, Normal Fell, Ned Romero, Richard Anderson. *Guests:* Peter Brown, David Soul, Mickey Rooney, Keith Andes, Barney Phillips, Billy Dee Williams.

Gunsmoke—"The Sodbusters"
First broadcast on November 20, 1972, on CBS. *Starring:* James Arness. *Guests:* Morgan Woodward, Alex Cord, Kathrine Justice, Leif Garrett, Dawn Lyn, Robert Viharo, Richard Bull, Joe di Reda.

Gunsmoke—"Whelan's Men"
First broadcast on February 5, 1973, on CBS. *Starring:* James Arness, Amanda Blake. *Guests:* Robert Burr, William Bramley, Noble Willingham, Frank Ramirez, Gerald McRaney, Bobby Hall.

Kung Fu—"Crossties"
First broadcast on February 12, 1974, on ABC. *Starring:* David Carradine. *Guests:* Barry Sullivan, Andy Robinson, Denver Pyle, John Anderson, Dennis Fimple.

Petrocelli—"Edge of Evil"
First broadcast on October 2, 1974, on NBC. *Starring:* Barry Newman, Susan Howard, Albert Salmi, David Huddleston. *Guests:* William Shatner, Susan Oliver, Lynn Carlin, Dana Elcar, Morgan Paull, Glenn Corbett.

Television Films/Pilots/Movies of the Week

The Intruders
First broadcast on November 10, 1970, on NBC. *Director:* William A. Graham. *Producer:* James Duff McAdams. *Writer:* Dean E. Riesner (from a story by William Douglas Lansford). *Starring:* Anne Francis, Don Murray, Edmond O'Brien, John Saxon, Shelly Novack, Dean Stanton, Zalman King, Stuart Margolin, Gene Evans, Edward Andrews.

Judgment: The Court Martial of Lt. William Calley
First broadcast on January 12, 1975, on ABC. *Director:* Stanley Kramer. *Producer:* Stanley Kramer. *Writer:* Henry Denker.

Starring: Tony Musante, Richard Basehart, Bo Hopkins, G.D. Spradlin, Bill Lucking, Linda Haynes, Olive Clark, Ben Piazza, Leon Russon, Fredd Wayne.

James A. Michener's Dynasty

First broadcast on March 13, 1976, on NBC. *Director:* Lee Philips. *Producer:* David Paradine. *Writer:* Sidney Carroll (from a story by James A. Michener). *Starring:* Sarah Miles, Stacy Keach, Harris Yulin, Amy Irving, Granville Van Dusen, Charles Weldon, Gerrit Graham.

The Possessed

First broadcast on May 1, 1977, on NBC. *Director:* Jerry Thorpe. *Producer:* Philip Mandelker. *Writer:* John Sacret Young. *Starring:* James Farentino, Joan Hackett, Claudette Nevins, Eugene Roche, Ann Dusenberry, Diana Scarwid, Dinah Manoff, Carol Jones, P.J. Soles.

FEATURE FILMS

Dead Heat on a Merry-Go-Round (1967, Columbia)

Director: Bernard Girard. *Producer:* Carter de Haven. *Writer:* Bernard Girard. *Starring:* James Coburn, Camilla Sparv, Aldo Ray, Nina Wayne, Severn Darden, Todd Armstrong, Rose Marie, Robert Weller.

A Time for Killing (aka The Long Ride Home) (1967, Columbia)

Director: Phil Karlson. *Producer:* Harry Joe Brown. *Writer:* Halsted Welles (from a novel by Nelson and Shirley Wolford). *Starring:* Glenn Ford, George Hamilton, Inger Stevens, Max Baer, Paul Petersen, Todd Armstrong.

Luv (1967, Columbia)

Director: Clive Donner. *Producer:* Martin Manulis. *Writers:* Elliott Baker (from a play by Murray Shisgal). *Starring:* Jack Lemmon, Peter Falk, Elaine May, Nina Wayne, Severn Darden, Paul Hartman, Eddie Mayehoff.

Journey to Shiloh (1967, Universal)

Director: William Hale. *Producer:* Howard Christie. *Writers:* Gene Coon (from a novel by Will Henry). *Starring:* James Caan, Michael Sarrazin, Brenda Scott, Paul Petersen, Don Stroud, Jan Michael Vincent, John Doucette, Noah Beery, Jr.

Zabriskie Point (1969, MGM)

Director: Michelangelo Antonioni. *Producer:* Carlo Ponti. *Writers:* Michelangelo Antonioni, Fred Gardner, Sam Shepard, Tonino Guerra, Clare Peploe. *Starring:* Mark Frechetter, Daria Halprin, Rod Taylor, Paul Fix, G.D. Spradlin, Bill Garaway, Kathleen Cleaver.

Getting Straight (1970, Columbia)

Producer-Director: Richard Rush. *Writers:* Robert Kaufman (based on a novel by Ken Kolb). *Starring:* Elliott Gould, Candice Bergen, Robert F. Lyons, Jeff Corey, Max Julien, Cecil Kellaway, Jon Lormer, Leonard Stone, William Bramley, Jenny Sullivan.

American Graffiti (1973, Universal)

Director: George Lucas. *Producers:* Francis Coppola, Gary Kurtz. *Writer:* George Lucas. *Starring:* Richard Dreyfuss, Candy Clark, Ron Howard, Paul Le Mat, Charles Martin Smith, Cindy Williams, Mackenzie Philips.

The Conversation (1974, Paramount)

Writer-Producer-Director: Francis Coppola. *Starring:* Gene Hackman, Frederic Forrest, John Cazale, Allen Garfield, Cindy Williams.

Star Wars (1977, 20th Century–Fox)

Writer-Director: George Lucas. *Producer:* Gary Kurtz. *Starring:* Mark Hamill, Carrie Fisher, Sir Alec Guinness, Peter Cushing, David Prowse, Anthony Daniels, Peter Mayhew, Kenny Baker.

Heroes (1977, Universal)

Director: Jeremy Paul Kagan. *Producers:* David Foster, Lawrence Turman. *Writers:* James Carabatsos, David Freeman (uncredited). *Starring:* Henry Winkler, Sally Field, Val Avery.

Force Ten from Navarone (1979, Columbia)

Director: Guy Hamilton. *Producer:* Oliver A. Unger. *Writers:* Robin Chapman (from a novel by Alistair MacLean). *Starring:* Robert

Shaw, Carl Weathers, Franco Nero, Edward Fox, Barbara Bach, Richard Kiel.

Hanover Street (1979, Columbia)

Writer-Director: Peter Hyams. *Producer:* Paul N. Lazarus III. *Starring:* Lesley-Anne Down, Christopher Plummer, Alec McCowen, Max Wall, Michael Sacks, Richard Masur.

The Frisco Kid (1979, Warner Bros.)

Director: Robert Aldrich. *Producer:* Mace Neufeld. *Writers:* Michael Elias, Frank Shaw. *Starring:* Gene Wilder, Romon Bieri, Penny Peyser, Leo Fuchs, Val Bisoglio, William Smith.

Apocalypse Now (1979, Zeotrope)

Producer-Director: Francis Coppola. *Writers:* Francis Coppola, John Milius. *Starring:* Martin Sheen, Marlon Brando, Robert Duvall, Frederic Forrest, Dennis Hopper, Larry Fishburne, Samuel Bottoms.

The Empire Strikes Back
(1980, 20th Century–Fox)

Director: Irvin Kershner. *Producer:* Gary Kurtz. *Writer:* Leigh Brackett, Lawrence Kasdan (from a story by George Lucas). *Starring:* Mark Hamill, Carrie Fisher, Billy Dee Williams, Sir Alec Guinness, David Prowse, Anthony Daniels, Peter Mayhew, Kenny Baker.

Raiders of the Lost Ark
(1981, Paramount)

Director: Steven Spielberg. *Producer:* Frank Marshall. *Writer:* Lawrence Kasdan. *Starring:* Karen Allen, Paul Freeman, John Rhys Davies, Denholm Elliott, Ronald Lacey.

Blade Runner (1982, Warner Bros.)

Director: Ridley Scott. *Producer:* Michael Deeley. *Writers:* Hampton Fancher, David Peoples (based upon a novel by Philip K. Dick). *Starring:* Sean Young, Rutger Hauer, Edward James Olmos, Daryl Hannah, M. Emmet Walsh.

Return of the Jedi
(1983, 20th Century–Fox)

Director: Richard Marquand. *Producer:* Howard Kazanjian. *Writers:* Lawrence Kasdan, George Lucas. *Starring:* Mark Hamill, Carrie Fisher, Billy Dee Williams, Sir Alec Guinness, David Prowse, Anthony Daniels, Peter Mayhew, Kenny Baker.

Indiana Jones and the Temple of Doom (1984, Paramount)

Director: Steven Spielberg. *Producer:* Robert Watts. *Writers:* Willard Huyck, Gloria Katz (from a story by George Lucas). *Starring:* Kate Capshaw, Denholm Elliott, Ke Huy Quan, Amrish Puri, Roshan Seth.

Witness (1985, Paramount)

Director: Peter Weir. *Producer:* Edward Feldman. *Writers:* W. Earl Wallace, William Kelley. *Starring:* Kelly McGillis, Danny Glover, Lukas Haas, Alexander Godunov, Jan Rubes, Josep Sommer, Patti LuPone.

The Mosquito Coast
(1986, Warner Bros.)

Director: Peter Weir. *Producers:* Saul Zaentz, Jerome Hellman. *Writers:* Paul Schrader (from a novel by Paul Theroux). *Starring:* Helen Mirren, River Phoenix, Jadrien Steele, Andre Gregory.

Frantic (1987, Warner Bros.)

Director: Roman Polanski. *Producers:* Thom Mount, Tim Hampton. *Writers:* Roman Polanski, Gerard Brach. *Starring:* Emmanuelle Seigner, Betty Buckley, John Mahoney.

Working Girl (1988, 20th Century–Fox)

Director: Mike Nichols. *Producer:* Douglas Wick. *Writer:* Kevin Wade. *Starring:* Melanie Griffith, Sigourney Weaver, Joan Cusack, Alec Baldwin, Oliver Platt, Olympia Dukakis, Nora Dunn, Philip Bosco.

Indiana Jones and the Last Crusade
(1989, Paramount)

Director: Steven Spielberg. *Producer:* Robert Watts. *Writers:* Jeffrey Boam (from a story by George Lucas). *Starring:* Sean Connery, Alison Doody, Julian Glover, John Rhys-Davies, Denholm Elliott, River Phoenix, Michael Byrne, Alexei Sayle.

Presumed Innocent (1990, Paramount)

Director: Alan Pakula. *Producers:* Sydney Pollack, Mark Rosenberg. *Writers:* Alan Pakula, Frank Pierson (from a novel by Scott Turow). *Starring:* Greta Scacchi, Bonnie Bedelia, Brian Dennehy, Raul Julia, Paul Winfield, Paul Spencer, Sab Shimono, Joe Grifasi.

Regarding Henry (1991, Paramount)

Director: Mike Nichols. *Producers:* Scott Rudin, Mike Nichols. *Writer:* Jeffrey Abrams. *Starring:* Annette Bening, Bill Nunn, Mikki Allen, Donald Moffat, Aida Linares, Bruce Altman.

Patriot Games (1992, Paramount)

Director: Philip Noyce. *Producers:* Mace Neufeld, Robert Rehme. *Writer:* W. Peter Iliff, Donald Stewart (from a novel by Tom Clancy). *Starring:* Anne Archer, Sean Bean, James Earl Jones, James Fox, Patrick Bergin, Thora Birch, Samuel L. Jackson, Richard Harris, Polly Walker.

The Fugitive (1993, Warner Bros.)

Director: Andrew Davis. *Producer:* Arnold Kopelson. *Writers:* Jeb Stuart, David Twohy (based upon characters created by Roy Huggins). *Starring:* Tommy Lee Jones, Jeroen Krabbe, Sela Ward, Joe Pantoliano, Andreas Katsulas.

Clear and Present Danger (1994, Paramount)

Director: Philip Noyce. *Producers:* Mace Neufeld, Robert Rehme. *Writers:* Donald Stewart, Steven Zaillian, John Milius (from a novel by Tom Clancy). *Starring:* Anne Archer, James Earl Jones, Willem Dafoe, Henry Czerny, Joaquim De Almeida, Donald Moffat, Harris Yulin, Thora Birch, Miguel Sandoval.

Sabrina (1995, Paramount)

Director: Sydney Pollack. *Producers:* Sydney Pollack, Scot Rudin. *Writers:* Barbara Benedek, David Rayfiel. *Starring:* Julia Ormond, Greg Kinnear, Nancy Marchand, John Wood, Lauren Holly, Richard Crenna, Angie Dickinson.

The Devil's Own (1997, Columbia)

Director: Alan Pakula. *Producers:* Lawrence Gordon, Robert F. Colesberry. *Writers:* David Aaron Cohen, Vincent Patrick, Kevin Jarre. *Starring:* Brad Pitt, Margaret Colin, Ruben Blades, Treat Williams, Natascha McElhone.

Air Force One (1997, Columbia)

Director: Wolfgang Peterson. *Producer:* Gloria Katz. *Writer:* Andrew Marlowe. *Starring:* Gary Oldman, Glenn Close, Wendy Crewson, Liesel Matthews, Paul Guilfoyle, Xander Berkeley, William H. Macy, Dean Stockwell.

Six Days, Seven Nights (1998, Touchstone)

Director: Ivan Reitman. *Producers:* Ivan Reitman, Roger Birnbaum, Wallis Nicita. *Writer:* Michael Browning. *Starring:* Anne Heche, David Schwimmer, Jacqueline Obradors.

Random Hearts (1999, Paramount)

Director: Sydney Pollack. *Producers:* Sydney Pollack, Marykay Powell. *Writer:* Kurt Luedtke (from a novel by Warren Adler). *Starring:* Kristen Scott Thomas, Charles Dutton, Bonnie Hunt, Dennis Haysbert, Sydney Pollack, Richard Jenkins, Paul Guilfoyle.

What Lies Beneath (2000, Dreamworks)

Director: Robert Zemeckis. *Producers:* Robert Zemeckis, Steve Starkey, Jack Rapke. *Writer:* Clark Gregg. *Starring:* Michelle Pfeiffer, Diana Scarwid, Joe Morton, James Remar, Miranda Otto.

K-19: The Widowmaker (2002, Paramount)

Director: Kathryn Bigelow. *Producers:* Kathryn Bigelow, Edward S. Feldman, Sigurjon Sighvatsson, Chris Whitaker. *Writer:* Christopher Kyle. *Starring:* Liam Neeson

Hollywood Homicide (2003, Columbia)

Director: Ron Shelton. *Producers:* Ron Shelton, Lou Pitt. *Writers:* Ron Shelton, Robert Souza. *Starring:* Josh Hartnett, Lena Olin, Bruce Greenwood, Isaiah Washington, Lolita Davidovitch, Keith David, Master P, Dwight Yoakam, Martin Landau.

Chapter Notes

Prologue
1. Pye, Michael. "The Reluctant Hero." *Esquire* Sept. 1993: 52.
2. Ibid.

Chapter 1
1. Pye, Michael. "The Reluctant Hero." *Esquire* Sept. 1993: 52.
2. Corliss, Richard. "What's Old Is Gold: A Triumph for Indy 3." *Time* 29 May 1989.
3. Wuntch, Philip. "Ford and Gere Step Out of Character." *Dallas Morning News* 14 Dec. 1986.
4. Pfeiffer, Lee, and Michael Lewis. *The Films of Harrison Ford*. New York: Citadel Press, 1996: 2.
5. Ibid.

Chapter 2
1. Miller, Edwin. "Harrison Ford: A Very Private Guy." *Seventeen* July 1983.
2. The Crimson Yearbook of Ripon College 1963.
3. Oney, Steve. "Just Another Cowboy." *North Shore* May 1990.
4. Zehme, Bill. "Harrison Ford: 20 Questions." *Playboy* April 1988.
5. Pye, Michael. "The Reluctant Hero." *Esquire* Sept. 1993.
6. Ebert, Roger. *St. Paul Sunday Pioneer Press* 27 June 1982.
7. Byrge, Duane. "Self-Made Man." *Hollywood Reporter* 4 March 1994.
8. Pfeiffer, Lee, and Michael Lewis. *The Films of Harrison Ford*. New York: Citadel Press, 1996: 3.
9. Ibid., Miller.
10. Vare, Ethlie Ann, and Mary Toledo, *Harrison Ford*. St. New York: Martin's Press, 1987: 11.

Chapter 3
1. Rogues Gallery: Unofficial Harrison Ford fanzine. Issue #4, 1982: 6.

Chapter 4
1. Hellicar, Michael. "The £100m Hermit of Snake Ridge." *Daily Star* 23 Sept. 1993.
2. Oney, Steve. "Just Another Cowboy." *North Shore* May 1990.
3. Kaplan, James. "Harrison Ford's Natural Drive." *Vanity Fair* Aug. 1990.
4. McCanny, Roy A. "Laguna Playhouse Performances Superb." *McCanny's Notes* 6 March 1965.
5. Torgerson, Ellen. "It's History, Art — It's Great." 4 March 1965.
6. Silverman, Jeff. "Harrison Ford Breaks the Mold to Pieces in 'Witness.'" *Chicago Tribune* 10 Feb. 1985.

Chapter 5
1. Thomas, Bob. "Star Watch: Despite Stalwart Roles, Ford Is Really Quiet Man." *Associated Press* 28 Feb. 2000.
2. Rowland, Mark. "Harrison Ford." *Playgirl* Dec. 1983.
3. Crawley Tony. *Films Illustrated* 1978.
4. "Ford, Harrison." *Current Biography Yearbook*. 1984 ed.
5. Carter, Alan. "Down to Earth." *New York Daily News* 28 Feb. 1988.

Chapter 6
1. Grobel, Lawrence. "Off the Beaten Path." *Movieline* July 1997.
2. Clinch, Minty. *Harrison Ford*. Great Britain: New English Library, 1987: 18.
3. Ford, Harrison. Interview. *Harrison Ford: The Last Crusade*. MTV: Music Television. New York. 1989.
4. Jenkins, Gary. *Harrison Ford: Reluctant Star*. Great Britain: Birch Lane Press, 1998: 90.
5. Oney, Steve. "Just Another Cowboy." *North Shore* May 1990.
6. Ibid., Jenkins.
7. Ibid.
8. Ibid., Oney.
9. Ibid., Grobel.
10. Miller, Edwin. "Harrison Ford: A Very Private Guy." *Seventeen* July 1983.
11. Robinson, David. "I, Harrison Ford, Solemnly Declare…" *The Times* 14 Sept. 1994.

Chapter 7
1. Ford, Harrison. Interview. *Larry King Live!* CNN: Cable News Network. New York. 21 Dec. 1995.
2. *Milwaukee Journal* 15 May 1983.
3. Ford, Harrison. Interview. *The Mike Douglas Show* 30 March 1979.
4. Vale, Ethlie Ann. *Harrison Ford*. New York: St. Martin's Press, 1987.
5. Spencer, John. "Han Solo." *US* 20 June 1983.
6. Abele, Robert. *People Profiles: Harrison Ford*. New York: Time, 2000: 57.
7. Weiner, Rex. "Helping Build a Lasting Career." *Daily Variety* 4 March 1994.
8. Scott, Vernon. "Scott's World; Talk to My Manager." *Hollywood Reporter* 20 Nov. 1987.

293

9. Coleman, Todd. "On the Run." *Hollywood Reporter* 4 March 1994.
10. Honeycutt, Kirk. "Harrison Ford on Harrison Ford." *L.A. Daily News* 26 Nov. 1986.

Chapter 8

1. Pollack, Dale. *Skywalking: The Life and Films of George Lucas.* New York: Harmony Books, 1983: 104.
2. Ibid.
3. Ibid.
4. Clinch, Minty. *Harrison Ford.* Great Britain: New English Library, 1987: 37.
5. Coleman, Todd. "On the Run." *Hollywood Reporter* 4 March 1994.
6. Campbell, Virginia. "Still Sane After All These Years." *Movieline* Dec. 1995: 84.
7. Schiano, Marina. "The Fugitive Star." *Vanity Fair* July 1993: 127.
8. Fitzpatrick, Kevin. "'American Graffiti': George Lucas' First Blockbuster." *Star Wars Insider* Issue #30: 45–46.
9. Ibid., Pollock.
10. Ibid.
11. Ibid.
12. Ibid., Fitzpatrick 47.
13. Ibid., Schiano 127.

Chapter 9

1. Goodwin, Michael, and Naomi Wise. *On the Edge: The Life & Times of Francis Coppola.* New York: William Morrow, 1989: 144.
2. Ibid.
3. Ibid.
4. Ibid.
5. Ibid.
6. Ibid.
7. Oney, Steve. "Just Another Cowboy." *North Shore* May 1990: 122.

Chapter 10

1. Ford, Harrison. Interview. *Late Night with David Letterman.* CBS. New York. 22 June 1982.
2. Dorf, Shel. "Interview: Harrison Ford." *Movie Writes* 1977: 76.
3. Brantley, Robin. "New Face: Harrison Ford. A Star Warrior." *New York Times* 1 July 1977.
4. Ibid., Dorf 78.
5. Rosenthal, Lee. "The Empire Talks Back." *Details* Feb. 1997: 143–144.
6. Clinch, Minty. *Harrison Ford.* Great Britain: New English Library, 1987: 61.
7. Ibid.
8. *Rogues Gallery:* issue #9. Unofficial Harrison Ford fanzine. 1983: 17.
9. Ibid., Dorf 77–78.
10. Vale, Ethlie Ann, and Mary Toledo. *Harrison Ford.* New York: St. Martin's Press, 1987.
11. Pollack, Dale. *Skywalking: The Life and Films of George Lucas.* New York: Harmony Books, 1983: 180.
12. Jenkins, Gary. *Harrison Ford: Imperfect Hero.* New Jersey: Birch Lane Press, 1998: 180.
13. Ibid., Pollack: 182.
14. Ibid., Jenkins: 123–124.
15. Ibid., Clinch: 63.
16. Ibid.

Chapter 11

1. Schumacher, Michael. *Francis Ford Coppola: A Filmmaker's Life.* New York: Crown, 1999: 253.
2. Goodwin, Michael, and Naomi Wise. *On the Edge: The Life & Times of Francis Coppola.* New York: William Morrow, 1989.
3. Roderick, Mann. "Ford in the Fast Lane." *Los Angeles Times* 6 Sept. 1981: Cal: 3.

Chapter 12

1. *Teen Bag* March 1982.
2. Spencer, John. "Han Solo." *US* 20 June 1983.
3. Abele, Robert. *People Profiles: Harrison Ford.* New York: Time, 2000: 70.
4. Ibid.
5. Miller, Edwin. "Harrison Ford: A Very Private Guy." *Seventeen* July 1983.
6. Canby, Vincent. *New York Times* 19 Feb. 1978.
7. Ansen, David. "Hit the Road, Jack." *Newsweek* 14 Nov. 1977.
8. Schaefer, Stephen. "Harrison Ford Bids Farewell to Indiana Jones." *Boston Globe* 21 May 1989.
9. Weiner, Rex. "Helping Build a Lasting Career." *Daily Variety* 4 March 1994.

Chapter 13

1. Radin, Victoria. "Storm Clouds Over Navarone." *Observer* 29 Jan. 1978.
2. Arnold, Alan. *Once Upon a Galaxy: A Journal of the Making of "The Empire Strikes Back."* New York: Ballantine, 1980.
3. Rogues Gallery: Unofficial Harrison Ford fanzine. Issue #6, 1978: 13.
4. Ibid., Radin.
5. Clinch, Minty. *Harrison Ford.* Great Britain: New English Library, 1987: 80–81.
6. *Teen Bag* March 1982.
7. Vale, Ethlie Ann, and Mary Toledo. *Harrison Ford.* New York: St. Martin's Press, 1987: (monomaniacal attitude)
8. *She* 1978.
9. Pfeiffer, Lee, and Michael Lewis. *The Films of Harrison Ford.* New York: Citadel Press, 1996: (totally sexless)
10. Roderick, Mann. "Ford in the Fast Lane." *Los Angeles Times* 6 Sept. 1981: Cal: 3.
11. Etherington, Jan. *Prevue* 16 Nov. 1978.
12. Champlin, Charles. "War, Love on 'Hanover Street.'" *Los Angeles Times* 1979: IV: 22.
13. Campbell, Virginia. "The Way to 'The Mosquito Coast.'" *Movieline* 5 Dec. 1986.
14. Ibid.
15. Williamson, Bruce. "Hanover Street." *Playboy* June 1979.
16. Peter Hyams commentary for *Hanover Street* DVD, Columbia Pictures. 2001.
17. *Circus Weekly* 3 April 1979.
18. Cunneff, Tom, and Elizabeth Sporkin. "Checking 'Em Out." *People* 17 Nov. 1997.
19. Ibid., Mann.
20. *Superstars of Action: Harrison Ford.* Videotape. ABC Video, 1995.
21. Skow, John. "Blazing Bagels." *Time* 30 July 1979.
22. "Screen: Gene Wilder in Aldrich's 'The Frisco Kid.'" *New York Times* 6 July 1979.

Chapter 14

1. Spencer, John. "Han Solo." *US* 20 June 1983.
2. Lennon, Rosemarie. "Revealed! Harrison Ford is a Hush-Hush Grandpa." *Star* Aug. 1997: 22.
3. Ibid., Spencer.

4. Clinch, Minty. *Honey* Dec. 1982.
5. Ibid., Lennon.
6. Jenkins, Gary. *Harrison Ford: Imperfect Hero*. New Jersey: Birch Lane Press, 1998: 142.
7. Oney, Steve. "A Very Ordinary Man." *Premiere* March 1988.
8. Crawley, Tony. *Starburst* Winter 1982–83.

Chapter 15

1. May, John, ed. *The Empire Strikes Back Official Collectors Edition*. Connecticut: Paradise Press, 1980: 40.
2. Buckley, Tim. "The 'Force' Behind 'Empire Strikes Back.'" *New York Times* 16 May 1980.
3. Packer, David. "An Interview with Harrison Ford." *Starlog* Aug. 1980.
4. Ibid., May.
5. Dovlin, Rod. "The Force of Mark Hamill." *Axcess* 1997. 62–63.
6. Clinch, Minty. *Harrison Ford*. Great Britain: New English Library, 1987.
7. "The Empire Strikes Back" *Presskit*. Beverly Hills: 20th Century-Fox Films, 1980: 1.
8. Arnold, Alan. *Once Upon a Galaxy: A Journal of the Making of "The Empire Strikes Back."* New York: Ballantine, 1980.
9. Madsen, Dan. "Irvin Kershner: Remembering 'The Empire Strikes Back.'" *The Lucasfilm Fan Club*, #11 Spring, 1990: 4.
10. Ibid., May.
11. Ibid., Madsen 6.
12. Ibid., 7.
13. Ibid., 5.
14. "Furthermore." *People* 16 June 1980.
15. Ibid., Packer.
16. Ibid., Madsen 4.
17. Ibid., Arnold.
18. Ibid., Packer.
19. Ibid., Clinch: 98–99.
20. Ibid., Arnold.
21. Baxter, John. *Mythmaker: The Life and Work of George Lucas*. New York: Avon Books, 1999: 208.
22. Ibid.
23. Steranko, James. "Mark Hamill Bids Farewell to the Force in a Final Star-Slamming Interview." *Prevue* Oct. 1983.
24. Ibid., May.
25. *Aquarian* 1980.
26. White, Timothy. "Slaves to the Empire; The 'Star Wars' Kids Talk." *Rolling Stone* 24 July 1980.
27. Ibid.
28. Harmetz, Aljean. "'Shining' and 'Empire' Set Records." *New York Times* 28 May 1980.
29. Ansen, David. "The Force Is Back with Us." *Newsweek* 19 May 1980.
30. "The Empire Strikes Back." *Variety* 14 May 1980.
31. Maslin, Janet. "Film: Robots Return in 'Empire Strikes.'" *New York Times* May 1980.
32. Ibid., Clinch.
33. Ibid.

Chapter 16

1. Taylor, Derek. *The Making of Raiders of the Lost Ark*. New York: Ballantine Books, 1981: 14.
2. Holler, Ann. *Raiders of the Lost Ark Collector's Album*. New York: S. W. Ventures, 1981: 8.
3. Ibid.
4. Ibid.
5. Crawley, Tony. *The Steven Spielberg Story*. New York: Quill Press, 1983.
6. Ibid.
7. Ibid., Holler.
8. Ibid.
9. Rico, Perto. *San Juan Star* 30 April 1982.
10. *Photoplay* Feb. 1982.
11. Ibid., Taylor:165.
12. Ibid., Holler: 16.
13. Ibid., Holler: 46.
14. Ibid., 47.
15. Ibid., Taylor: 66.
16. Sragow, Michael. "'Raiders of the Lost Ark': The Ultimate Saturday Matinee." *Rolling Stone* 25 June 1981.
17. Ibid., Holler: 51.
19. Ibid., Taylor: 115.
19. *Kansas City Star* 21 June 1981.
20. "Of Narrow Misses and Close Calls." *American Cinematographer* Nov. 1981.
21. *The Register* 17 June 1981.
22. Ibid., Taylor: 7.
23. *Cinema Odyssey* Vol. 1, No. 1.
24. Ibid., Taylor: 7.
25. Ibid., Holler: 54.
26. *Family Weekly* 2 Aug. 1981.
27. Ibid., Sragow.
28. *Moviegoer* March 1982.
29. Ibid., *Cinema Odyssey*.
30. Ibid., Holler.
31. Jagger, Bianca, and Andy Warhol. "Steven Spielberg." *Interview* July 1982.
32. Canby, Vincent. "Film: 'Raiders of the Lost Ark.'" *New York Times* 12 June 1981.
33. Sarris, Andrew. "Surprise! Two Super Films." *Village Voice* 10–16 June 1981: 51.
34. *Kansas City Star* June 1981.
35. *Variety* 22 Sept. 1981.
36. Soll, Rick. *Chicago Sun Times* July 1981.
37. Kantrowitz, Barbara. "A Star Minus Vehicle." *Philadelphia Inquirer* 30 June 1981.
38. Hirschhorn, Clive. *Sunday Express* 20 Sept. 1981.
39. Goodwin, Jan. *New Idea*.
40. Grobel, Lawrence. "Off the Beaten Path." *Movieline* July 1997.
41. Powell, Joanna. "Harrison's Passions." *Good Housekeeping* Oct. 1999.

Chapter 17

1. Sammon, Paul M. *Future Noir: The Making of Blade Runner*. New York: Harper Collins, 1996: 34.
2. Ibid., 43.
3. Loud, Lance, Kristian Hoffman, and Paul M. Sammon. "'Blade Runner.'" *Details* Oct. 1982.
4. Ibid., Sammon, 68.
5. Ibid., 88.
6. Clinch, Minty. *Harrison Ford*. Great Britain: New English Library, 1987: 142.
7. Ibid., Sammon, 86.
8. Bulluck, Vic, ed. *Blade Runner Souvenir Magazine*. New York: Ira Friedman, 1982: 22.
9. *Chicago Tribune* 20 June 1982.
10. Ibid., Sammon, 82.
11. *"Blade Runner" Presskit*. Los Angeles: Warner Bros., 1982.
12. Ibid., Bulluck, 41.
13. Ibid., 53.
14. Ibid., Sammon.
15. Ibid., 156.
16. Ibid., 157.
17. Ibid., Bulluck, 54.
18. Ibid., Sammon, 192.
19. Ibid., 202.
20. Ibid., 216.
21. Ibid., Loud.
22. Ibid., Sammon, 387.
23. Ibid., 214.
24. Ibid., 218.
25. Ibid., 214.
26. Ibid., 163.
27. Ibid., Loud.
28. Steranko, James. *Prevue* July 1982.

29. Ibid., Sammon, 390.
30. Ibid., 296.
31. Ibid., Loud.
32. Denby, David. "'Blade Runner.'" *New York* 28 June 1982.
33. Travers, Peter. "'Blade Runner.'" *People* 2 Aug. 1982.
34. "'Blade Runner.'" *Variety* 16 July 1982.
35. Williamson, Bruce. "'Blade Runner.'" *Playboy* Sept. 1982.
36. Corliss, Richard. "The Pleasures of Texture." *Time* 12 July 1982.
37. Ibid., Loud.
38. Ibid., Sammon, 284.
39. Ibid., Bulluck, 8.
40. Ibid.

Chapter 18

1. *Family Weekly* 2 Aug. 1981.
2. "Why Fatherhood at 44 Scares Indiana Jones." *Daily Mail* 12 Jan. 1987.
3. Rowland, Mark. "Harrison Ford." *Playgirl* Dec. 1983: 108.
4. Shephard, Montgomery. "Harrison Ford: The 'Last Real Man' in Hollywood." *Celebrity Plus* Sept. 1989.
5. Epstein, Andrew. "Melissa Mathison: The Hands of E.T." *Los Angeles Times* 24 July 1982: 6.
6. *The Making of "E.T.: The Extra Terrestrial."* From the Limited Edition laserdisc edition of *E.T. The Extra Terrestrial*. MCA Universal. 1996.
7. Silverman, Jeff. *Los Angeles Herald Examiner* 27 July 1981.
8. Ibid.
9. Ibid.
10. Ibid.
11. Champlin, Charles. *George Lucas: The Creative Impulse — Special Abridged Edition*. New York: Harry N. Abrams, 1992.
12. Bock, Audie. "Secrecy Shrouds a 'Star Wars' Sequel." *New York Times* 11 July 1982: 24.
13. Goodwin, Jane. *The Face* 1982.
14. *In Touch* 28 July 2003.
15. *"Return of the Jedi" Presskit*. Beverly Hills: 20th Century–Fox Pictures, 1983: 4.
16. Clarke, Gerald. "Great Galloping Galaxies." *Time* 23 May 1983: 63.
17. Ibid., Clarke 65.
18. "'Return of the Jedi.'" *Variety* 18 May 1983.
19. Miller, Edwin. "Harrison Ford: A Very Private Guy." *Seventeen* July 1983.
20. Ibid.
21. Adamo, Susan. "Mark Hamill." *Starlog* #65.
22. Ibid.
23. Steranko, James. "Mark Hamill Bids Farewell to the Force in a Final Star-Slamming Interview." *Prevue* Oct. 1983.
24. *Morristown Herald News* 22 May 1983.
25. Haddad-Garcia, George. *Photoplay* May 1982.
26. Haddad-Garcia, George. *Movie Star* 1982.
27. Ibid., Clarke 65.
28. Ibid. Miller.

Chapter 19

1. Siskel, Gene. "And After 10 Years, Lucas Is Taking a Break." *Chicago Tribune* 15 May 1983: 6: 6.
2. Crawley, Tony. *The Steven Spielberg Story*. New York: Quill Press, 1983.
3. *Daily Variety* 4 Aug. 1983.
4. *Star Blazer* Summer 1984.
5. Clinch, Minty. *Harrison Ford*. Great Britain: New English Library 1987.
6. Collins, Glenn. "In 'Indiana Jones,' Stunts Get Star Billing." *New York Times* 20 May 1984.
7. *Star* 12 June 1984.
8. Ibid., Collins.
9. Ibid.
10. Brodie, Ian. *Family Weekly* 20 May 1984.
11. Ibid., Collins.
12. Span, Paula. "'Doom' and Destiny: The Sudden Success of Actress Kate Capshaw." *Washington Post* 20 May 1984: H13.
13. Ibid.
14. Freeman, Susan, ed. *Indiana Jones and the Temple of Doom: Official Collector's Edition*. New York: Paradise Press, 1984: 37.
15. Cleaver, Thomas McKelvey. "Frank Marshall: Adventuring Alongside 'Indiana Jones and the Temple of Doom.'" *Starlog* June 1984.
16. Pfeiffer, Lee, and Michael Lewis. *The Films of Harrison Ford*. New York: Citadel Press, 1996: 141.
17. Ford, Harrison. Interview. *The Today Show*. NBC. New York. 15 May 1984.
18. Cherubin, Jan. *Los Angeles Herald Examiner* May 1984.
19. Broeske, Pat H. *San Francisco Examiner* 27 May 1984.
20. Ibid.
21. Koltnow, Barry. "Ford Sees Jones as Ordinary Guy." *Providence Journal-Bulletin* 24 May 1989.
22. Ibid., Pfeiffer.
23. Barry Koltnow, "Indiana Jones Is Back, but Don't Call Him a Hero." *Anderson Independent Mail* 26 May 1989.
24. Canby, Vincent. "Screen: 'Indiana Jones' Directed by Spielberg." *New York Times* 23 May 1984.
25. Benson, Sheila. "Indy's 'Temple of Doom' Desecrated by Too Much Worship of Special Effects." *Los Angeles Times* 23 May 1984: Cal: 1.
26. Blowen, Michael. "Steven Spielberg." *Boston Globe* 16 Dec. 1984.
27. Ibid., Collins.
28. Barnes, Harper. "Harrison Ford." *St. Louis Post-Dispatch* 7 Feb. 1985.

Chapter 20

1. Maslin, Janet. "At the Movies." *New York Times* 8 Feb. 1985: C12.
2. Clinch, Minty. *Harrison Ford*. Great Britain: New English Library, 1987: 182.
3. Duncan, Andrew. "In and Out of Oz." *The Observer* 19 May 1985.
4. *"Witness" Presskit*. Hollywood: Paramount Pictures, 1985: 10.
5. Silverman, Jeff. "Harrison Ford Takes Off Fedora — and Turns Humble." *L. A. Herald Examiner* 1985.
6. Arnold, John. "From Woodwork to 'Witness.'" *Miami Herald* 3 Feb. 1985.
7. Ibid., *"Witness" Presskit*: 12.
8. Ibid., Arnold.
9. Ibid.
10. Ibid.
11. Ibid., *"Witness" Presskit*: 11.
12. Beale, Lewis. "Witness and the Amish — The Debate That Stirred Up Lancaster County." *Chicago Tribune* 10 Feb. 1985.
13. Coleman, Todd. "The Voice of Experience." *Hollywood Reporter* 4 March 1994.
14. Eyman, Scott. "The Swat Team." *Moviegoer* Dec. 1986.
15. Ibid., Coleman.
16. Fay, Stephen. "Harrison Ford Delivers the Groceries." 1985.

17. "Ford Changes Pace in 'Witness.'" *Norwalk [Connecticut] Hour* 14 Feb. 1985.
18. "Shy Harrison Ford Builds Solid Career." *Chicago Sun-Times* 3 Feb. 1985.
19. Hall, Carla. "Witness in the Amish Land." *Washington Post* 8 Feb. 1985.
20. Maychick, Diana. "'Witness' Draws Fire from the Amish." *New York Post* 1985.
21. "The Amish Under Siege." *The Inquirer* 1985: 21.
22. Clayton, Dawn. "John Hostetler Bears Witness to Amish Culture and Calls the Movie 'Witness' 'a Mockery.'" *People* 1985: 64.
23. "Amish Upset by Filming," *Washington Post* 28 June 1984.
24. Ibid., Beale.
25. Cole, Tom. "Amish Group Seeks Boycott of Movie." *Washington Post* 19 Feb. 1985.
26. Ibid., "The Amish Under Seige." 20.
27. Ibid., 21.
28. Ibid.
29. Kilmuska, Ed. "Actor Harrison Ford, 'Witness,' Star, Aids Farm Preserve Effort." *Lancaster New Era* 9 April 1990.
30. Ibid.
31. "Text of Harrison Ford's Letter." *Lancaster New Era* 9 April 1990.
32. Ibid., Kilmuska.
33. Clinch, Minty. *Harrison Ford.* Great Britain: New English Library, 1987: 187–88.
34. Verniere, James. "The Ford Charm." *Boston Herald* 14 Dec. 1986.
35. Hunter, Allan. *Films and Filming* Feb. 1987.
36. Ibid., Fay.
37. Carter, Alan. "He's Down to Earth." *Daily News* 28 Feb 1985.
38. Wuntch, Philip. *Dallas Morning News* 14 Dec. 1986.
39. Darnton, Nina. "At the Movies." *New York Times* 21 Nov. 1986.
40. Diehl, Digby. "The Road to Belize." *American Film* Dec. 1986.
41. Cook, Bruce. "Ford, Weir Team Up Again." *Boston Globe* 5 Dec. 1986.
42. *"The Mosquito Coast" Presskit.* Hollywood: Warner Bros. Pictures, 1986: 4.
43. Strauss, Bob. "It Took Peter Weir to Make Paul Theroux's 'Mosquito Coast' Fly." *Chicago Sun Times* 14 Dec. 1986.

44. Ibid., Hunter.
45. McGrady, Mike. "Harrison Ford Wins Star Wars." *Providence Journal-Bulletin* 19 Dec. 1986.
46. Ibid., *"The Mosquito Coast" Presskit.*
47. Lawson, Terry. "A Star in Reserve." *Dayton Daily News and Journal Herald* 14 Dec. 1986.
48. Ibid., Coleman.
49. Ibid., Strauss.
50. Ibid., Diehl.
51. Strauss, Bob. "Getting a Handle on Harrison Ford." *Los Angeles Herald Examiner* 30 Nov. 1986.
52. Mann, Roderick. "'Mosquito' Star Bitten by Fan Bug." *Los Angeles Times* 18 Oct. 1986.
53. Harrison Ford interviewed by Charles Champlin on Film Scene.
54. Ibid., *"The Mosquito Coast" Presskit.*: 7–8.
55. Rabinovitch, Dina. "Harrison, the Model Ford." *The Independent* 23 Jan. 1988.
56. Diehl, Digby. "Star Worries." *Daily News Magazine* 23 Nov. 1986.
57. Bandler, Michael J. "Acting the Hero." *American Way* 1 Feb. 1986.
58. Film 87. Harrison Ford interviewed by Barry Norman. 27 Jan. 1987.
59. Attanasio, Paul. "Harrison Ford: Currents of a Collaborator." *Washington Post* 24 Dec. 1986.
60. Theroux, Paul. "Where the Mosquito Bites." *Vanity Fair* Dec. 1986.
61. Lee, Nora. "'Mosquito Coast': A Jungle Utopia Gone Awry." *American Cinematographer* Feb. 1987.
62. Ibid., Eyman.
63. Ibid., *"The Mosquito Coast" Presskit* 9.
64. Ibid., Diehl.
65. Thomas, Bob. "Ford Surprised by Reaction to Latest Film." *Morning Advocate* 3 Jan. 1987.
66. Ibid.
67. Siskel, Gene. "A Very Proud Papa." *Chicago Tribune* 14 Dec. 1986.
68. Ibid.
69. Theroux, Paul. "Author's Review." *Time* 2 Jan. 1987.
70. Ibid., Eyman.
71. Ebert, Roger. "'Mosquito Coast.'" *Chicago Sun-Times* 19 Dec. 1986.

72. Benson, Sheila. "'The Mosquito Coast.'" *Los Angeles Times* 26 Nov. 1986.
73. Healy, Michael. "Ambition Put Harrison Ford in an Odd Role." *Denver Post* 14 Dec. 1986.

Chapter 21

1. McBride, Stewart. "Rebel Without Pause." *Premiere* March 1988.
2. Oney, Steve. "A Very Ordinary Man." *Premiere* March 1988.
3. Wuntch, Philip. "Harrison Ford: Comfortable with Stardom." *Dallas Morning News* 1989.
4. Ibid., Oney.
5. Minton, Lynn. "Harrison Ford Searches for Wife in Thriller." *Parade Magazine* 7 Feb. 1988.
6. Ibid., McBride.
7. Polanski, Roman. Interview. *Cinema* RAI (Italian Television). March 1988.
8. *Frantic Presskit.* Los Angeles: Warner Bros., 1987: 2–3.
9. Siskel, Gene. "Roman Relaxes." *Chicago Tribune* 6 March, 1988.
10. Williams, Jeannie. "The Magnetic 'Frantic' Star Stays Mellow." *USA Today* 10 March 1988.
11. Mills, Nancy. "Avoiding the Star Wars." *Elle* Feb. 1988.
12. Ibid., *"Frantic" Presskit* 5.
13. Zehme, Bill. "Harrison Ford: 20 Questions." *Playboy* March 1988.
14. Ibid., *"Frantic" Presskit* 8.
15. *Zest* 8 May 1988.
16. Paulsen-Nalle, Amy. "Paris'N'Ford." *US* 22 Feb. 1988.
17. *"Frantic" Presskit*: 6.
18. Freeman, Paul. "Talking After Hours with the Working Girl's Man ... Harrison Ford." *Prevue* Dec./March 1989.
19. Ford, Harrison. Interview. *The Today Show.* NBC. New York. 25 Feb 1988.
20. *"Frantic" Presskit*: 9.
21. Malkiewicz, Kris. "Camera Becomes Storyteller for 'Frantic.'" *American Cinematographer* June 1988.
22. Ibid., Paulsen-Nalle.
23. "The Lady Vanishes." *Newsweek* 7 March 1988.
24. Simon, John. "'Frantic.'" *National Review* 15 April 1987.
25. Ibid., Siskel.

Chapter 22

1. Freeman, Paul. "Talking After Hours with the Working Girl's Man ... Harrison Ford," *Prevue* Dec./March 1989.
2. *"Working Girl" Presskit*. Beverly Hills: 20th Century–Fox Film Corporation, 1988: 1–2.
3. Ibid., 2.
4. Milward, John. "A Private Star." *Philadelphia Inquirer* 30 Nov. 1988.
5. Ibid.
6. Armstrong, Douglas. "Ford at the Wheel." *Milwaukee Journal* 22 Jan. 1989.
7. Ibid., Freeman.
8. Ford, Harrison. Interview. *Movietime* interview with Greg Kinnear Dec. 1988.
9. Ibid., Freeman.
10. *"Working Girl" Presskit*: 2–3.
11. Ibid., 3.
12. Ibid.
13. Mawson, Dave. "Harrison Ford: Just Like Han Solo or Indy, This Actor Is Nobody's Sidekick." *Leisure* 11 Dec. 1988.
14. Ibid. Armstrong.
15. Strauss, Bob. "Workingman's Ford." *Movieline* 9 Dec. 1988.
16. Johnson, Brian D. "Working Girl." *Maclean's* 19 Dec. 1988: 52.
17. Ibid., *Working Girl Presskit* 3.
18. Ibid., 4.
19. Nichols, Mike. Interview. *The Today Show*. NBC. New York. 22 Dec. 1988.

Chapter 23

1. Griffin, Nancy. "Manchild in the Promised Land." *Premiere* June 1989.
2. "George Lucas." *Lucasfilm Fan Club Magazine* Winter 1989.
3. Shapiro, Marc. "Indiana Jones Rides Again." *Starlog* May 1989.
4. Ibid.
5. Madsen, Dan. "Steven Spielberg." *Lucasfilm Fan Club Magazine* Summer 1989: 3–4.
6. Woodward, Richard. "Indy Takes Final Bow." *Plain Dealer* 26 May 1989.
7. Ibid.
8. Koltnow, Barry. "Ford Sees Jones as Ordinary Guy." *Providence Journal-Bulletin* 24 May 1989.
9. Garner, Jack. "'Indiana Jones' Opens with Ford and Connery." *Rochester Democrat and Chronicle* 21 May 1989.
10. Ibid.
11. Schaefer, Stephen. "Harrison Ford Bids Farewell to Indiana Jones." *Boston Herald* 21 May 1989.
12. Madsen, Dan. "The Villains of the Last Crusade." *Lucasfilm Fan Club Magazine* Winter 1989: 5.
13. *"Indiana Jones and the Last Crusade" Presskit*. Los Angeles: Paramount Pictures, CA. 1989: 5.
14. Shapiro, Marc. "Indiana Jones' Final Adventures." *Starlog* June 1989.
15. Spielberg, Steven. Interview. *Premiere: Inside the Summer Blockbusters*. 3 June 1989.
16. Ibid.
17. Roller, Pamela E. "Vic Armstrong: The Other Indy Behind the Bullwhip." *Lucasfilm Fan Club Magazine* #13 1991.
18. Ibid., Koltnow.
19. Ibid., *Premiere: Inside the Summer Blockbusters*.
20. Reich, Holly. "Oh, My Aching Back." *New York Daily News* 5 June 1989.
21. Ibid.
22. Ibid., Roller 5.
23. Dillow, Gordon. "'Indiana Jones': The Most Perilous Moments on the Set." *TV Guide* 27 Jan. 1990.
24. Heuring, David. "'Indiana Jones and the Last Crusade.'" *American Cinematographer* June 1989.
25. Spielberg, Steven. Interview. *The Today Show*. NBC. New York. 12 May 1989.
26. Banner, Simmon. "'This Ford Never Runs Out of Gas." *Star* 4 July 1989.
27. "Harrison Ford's Last Crusade." *Fantazone II* Summer 1989.
28. "Crusade for Spielberg: Saving a British Studio." *New York Times* 1 Aug. 1988.
29. Ibid., Shapiro.
30. Ibid.
31. Garner, Jack. "Out West with Indy as a Teen-Age Adventurer." *Rochester Democrat and Chronicle* 28 May 1989.
32. Yakir, Dan. "American Dreamer." *Empire* 1989.
33. Immergut, Scott, and Kim Masters. "Premiere's Ultimate Summer Preview." *Premiere* June 1989.
34. Ibid., Madsen. "Steven Spielberg." 3.
35. Cullen, Jenny. "Indy Finds an Irish Beauty." *Sunday Telegraph* 4 June 1989.
36. Corliss, Richard. "What's Old Is Gold: A Triumph for 'Indy 3.'" *Time* 29 May 1989.
37. Ibid., Madsen. "Steven Spielberg." 4.
38. Ibid., Griffin.
39. *Fantazone II*.
40. Connery, Sean. Interview. *Hollywood Hotline online* 25 May 1989.
41. Ibid.
42. Ibid., Cullen.
43. Ibid.
44. "'Flintstones' Bring in the Yabba-Dabba Dough." *Boston Globe* 30 May 1994.
45. "'Indiana Jones and the Last Crusade.'" *Variety* 7–13 June 1989.
46. Spielberg, Steven. Interview. *The Today Show*. NBC. New York. 12 May 1989.
47. Ford, Harrison. Interview. *Good Morning America*. ABC. New York. 23 May 1989.
48. Spelling, Ian. "Harrison Ford's Last (and Extremely Brief) Crusade." *Starlog* April 1989.
49. Ibid., Madsen. "Steven Spielberg." 4.

Chapter 24

1. Falk, Quentin. "Trapped in a Web of Murder." *Flicks* Oct. 1990.
2. Terry, Clifford. "What Drives Harrison Ford?" *Chicago Tribune* 22 July 1990.
3. Ibid.
4. Lazar, Jerry. "An American Classic." *US* 20 Aug. 1990.
5. Yakir, Dan. "An Innocent Man?" *Empire* Sept. 1990.
6. Appelo, Tim. "Making Book." *Entertainment Weekly* 10 Aug. 1990.
7. Champlin, Charles. "Order in Pakula's Court." *Los Angeles Times* 12 Oct. 1989.
8. Tibbetts, John C. "For Presumed Innocent Star Harrison Ford, a Strong Performance Depends on Details." *Christian Science Monitor* 30 July 1990.
9. Carr, Jay. "Presumed Innocent." *Boston Sunday Globe* 15 July 1990.
10. Wallace, David. "Screen Gem." *Phillip Morris Magazine* Winter 1991.
11. Ibid., Lazar.

12. Siegel, Rochelle. "Presumed Accurate." *Chicago Tribune* 29 July 1990.
13. Charles Champlin. "Harrison Ford: More Than Slam-Bam." *Los Angeles Times* 22 July 1990.
14. Bob Thomas. "Don't Ask Harrison Ford to Talk About Himself." *St. Louis Post Dispatch* 1990.
15. Ibid., Tibbetts.
16. *Entertainment Weekly* 28 Dec 1990.
17. Abrams, Jeffrey. "Regarding Harrison." *USA Weekend* 5 July 1991.
18. Ibid., Champlin.
19. Ibid.
20. Ibid.
21. Siegler, Bonnie. *Movies USA* Aug. 1990.
22. Ibid.
23. Ibid., Champlin.
24. Musial, Robert. "Movie Picture Moves Slowly." *Detroit Free Press* 4 Aug. 1989.
25. Hoban, Phoebe. "Court and Spark." *Premiere* Aug. 1990.
26. Rea, Steven. "Harrison Ford's Trial in a New Kind of Role." *Philadelphia Inquirer* 29 July 1990.
27. Roeper, Richard. "Harrison Ford Gives Up His Defenses in *Presumed Innocent*." *Chicago Sun-Times* 15 July 1990.
28. Pfeiffer, Lee, and Michael Lewis. *The Films of Harrison Ford.* New York: Citadel Press, 1996: 187–188.
29. Ibid., Siegel.
30. Ibid.
31. Ibid.
32. Corliss, Richard. "All Rise! Action!" *Time* 11 June 1990.
33. Wolf, Jeanne. "Torrid Scenes in 'Innocent' Part of Acting." *Denver Post* 18 July 1990.
34. Grobel, Lawrence. "Off Camera: Actor Harrison Ford." *Playboy* Sept. 1993.
35. Ibid., Wolf.
36. Keough, Peter. "Scott Free?" *Boston Phoenix* 27 July 1990.
37. Plaskin, Glenn. "Harrison Ford Nails Down Spot as Movie Hero." *Milwaukee Sentinel* 25 July 1990.
38. Wuntch, Philip. "On the Defense." *Dallas Morning News* 26 July 1990.
39. Usher, Shaun. *Daily Mirror* Oct. 1990.
40. Ibid.
41. Ibid., Lazar.
42. Ibid., Wolf.
43. Master, Kim, and John H. Richardson. "The Ultimate Movie Guide." *Premiere* June 1990.
44. Ibid., Champlin. "Harrison Ford: More Than Slam-Bam."
45. Yakir, Dan. "Innocence Proves Ambivalence." *Boston Globe* 21 Aug. 1990.
46. Ibid.
47. Dennehy, Brian. Interview. *Arsenio Hall Show*. Fox. New York. July 1990.
48. Rea, Stephen. "Bonnie Bedelia's Big Summer." *Philadelphia Enquirer* 29 July 1990.
49. Kaplan, James. "Harrison Ford's Natural Drive." *Vanity Fair* Aug. 1990: 149.
50. Milling, Robin. "Harrison Ford." *Inside Hollywood* Nov./Dec. 1991.

Chapter 25

1. "Regarding Henry" Presskit. Hollywood: Paramount Pictures. 1991: 2.
2. Koltnow, Barry. "Harrison Ford Jumps at the Chance to Play an Attorney Again in 'Henry.'" *Dallas Morning News* 14 July 1991.
3. Ibid., Koltnow.
4. Ibid.
5. Ibid., *"Regarding Henry"* Presskit 2.
6. "Regarding Harrison." *Empire* Oct. 1991.
7. Ibid., *"Regarding Henry"* Presskit 3.
8. Ibid., "Regarding Harrison."
9. Milling, Robin. "Harrison Ford." *Inside Hollywood* Nov./Dec. 1991.
10. Turner, Dylan. "'Regarding Henry.'" *Inside Hollywood* July/Aug. 1991.
11. Johnson, Brian D. "The Reluctant Star." *Maclean's* 15 July 1991.
12. Mills, Bart. *Bergen County Record*.
13. Berlin, J. "Harrison Ford." *Video Software Magazine* Nov. 1991.
14. Ibid.
15. Phillips, Michelle. "Regarding Harrison." *San Diego Union* 7 July 1991.
16. Ibid., *Regarding Henry* Presskit 4.
17. Ibid., Turner.
18. Billen, Stephanie. "Learning to Love Again." *Flicks* Sept. 1991.
19. Ibid., *"Regarding Henry"* Presskit 6.
20. Ibid., *"Regarding Henry"* Presskit 9.
21. Ibid., *"Regarding Henry"* Presskit 7.
22. Ibid., *"Regarding Henry"* Presskit 8.
23. Ibid., Koltnow.
24. Ibid., Phillips.
25. "We're Sorry Harrison Ford." *News of the World* 2 Sept. 1990.
26. Ibid., Phillips.
27. Kilday, Gregg. "Regarding Harrison." *Entertainment Weekly* 12 June 1992.
28. *Sunday Express Magazine* 14 July 1991.
29. "Regarding Harrison." *News Extra* 19 Nov. 1991.
30. Ibid.
31. Ibid.

Chapter 26

1. Kilday, Gregg. "Dangerous Games." *Entertainment Weekly* 12 June 1992.
2. Richardson, John H. "Ford Frenzy." *Premiere* Nov. 1991.
3. Ibid.
4. Griffin, Nancy. "I, Spy." *Premiere* June 1992.
5. Murphy, Ryan. "Patriot Missile." *New York Daily News* 31 May 1992.
6. Stimac, Elias. "Harrison Ford." *Drama-Logue* 4–10 June 1992.
7. Cooney, Jenny. "The Spy Who Came in from the Cold." *Empire* 1992: 78.
8. Stimac, Elias. "Mace Neufeld." *Drama-Logue* 4–10 June 1992.
9. Ibid., Kilday.
10. Welkos, Robert W. "Mr. Nice Guy Dives Back Into Action." *Los Angeles Times* 22 March 1992: 3.
11. Ibid., Kilday.
12. Cox, Meg. "To Tom Clancy: The Real Bad Guys Work in Hollywood." *Wall Street Journal* 22 January 1992.
13. Ibid., Stimac, "Mace Neufeld."
14. Angeli, Michael. "Have You Directed a Ford Lately?" *Movieline* June 1992.
15. "Patriot Games" Presskit. Hollywood: Paramount Pictures. 1992: 7–8.
16. Ibid., Angeli.

17. Ibid., Stimac, "Mace Neufeld."
18. Ibid., Murphy.
19. Stimac, Elias. "Philip Noyce." *Drama-Logue* 4–10 June 1992.
20. Ibid., Stimac, "Harrison Ford."
21. Ibid., *"Patriot Games"* Presskit 6.
22. Stimac, Elias. "Anne Archer." *Drama-Logue* 4–10 June 1992.
23. Ibid., *"Patriot Games"* Presskit 5.
24. Stimac, Elias. "Anne Archer." *Drama-Logue* 4–10 June 1992.
25. Ibid., Griffin 82.
26. Ibid.
27. Ibid., *"Patriot Games"* Presskit 9.
28. Ibid.
29. Griffin, Nancy. "Shot by Shot." *Premiere* June 1992: 79.
30. Ibid., Stimac, "Harrison Ford."
31. Stanley, John. "A Deadly Patriot's Game: Harrison Ford in New Suspense Thriller." *San Francisco Chronicle* 31 May 1992.
32. Ibid., Angeli.
33. Ibid., Stimac, "Philip Noyce."
34. Kronke, David. "A Clear and Present Actor." *Daily Variety* 4 March 1994.
35. Hall, Carla. "The Old Ford, Back in Action." *Washington Post* 5 June 1992.
36. Frankel, Martha. "Mr. Lucky." *Movies USA* May 1992.
37. Willistein, Paul. "It Took No Intrigue to Get Ford for CIA Thriller." *Morning Call* 31 May 1992.
38. Michael, Dennis. "'Patriot Games' Goes Deep Into the CIA." *CNN Headline News.* CNN: Cable News Network. New York. 20 May 1992.
39. Ibid., *"Patriot Games"* Presskit 10.
40. Ibid., Hall.
41. Ibid., Stimac, "Philip Noyce."
42. Kilday, Gregg. "Getting Tanked." *Entertainment Weekly* 12 June 1992.
43. Ibid., Cooney 76.
44. Ibid., *"Patriot Games"* Presskit 14.
45. Ibid., Stanley.
46. Rea, Steven. "Behind the Scenes, 'Patriot Games' Navigated Rough Waters." *Philadelphia Enquirer* 14 June 1992.
47. Ibid., Cooney 76.
48. McBride, Joseph. "Patriot Games." *Variety* 8 June 1992.

49. Ford, Harrison. Interview. Amazon.com interview to promote *What Lies Beneath*. 2000.

Chapter 27

1. Keets, Heather. "The First Fugitive." *Entertainment Weekly* 9 July 1993.
2. *"The Fugitive"* Presskit. Hollywood: Warner Bros., 1993: 2.
3. Hearty, Kitty Bowe. "Born to Run." *Premiere* Sept. 1993.
4. Koltnow, Barry. "Fugitive from Stardom." *Orange County Register* 6 Aug. 1993.
5. Ibid., *"The Fugitive"* Presskit: 3.
6. Ibid.
7. Ibid., 4.
8. Brace, Eric. "Six Questions for Andrew Davis." *Washington Post* 8 Aug. 1993.
9. Ibid.
10. Dutka, Elaine. "Producer Captures a Classic Fugitive." *Calendar* 8 July 1993.
11. Portman, Jamie. "Fugitive Ford Suffers Through More On-the-Job Injuries." *Ottawa Citizen* 6 Aug. 1993.
12. Ibid., *"The Fugitive"* Presskit 4.
13. Ibid., *"The Fugitive"* Presskit 3.
14. Ibid., Brace.
15. Ibid., *"The Fugitive"* Presskit 4.
16. Ibid.
17. Ibid.
18. "An Affair to Remember." *TV Guide* 21–27 Aug. 1993.
19. Ibid., *"The Fugitive"* Presskit 8–9.
20. Strauss, Bob. "Harrison Ford Brings Thought to Action Figures." *Providence Journal-Bulletin* 22 Aug. 1993: E5.
21. Ibid., Strauss.
22. Coleman, Todd. "The Voice of Experience." *Hollywood Reporter* 6 March 1994.
23. Ford, Harrison. Interview. *The Today Show*. NBC. New York. 25 May 1993.
24. "Carved in Celluloid." *Birmingham Post* 24 Sept. 1993.
25. "'Doc' Ford Gets a Big Taste of His Own Medicine." *Globe* 3 Aug. 1993.
26. Pearlman, Cindy. "Medical Research." *Entertainment Weekly* 23 April 1993.
27. Ibid., *"The Fugitive"* Presskit 9–10.

28. Film '93 20 Sept. 1993.
29. Ibid., *"The Fugitive"* Presskit 6.
30. "Marathon Man." *Entertainment Weekly* 20 Aug. 1993.
31. Ibid., *"The Fugitive"* Presskit 6–7.
32. Ibid., "Marathon Man."
33. Grobel, Lawrence. "Off the Beaten Path." *Movieline* July 1997.
34. *Entertainment Weekly* 20 Aug. 1993.
35. Ryan, James. "Harrison Ford Doesn't Run from Work." *Houston Post* 1 Aug. 1993.
36. Pfeiffer, Lee, and Michael Lewis. *The Films of Harrison Ford*. New York: Citadel Press, 1996: 209.
37. Ibid., *"The Fugitive"* Presskit 5.
38. Ibid., Brace.
39. Ibid., Ford, Harrison. Interview. *The Today Show*.
40. Ibid., Hearty.
41. Ibid., Ryan.
42. Spillman, Susan. "An Action-Packed Career Keeps Ford Running. Feats of Film Derring-Do Often Leave Him Limping." *USA Today* 9 Aug. 1993.
43. Ibid., *"The Fugitive"* Presskit 8.
44. Ibid.
45. Ibid.
46. Ibid., *"The Fugitive"* Presskit 10.
47. Mark, Lois Alter. "Rundown Neighborhood." *Entertainment Weekly* 10 Sept. 1993.
48. Ibid., *The Fugitive* Presskit 10.
49. Ibid., Hearty.
50. Stuart, Charles. "A Fugitive from Fame." *Today* 24 Sept. 1993.
51. "Fugitive Heartthrob Ford: When I'm On the Run I Always Take My Wife." *Star* 24 Aug. 1993.
52. Ibid., Stuart.
53. Ibid.
54. Kronke, David. "A Clear and Present Actor." *Daily Variety* 4 March 1994.
55. Ibid., Coleman.
56. Ibid.
57. Ibid., Coleman.
58. Gristwood, Sarah. *Daily Telegraph* 9 Oct. 1993.
59. Kronke, David. "Catching Up with Harrison Ford." *Dallas Morning News* 7 Aug. 1993.
60. Arnold, Gary. "He Can Run but He Can't Hide; Harrison Ford Can Act Any Role but Film Star." *Washington Times* 6 Aug. 1993.

61. Ibid., Brace.
62. Ibid., Kronke.
63. Ibid., Strauss E5.
64. Gable, Donna. "'Fugitive' from Her Sisters." *USA Today* 26 Aug. 1993: 3D.
65. Thompson, Malissa. "Talk About a Manhunt." *Premiere* Oct. 1993.
66. "A Run of Good Luck." *Entertainment Weekly* 20 Aug. 1993.
67. Jones, Tommy Lee. Best Supporting Actor acceptance speech. 66th Academy Awards. 21 March 1994.
68. Marx, Andy. "Savoy Pix Develops on Cash-Cushioned Curve." *Variety* 18 Oct. 1993.
69. Pearlman, Cindy. "Role Redux." *Entertainment Weekly* 12 Aug. 1993.
70. Pearlman, Cindy. "Dead Reckoning." *Entertainment Weekly* 24 Sept. 1993.
71. Ford, Harrison. Interview. *The Little Picture Show*. United Kingdom. 24 Sept. 1993.
72. Grobel, Lawrence. "Off Camera: Actor Harrison Ford." *Playboy* Sept. 1993.

Chapter 28

1. Shapiro, Marc. "Clear & Present Thriller." *Action Heroes* 1994.
2. *"Clear and Present Danger"* Presskit. Hollywood: Paramount Pictures, 1994.
3. "Noyce and Ford Join Tom-Tom Club, Re-Up for Clancy's Danger." *Premiere* Dec. 1994.
4. Fretts, Bruce. "After Surviving One Clash with Tom Clancy, Harrison Ford and the 'Patriot Games' Team Head Back Into the Danger Zone." *Entertainment Weekly* 19 Aug. 1994: 23.
5. Ibid., Fretts 24.
6. Ibid.
7. "Summer Movie Preview: 'Clear and Present Danger.'" *Entertainment Weekly* 27 May 1994.
8. Ibid., Fretts 24.
9. Ibid., *Premiere* Dec. 1994.
10. Susman, Gary. "A Model Ford." *Boston Phoenix* 5 Aug. 1994.
11. Kehr, Dave. "Clancy's 'Danger' Is No Killer in the Thriller Department." *New York Post* 3 Aug. 1994.
12. Ibid., Kehr.

13. Willistein, Paul. "Filming of 'Danger' Lives Up to Its Title." *Morning Call* 31 July 1994.
14. Ibid.
15. Ibid.
16. Oldenburg, Ann. "A Clear and Present Frost: Ford and Company Find Set of Clancy Thriller a Chiller." *USA Today* 17 Jan. 1994: D4.
17. Ibid., *"Clear and Present Danger"* Presskit.
18. Ibid., Shapiro.
19. "Clearing the Path to 'Danger.'" *USA Today* 15 Aug. 1994.
20. Ibid., Fretts 25.
21. Ibid.
22. Grimes, William. "Things That Go BLAM! KA-CHUNG! In the Night." *New York Times* 29 June 1994.
23. Mansfield, Stephanie. "Harrison Hams It Up." *GQ* June 1994.
24. Ibid., Fretts 25.
25. Wayne White, Randy. "The Ryan Game." *Premiere* Sept 1994: 60.
26. Robinson, David. "I, Harrison Ford, Solemnly Declare..." *The Times* 14 Sept. 1994.
27. Ibid., Shapiro.
28. Ibid., Fretts 24.
29. Ibid., White.
30. Michael, Dennis. *Showbiz Today* 5 Aug. 1994.
31. Coleman, Todd. "The Voice of Experience." *Hollywood Reporter* 6 March 1994.
32. *Ottawa Citizen* 2 Aug. 1992.
33. Sandler, Adam. "PGA Honors Neufeld, Rehme." *Daily Variety* 14 Jan. 1994.
34. Schultz, Rick. "Clear Vision." *Boxoffice* July 1994: 19.
35. Ibid., Schultz.
36. Bennett, Ray. "Tall, Dark and Bankable." *Hollywood Reporter* 6 March 1994.
37. "Bally High." *Premiere* June 1994: 24.
38. Ibid.
39. "A Really Big Sho." *Entertainment Weekly* 1994.
40. Ibid., Coleman.
41. Ibid., Mansfield 219.
42. *Toronto Star* 29 July 1994.
43. *Ottawa Citizen* 12 Aug. 1994.
44. Ibid., Coleman.
45. Ibid., Mansfield 162.
46. Higgins, Bill. "Harrison Ford Makes the Party." *Los Angeles Times* 5 Aug. 1994.
47. Staggs, Jeffrey. "'Danger' at KenCen Helps AFI." *Washington Times* 28 July 1994.

48. Galbraityh, Jane. "Clear and Present Hardware." *New York Newsday* 8 Aug. 1994.
49. "'Clear and Present Danger' Generates Spectacular Box Office Action to Become No. 1 During Premiere Weekend with $20.3 Million Gross." *PR Newswire* 8 Aug. 1994.
50. *PR Newswire* 1 Feb. 1995.
51. Ibid., Fretts 26.
52. *Variety* 30 May–5 June 1994.
53. Ibid., Fretts.

Chapter 29

1. Thompson, Gary. "Ford's Roles Suit Him to a Tee." *Philadelphia Daily News* 15 Dec. 1995.
2. Schaefer, Stephen. "Fugitive from Publicity." *Boston Herald* 12 Dec. 1995: 43.
3. Willistein, Paul. "A Remake Not a Copy." *The Morning Call* 15 Dec. 1995.
4. Stivers, Cyndi. "Scions of the Times." *Premiere* Nov. 1995: 73.
5. Ibid., Stivers 72.
6. Wloszczyna, Susan. "The Perils of Giving 'Sabrina' a '90s Makeover." *USA Today* 1995: 2D.
7. *"Sabrina"* Presskit. Hollywood: Paramount Pictures. 1995: 7.
8. Campbell, Virginia. "Still Sane After All These Years." *Movieline* Dec. 1995.
9. Blum, David. "The Conception, Production and Distribution of Julia Ormond." *New York Times Magazine* 9 April 1995: 78.
10. Ibid., Thompson.
11. Schaefer, Stephen. "Thanks, but No Thanks, 'Sabrina.'" *US* March 1995.
12. Ibid., Stivers 72.
13. Ibid.
14. Frankel, Martha. "Golden Boy." *Movieline* Dec. 1995: 64.
15. Grimes, William. "Harrison Ford's Fashion Statement." *Elle* 1995: 103.
16. Ibid.
17. Ibid.
18. Ibid.
19. Ibid.
20. Ibid.
21. Schaefer, Stephen. "Ordinary People." *Entertainment Weekly* 11 Aug. 1995.
22. Richmond, Peter. "When Julia Gets Blue." *GQ* May 1996: 147.
23. Ibid., Stivers 74.

24. Ibid., Wloszczyna 1D.
25. Garner, Jack. "Tackling the Great Billy Wilder." *Rochester Democrat and Chronicle*
26. Ibid., Frankel: 86.
27. Ibid., Frankel: 65.
28. Ibid., Stivers: 73.
29. Ibid.
30. Hensley, Dennis. "On the Brink." *Movieline* Nov. 1995: 46.
31. Szymanski, Mike. "Ford Gets Their Motors Running." *First* 11 March 1995: 121.
32. Carr, Jay. "Harrison Ford: The Ordinary Hero." *Boston Sunday Globe* 31 July 1994.
33. Leydon, Joe. "Harrison Ford Cultivates His Privacy as Carefully as He Picks Film Roles." *Providence Journal-Bulletin*
34. Ibid., Thompson.
35. Rea, Stephen. "Ford Loves Slapstick — Played by Someone Else." *Philadelphia Enquirer* 17 Dec. 1995.
36. Ibid., Thompson.

Chapter 30

1. Hobson, Louis B. "Brad's Unbeatable." *Calgary Sun* 16 March 1997.
2. Pener, Degen. "Dealing with the Devil." *Entertainment Weekly* 11 April 1997: 34.
3. Anne Thompson, "The 'Devil' in the Details."
4. *"The Devil's Own" Presskit*. Hollywood: Paramount Pictures. 1997.
5. Fisher, Ian. "Devil of a Shoot." *Providence Journal-Bulletin* 1996.
6. Ibid., Pener 34.
7. Ibid., Thompson.
8. "The 100 Dumbest Things Hollywood's Done Lately." *Movieline* May 1996: 70.
9. Ibid., Pener 37.
10. Ibid., Thompson.
11. Ibid., Pener 36.
12. Ibid., Pener 34.
13. Ibid., Pener 36.
14. Ibid.
15. Ibid.
16. Ibid., *"The Devil's Own" Presskit*.
17. Giles, Jeff. "Cool. Excellent. Thanks." *Newsweek* 3 Feb. 1997: 51.
18. Ibid., Pener 37.
19. Ibid.
20. Ibid., Pener 37.
21. Ibid., Thompson.
22. Ibid.

23. Ibid., Pener 37.
24. Kirkland, Bruce. "Devil's Advocate." *Toronto Sun* 23 March 1997.
25. Ibid.
26. Ibid., Pener 37.
27. Ibid., Thompson.
28. Ibid.
29. Ibid., Kirkland.
30. Ibid.
31. Ibid.
32. *Detour* April 1997: 101.
33. Ibid., Thompson.
34. Rush, George, and Joanna Malloy. "'Devil' of a Time." *New York Daily News* 29 March 1996.
35. Ibid., *"The Devil's Own" Presskit*.
36. Ibid.
37. Ibid., Pener 38.
38. Sales, Nancy Jo. "Shoot Out." *New York* 16 Sept. 1996: 36.
39. Ibid.
40. Baran, Walter. "Married Harrison Ford and Sexy Galpal Get Down and Dirty in Biker Bar." *Star* 28 May 1996: 21.
41. South, John, and Michael Hanrahan, "Harrison Ford in Wild Fling with Mystery Blonde." *National Enquirer* May 1996.
42. Ibid., Baran: 20.
43. O'Neill, Tom. "Harrison Ford." *US* June 1997: 78.
44. Ibid., Giles 50.
45. Ibid., Pener 38.
46. Seiler, Andy. "Pitt, Pakula Found 'Devil' Details a Source of Conflict." *USA Today* 26 March 1997.
47. Ibid., Kirkland.
48. Pitt, Brad. "The Devil Made Me Do It." *Newsweek* 10 Feb. 1997.
49. Ibid., Seiler.
50. Ibid., *"The Devil's Own" Presskit*.
51. Malkin, Mark S. "The Devil, You Say." *Premiere* May 1997: 52.
52. Hobson, Louis B. "Harrison Ford's Solo Career." *Calgary Sun* 16 March 1997.
53. Dunn, Jancee. "Rebel Star, Top Dog." *Rolling Stone* 3 April 1997.
54. Ibid., *"The Devil's Own" Presskit*.
55. Thompson, Anne. "'The Devil's Own.'" *Premiere* 1996.
56. Maslin, Janet. "Wake Up, Sergeant. There's a Terrorist in Your Basement." *New York Times* 26 March 1997: C21.
57. Wilmington, Michael. "'Devil's Own' is Troubled by Lack of Emotional Core." *Chicago Tribune* 26 March 1997: 5: 3.
58. Clark, Mike. "No Sparks from This Star Pairing." *USA Today* 26 March 1997.
59. Siskel, Gene. "Devil's Own" review. *Siskel and Ebert* 29 March 1997.
60. McCarthy, Todd. "'Devil' Punctuates Moral Issue." *Variety* 24 March 1997.

Chapter 31

1. Fleming, Michael. "'Air Force One.'" *Daily Variety* 9 Jan. 1996.
2. Ibid.
3. *"Air Force One" Presskit*. Columbia Pictures. 1997.
4. Ibid.
5. Blair, Iain. "Ford Takes Off in 'Air Force One.'" *Boston Herald* 25 July 1997: S7.
6. Mooney, Joshua. *Entertainment News Wire* 16 July 1997.
7. Ibid.
8. Ibid., *"Air Force One" Presskit*.
9. Ibid.
10. Ibid.
11. Schneider, Karen S. "Vintage Ford." *People* 4 Aug. 1997.
12. Fineman, Howard. "Last Action President." *Newsweek* 21 July 1997: 67.
13. Young, Josh. "Upright & Personal." *George* Aug. 1997: 66.
14. Ford, Harrison. Interview. *Flicks with Patrick Stoner*. WHYY-TV. Philadelphia. July 1997.
15. "President Ford Flies High on 'Air Force One.'" *Premiere* Feb. 1997: 27.
16. Hochman, David. "The Plane and Simple Truth." *Entertainment Weekly* 1 Aug. 1997: 24.
17. Ibid., 22.
18. Ibid., Blair S7.
19. *Better Idea Zine*: issue #35. Unofficial Harrison Ford fanzine. 1997: 24.
20. Ibid., Hochman 24.
21. Ibid.
22. Ibid.
23. *Air Force One* DVD line notes. Columbia Pictures. 1997.
24. Ibid., Mooney.
25. Ibid., *"Air Force One" Presskit*.
26. Ibid., *Air Force One* DVD linear notes.
27. Ford, Harrison. Interview. *Mr. Showbiz.com*. 23 July 1997.
28. King, Larry. "Trump, Ford,

Foster: In Love with Work." *USA Today* 28 July 1997.
29. Ibid., *"Air Force One" Presskit*.
30. *E! Behind the Scenes: 'Air Force One.'* Los Angeles: E! Entertainment Television. 1997.
31. Ibid., Schneider.
32. Ibid., *Mr. Showbiz.com*.
33. Ibid., Young 96.
34. Ibid., *E! Behind the Scenes: 'Air Force One.'*
35. Woods, Vicki. "The Ford in Our Future." *Vogue* March 1997.
36. Ibid., *Mr. Showbiz.com*.
37. Grobel, Lawrence. "Off the Beaten Path." *Movieline* July 1997.
38. Mills, Bart. "Harrison Ford: Rugged Romantic." *Biography* Oct. 1999: 53.
39. Ibid., *Mr. Showbiz.com*.
40. Ibid., Young 97.
41. Ibid., 96.
42. "Acting Presidents." *Time* 14 April 1997.
43. Williams, Jeannie. "Sean Connery Bonds with America at His Film Tribute." *USA Today* 5 May 1997.
44. "No Nostalgia, Thanks." *People* 1997.
45. "Harrison Ford Fights for New Film." Mr. Showbiz.com online article. 9 May 1997.
46. Wloszczyna, Susan. "A Well-Piloted Career Pays Off with Power, Privilege." *USA Today* 25 July 1997.
47. Peters, Jenny. "Ford Tough." *Woonsocket Call* 1997.
48. Strauss, Bob. "Ford Takes on Job 'One.'" *Boston Globe* 20 July 1997: N12.
49. Sobieraj, Sandra. "Clinton Dishes on 'Air Force One.'" *Associated Press* 18 July 1997.
50. Ibid., Hochman 25.
51. Schaefer, Stephen. "President Ford." *Boston Sunday Herald* 20 July 1997: 41.
52. Ibid., Young 66.
53. Ibid., Young 97.
54. Ibid., *E! Behind the Scenes: "Air Force One."*
55. Kirkland, Bruce. "Han Solo Makes Him Blush." *Toronto Sun* 17 March 1997.
56. Ibid.

Chapter 32

1. Booth, Cathy. "Out on Her Own." *Time* 1998. p. 70.
2. Pond, Steve. "Pleasure Island." *Premiere* July 1998: 44.
3. *"Six Days, Seven Nights" Presskit*. Touchstone Pictures. 1998.
4. Ibid.
5. Ibid.
6. Carr, Jay. "Ford Flies at Fun." *Sunday Telegraph* 28 June 1998.
7. Ibid., *"Six Days, Seven Nights" Presskit*.
8. Ibid.
9. Ibid.
10. Ibid., Pond 44.
11. Ibid., *"Six Days, Seven Nights" Presskit*.
12. Worth, Larry. "The Leading Man Is Built Ford Tough." *New York Post* 1998.
13. Lynch, Lorrie. "To Me, Success Is a Choice." *USA Weekend* 12–14 June 1998: 5.
14. Ibid., *Six Days, Seven Nights Presskit*.
15. Kamps, Louisa. "Deconstructing Harrison." *Elle* July 1998.
16. Ibid.
17. Ibid., Carr.
18. Ibid., *Six Days, Seven Nights Presskit*.
19. Ibid.
20. Touchstone Pictures press release. 20 Feb. 1998.
21. Schickel, Richard. "Been There, Seen That." *Time* 15 June 1998
22. Maslin, Janet. "A Couple of Strangers in Paradise." *New York Times* 12 June 1998.
23. Turan, Kenneth. "'Six Days,' Many Echoes." *Los Angeles Times* 12 June 1998.
24. Ibid., *"Six Days, Seven Nights" Presskit*.
25. Ibid.

Chapter 33

1. Schneider, Wolf. "Leading with His Heart." *Blackstone Valley Advocate* 1999.
2. Koltnow, Barry. "Kristin Scott Thomas Keeps Her Distance." *Providence Journal-Bulletin* 8 Oct. 1999.
3. Williams, Jeannie. "Pollack Keeps Shirt On in Sultry Tale of Adultery." *USA Today* 10 Aug. 1999.
4. *HBO: First Look — The Making of "Random Hearts."* New York: HBO Productions. 1999.
5. Ibid.
6. Stanton, Doug. "The Perfection of Harrison Ford." *Men's Journal* Sept. 1999.
7. Ibid., *HBO: First Look — The Making of "Random Hearts."*
8. Ibid.
9. Ibid.
10. Ibid.
11. Pearlman, Cindy. "Harrison Ford Tough." *Chicago Tribune* 3 Oct. 1999.
12. McCarthy, Todd. "'Random Hearts.'" *Variety* 4–10 Oct. 1999.
13. Keller, Julie. "No Love for 'Random Hearts.'" E! Online 23 Oct. 1999.
14. Maslin, Janet. "Thrown Together by a Twist of Fate." *New York Times* 8 Oct. 1999.
15. Janusonis, Michael. "'Hearts' Needs a Pacemaker." *Providence Journal-Bulletin* 8 Oct. 1999.
16. Kennedy, Colin. "…And Beneath Lies, the Truth." *Empire* Nov. 2000: 76.

Chapter 34

1. Ford, Harrison. Interview. Deauville Film Festival press conference. 8 Sept. 2000.
2. *"What Lies Beneath" official website*. Dreamworks SKG. 2000.
3. *"What Lies Beneath" Presskit*. Dreamworks. 2000.
4. Hobson, Louis B. "Acting Enigma." *Calgary Sun* 17 July 2000.
5. Gregg, Clark. Interview. WGA.org online. 2000.
6. Colin Kennedy. "…And Beneath Lies, the Truth," *Empire* Nov. 2000: 69.
7. O'Neill, Anne-Marie. "Built to Last." *People* 7 Aug. 2000.
8. Schwarzbaum, Lisa. "Grand Allusion." *Entertainment Weekly* 28 July 2000.
9. Rynning, Roald. "Bathroom Sink Drama." *Film Review* Nov. 2000: 69.
10. "Will the Real Harrison Ford Stand Up?" *Urban Cinefile* 2 Nov. 2000.
11. "Hollywood 100 Most…" *Movieline* Nov. 2000.
12. Morgenstern, Joe. "A Hollow Shell Is 'What Lies Beneath' Creepy New Thriller." *Wall Street Journal* 21 July 2000.
13. Rainer, Peter. "Breathtaking." *New York* 21 July 2000.
14. Janusonis, Michael. "A Thrilling, Chilling Terrifying Ride." *Providence Journal-Bulletin* 21 July 2000: E1.
15. Lumenick, Lou. "Reel Scary Movie — 'Beneath' Uses All the

Tricks." *New York Post* 21 July 2000.
16. Rebello, Stephen. "Steven Soderbergh Is So Money." *Movieline* Dec. 2001.
17. Ibid., Kennedy 73.
18. Beck Marilyn, and Stacy Jenel Smith. "A New 'Indiana Jones'? Could be, Says the Hero." *Philadelphia Inquirer* 15 Sept. 1999.
19. Ibid., "Will the Real Harrison Ford Stand Up?"
20. "A Change at the CIA." *People* 25 Sept. 2000: 14.
21. Ibid.

Chapter 35

1. *"K-19: The Widowmaker"* Presskit. Hollywood: Paramount Pictures. 2002: 4.
2. Darlington, Shasta. "Harrison Ford Defends Controversial 'K-19' Role." *Reuters* 1 Sept. 2002.
3. Ford, Harrison. Interview. *Film 2002*. London: BBC1. 21 Oct. 2002.
4. Fleming, Michael. "Playboy Interview: Harrison Ford." *Playboy* Aug. 2002: 60.
5. Ibid., 64.
6. Ibid., 60.
7. Ibid.
8. Ibid.
9. Honeycutt, Kirk. "'K-19: The Widowmaker.'" *Hollywood Reporter* 15 July 2002.
10. Scott, A. O. "Testosterone Put to a Test." *New York Times* 19 July 2002.
11. Germain, David. "'K-19: The Widowmaker.'" *Associated Press* July 2002.
12. "New Film Is Not a Failure, Says Ford." *Ananova online* 1 Sept. 2002.
13. *K19: The Widowmaker* DVD commentary with director Kathryn Bigelow. Paramount Pictures. 2002.
14. Thompson, Bob. "Harrison Ford: Not Just Another Playboy." *Sympatico.ca* July 2002.
15. Stauss, Bob. "Below the Surface." *Los Angeles Daily News* 14 July 2002.
16. Trescott, Jacqueline. "A Different Ford in Our Future." *Washington Post* 14 July 2002.

Chapter 36

1. Pearlman, Cindy. "Ford Stays Focused Despite Hollywood Hardships." *Chicago Sun Times* 8 June 2003.
2. Hart, Hugh. "Harrison Ford Lightens Up (A Little)." *Boston Sunday Globe* 8 June 2000: N19.
3. *Hollywood Homicide* Presskit. Columbia Pictures 2003: 2.
4. *Hollywood Homicide* DVD commentary with director Ron Shelton. Columbia Pictures 2003.
5. Ibid., Hart N19.
6. Germain, David. "Harrison Ford Plays with Tough Guy Image." *Associated Press* 11 June 2003.
7. Ibid.
8. Ibid., Hart.
9. Topel, Fred. "Harrison Ford Interview: Part One—'Hollywood Homicide' and Acting." *About.com* 2003.
10. Ibid.
11. Ibid., Hart.
12. Ibid.
13. Slotek, Jim. "Sneer We Go." *Toronto Sun* 8 June 2003.
14. "CS! Interview: Hartnett on 'Hollywood Homicide.'" *Comingsoon.net* 10 June 2003.
15. Lee, Alana. "Harrison Ford: 'Hollywood Homicide.'" *BBCi Films* 20 Aug. 2003.
16. Whipp, Glenn. "A Trusting Ford Accepts His Lot." *San Bernardino County Sun* 26 April 2003.
17. Loewenstein, Lael. "The Buddy Factor." *New York Daily News* 8 June 2003.
18. LaSalle, Mick. "Grit and Wit: Ford, Hartnett and Odd Pair of Detectives in a Decaying Hollywood in 'Homicide.'" *San Francisco Chronicle* 13 June 2003.
19. Burr, Ty. "'Homicide' Dead from Script Down." *Boston Globe* 13 June 2003.
20. MacDonald, Addison. "'Hollywood Homicide.'" *Premiere* 2003.
21. Bernard, Jami. "'Homicide' Is a Crime." *New York Daily News* 13 June 2003.
22. Ebert, Roger. "'Hollywood Homicide.'" *Chicago Sun Times* 13 June 2003.
23. Ibid., Burr.
24. "CS! Interview: Lena Olin on 'Hollywood Homicide.'" *Comingsoon.net* 11 June 2003.
25. Dziemianowicz, Joe. "Harrison Ford: Enjoying the Ride." *Biography* June 2003.
26. Ibid., Slotek.
27. "Isaiah Washington Follows Harrison Ford's Lead in New Movie." *Associated Press* 2 Feb. 2003.
28. Ibid., Topel.
29. C.J. "Was Hartnett's Heat Too Much for Harrison Ford?" *Star Tribune* 30 May 2003.

Chapter 37

1. Samantha Miller, "Brand New Ford." *People* 23 June 2003: 90.
2. Tresniowski, Alex. "New Model Ford." *People* 20 April 1998: 130.
3. Ibid., 129.
4. Mills, Bart. "Harrison Ford: Rugged Romantic." *Biography* Oct. 1999: 94.
5. Mills, Bart. *Bergen County Record* 1990.
6. Stuart, Charles. "A Fugitive from Fame." *Today* 24 Sept. 1993.
7. Pearce, Guy. "Why Harrison's Keeping His Family Top Secret!" *Woman's Own* 21 Sept. 1992.
8. Morrison, Mark. "Low-Key Leading Man." *Movies* May 1989.
9. Mills, Bart. "The Quiet American." *For Him* Aug.-Sept. 1990.
10. Kaplan, James. "Harrison Ford's Natural Drive." *Vanity Fair* Aug. 1990.
11. Green, Tom. "Not-So-Driven Harrison Ford." *USA Today* 5 June 1992.
12. Lurie, Rod. "Family, Fame and Harrison Ford." *OK!* Issue 19. 1994: 51.
13. "Land Trust Names Ford to Board." *Jackson Hole Daily* 26 Nov. 1991.
14. "Ford, Mathison Protect More Snake Property." *Jackson Hole News* 5 Jan. 1994.
15. Oney, Steve. "Just Another Cowboy." *North Shore* May 1990.
16. Corcoran, Monica. "Surreal Estate." *In Style* 2000.
17. Carr, Jay. "Ford Looks Beyond Indy's Last Hurrah." *Boston Globe* 21 May 1989.
18. Gabriel, Trip. "Facing His Biggest Risk of All: Romantic Comedy." *New York Times* 14 Dec. 1995.
19. Thomas, Bob. "'Fugitive' Hides from Limelight." *Delaware County Daily Times* 19 Aug. 1993.
20. Grobel, Lawrence. "Off the Beaten Path." *Movieline* July 1997.
21. *City Harvest Press Release* 17 July 2002.

22. Artists Rights Foundation website: http://www.artistsrights.org.
23. "Suriname Preserves 10 Percent of Its Tropical Wilderness." *Boston Globe* 17 June 1998.
24. Powell, Joanna. "Harrison's Passions." *Good Housekeeping* Oct. 1999.
25. Ibid.
26. Ibid.
27. Jay Carr, "Ford Flies at Fun," *[Sydney] Sunday Telegraph* 28 June 1998.
28. Ibid., Grobel.
29. Ford, Harrison. "Realizing the Dream: A Promise Kept." *AOPA Pilot Magazine* June 1998.
30. Stanton, Doug. "The Perfection of Harrison Ford." *Men's Journal* Sept. 1999.
31. "Chatting with Harrison," *Amica* Oct. 2000.
32. Ibid., Ford.
33. Ford, Harrison. Interview. *Larry King Live!* CNN: Cable News Network. New York. 26 July 1997.
34. "50 Most Beautiful People in the World." *People* May 1997.
35. Ford, Harrison. Interview. *Tonight Show with Jay Leno.* NBC. New York. 3 Aug. 1994.
36. Reed, J. D. "The Sexiest Man Alive '98 ... Harrison Ford." *People* 16 Nov. 1998.
37. Ibid.
38. Bennett, Ray. "Tall, Dark and Bankable." *Hollywood Reporter* March 1994.
39. *Hasty Pudding Theatricals 148 Man of the Year Press Kit.* Cambridge: Harvard University. 1996.
40. Falcone, David. "Ford & Sarandon Have a Pudding Pot in Their Future." *Boston Herald* 30 Jan. 1996: 17.
41. Thomas, Bob. "Star Watch: Harrison Ford." *Associated Press* 2 March 2000.
42. Abele, Robert. *People Profiles: Harrison Ford.* New York: Time, 2000: 103.
43. "Model Ford." *People* 6 March 2000.
44. Tscharner-Patao, Gabriela. "Harrison Ford on Playing Heroes, Handling the Paparazzi, and Returning as Indiana Jones." *Star Wars Insider* Issue #71: 65.
45. Ibid.
46. Hellicar, Michael. "The £100m Hermit of Snake Ridge: Part 2." *Daily Star* 22 Sept. 1992.

BIBLIOGRAPHY

Books

Abele, Robert. *People Profiles: Harrison Ford.* New York: Time, 2000.
Arnold, Alan. *Once Upon a Galaxy: A Journal of the Making of The Empire Strikes Back.* New York: Ballantine, 1980.
Baxter, John. *Mythmaker: The Life and Work of George Lucas.* New York: Avon Books, 1999: 208.
Bulluck, Vic, ed. *Blade Runner Souvenir Magazine.* New York: Ira Friedman, 1982.
Champlin, Charles. *George Lucas: The Creative Impulse — Special Abridged Edition.* New York: Harry N. Abrams, 1992.
Clinch, Minty. *Harrison Ford.* Great Britain: New English Library, 1987.
Crawley, Tony. *The Steven Spielberg Story.* New York: Quill Press, 1983.
"Ford, Harrison." *Current Biography Yearbook.* 1984 ed.
Freeman, Susan, ed., *Indiana Jones and the Temple of Doom: Official Collector's Edition.* New York: Paradise Press, 1984.
Goodwin, Michael, and Naomi Wise. *On the Edge: The Life & Times of Francis Coppola.* New York: William Morrow, 1989.
Holler, Ann. *Raiders of the Lost Ark Collector's Album.* New York: S. W. Ventures, 1981: 8.
Jenkins, Gary. *Harrison Ford: Imperfect Hero.* New Jersey: Birch Lane Press, 1998.
_____. *Harrison Ford: Reluctant Star.* Great Britain: Birch Lane Press, 1998.
May, Johnm ed. *The Empire Strikes Back Official Collectors Edition.* Connecticut: Paradise Press, 1980.
Pfeiffer, Lee, and Michael Lewis. *The Films of Harrison Ford.* New York: Citadel Press, 1996.
Pollack, Dale. *Skywalking: The Life and Films of George Lucas.* New York: Harmony Books, 1983.
Sammon, Paul M. *Future Noir: The Making of Blade Runner.* New York: Harper Collins, 1996.
Schumacher, Michael. *Francis Ford Coppola: A Filmmaker's Life.* New York: Crown, 1999.
Taylor, Derek. *The Making of Raiders of the Lost Ark.* New York: Ballantine Books, 1981.
Vale, Ethlie Ann, and Mary Toledo. *Harrison Ford.* New York: St. Martin's Press, 1987.

Periodical Articles

Abrams, Jeffrey. "Regarding Harrison." *USA Weekend* 5 July 1991.
"Acting Presidents." *Time* 14 April 1997.
Adamo, Susan. "Mark Hamill." *Starlog* #65.
"An Affair to Remember." *TV Guide* 21–27 Aug. 1993.
Air Force One Presskit. Columbia Pictures. 1997.
"The Amish Under Siege." *The Inquirer* 1985: 21.
"Amish Upset by Filming," *Washington Post* 28 June 1984.
Angeli, Michael. "Have You Directed a Ford Lately?" *Movieline* June 1992.
Ansen, David. "Cliffhanger Classic." *Newsweek* 15 June 1981.
_____. "The Force Is Back with Us." *Newsweek* 19 May 1980.
_____. "Hit the Road, Jack." *Newsweek* 14 Nov. 1977.
Appelo, Tim. "Making Book." *Entertainment Weekly* 10 Aug. 1990.
Aquarian 1980.
Armstrong, Douglas. "Ford at the Wheel." *Milwaukee Journal* 22 Jan. 1989.

Arnold, Gary. "He Can Run but He Can't Hide; Harrison Ford Can Act Any Role but Film Star." *Washington Times* 6 Aug. 1993.
Arnold, John. "From Woodwork to *Witness*." *Miami Herald* 3 Feb. 1985.
Artists Rights Foundation website: http://www.artistsrights.org.
Attanasio, Paul. "Harrison Ford: Currents of a Collaborator." *Washington Post* 24 Dec. 1986.
"Bally High." *Premiere* June 1994: 24.
Bandler, Michael J. "Acting the Hero." *American Way* 1 Feb. 1986.
Banner, Simmon. "This Ford Never Runs Out of Gas." *Star* 4 July 1989.
Baran, Walter. "Married Harrison Ford and Sexy Galpal Get Down and Dirty in Biker Bar." *Star* 28 May 1996: 21.
Barnes, Harper. "Harrison Ford." *St. Louis Post-Dispatch* 7 Feb. 1985.
Beale, Lewis. "Witness and the Amish — The Debate That Stirred Up Lancaster County." *Chicago Tribune* 10 Feb. 1985.
Beck, Marilyn, and Stacy Jenel Smith. "A New *Indiana Jones*? Could Be, Says the Hero." *Philadelphia Inquirer* 15 Sept. 1999.
Bennett, Ray. "Tall, Dark and Bankable." *Hollywood Reporter* 6 March 1994.
Benson, Sheila. "Indy's *Temple of Doom* Desecrated by Too Much Worship of Special Effects." *Los Angeles Times* 23 May 1984.
_____. "The Mosquito Coast." *Los Angeles Times* 26 Nov. 1986.
Berlin, J. "Harrison Ford." *Video Software Magazine* Nov. 1991.
Bernard, Jami. "*Homicide* Is a Crime." *New York Daily News* 13 June 2003.
Better Idea Zine: issue #35. Unofficial Harrison Ford fanzine. 1997: 24.
Billen, Stephanie. "Learning to Love Again." *Flicks* Sept. 1991.
"*Blade Runner*." *Variety* 16 July 1982.
Blade Runner Presskit. Los Angeles: Warner Bros., 1982.
Blair, Iain. "Ford Takes Off in *Air Force One*." *Boston Herald* 25 July 1997.
Blowen, Michael. "Steven Spielberg." *Boston Globe* 16 Dec. 1984.
Blum, David. "The Conception, Production and Distribution of Julia Ormond." *New York Times Magazine* 9 April 1995: 78.
Bock, Audie. "Secrecy Shrouds a *Star Wars* Sequel." *New York Times* 11 July 1982. Booth, Cathy. "Out on Her Own." *Time* 1998. p. 70.
Brace, Eric. "Six Questions for Andrew Davis." *Washington Post* 8 Aug. 1993.
Brantley, Robin. "New Face: Harrison Ford. A Star Warrior." *New York Times* 1 July 1977.
Brodie, Ian. *Family Weekly* 20 May 1984.
Broeske, Pat H. *San Francisco Examiner* 27 May 1984.
Buckley, Tim. "The 'Force' Behind *Empire Strikes Back*." *New York Times* 16 May 1980.
Burr, Ty. "*Homicide* Dead from Script Down." *Boston Globe* 13 June 2003.
Byrge, Duane. "Self-Made Man." *Hollywood Reporter* 4 March 1994.
C.J. "Was Hartnett's Heat Too Much for Harrison Ford?" *Star Tribune* 30 May 2003.
Campbell, Virginia. "Still Sane After All These Years." *Movieline* Dec. 1995.
_____. "The Way to *The Mosquito Coast*." *Movieline* 5 Dec. 1986.
Canby, Vincent. "Film: *Raiders of the Lost Ark*." *New York Times* 12 June 1981.
_____. *New York Times* 19 Feb. 1978.
_____. "Screen: 'Indiana Jones' Directed by Spielberg." *New York Times* 23 May 1984.
Carr, Jay. "Ford Flies at Fun." *Sunday Telegraph* 28 June 1998.
_____. "Ford Looks Beyond Indy's Last Hurrah." *Boston Globe* 21 May 1989.
_____. "Harrison Ford: The Ordinary Hero." *Boston Sunday Globe* 31 July 1994.
_____. "Presumed Innocent." *Boston Sunday Globe* 15 July 1990.
Carter, Alan. "Down to Earth." *New York Daily News* 28 Feb. 1988.
_____. "He's Down to Earth." New York *Daily News* 28 Feb 1985.
"Carved in Celluloid." *Birmingham Post* 24 Sept. 1993.
Champlin, Charles. "Harrison Ford: More Than Slam-Bam." *Los Angeles Times* 22 July 1990.
_____. "Order in Pakula's Court." *Los Angeles Times* 12 Oct. 1989.
_____. "War, Love on *Hanover Street*." *Los Angeles Times* 1979.
"A Change at the CIA." *People* 25 Sept. 2000: 14.
"Chatting with Harrison," *Amica* Oct. 2000.
Cherubin, Jan. *Los Angeles Herald Examiner* May 1984.
Chicago Tribune 20 June 1982.
Cinema Odyssey Vol. 1, No. 1.
Circus Weekly 3 April 1979.

City Harvest Press Release 17 July 2002.
Clark, Mike. "No Sparks from This Star Pairing." *USA Today* 26 March 1997.
Clarke, Gerald. "Great Galloping Galaxies." *Time* 23 May 1983: 63.
Clayton, Dawn. "John Hostetler Bears Witness to Amish Culture and Calls the Movie *Witness* 'a Mockery.'" *People* 1985: 64.
"*Clear and Present Danger* Generates Spectacular Box Office Action to Become No. 1 During Premiere Weekend with $20.3 Million Gross." *PR Newswire* 8 Aug. 1994.
Clear and Present Danger Presskit. Hollywood: Paramount Pictures, 1994.
"Clearing the Path to *Danger.*" *USA Today* 15 Aug. 1994.
Cleaver, Thomas McKelvey. "Frank Marshall: Adventuring Alongside *Indiana Jones and the Temple of Doom.*" *Starlog* June 1984.
Clinch, Minty. *Honey* Dec. 1982.
Cole, Tom. "Amish Group Seeks Boycott of Movie." *Washington Post* 19 Feb. 1985.
Coleman, Todd. "On the Run." *Hollywood Reporter* 4 March 1994.
_____. "The Voice of Experience." *Hollywood Reporter* 6 March 1994.
Collins, Glenn. "In *Indiana Jones*, Stunts Get Star Billing."
Connery, Sean. Interview. *Hollywood Hotline online* 25 May 1989.
Cook, Bruce. "Ford, Weir Team Up Again." *Boston Globe* 5 Dec. 1986.
Cooney, Jenny. "The Spy Who Came In from the Cold." *Empire* 1992: 78.
Corcoran, Monica. "Surreal Estate." *In Style* 2000.
Corliss, Richard. "All Rise! Action!" *Time* 11 June 1990.
_____. "The Pleasures of Texture." *Time* 12 July 1982.
_____. "What's Old Is Gold: A Triumph for Indy 3." *Time* 29 May 1989.
Cox, Meg. "To Tom Clancy: The Real Bad Guys Work in Hollywood." *Wall Street Journal* 22 January 1992.
Crawley, Tony. *Films Illustrated* 1978.
_____. *Starburst* Winter 1982–83.
The Crimson Yearbook of Ripon College 1963.
"Crusade for Spielberg: Saving a British Studio." *New York Times* 1 Aug. 1988.
"CS! Interview: Hartnett on *Hollywood Homicide.*" Comingsoon.net 10 June 2003.
"CS! Interview: Lena Olin on *Hollywood Homicide.*" Comingsoon.net 11 June 2003.
Cullen, Jenny. "Indy Finds an Irish Beauty." *Sunday Telegraph* 4 June 1989.
Cunneff, Tom and Elizabeth Sporkin, "Checking 'Em Out." *People* 17 Nov. 1997.
Daily Variety 4 Aug. 1983.
Darlington, Shasta. "Harrison Ford Defends Controversial *K-19* Role." *Reuters* 1 Sept. 2002.
Darnton, Nina. "At the Movies." *New York Times* 21 Nov. 1986.
Denby, David. "*Blade Runner.*" *New York* 28 June 1982.
Detour April 1997: 101.
The Devil's Own Presskit. Hollywood: Paramount Pictures. 1997.
Diehl, Digby. "The Road to Belize." *American Film* Dec. 1986.
_____. "Star Worries." *Daily News Magazine* 23 Nov. 1986.
Dillow, Gordon. "*Indiana Jones*: The Most Perilous Moments on the Set." *TV Guide* 27 Jan. 1990.
"'Doc' Ford Gets a Big Taste of His Own Medicine." *Globe* 3 Aug. 1993.
Dorf, Shel. "Interview: Harrison Ford." *Movie Writes* 1977: 76.
Dovlin, Rod. "The Force of Mark Hamill." *Axcess* 1997. 62–63.
Duncan, Andrew. "In and Out of Oz." *The Observer* 19 May 1985.
Dunn, Jancee. "Rebel Star, Top Dog." *Rolling Stone* 3 April 1997.
Dutka, Elaine. "Producer Captures a Classic Fugitive." *Calendar* 8 July 1993.
Dziemianowicz, Joe. "Harrison Ford: Enjoying the Ride." *Biography* June 2003.
E! Behind the Scenes: Air Force One. Los Angeles: E! Entertainment Television. 1997.
Ebert, Roger. "Hollywood Homicide." *Chicago Sun Times* 13 June 2003.
_____. "*Mosquito Coast.*" *Chicago Sun-Times* 19 Dec. 1986.
_____. *St. Paul Sunday Pioneer Press* 27 June 1982.
"The Empire Strikes Back." *Variety* 14 May 1980.
The Empire Strikes Back Presskit. Beverly Hills: 20th Century–Fox Films, 1980.
Entertainment Weekly 28 Dec 1990.
_____ 20 Aug. 1993.
Epstein, Andrew. "Melissa Mathison: The Hands of *E.T.*" *Los Angeles Times* 24 July 1982.
Etherington, Jan. *Prevue* 16 Nov. 1978.
Eyman, Scott. "The Swat Team." *Moviegoer* Dec. 1986.

Falcone, David. "Ford & Sarandon Have a Pudding Pot in Their Future." *Boston Herald* 30 Jan. 1996.
Falk, Quentin. "Trapped in a Web of Murder." *Flicks* Oct. 1990.
Family Weekly 2 Aug. 1981.
Fantazone II.
Fay, Stephen. "Harrison Ford Delivers the Groceries." 1985.
"50 Most Beautiful People in the World." *People* May 1997.
Film '93 20 Sept. 1993.
Film 87. Harrison Ford interviewed by Barry Norman. 27 Jan. 1987.
Fineman, Howard. "Last Action President." *Newsweek* 21 July 1997: 67.
Fisher, Ian. "Devil of a Shoot." *Providence Journal-Bulletin* 1996.
Fitzpatrick, Kevin. "*American Graffiti*: George Lucas' First Blockbuster." *Star Wars Insider* Issue #30: 45–46.
Fleming, Michael. "*Air Force One*." *Daily Variety* 9 Jan. 1996.
_____. "*Playboy* Interview: Harrison Ford." *Playboy* Aug. 2002: 60.
"*Flintstones* Bring in the Yabba-Dabba Dough." *Boston Globe* 30 May 1994.
"Ford Changes Pace in *Witness*." *Norwalk Hour* (CT) 14 Feb. 1985.
Ford, Harrison. Interview. Amazon.com interview to promote *What Lies Beneath*. 2000.
_____. Interview. *Deauville Film Festival press conference*. 8 Sept. 2000.
_____. Interview. *Film 2002*. London: BBC1. 21 Oct. 2002.
_____. Interview by Charles Champlin on Film Scene.
_____. Interview. *Flicks with Patrick Stoner*. WHYY-TV. Philadelphia. July 1997.
_____. Interview. *Good Morning America*. ABC. New York. 23 May 1989.
_____. Interview. *Harrison Ford: The Last Crusade*. MTV.
_____. Interview. *Larry King Live!* CNN. New York. 26 July 1997.
_____. Interview. *Larry King Live!* CNN. New York. 21 Dec. 1995.
_____. Interview. *Late Night with David Letterman*. CBS. New York. 22 June 1982.
_____. Interview. *The Little Picture Show*. United Kingdom. 24 Sept. 1993.
_____. Interview. *Mr. Showbiz.com*. 23 July 1997.
_____. Interview. *Movietime* interview with Greg Kinnear Dec. 1988.
_____. Interview. *The Mike Douglas Show* 30 March 1979.
_____. Interview. *The Today Show*. NBC. New York. 15 May 1984.
_____. Interview. *The Today Show*. NBC. New York. 25 Feb 1988.
_____. Interview. *The Today Show*. NBC. New York. 25 May 1993.
_____. Interview. *Tonight Show with Jay Leno*. NBC. New York. 3 Aug. 1994.
_____. "Realizing the Dream: A Promise Kept." *AOPA Pilot Magazine* June 1998.
"Ford, Mathison Protect More Snake Property." *Jackson Hole News* 5 Jan. 1994.
Frankel, Martha. "Golden Boy." *Movieline* Dec. 1995: 64.
_____. "Mr. Lucky." *Movies USA* May 1992.
Frantic Presskit. Los Angeles: Warner Bros., 1987.
Freeman, Paul. "Talking After Hours with the Working Girl's Man ... Harrison Ford," *Prevue* Dec./March 1989.
Fretts, Bruce. "After Surviving One Clash with Tom Clancy, Harrison Ford and the *Patriot Games* Team Head Back Into the Danger Zone." *Entertainment Weekly* 19 Aug. 1994: 23.
"Fugitive Heartthrob Ford: When I'm On the Run I Always Take My Wife." *Star* 24 Aug. 1993.
The Fugitive Presskit. Hollywood: Warner Bros., 1993.
"Furthermore." *People* 16 June 1980.
Gable, Donna. "*Fugitive* from Her Sisters." *USA Today* 26 Aug. 1993: 3D.
Gabriel, Trip. "Facing His Biggest Risk of All: Romantic Comedy." *New York Times* 14 Dec. 1995.
Galbraityh, Jane. "Clear and Present Hardware." *New York Newsday* 8 Aug. 1994.
Garner, Jack. "*Indiana Jones* Opens with Ford and Connery." *Rochester Democrat and Chronicle* 21 May 1989.
_____. "Out West with Indy as a Teen-Age Adventurer." *Rochester Democrat and Chronicle* 28 May 1989.
_____. "Tackling the Great Billy Wilder." *Rochester Democrat and Chronicle*
Germain, David. "Harrison Ford Plays with Tough Guy Image." *Associated Press* 11 June 2003.
Germain, David. "*K-19: The Widowmaker*." *Associated Press* July 2002.
"George Lucas." *Lucasfilm Fan Club Magazine* Winter 1989.
Giles, Jeff. "Cool. Excellent. Thanks." *Newsweek* 3 Feb. 1997: 51.
Goodwin, Jan. *New Idea*.

Goodwin, Jane. *The Face* 1982.
Green, Tom. "Not-So-Driven Harrison Ford." *USA Today* 5 June 1992.
Gregg, Clark. Interview. WGA.org online. 2000.
Griffin, Nancy. "I, Spy." *Premiere* June 1992.
_____. "Manchild in the Promised Land." *Premiere* June 1989.
_____. "Shot by Shot." *Premiere* June 1992: 79.
Grimes, William. "Harrison Ford's Fashion Statement." *Elle* 1995: 103.
_____. "Things That Go BLAM! KA-CHUNG! in the Night." *New York Times* 29 June 1994.
Gristwood, Sarah. *Daily Telegraph* 9 Oct. 1993.
Grobel, Lawrence. "Off Camera: Actor Harrison Ford." *Playboy* Sept. 1993.
_____. "Off the Beaten Path." *Movieline* July 1997.
Haddad-Garcia, George. *Movie Star* 1982.
_____. *Photoplay* May 1982.
Hall, Carla. "The Old Ford, Back in Action." *Washington Post* 5 June 1992.
_____. "Witness in the Amish Land." *Washington Post* 8 Feb. 1985.
Harmetz, Aljean. "*Shining* and *Empire* Set Records." *New York Times* 28 May 1980.
"Harrison Ford Fights for New Film." Mr. Showbiz.com online article. 9 May 1997.
"Harrison Ford's Last Crusade." *Fantazone II* Summer 1989.
Hart, Hugh. "Harrison Ford Lightens Up (A Little)." *Boston Sunday Globe* 8 June 2000.
Hasty Pudding Theatricals 148 Man of the Year Presskit. Cambridge: Harvard University. 1996.
Healy, Michael. "Ambition Put Harrison Ford in an Odd Role." *Denver Post* 14 Dec. 1986.
Hearty, Kitty Bowe. "Born to Run." *Premiere* Sept. 1993.
Hellicar, Michael. "The £100m Hermit of Snake Ridge." *Daily Star* 23 Sept. 1993.
Hensley, Dennis. "On the Brink." *Movieline* Nov. 1995: 46.
Heuring, David. "*Indiana Jones and the Last Crusade*." *American Cinematographer* June 1989.
Higgins, Bill. "Harrison Ford Makes the Party." *Los Angeles Times* 5 Aug. 1994
Hirschhorn, Clive. *Sunday Express* 20 Sept. 1981.
Hoban, Phoebe. "Court and Spark." *Premiere* Aug. 1990.
Hobson, Louis B. "Acting Enigma." *Calgary Sun* 17 July 2000.
_____. "Brad's Unbeatable." *Calgary Sun* 16 March 1997.
_____. "Harrison Ford's Solo Career." *Calgary Sun* 16 March 1997.
Hochman, David. "The Plane and Simple Truth." *Entertainment Weekly* 1 Aug. 1997: 24.
Hollywood Homicide Presskit. Columbia Pictures 2003: 2.
"Hollywood 100 Most…" *Movieline* Nov. 2000.
Honeycutt, Kirk. "Harrison Ford on Harrison Ford." *L.A. Daily News* 26 Nov. 1986.
_____. "K-19: The Widowmaker." *Hollywood Reporter* 15 July 2002.
Hunter, Allan. *Films and Filming* Feb. 1987.
Immergut, Scott, and Kim Masters. "Premiere's Ultimate Summer Preview." *Premiere* June 1989.
In Touch 28 July 2003.
"Indiana Jones and the Last Crusade." *Variety* 7–13 June 1989.
Indiana Jones and the Last Crusade Presskit. Los Angeles: Paramount Pictures, CA. 1989: 5.
"Isaiah Washington Follows Harrison Ford's Lead in New Movie." *Associated Press* 2 Feb. 2003.
Jagger, Bianca, and Andy Warhol. "Steven Spielberg." *Interview* July 1982.
Janusonis, Michael. "'Hearts' Needs a Pacemaker." *Providence Journal-Bulletin* 8 Oct. 1999.
_____. "A Thrilling, Chilling Terrifying Ride." *Providence Journal-Bulletin* 21 July 2000.
Jay, Carr. "Ford Flies at Fun." *[Sydney] Sunday Telegraph* 28 June 1998.
Johnson, Brian D. "The Reluctant Star." *Maclean's* 15 July 1991.
_____. "Working Girl." *Maclean's* 19 Dec. 1988: 52.
K-19: The Widowmaker Presskit. Hollywood: Paramount Pictures. 2002: 4.
Kamps, Louisa. "Deconstructing Harrison." *Elle* July 1998.
Kansas City Star 21 June 1981.
Kantrowitz, Barbara. "A Star Minus Vehicle." *Philadelphia Inquirer* 30 June 1981.
Kaplan, James. "Harrison Ford's Natural Drive." *Vanity Fair* Aug. 1990.
Keets, Heather. "The First Fugitive." *Entertainment Weekly* 9 July 1993.
Kehr, Dave. "Clancy's *Danger* Is No Killer in the Thriller Department." *New York Post* 3 Aug. 1994.
Keller, Julie. "No Love for *Random Hearts*." E! Online 23 Oct. 1999.
Kennedy, Colin. "…And Beneath Lies, the Truth." *Empire* Nov. 2000.
Keough, Peter. "Scott Free?" *Boston Phoenix* 27 July 1990.
Kilday, Gregg. "Dangerous Games." *Entertainment Weekly* 12 June 1992.
_____. "Getting Tanked." *Entertainment Weekly* 12 June 1992.

_____. "Regarding Harrison." *Entertainment Weekly* 12 June 1992.
Kilmuska, Ed. "Actor Harrison Ford, *Witness* Star, Aids Farm Preserve Effort." *Lancaster New Era* 9 April 1990.
King, Larry. "Trump, Ford, Foster: In Love with Work." *USA Today* 28 July 1997.
Kirkland, Bruce. "*Devil's Advocate.*" *Toronto Sun* 23 March 1997.
_____. "Han Solo Makes Him Blush." *Toronto Sun* 17 March 1997.
Koltnow, Barry. "Ford Sees Jones as Ordinary Guy." *Providence Journal-Bulletin* 24 May 1989.
_____. "Fugitive from Stardom." *Orange County Register* 6 Aug. 1993.
_____. "Harrison Ford Jumps at the Chance to Play an Attorney Again in *Henry*." *Dallas Morning News* 14 July 1991.
_____. "Indiana Jones Is Back, but Don't Call Him a Hero." *Anderson Independent Mail* 26 May 1989.
_____. "Kristin Scott Thomas Keeps Her Distance." *Providence Journal-Bulletin* 8 Oct. 1999.
Kronke, David. "Catching Up With Harrison Ford." *Dallas Morning News* 7 Aug. 1993.
_____. "A Clear and Present Actor." *Daily Variety* 4 March 1994.
"The Lady Vanishes." *Newsweek* 7 March 1988.
"Land Trust Names Ford to Board." *Jackson Hole Daily* 26 Nov. 1991.
LaSalle, Mick. "Grit and Wit: Ford, Hartnett and Odd Pair of Detectives in a Decaying Hollywood in *Homicide*." *San Francisco Chronicle* 13 June 2003.
Lawson, Terry. "A Star in Reserve." *Dayton Daily News and Journal Herald* 14 Dec. 1986.
Lazar, Jerry. "An American Classic." *US* 20 Aug. 1990.
Lee, Alana. "Harrison Ford: *Hollywood Homicide*." *BBCi Films* 20 Aug. 2003.
Lee, Nora. "*Mosquito Coast*: A Jungle Utopia Gone Awry." *American Cinematographer* Feb. 1987.
Lennon, Rosemarie. "Revealed! Harrison Ford Is a Hush-Hush Grandpa." *Star* Aug. 1997: 22.
Leydon, Joe. "Harrison Ford Cultivates His Privacy as Carefully as He Picks Film Roles." *Providence Journal-Bulletin*
Loewenstein, Lael. "The Buddy Factor." *New York Daily News* 8 June 2003.
Loud, Lance, Kristian Hoffman, and Paul M. Sammon, "*Blade Runner*." *Details* Oct. 1982.
Lumenick, Lou. "Reel Scary Movie—*Beneath* Uses All the Tricks." *New York Post* 21 July 2000.
Lurie, Rod. "Family, Fame and Harrison Ford." *OK!* Issue 19 1994: 51.
Lynch, Lorrie. "To Me, Success Is a Choice." *USA Weekend* 12–14 June 1998: 5.
MacDonald, Addison. "*Hollywood Homicide*." *Premiere* 2003.
Madsen, Dan. "Irvin Kershner: Remembering *The Empire Strikes Back*." *The Lucasfilm Fan Club*, #11 Spring, 1990: 4.
_____. "Steven Spielberg." *Lucasfilm Fan Club Magazine* Summer 1989: 3–4.
_____. "The Villains of *The Last Crusade*." *Lucasfilm Fan Club Magazine* Winter 1989: 5.
Malkiewicz, Kris. "Camera Becomes Storyteller for *Frantic*." *American Cinematographer* June 1988.
Malkin, Mark S. "The Devil, You Say." *Premiere* May 1997: 52.
Mann, Roderick. "*Mosquito* Star Bitten by Fan Bug." *Los Angeles Times* 18 Oct. 1986.
Mansfield, Stephanie. "Harrison Hams It Up." *GQ* June 1994.
"Marathon Man." *Entertainment Weekly* 20 Aug. 1993.
Mark, Lois Alter. "Run-down Neighborhood." *Entertainment Weekly* 10 Sept. 1993.
Marx, Andy. "Savoy Pix Develops on Cash-Cushioned Curve." *Variety* 18 Oct. 1993.
Maslin, Janet. "At the Movies." *New York Times* 8 Feb. 1985: C12.
_____. "A Couple of Strangers in Paradise." *New York Times* 12 June 1998.
_____. "Film: Robots Return in *Empire Strikes*." *New York Times* May 1980.
_____. "Thrown Together by a Twist of Fate." *New York Times* 8 Oct. 1999.
_____. "Wake Up, Sergeant. There's a Terrorist in Your Basement." *New York Times* 26 March 1997: C21.
Master, Kim, and John H. Richardson. "The Ultimate Movie Guide." *Premiere* June 1990.
Mawson, Dave. "Harrison Ford: Just Like Han Solo or Indy, This Actor Is Nobody's Sidekick." *Leisure* 11 Dec. 1988.
Maychick, Diana. "*Witness* Draws Fire from the Amish." *New York Post* 1985.
McBride, Joseph. "Patriot Games." *Variety* 8 June 1992.
McBride, Stewart. "Rebel Without Pause." *Premiere* March 1988.
McCanny, Roy A. "Laguna Playhouse Performances Superb." *McCanny's Notes* 6 March 1965.
McCarthy, Todd. "*Devil* Punctuates Moral Issue." *Variety* 24 March 1997.
_____. "*Random Hearts*." *Variety* 4–10 Oct. 1999.
McGrady, Mike. "Harrison Ford Wins Star Wars." *Providence Journal-Bulletin* 19 Dec. 1986.
Michael, Dennis. "'Patriot Games' Goes Deep Into the CIA." *CNN Headline News*. CNN. 20 May 1992.

Michael, Dennis. *Showbiz Today* 5 Aug. 1994.
Miller, Edwin. "Harrison Ford: A Very Private Guy." *Seventeen* July 1983.
Miller, Samantha. "Brand New Ford." *People* 23 June 2003: 90.
Milling, Robin. "Harrison Ford." *Inside Hollywood* Nov./Dec. 1991.
Mills, Bart. *Bergen County Record* 1990.
_____. "Harrison Ford: Rugged Romantic." *Biography* Oct. 1999: 94.
_____. "The Quiet American." *For Him* Aug.-Sept. 1990.
Mills, Nancy. "Avoiding the Star Wars." *Elle* Feb. 1988.
Milward, John. "A Private Star." *Philadelphia Inquirer* 30 Nov. 1988.
Milwaukee Journal 15 May 1983.
Minton, Lynn. "Harrison Ford Searches for Wife in Thriller." *Parade Magazine* 7 Feb. 1988.
Mooney, Joshua. *Entertainment News Wire* 16 July 1997.
Morgenstern, Joe. "A Hollow Shell Is *What Lies Beneath* Creepy New Thriller." *Wall Street Journal* 21 July 2000.
Morrison, Mark. "Low-Key Leading Man." *Movies* May 1989.
Morristown Herald News 22 May 1983.
The Mosquito Coast Presskit. Hollywood: Warner Bros. Pictures, 1986.
Moviegoer March 1982.
Murphy, Ryan. "Patriot Missile." *New York Daily News* 31 May 1992.
Musial, Robert. "Movie Picture Moves Slowly." *Detroit Free Press* 4 Aug. 1989.
"New Film Is Not a Failure, Says Ford." *Ananova online* 1 Sept. 2002.
New York Times 20 May 1984.
"No Nostalgia, Thanks." *People* 1997.
"Noyce and Ford Join Tom-Tom Club, Re-Up for Clancy's Danger." *Premiere* Dec. 1994.
O'Neill, Anne-Marie. "Built to Last." *People* 7 Aug. 2000.
O'Neill, Tom. "Harrison Ford." *US* June 1997: 78.
"Of Narrow Misses and Close Calls." *American Cinematographer* Nov. 1981.
Oldenburg, Ann. "A Clear and Present Frost: Ford and Company Find Set of Clancy Thriller a Chiller." *USA Today* 17 Jan. 1994: D4.
"The 100 Dumbest Things Hollywood's Done Lately." *Movieline* May 1996: 70.
Oney, Steve. "Just Another Cowboy." *North Shore* May 1990: 122.
_____. "A Very Ordinary Man." *Premiere* March 1988.
Ottawa Citizen 2 Aug. 1992.
_____ 12 Aug. 1994.
Packer, David. "An Interview with Harrison Ford." *Starlog* Aug. 1980.
Patriot Games Presskit. Hollywood: Paramount Pictures. 1992: 7–8.
Paulsen-Nalle, Amy. "Paris'N'Ford." *US* 22 Feb. 1988.
Pearce, Guy. "Why Harrison's Keeping His Family Top Secret!" *Woman's Own* 21 Sept. 1992.
Pearlman, Cindy. "Dead Reckoning." *Entertainment Weekly* 24 Sept. 1993.
_____. "Ford Stays Focused Despite Hollywood Hardships." *Chicago Sun Times* 8 June 2003.
_____. "Harrison Ford Tough." *Chicago Tribune* 3 Oct. 1999.
_____. "Medical Research." *Entertainment Weekly* 23 April 1993.
_____. "Role Redux." *Entertainment Weekly* 12 Aug. 1993.
Pener, Degen. "Dealing with the Devil." *Entertainment Weekly* 11 April 1997: 34.
Peters, Jenny. "Ford Tough." *Woonsocket Call* 1997.
Phillips, Michelle. "Regarding Harrison." *San Diego Union* 7 July 1991.
Photoplay Feb. 1982.
Pitt, Brad. "The Devil Made Me Do It." *Newsweek* 10 Feb. 1997.
Plaskin, Glenn. "Harrison Ford Nails Down Spot as Movie Hero." *Milwaukee Sentinel* 25 July 1990.
Pond, Steve. "Pleasure Island." *Premiere* July 1998: 44.
Portman, Jamie. "Fugitive Ford Suffers Through More On-the-Job Injuries." *Ottawa Citizen* 6 Aug. 1993.
Powell, Joanna. "Harrison's Passions." *Good Housekeeping* Oct. 1999.
PR Newswire 1 Feb. 1995.
"President Ford Flies High on *Air Force One*." *Premiere* Feb. 1997: 27.
Pye, Michael. "The Reluctant Hero." *Esquire* Sept. 1993.
Rabinovitch, Dina. "Harrison, the Model Ford." *The Independent* 23 Jan. 1988.
Radin, Victoria. "Storm Clouds Over Navarone." *Observer* 29 Jan. 1978.
Rainer, Peter. "Breathtaking." *New York* 21 July 2000.

Rea, Stephen. "Behind the Scenes, *Patriot Games* Navigated Rough Waters." *Philadelphia Enquirer* 14 June 1992.
_____. "Bonnie Bedelia's Big Summer." *Philadelphia Enquirer* 29 July 1990.
_____. "Ford Loves Slapstick — Played by Someone Else." *Philadelphia Enquirer* 17 Dec. 1995.
_____. "Harrison Ford's Trial in a New Kind of Role." *Philadelphia Inquirer* 29 July 1990.
"A Really Big Show." *Entertainment Weekly* 1994.
Rebello, Stephen. "Steven Soderbergh Is So Money." *Movieline* Dec. 2001.
Reed, J. D. "The Sexiest Man Alive '98 ... Harrison Ford." *People* 16 Nov. 1998.
"Regarding Harrison." *Empire* Oct. 1991.
"Regarding Harrison." *News Extra* 19 Nov. 1991.
Regarding Henry Presskit. Hollywood: Paramount Pictures. 1991.
The Register 17 June 1981.
Reich, Holly. "Oh, My Aching Back." *New York Daily News* 5 June 1989.
"Return of the Jedi." *Variety* 18 May 1983.
Return of the Jedi Presskit. Beverly Hills: 20th Century–Fox Pictures, 1983.
Richardson, John H. "Ford Frenzy." *Premiere* Nov. 1991.
Richmond, Peter. "When Julia Gets Blue." *GQ* May 1996: 147.
Rico, Perto. *San Juan Star* 30 April 1982.
Robinson, David. "I, Harrison Ford, Solemnly Declare..." *The Times* 14 Sept. 1994.
Roderick, Mann. "Ford in the Fast Lane." *Los Angeles Times* 6 Sept. 1981.
Roeper, Richard. "Harrison Ford Gives Up His Defenses in Presumed Innocent." *Chicago Sun-Times* 15 July 1990.
Rogues Gallery: Unofficial Harrison Ford fanzine. Issue #4, 1982.
_____. Issue #9, 1983.
_____. Issue #6, 1978.
Roller, Pamela E. "Vic Armstrong: The Other Indy Behind the Bullwhip." *Lucasfilm Fan Club Magazine* #13 1991.
Rosenthal, Lee. "The Empire Talks Back." *Details* Feb. 1997: 143–144.
Rowland, Mark. "Harrison Ford." *Playgirl* Dec. 1983.
"A Run of Good Luck." *Entertainment Weekly* 20 Aug. 1993.
Rush, George, and Joanna Malloy. "*Devil* of a Time." *New York Daily News* 29 March 1996.
Ryan, James. "Harrison Ford Doesn't Run from Work." *Houston Post* 1 Aug. 1993.
Rynning, Roald. "Bathroom Sink Drama." *Film Review* Nov. 2000: 69.
Sabrina Presskit. Hollywood: Paramount Pictures. 1995: 7.
Sales, Nancy Jo. "Shoot Out." *New York* 16 Sept. 1996: 36.
Sandler, Adam. "PGA Honors Neufeld, Rehme." *Daily Variety* 14 Jan. 1994.
Sarris, Andrew. "Surprise! Two Super Films." *Village Voice* 10–16 June 1981: 51.
Schaefer, Stephen. "Fugitive from Publicity." *Boston Herald* 12 Dec. 1995: 43.
_____. "Harrison Ford Bids Farewell to Indiana Jones." *Boston Herald* 21 May 1989.
_____. "Ordinary People." *Entertainment Weekly* 11 Aug. 1995.
_____. "President Ford." *Boston Sunday Herald* 20 July 1997: 41.
_____. "Thanks, but No Thanks, 'Sabrina.'" *US* March 1995.
Schiano, Marina. "The Fugitive Star." *Vanity Fair* July 1993: 127.
Schickel, Richard. "Been There, Seen That." *Time* 15 June 1998
Schneider, Karen S. "Vintage Ford." *People* 4 Aug. 1997.
Schneider, Wolf. "Leading with His Heart." *Blackstone Valley Advocate* 1999.
Schultz, Rick. "Clear Vision." *Boxoffice* July 1994: 19.
Schwarzbaum, Lisa. "Grand Allusion." *Entertainment Weekly* 28 July 2000.
Scott, A. O. "Testosterone Put to a Test." *New York Times* 19 July 2002.
Scott, Vernon. "Scott's World; Talk to My Manager." *Hollywood Reporter* 20 Nov. 1987.
"Screen: Gene Wilder in Aldrich's *The Frisco Kid*." *New York Times* 6 July 1979.
Seiler, Andy. "Pitt, Pakula Found *Devil* Details a Source of Conflict." *USA Today* 26 March 1997.
Shapiro, Marc. "Clear & Present Thriller." *Action Heroes* 1994.
_____. "Indiana Jones Rides Again." *Starlog* May 1989.
_____. "Indiana Jones' Final Adventures." *Starlog* June 1989.
She 1978.
Shephard, Montgomery. "Harrison Ford: The 'Last Real Man' in Hollywood." *Celebrity Plus* Sept. 1989.
"Shy Harrison Ford Builds Solid Career." *Chicago Sun-Times* 3 Feb. 1985.
Siegel, Rochelle. "Presumed Accurate." *Chicago Tribune* 29 July 1990.

Siegler, Bonnie. *Movies USA* Aug. 1990.
Silverman, Jeff. "Harrison Ford Breaks the Mold to Pieces in *Witness*." *Chicago Tribune* 10 Feb. 1985.
_____. "Harrison Ford Takes Off Fedora — and Turns Humble." *L. A. Herald Examiner* 1985.
_____. *Los Angeles Herald Examiner* 27 July 1981.
Simon, John. "*Frantic*." *National Review* 15 April 1987.
Siskel, Gene. "And After 10 Years, Lucas Is Taking a Break." *Chicago Tribune* 15 May 1983.
_____. *Devil's Own* review. *Siskel and Ebert* 29 March 1997.
_____. "Roman Relaxes." *Chicago Tribune* 6 March, 1988.
_____. "A Very Proud Papa." *Chicago Tribune* 14 Dec. 1986.
Six Days, Seven Nights Presskit. Touchstone Pictures. 1998.
Skow, John. "Blazing Bagels." *Time* 30 July 1979.
Slotek, Jim. "Sneer We Go." *Toronto Sun* 8 June 2003.
Sobieraj, Sandra. "Clinton Dishes on *Air Force One*." *Associated Press* 18 July 1997.
Soll, Rick. *Chicago Sun Times* July 1981.
South, John, and Michael Hanrahan. "Harrison Ford in Wild Fling with Mystery Blonde." *National Enquirer* May 1996.
Span, Paula. "*Doom* and Destiny: The Sudden Success of Actress Kate Capshaw." *Washington Post* 20 May 1984: H13.
Spelling, Ian. "Harrison Ford's Last (and Extremely Brief) Crusade." *Starlog* April 1989.
Spencer, John. "Han Solo." *US* 20 June 1983.
Spielberg, Steven. Interview. *Premiere: Inside the Summer Blockbusters.* 3 June 1989.
Spillman, Susan. "An Action-Packed Career Keeps Ford Running. Feats of Film Derring-Do Often Leave Him Limping." *USA Today* 9 Aug. 1993.
Sragow, Michael. "*Raiders of the Lost Ark*: The Ultimate Saturday Matinee." *Rolling Stone* 25 June 1981.
Staggs, Jeffrey. "*Danger* at KenCen Helps AFI." *Washington Times* 28 July 1994.
Stanley, John. "A Deadly Patriot's Game: Harrison Ford in New Suspense Thriller." *San Francisco Chronicle* 31 May 1992.
Stanton, Doug. "The Perfection of Harrison Ford." *Men's Journal* Sept. 1999.
Star 12 June 1984.
Star Blazer Summer 1984.
Stauss, Bob. "Below the Surface." *Los Angeles Daily News* 14 July 2002.
Steranko, James. "Mark Hamill Bids Farewell to the Force in a Final Star-Slamming Interview." *Prevue* Oct. 1983.
_____. *Prevue* July 1982.
Stimac, Elias. "Anne Archer." *Drama-Logue* 4–10 June 1992
_____. "Harrison Ford." *Drama-Logue* 4–10 June 1992.
_____. "Mace Neufeld." *Drama-Logue* 4–10 June 1992.
_____. "Philip Noyce." *Drama-Logue* 4–10 June 1992.
Stivers, Cyndi. "Scions of the Times." *Premiere* Nov. 1995: 73.
Strauss, Bob. "Ford Takes on Job 'One.'" *Boston Globe* 20 July 1997: N12.
_____."Getting a Handle on Harrison Ford." *Los Angeles Herald Examiner* 30 Nov. 1986.
_____. "Harrison Ford Brings Thought to Action Figures." *Providence Journal-Bulletin* 22 Aug. 1993: E5.
_____. "It Took Peter Weir to Make Paul Theroux's *Mosquito Coast* Fly." *Chicago Sun Times* 14 Dec. 1986.
_____. "Workingman's Ford." *Movieline* 9 Dec. 1988.
Stuart, Charles. "A Fugitive from Fame." *Today* 24 Sept. 1993.
"Summer Movie Preview: *Clear and Present Danger*." *Entertainment Weekly* 27 May 1994.
Sunday Express Magazine 14 July 1991.
"Suriname Preserves 10 Percent of Its Tropical Wilderness." *Boston Globe* 17 June 1998.
Susman, Gary. "A Model Ford." *Boston Phoenix* 5 Aug. 1994.
Szymanski, Mike. "Ford Gets Their Motors Running." *First* 11 March 1995: 121.
Teen Bag March 1982.
Terry, Clifford. "What Drives Harrison Ford?" *Chicago Tribune* 22 July 1990.
"Text of Harrison Ford's Letter." *Lancaster New Era* 9 April 1990.
Theroux, Paul. "Author's Review." *Time* 2 Jan. 1987.
_____."Where the Mosquito Bites." *Vanity Fair* Dec. 1986.
Thomas, Bob. "Don't Ask Harrison Ford to Talk About Himself." *St. Louis Post Dispatch* 1990.

_____. "Ford Surprised by Reaction to Latest Film." *Morning Advocate* 3 Jan. 1987.
_____. "'Fugitive' Hides from Limelight." *Delaware County Daily Times* 19 Aug. 1993.
_____. "Star Watch: Despite Stalwart Roles, Ford Is Really Quiet Man." *Associated Press* 28 Feb. 2000.
_____. "Star Watch: Harrison Ford." *Associated Press* 2 March 2000.
Thompson, Anne. "The *Devil* in the Details."
_____. "*The Devil's Own*." *Premiere* 1996.
Thompson, Bob. "Harrison Ford: Not Just Another Playboy." *Sympatico.ca* July 2002.
Thompson, Gary. "Ford's Roles Suit Him to a Tee." *Philadelphia Daily News* 15 Dec. 1995.
Thompson, Malissa. "Talk About a Manhunt." *Premiere* Oct. 1993.
Tibbetts, John C. "For Presumed Innocent Star Harrison Ford, a Strong Performance Depends on Details." *Christian Science Monitor* 30 July 1990.
Topel, Fred. "Harrison Ford Interview: Part One—*Hollywood Homicide* and Acting." *About.com* 2003.
Torgerson, Ellen. "It's History, Art—It's Great." 4 March 1965.
Toronto Star 29 July 1994.
Touchstone Pictures press release. 20 Feb. 1998.
Travers, Peter. "*Blade Runner*." *People* 2 Aug. 1982.
Trescott, Jacqueline. "A Different Ford in Our Future." *Washington Post* 14 July 2002.
Tresniowski, Alex. "New Model Ford." *People* 20 April 1998: 130.
Turan, Kenneth. "*Six Days*, Many Echoes." *Los Angeles Times* 12 June 1998.
Turner, Dylan. "*Regarding Henry*." *Inside Hollywood* July-Aug. 1991.
Usher, Shaun. *Daily Mirror* Oct. 1990.
Variety 22 Sept. 1981.
Variety 30 May–5 June 1994.
Verniere, James. "The Ford Charm." *Boston Herald* 14 Dec. 1986.
Wallace, David. "Screen Gem." *Phillip Morris Magazine* Winter 1991.
Weiner, Rex. "Helping Build a Lasting Career." *Daily Variety* 4 March 1994.
Welkos, Robert W. "Mr. Nice Guy Dives Back Into Action." *Los Angeles Times* 22 March 1992.
"We're Sorry Harrison Ford." *News of the World* 2 Sept. 1990.
White, Randy Wayne. "The Ryan Game." *Premiere* Sept 1994: 60.
What Lies Beneath official website. Dreamworks SKG. 2000.
What Lies Beneath Presskit. Dreamworks. 2000.
Whipp, Glenn. "A Trusting Ford Accepts His Lot." *San Bernardino County Sun* 26 April 2003.
White, Timothy. "Slaves to the Empire; The *Star Wars* Kids Talk." *Rolling Stone* 24 July 1980.
"Why Fatherhood at 44 Scares Indiana Jones." *Daily Mail* 12 Jan. 1987.
"Will the Real Harrison Ford Stand Up?" *Urban Cinefile* 2 Nov. 2000.
Williams, Jeannie. "The Magnetic *Frantic* Star Stays Mellow." *USA Today* 10 March 1988.
_____. "Pollack Keeps Shirt On in Sultry Tale of Adultery." *USA Today* 10 Aug. 1999.
_____. "Sean Connery Bonds with America at his Film Tribute. " *USA Today* 5 May 1997.
Williamson, Bruce. "*Blade Runner*." *Playboy* Sept. 1982.
_____. "*Hanover Street*." *Playboy* June 1979.
Willistein, Paul. "Filming of *Danger* Lives Up to Its Title." *Morning Call* 31 July 1994.
_____. "It Took No Intrigue to Get Ford for CIA Thriller." *Morning Call* 31 May 1992.
_____. "A Remake Not a Copy." *The Morning Call* 15 Dec. 1995.
Wilmington, Michael. "*Devil's Own* Is Troubled by Lack of Emotional Core." *Chicago Tribune* 26 March 1997.
Witness Presskit. Hollywood: Paramount Pictures. 1985: 10.
Wloszczyna, Susan. "The Perils of Giving *Sabrina* a '90s Makeover." *USA Today* 1995: 2D.
_____. "A Well-Piloted Career Pays Off with Power, Privilege." *USA Today* 25 July 1997.
Wolf, Jeanne. "Torrid Scenes in *Innocent* Part of Acting." *Denver Post* 18 July 1990.
Woods, Vicki. "The Ford in Our Future." *Vogue* March 1997.
Woodward, Richard. "Indy Takes Final Bow." *Plain Dealer* 26 May 1989.
Working Girl Presskit. Beverly Hills: 20th Century–Fox Film Corporation, 1988.
Worth, Larry. "The Leading Man Is Built Ford Tough." *New York Post* 1998.
Wuntch, Philip. *Dallas Morning News* 14 Dec. 1986.
_____. "Ford and Gere Step Out of Character." *Dallas Morning News* 14 Dec. 1986
_____. "Harrison Ford: Comfortable with Stardom." *Dallas Morning News* 1989.
_____. "On the Defense." *Dallas Morning News* 26 July 1990.
Yakir, Dan. "American Dreamer." *Empire* 1989.

_____. "An Innocent Man?" *Empire* Sept. 1990.
_____. "Innocence Proves Ambivalence." *Boston Globe* 21 Aug. 1990.
Young, Josh. "Upright & Personal." *George* Aug. 1997: 66.
Zehme, Bill. "Harrison Ford: 20 Questions." *Playboy* March 1988.
Zest 8 May 1988.

INDEX

Abbott, Bud 57
ABC (American Broadcast Corporation) 121, 188, 191
Abele, Robert 48
Above the Law 189
Abrams, Jeffrey 169, 170
Absence of Malice 252
Academy of Motion Picture Arts and Sciences (MPAA) 198, 220, 233, 238
Academy of Science Fiction, Fantasy and Horror Films 284
Addison, VT 258
Adler, Warren 252, 255
"The Adventures of Luke Skywalker as Taken from the Journal of the Whills: Saga One: The Star Wars" 35
Aero Commander (plane) 205
Affair, Kurt 15
Affleck, Ben 261
AFO 237
After Hours 147
Age of Aquarius 251
"Air Force Fun" 239
Air Force One (film) 233–241, 242–243, 244, 247, 251, 260, 282
Air Force One (plane) 233, 236, 237, 238, 239, 241, 243
Alaska 64
Albee, Edward 9
Aldrich, Robert 52, 56, 57, 145, 176
Aldrin, Buzz 210
Aldrin, Lois 210
Alexandre III Bridge (Paris) 217
Alexandria, VA 253
Alien 88
All the President's Men 161, 166
Allen, Karen 79, 81
Allen, Mikki 172, 174
Allen, Woody 42, 252
Allendale, NJ 164
Ally McBeal 3, 270, 273
Almeria, Spain 152
Altman, Robert 252
Amadeus 130

Amarillo, TX 158
Amazon.com 187
Ambergris Caye (Belize) 134
America 159, 188
American Beauty 171, 256
American Cancer Society 278
American Cinema 284
American Film Institute 210, 285
American Graffiti 25, 26–30, 31, 32, 33, 34, 36, 37, 41, 42, 48, 52, 54, 76, 109, 285
American Himalayan Foundation 280
American Museum of Natural History 278
American River 115
American Zeotrope 44
America's Society (building) 217
America's Young Eagles 282
Amish 121, 122, 123, 124, 125, 126, 127
Amos and Andrew 223
Andersen, Hans Christian 284
Anderson, Richard 86
Anderson, Steve 158
Andrews Air Force Base 204
"Android" 88
The Andy Griffith Show 27
Annapolis, MD 184
Annapolis Naval Academy 181
Annie Hall 42
Another World 140
Ansen, David 49, 72
Antonioni, Michelangelo 21
"Anything Goes" 110
Anzevino, Amy 191
AOPA (Aircraft Owners and Pilot's Association) Pilot Magazine 281
Apocalypse Now 43–45, 50, 60, 90, 201
Apocalypse Now Redux 45
Apollo 13 228, 235
Apted, Michael 89
Arafat, Yasser 211
Arbogast, Roy 191
Archaeology Advisory Group

(of Colorado, Alaska, Mississippi, Arizona, North Carolina, New Mexico) 278
Archer, Anne 177, 180, 200, 286
Arches National Park (UT) 157
Arctic Circle 64
Arctic Ocean 264
Ardent, Fanny 217
Argosy 15
Arizona 57, 103
Arkin, Alan 144
Arlington National Cemetery 204
Armstrong, Vic 112, 113, 152, 153, 154
Armuchee, GA 136
Arnold, Alan 65
Arnold, Tom 210
Arthur, Beatrice 62
Artists Rights Foundation 278
As Good As It Gets 215
As the World Turns 140
"Ass-Kicking President" 236
Associated Press 265
Astaire, Fred 285
Atlantic Theater Company 258
Auschwitz 138
Australia 136
Avery Fisher Hall (NY) 241
Aviat Husky (plane) 281
Avis 203
Aykroyd, Dan 115, 284

Babe Ruth League
Baby ... Secret of the Lost Legend 53
Bacall, Lauren 219–220
Bach, Barbara 51
Bains Douches (Paris) 141
Baker, Kenny 37
Baker, Tammy Faye 62
Baldwin, Alec 145, 176, 187, 214, 261
Ballhaus, Michael 147–148, 236, 238, 239, 240, 241
Ballhaus, Sebastian 239
Bally's Hotel (Las Vegas) 208
Baltimore, MD 136
Bambi 5

Band-Aid 185
Bangkok 188
Barish, Keith 188
Barry, John (composer) 54
Barry, John (production designer) 37, 39, 66–67
Bart, Peter 186
Baruch College (NY) 228
Barwood, Hal 41
Baskin, Elya 235
Bass Ale 229
Batman 88
Bay Street Landing (NY) 148
BBC (British Broadcasting Corporation) 269
Bean, Sean 177, 180, 185
Beard Street (NY) 228
Beastie Boys 280
Beatty, Warren 144, 285
Beaumont Gardens (Hampstead, North London) 156
A Beautiful Mind 286
Beckett, Samuel 212
Bedelia, Bonnie 162, 165, 168,
Beech B36TC Bonanza (plane) 281
Behind the Scenes: A Portrait of Pierre Guffroy 284
Bel Air, CA 138
Belfast (Ireland) 225
Belfry Players 10, 11
The Believers 200
Belize 128, 130, 133, 134, 135, 136
Belize City 130, 134, 136
Belize Zoo 279
Bell (helicopter) 253, 279, 281
Bell School (TX) 281
Benedek, Barbara 212, 213
Benedict Canyon, CA 46, 110
Benet, Stephen Vincent 14
Bening, Annette 171, 172
Benson, Sheila 117, 137
Bentsen, Lloyd (U.S. Treasury Secretary) 210
Berenger, Tom 75
Beresford, Bruce 89
Bergen, Candice 20
Bergen, Norway 64
Bergin, Patrick 178–179
Bergman, Alan 220
Bergman, Marilyn 220
Bergstrum, Richard (Prof.) 10
Berkeley (college) 61
Berkeley, CA 136
Berkeley, Xander 235
Bernard, Ian 14
Bernstein, Armyan 116, 233, 242
Bertolucci, Bernardo 93
The Best Years of Our Lives 166
Bettany, Paul 286
Beverly Hills, CA 46, 56, 274
Beverly Hills Cop 117, 130
Beverly Hills Hotel 46
The Beverly Hilton Hotel 208, 286

The Bible 170
Bies, Don 156
Big (film) 138, 170
Big Bear, CA 98
The Big Chill 212
Bigelow, Kathryn 262–263, 264–265, 266
Billington, James H (U.S. Librarian of Congress) 30, 210
Binoche, Juliette 214, 245
Birch, Thora 177, 200
The Birdcage 273
Birmingham, England 81
Birnbaum, Roger 246
Bitter Moon 140
Black Hawk Down 267
The Black Stallion 61
Blade Runner 88–99, 186, 265
Blade Runner: The Director's Cut 186–187
Blades, Ruben 223
Blazing Saddles 56
Blow Up 21
Blown Away 189
"Blue Harvest (Horror Beyond Imagination)" 104–105
Blue Velvet 235
Boam, Jeffrey 150, 151, 157
Bob & Carol & Ted & Alice 20
Body by Jake 113, 154
Body Heat 101
The Bodyguard 163
Boeing Aircraft 36
Boeing 707 233
Boeing 747 238
Bogart, Humphrey 85, 160, 212, 218, 219–220
Bogart, Stephen 219–220
Bogota, Colombia 205
Das Boot 76, 234, 235, 238, 265
Borehamwood, England 102–103
Bosco, Philip 148
Bosnia 251
Boston Globe 271
Boy Scouts of America 281
Boyle, Lara Flynn 273
Boys Don't Cry 266
A Boy's Life 61
Boyum, Steve 185
Brach, Gerard 138, 142
Brackett, Leigh 63, 69
Bradbury Building (L.A.) 93, 94
Bradley, Ed 283
Branagh, Kenneth 174
Brandenstein, Patrizia Von 148
Brando, Marlon 31, 44, 229
Brentwood, CA 269, 273, 277
The Bridge on the River Kwai 51
Bridger Wilderness Act 277
Brief Encounter 255–256
British Academy of Film and Television Arts (BAFTA) 99, 128
British Board of Censors 117

British Broadcasting Corporation (BBC) 35
British Critics' Circle 99
British Honduras (Belize) 130
British Special Air Service (SAS) 178
Broadcast News 148
Broadway 18, 121, 148
Broderick, Matthew 144
Bronx, NY 228
The Brooklyn Bridge 148
Brooks, James 148
Brooks, Mel 56
The Brothers Gross 9
Brown, Garret 112
Browning, Michael 249
Bruel, Patrick 217
Buck Rogers 35
Buckingham Palace 181
Buckley, Betty 140
Buddhism 280
Buffett, Jimmy 134, 283
Bujold, Genevieve 53
Bull Durham 267
Bulloch, Jeremy 68
Bullock, Donna 235
Bullock, Sandra 245
Bullock's (dept. store) 13
Burbank, CA 182
Burbank Studios 57, 91, 93, 166
Burke Institute (NY) 170
Burlington, VT 258
Burr, Ty 271
Burroughs, William S. 88
Burtt, Ben 42, 71, 72, 78, 86, 152
Bush, George (Sr.) 204
Bussell, Darcy 214
Butch Cassidy and the Sundance Kid 54, 158
Buttercup Valley, UT 103
Byrne, Michael 152

C-5A Galaxy (plane) 238
C-130 (plane) 238
C-141 Starlifter (plane) 238
CAA (Creative Artists Agency) 227
Caan, James 20, 24
Cadell, Pat (White House speechwriter) 239
Cagney, James 285
The Caine Mutiny 22
Cairo, Egypt 83
Cali, Columbia 202, 210
California 3, 13, 14, 19, 21, 26, 57, 93, 103, 105, 115, 138, 173, 204, 277
California Culinary Institute 274
California Institution for Men at Chino 138
California National Guard 239
Called Home 119
Calponia harrisonfordi Platnick 285

Index

Cambridge, MA 285
Cameron, James 242, 262, 286
Camp David 52
"Camp Larrabee" 215
Camp Pendleton, CA 203
Canada 64, 210, 264
Canby, Vincent 49, 57, 85, 117
Cannes Film Festival 32, 43, 44
Cannon Group, Inc. 156
Canton, Mark 222, 226, 227
Cape Cod 129
Capital Hill (D.C.) 202
Capri (island) 251
Capri Cinema 172
Capricorn One 55
Capshaw, Kate 110, 112, 114, 116
Caravan Pictures 233
Caribbean 130
Carnal Knowledge 144
Carney, Art 62
The Carolinas (North, South) 258
Carpenter, John 97, 237
carpentry 23–25, 33
Carradine, Keith 133
Carrey, Jim 243, 268, 282
Carrie 34, 140
Carroll farmstead (GA) 136
Carter, Jimmy 52
Cassidy, Joanna 91, 94
Cast Away 258
Catch-22 144
Cats 140
Cazale, Jerry 32
CBS 62, 252
Cecil B. DeMille Award 273
Les Cent et Une Nuits (*The Hundred and One Nights*) 216
Centinela Hospital (LA) 113
Central America 129, 130, 131
Central Park (NY) 228, 277
Central Park West 273, 277
Century City, CA 242
Cerruti, Nino 215–216, 220, 240
CGI (computer generated imagery) 238
Chadwick, Alan 274
Chadwick's (restaurant) 274
Chadwick's Fine Food and Special Events 274
Champlin, Charles 55
Chandler, Jared 203
Chapman, Robert 51
Charlie's Angels: Full Throttle 269, 271
Charlotte, VT 259
Charman, Roy 86
Chechnya 278
Cheers 145
Chelsea, NY 273
Chelsea Piers (NY) 229
Cheoah Dam (NC) 194
Cher 144
Chesapeake Bay, MD 184
Chevrolet 28, 185
Chevrolet Nova 15

Chevrolet Suburban 205
Chicago, IL 5, 27, 164, 191, 194, 196
The Chicago Hilton 196
Chicago Sun Times 271
Chicago Tribune 9, 117, 232
Chilmark, MA 218
China 280
Chinatown (film) 138
Chinatown, LA 30, 110
Chinatown, PA 125
Christian (family) 158
Christian missionaries 131
Christiana, PA 124
Christie's (auction house) 160
CIA (Central Intelligence Agency) 178, 181, 182, 183, 202, 203
Cinema Score 198
Cineplex Odeon (CA) 242
Citizen Kane 201
City Hall (Chicago) 191, 195
City Harvest 278
Civil War (American) 19
Clancy, Tom 176, 177, 178, 180, 200, 201, 203, 207, 211, 261
Clarke, Candy 24, 30, 53
Clarke, Mike 232
Clear and Present Danger (film) 200–211, 215, 283
Clear and Present Danger (novel) 178, 201
Cleveland, OH 166, 239
Cleveland Philharmonic Orchestra 239
The Client 189
Clinton, Bill 218, 235, 236, 243
Clinton, Hillary Rodham 6
Cloisters Museum (NY) 228
Close, Glenn 174, 235
Close Encounters of the Third Kind 50
CNN (Cable News Network) 237
Coal Miner's Daughter 189
Coatepec, Mexico 202
Cobb 189
Coburn, James 16, 24
Cocks, Jay 41
Code of Silence 189
Cohen, David Aaron 224, 226
Colangelo, Matthew 285
The Cold War 262
Coleman, George Churchill 178
Colesberry, Robert F. 228
Colin, Margaret 223
Coliseum (Rome) 155
College Days 8
Colombia 202
The Color of Money 147
The Color Purple 150
Colorado 57
Colorado River 103
Columbia (America's Cup yacht) 13
Columbia Pictures 14, 15–16 17,

18, 19, 20, 51, 55, 56, 112, 222, 224, 228, 233, 236, 252, 270
Columbus, Chris 150
Columbus, OH 238
Combs, Gary 94, 95
Coming Home 129
Committee on Exceptional Films 33
Communism 20
Compass Management 24
Conan the Barbarian 201
Condor (equipment) 218
Conference of Personal Managers 24
The Conformist 93
Congress (U.S.) 207
Connecticut 14
Connery, Sean 52, 151, 152, 153, 155, 156, 158, 159, 160, 177, 222, 241
Conrad, Joseph 43
Conservation International (CI) 265, 278
Conspiracy Theory 242, 243
The Conversation 31–33, 42, 43, 90
Converse All-Stars 186
Cook, Dick 250
Cook County Hospital 191
Cooke, Sam 123
Cooper, Gary 119
Coppola, Eleanor 61
Coppola, Francis Ford 26–27, 30, 31, 32, 33, 43, 44, 45, 50, 60, 61
Corliss, Richard 98
Corrina, Corrina 235
Costa Rica 130
Costner, Kevin 163, 176, 221, 233
Coyote, Peter 75, 253
Crane Hall 11
Creative Artist's Agency (CAA)
Crenna, Richard 219
Crescent City, CA 105, 106
Crewson, Wendy 235, 240, 242
Crimson Tide 89
Crisis in the Hot Zone 187
Crittenden, Diane 34
Cronenweth, Jeff 265
Cronenweth, Jordan 265
Cruise, Tom 120, 214, 244, 252, 282
Cruz, Raymond 203
Cuernavaca, Mexico 202, 206
Culkin, Macaulay 209
Culling, Mike 79
Culver City, CA 203, 255
Culver City Studios 237
Cumbres and Toltec Scenic Railroad (NM) 157
Cure Autism Now Foundation (CAN) 242
Curtis, Tony 16
Curtis-Hall, Vondie 203
Cusack, Joan 148–149

Cushing, Peter 39
Custer, General 134
Cutthroat Island 187
Czerny, Henry 200, 209, 210

Dafoe, Willem 200, 203, 207
Dalai Lama 229, 275
Daley, Richard (Mayor) 191
Daley Plaza (Chicago) 195
Dallas (TV) 188
Dallas, TX 97
Daly, Bob 242
Damn Yankees 11
Dan August 20–21
"Dangerous Days" 88
Dangerous Liasons 187
Daniels, Anthony 37, 106
Dante, Joe 150
Darabont, Frank 286
D'Arbanville, Patti 148
Dark Blue 267
Dark of the Moon 11
Das Boot 76, 234, 235, 238, 265
Daughters of the American Revolution (DAR) State Park (VT) 258
Dave 245
Davidovich, Lolita 171
Davieau, Allen 115
Davies, John Rhys 151
Davis, Andrew 188, 189, 190–191, 194, 195, 196, 197, 198–199
Davis, Warwick 106
DEA (Drug Enforcement Agency) 203, 210
Dead Heat on a Merry-Go-Round 16, 17
DeAlmeida, Joaquim 200, 206, 210
Death Valley, CA 40
Deauville Film Festival 256, 257, 270
Debont, Jan 252
Debt of Honor (novel) 211
Deeley, Michael 88, 89, 90, 91, 95, 97, 98
The Deep 52
The Deer Hunter 30, 88
DeGeneres, Ellen 245, 246
deHaviland Beaver (plane) 249, 250
Dell, Alan 229
DeMille, Cecil B. 185
Democratic party 244
Denby, David 98
De Niro, Robert 229, 241, 245, 285
Denmark 78
Dennehy, Brian 162, 168
Denver, CO 97, 157
DePalma, Brian 33, 34, 41
Department of Commerce Building (D.C.) 253
Department of Defense (U.S.) 203
DeScenna, Linda 99

"Desperation Samba" 134
Detective 140
Detroit, MI 163, 164,
Detroit River 164
The Devil's Own 221–232, 233, 243, 244, 251, 269, 282, 284
Diamonds Are Forever 50
DiCaprio, Leonardo 198
Dick, Philip K. 88, 89, 99
Dickinson, Angie 219
Didion, Joan 24
Die Hard 221, 233
Die Hard 2 167
Dilley, Leslie 86
The Dirty Dozen 56
The Discovery Channel 278
Disneyland 287
"Dive Daddy" 134
Do Androids Dream of Electric Sheep? 88
Do the Right Thing 170
The Doctor 235
Doctor Zhivago 57
Dog Day Afternoon 162
Doges Palace (Venice) 157
The Dogs of War 130
Dolgen, Jonathan 210, 242
Doody, Allison 152, 155, 158, 159
Dooley, Eugene (Detective Capt., Philadelphia PD) 121
The Doors (band) 19, 24
Dosoris Lane (Long Island) 215
Double Jeopardy 189
Douglas, Kirk 57
Douglas, Michael 252, 261
Down, Lesley-Anne 52, 54, 56, 60, 253
Dreamscape 110
Dreamworks SKG 251, 257, 259
Dreyfuss, Richard 24, 27, 29, 53
Driver, Minnie 273
Dryer, David 96–97, 99
Dublin, Ireland 229
Dulles International Airport 204
Dumb and Dumber 268
Dumb and Dumberer: When Harry Met Lloyd 271
Dunne, John Gregory 24
Dupont Circle (D.C.) 253
Dutch (language) 122
Dutton, Charles S. 253
Duval, Robert 32, 44
Dykstra, John 39, 40
"Dykstraflex" 40
Dynasty 22

E! Entertainment Television 214
Earl, Peter 156, 157
Earth 280
Earth and the American Dream 284
Earth Day 279
East Coast (U.S.) 129, 215
East Maine Township High School 6

East Orchard Street (NJ) 164
East Side (NY) 174
East 60th Street heliport 217
Eastern Market (Detroit) 164
Eastwood, Clint 209, 286
Ebel watches 283
Ebert, Roger 137, 271
Edge, Steve 79
Edlund, Richard 40, 86
The Edwardian Room (NY) 172
Eiffel Tower 217
Eight Is Enough 140
1889 Bar and Grill (NY) 228
Eisenhower, Dwight D. 233
Eisner, Michael 75
the El (Chicago subway) 194, 195
El Centro, CA 183
The Elephant Man 101
Elliot, Denholm 151
Ellis, Dave 185
Ellis Island (NY) 142
Elmhurst Hospital (Manhattan) 217
Elstree S.O.S. (Save Our Studios) 156
The Emerald Forest 135
(EMI) Elstree Studios 37, 54, 55, 66, 68, 69, 71, 76, 77, 78, 81, 102–103, 112, 113, 114, 151, 155, 156, 159, 223
Emmy Award 101
The Emperor's New Clothes: An All-Star Illustrated Retelling of the Classic Fairy Tale 284
Empire of the Sun 157
Empire State Building 148
The Empire Strikes Back 40, 63–73, 74, 75, 76, 77, 101, 102, 103, 106, 113, 116, 223
The Empire Strikes Back Special Edition 244
Encino, CA 23
Encino Public Library 23
England 34, 51, 52, 69, 76, 111, 156, 180, 264
The English Patient 253
Ennis-Brown House 93
Enter the Dragon 26
Entertainment Weekly 163, 241, 260
Environmental Media Association 278
Eraserhead 101
Ericson, Julia 278
Erin Brockovich 260
The Escape Artist 61
Escape from New York 97, 237
Escobar, Pablo (drug kingpin) 203
Essex County Courthouse (Newark) 164
E.T. The Extra-Terrestrial 3, 61, 98, 100, 101, 106, 115
Eugene, OR 20
Eureka, California 48

Index

Europe 15, 19, 37, 57, 64, 178
Everly, Don 29
Everly Brothers 29
Executive Decision 237
The Exorcist 26
Eye of the Needle 101
The Eyes of Laura Mars 63
Eyes Wide Shut 252

F/A18 (plane) 203
F-15 (plane) 238
Fail-Safe 233
Fairfax, CA 158
Falk, Peter 18
Family Business 224
Fancher, Hampton 88, 89, 95, 96
The Fantastiks 10
Far East (Asia) 89
Fargo 235
Fatal Attraction 180, 235
FBI (Federal Bureau of Investigation) 203
Fearless 120
Feast of Friends 19–20
Feldman, Edward S. 119, 120, 121, 122
"Female Star of Tomorrow" 220
Fenton, Mike 110
Ferrara, Paul 19
Field, Sally 47, 48
Field of Dreams 221, 251
Fiennes, Ralph 198
Fifth Avenue (NY) 148
The Fifth Element 234
Fiji 258
The Film Society of Lincoln Center 241
Filmways 89
Finland 64
Finse, Norway 64
The Firm 161, 213
First Family 218
First Knight 214
Fisher, Carrie 33, 34, 38, 62, 63, 69, 70, 72, 86, 102, 104, 106, 107, 116, 284, 286
Fisher, Eddie 34
Flash Gordon 35
Fleisher, Richard 24
The Flight Line: The Army Helicopters of Vietnam 278
The Flintstones 160
Flipper 88
Flockhart, Calista 3, 270, 273
"Floridays" 134
"The Flying Cow" 233
The Flying Nun 48
Flynn, Errol 85
Fonda, Henry 151
Fonda, Jane 148
Forbidden Planet 35
Force 10 from Navarone 50–52, 54, 60, 84
Ford, Benjamin 23, 60, 100, 137, 274, 275

Ford, Christopher 5–6, 254–255
Ford, Dorothy 5
Ford, Georgia 274, 275, 285
Ford, Glenn 18–19, 24
Ford, Harrison 3, 5–24, 25, 27, 28–29, 30, 31, 32, 33, 34–35, 37–38, 39, 40, 41, 42, 44–45, 46–49, 50, 51, 52, 53, 54, 55, 56–59, 60–61, 63, 65–66, 69–73, 75, 76, 77–78, 79, 81, 82–84, 85, 86–87, 88, 89–91, 92, 93, 94–96, 97, 98, 99–100, 101, 102, 103, 104–105, 106, 107–108, 109, 110, 111–112, 113, 115–116, 117–118, 119–121, 123, 124–125, 127, 128, 129, 130–133, 134–135, 136–137, 138–140, 142–143, 144–145, 146, 147, 148, 151, 152, 153–154, 155, 156, 158, 159–160, 161–163, 165, 166, 167–168, 169, 170–171, 172, 173–175, 176–177, 179–180, 181183, 184, 185, 186, 187, 188, 189–190, 191, 192, 193–194, 195, 196–197, 198, 199, 200–201, 203, 204, 205, 206–210, 211, 212–213, 214, 215, 216–217, 218, 219–220, 221, 222–223, 224, 225, 226–227, 228–230, 231, 232, 233, 234, 235–236, 237, 238, 239–242, 243–244, 245, 246–249, 250–251, 252, 253, 254–255, 256, 257–258, 260–261, 262, 263, 264, 265–266, 267, 268–269, 270, 271, 272, 273–287
Ford, Harrison (silent screen actor) 15–16
Ford, Harrison J. 16
Ford, John 157
Ford, John William 5
Ford, Malcolm 142, 156, 274, 275, 277
Ford, Michael 86
Ford, Terence 5, 6, 11, 24
Ford, Willard 23, 57, 60, 75, 100, 137, 274, 275
"The Ford Foundation" 24
Ford Tri-Motor 115
Fordes, Williams 166
Forest Stewardship Council 279
Forrest, Frederic 24, 31, 32
Forrest Gump 257
Fort George Hotel 134
Fort Lauderdale, FL 281
Fort Tryon Park (NY) 228
Fort Worth, TX 278, 281
48 HRS 221
Foster, Jodie 34
Four Seasons (NY restaurant) 232
Four Seasons Hotel (Chicago) 196
Fox, Edward 50
Fox, James 177
France 76, 138, 142, 270

The Francis Scott Key Bridge (MD) 253
Frank Murphy Hall of Justice (Detroit) 162
Frankovich, Frank 19
Frantic 138–143, 144, 163, 270
Fraser, Dr. Richard 170
Frasier 140
Frears, Stephen 187
Fred Cuny: The Lost American 278
Free Tibet 277
Freeborn, Stuart 38
Freeman, Paul 81
The Freeway Club (L.A.) 269
The French Connection 31
French Polynesia 247
Friedkin, William 31, 210
Friedman, Rob 210
Friendly Persuasion 119
Friends 246
The Frisco Kid 52, 56–59, 145, 176
From Justin to Kelly 271
From Russia with Love 52
Frontline (PBS) 278
Frost, Tom (attorney) 171
The Fugitive (film) 187, 188–199, 219–220, 227, 276
The Fugitive (TV) 188, 189
Fulton Opera House (PA) 127

Gable, Clark 160
Gaghan, Stephen 260–261, 261
Gallipoli 120
Gangbusters 6
Ganis, Sidney 112, 210
Gargoyles 53
Garland, Judy 160
Garner, James 128
Garr, Teri 24
Gaudix railway station (Spain) 155
Geilo, Norway 64
George (magazine) 241
George, Bill 97
George, Terry 226
Georgia 131
Gerald Durrell Visitor Center (Belize) 279
Gerber, Mitch 229
Gere, Richard 280
Germain, David 265
German (language) 122
Germany 81, 284
Getting Straight 20
Ghost 167
Ghostbusters 117, 245
G.I. Jane 235
Gibbs, George 112, 114, 152, 181
Gibson, Mel 119, 183, 242, 243, 285
Gidget 48
Giler, David 187
Giles, Jeff 230
Gillespie, Kevin 226

Index

Gil's Bar and Restaurant (Newark) 164
Ginsburg, Ruth Bader (U.S. Supreme Court Justice) 210
"Give Graffiti the Brush" 191
Glass, Philip 280
Glen Cove, Long Island 215
Gleneagles Hotel (Scotland) 156
Glory 221
Glover, Danny 121
Glover, Julian 152
God 18, 71, 80
Godard, Jean-Luc 140
The Godfather 30, 31, 32, 43
The Godfather II 61
Godspeed 286
Goldberg, Whoopi 148
Goldcrest 130
Golden Globe (award) 30, 32, 44, 119, 128, 137, 148, 180, 198, 220, 221, 256, 261, 273, 284
Goldfinger 50
Goldsmith, Jerry 242
Goldwyn Studios 33
Gone with the Wind 30, 133
Good Housekeeping 279
The Good Son 235
The Goodbye Girl 53
Goodfellas 280
Goonies 117
Gordon, Barry 14
Gordon, Hillary 131
Gordon, Lawrence 221, 222, 223, 227, 228
Gordon, Rebecca 131
Gore, Al 196
"Gotham City" 88
Gould, Elliot 20
Gower Street (L.A.) 14
Grace, Martin 78
Gracey Rock, Belize 135
The Graduate 144
Graeme Stewart Elementary 6
Gramercy Park (NY) 228, 229
Grammy Awards 223
Granada 155
Grand Canal (Venice) 157
Grand Hotel (Paris) 142
Grand Teton 276
Grant, Cary 66
Graumann's Chinese Theater 269
Great Lakes 8
Great Movie Stunts: "Raiders of the Lost Ark" 83
The Great Smoky Mountains Railway 192
The Green Mile 286
Greene, Graham 133
Greenport, Long Island 229
Greenwich Village (NY) 120, 172
Greenwood, Bruce 271
Gregg, Clark 257
Gregory, Andre 133
Griffith, Melanie 144, 145, 146, 147, 148

The Grifters 171, 187
Grimm, Tim 207
Guatemala 130
Gudonov, Alexander 121
Guffroy, Pierre 141
Guilfoyle, Paul 235, 242
Guinness, Sir Alec 38, 41, 68
Gulfstream G-IV (plane) 281
Gunn, Brendan 225
The Guns of Navarone (film) 50
The Guns of Navarone (novel) 51
Gunsmoke 21, 283

Haas, Lukas 121
Haber, Katherine 92, 96, 98
Hackman, Gene 31–32, 222
Halifax, Nova Scotia 263, 265
Halifax Shipyards 265
Haljum, Bill 8
Hamill, Mark 33, 34, 37, 38, 40, 42, 63, 64, 65, 66, 70, 71, 72, 86, 102, 104, 106, 107
Hamilton, George 18–19
Hamilton, Guy 50, 51, 52
Hamilton Air Force Base (CA) 115
Hamlet (play) 220
Hampton, Tim 141, 142
Hancock Park 202
Hanks, Tom 148, 170, 258, 285
Hannah, Daryl 91, 94, 286
Hanover Street 52, 53–56, 60, 84, 116, 253
Hanover Street (Annapolis Naval Academy) 184
Happy Days 48
Harcourt Brace and Co. 284
Hardanger Plateau, Norway 65
Harlin, Renny 187
Harper, Valerie 24, 83
Harris, David 10
Harris, Ed 228
Harrisburg, PA 123
Harrison, Jim 275
Harrison, Philip 55
"Harrison Ford Memorial Library" 24
"Harry Ford" 8
Hart, Tim 174
Hart Plaza (Detroit) 164
Hartnett, Josh 267, 268, 269, 270, 271, 272
Harvard Law School 223
Harvard University 129
Harwood, Jim 107
Hasty Pudding Men and Women of the Year 285
Hasty Pudding Theatricals (Harvard University) 284–285
Hauer, Rutger 91, 93, 96, 99
Havana (film) 213
Hawaii 74, 84, 130, 134, 250
Hawn, Goldie 148, 280
"The Hazing" 20

Hearn, George 223, 228
Heart of Darkness 43
Heart of the City Award 278
Heartburn 147
Heaven 209
Heaven and Earth 189
Heche, Anne 245, 246, 247, 248, 250
Hedren, Tippi 148
Helland, Roy J. 173
Hellman, Jerome 129, 130, 131, 134
Hendrix, Jimi 52
Henry, Will 20
Henry Forgets 169
Hepburn, Audrey 212, 214, 218
Herman, Miki 36, 105
Heroes 47–49, 51, 54, 55
Herr, Daniel 127
Hershey, Barbara 89
Herts, England 54
Hertz 203
Heston, Charlton 143
High Noon 22, 51
Hill, Walter 187
Historic Preservation Trust of Lancaster County 127
Hitchcock, Alfred 37, 143, 258, 260, 286
Hitler, Adolf 138, 156
Hoffman, Dustin 86, 89, 144, 187, 245, 252, 286
Hogs and Heifers (NY) 229
Holden, William 214
Holiday Inn 28
Holly, Lauren 213, 219
Hollywood, CA 5, 13, 14, 15, 16, 20, 21, 24, 27, 36, 42, 43, 46, 51, 60, 74, 86, 100, 157, 160, 161, 171, 186, 217, 221, 223, 267, 269, 277
Hollywood Boulevard 269
The Hollywood Bowl 46
Hollywood Hills 23
Hollywood Homicide 267–272, 286
The Hollywood Reporter 265
Holocaust 198
Holstein (cow) 275
Honda Motor Company 283
Honduras 130
Hong, James 93
Hong Kong 112
Hope, Bob 285
Hopkins, Bo 27
Horneff, Fran 154
Hostetler, John 126
House of Commons (UK) 156
Howard, Ron 27, 53
Howard Johnson (hotel) 28
Hudson River 279
Huffington, Michael (U.S. Republican Party Rep.) 210
Hugo Award 99
The Hulk 271
The Hunt for Red October

Index

176–177, 178, 184, 201, 206, 211, 261
Hunter College (Brookdale Campus) 228
Hurt, William 128
Husbands and Wives 252
Huston, John 141
Huvane, Kevin 227
Huyck, Willard 26, 41, 109, 110
Hyams, Peter 53, 54, 55, 56
Hyde Park-South Kenwood (IL) 191

I Love Trouble 187
Iberti, Joseph E. 215
Iceland 264
Ile aux Cygnes (Paris) 142
Iliff, W. Peter 177
Illinois 3, 8, 191
Immortal Beloved 234
In the Line of Fire 198, 234
"In the Moonlight" 220
In the Name of the Father 198, 226
Inchicore, Ireland 229
Independence Day (film) 206, 223
Independent (political party) 244
India 110–111
The Indian in the Cupboard 219–220
Indiana Jones and the Last Crusade 150–160, 174, 176
Indiana Jones and the Temple of Doom 86, 109–118 119, 150, 160, 181
"Indiana Jones and the Temple of Roses" 117
"The Indiana Jones Rating" 117
"Indiana Stoltzfus (and the Temple of Tobacco)" 124, 127
Industrial Light and Magic (ILM) 40, 68, 69, 85, 103, 105, 106, 115, 152, 247
Innerspace 150
Integraph (computer) 203
Intercourse, PA 125
Intermedia 264
Internal Affairs (LAPD) 268
International Mark Seven (tank) 153
International Plaza Garage (Detroit) 164
Interview with the Vampire 222, 243
The Intruders 22
IRA (Irish Republican Army) 179–180, 181, 226
Ireland 229, 264
Irma La Douce 139
Irving, Amy 116
Irvington, NY 229
Isham Park (NY) 228
The Italian Job 269

Jackie Stewart's Shooting School 156
Jackie's Bar and Restaurant (Detroit) 164
Jackson, Samuel L. 181, 184
Jackson Hole, WY 161, 191, 193, 235, 275, 276
Jackson Hole Land Trust 276
Jackson Hole Wildlife Film Festival 276
Jackson Land Trust Board of Directors 276
Jamaica 130
James, Brion 91, 94
James Bond 50, 52, 152, 160, 186, 200
Jane Goodall: Reason for Hope 278
Janssen, David 198
Janusonis, Michael 260
Japan 283
Japanese Float Plane (WWII) 247
Jarre, Kevin 221, 222, 224, 225
Jarre, Maurice 125, 133
Jaws 42, 52, 74
Jefferson Airplane 62
Jenkins, George 164, 166
Jennings, Brent 125
Jersey Channel Islands 52
Jesus (Christ) 167, 170, 192
Jewison, Norman 130
JFK (film) 176, 189, 234
Joel, Billy 218
John Brown's Body 14
John Wayne Airport 202
Johnson, Don 148
Johnston, Joe 86, 106
Jones, James Earl 39, 65, 200, 209
Jones, Tommy Lee 89, 189, 190, 198–199, 245
Jordan 157
Josephson, Barry 222, 228
A Journal of the Making of "The Empire Strikes Back" 65
Journey to Shiloh 20
"Judgment" (*Fugitive* episode) 188
Judgment at Neuremburg 22
Judgment: The Court Martial of Lt. William Calley (aka. *The Trial of Lt. Calley*) 22
Julia, Raul 161, 165
Juliett (Soviet submarine class) 262, 263
Julliard School of Music (NY) 120
Junction City, OR 84
The Junior League (Manhattan) 172
Jupiter Award 284
Jurassic Park 247

K-19 (submarine) 262, 263
K-19: The Widowmaker 262–266, 267
Kagan, Jeremy Paul 47, 48
Kahn, Michael 85, 86, 152
Kairouaun, Tunisia 83
Kamen, Robert Mark 227
Kanab, Utah 18
Kane, Bob 88
Kaplan, Michael 92, 96
Kaplan, Rick 174
Kasdan, Lawrence 63, 65, 70, 74, 75, 78, 101, 102
Katsulas, Andrew 190
Katt, William 34
Katz, Gayle 234, 242
Katz, Gloria 26, 41, 109, 110
Kauai, HI 84, 247, 249
Kaufman Astoria Studios 166, 167, 217, 229
Kazanjian, Howard 78, 104, 105, 108
Keaton, Buster 158
Keep Yellowstone Nuclear Free 279
Kellerman, Sally 24
Kelley, William 119, 128
Kelly, Brian 88
Kennedy, John F. 233
Kennedy, John F., Jr. 214, 241
Kennedy, Joseph P. (U.S. Democratic Representative) 210
Kennedy, Kathleen 77, 79
Kennedy, Robert F., Jr. 174
Kennedy, Ted (U.S. Democratic Senator) 210
Kennedy Center (D.C.) 210
Kern, Lis 182, 183
Kershner, Irvin 31, 63, 64, 65, 66, 68, 69, 70, 71, 102, 116
Kidman, Nicole 245
Kievsky Station (Russia) 264
King, John 123
King, Larry 23, 282
King, Pat 229
King, Rodney 186
Kingston Trio 9,
Kinnear, Greg 214–215, 219
Kipu Kai, HI 249
Kirin Beer 283
Kiss of the Spider Woman 128
Klute 161
Knight, Wilf 178
Knode, Charles 92
Kokak Theater (Hollywood) 270
Kopelson, Arnold 188, 196–197, 198, 199
Korman, Harvey 62
Kramer, Stanley 22
Kramer vs. Kramer 44
Kristofferson, Kris 53
Kroll, Jack 143
Kubrick, Stanley 35, 66, 98, 189, 252
Kundun 229

Kung Fu 21, 100, 274
Kurtz, Gary 39, 63
Kurupt 269
Kyle, Christopher 263

La Concepcion, Mexico 202
La Rochelle, France 76
Labor Day 160
Lacey, Ronald 79
Ladd, Alan, Jr. 36, 41, 89, 210
The Ladd Company 89
Lady Diana 117
Laguna Beach, CA 3
Laguna Beach Playhouse 14
Laguna Canyon 13
Lake Winnepeg 264
Lancaster, PA 123, 125
Lancaster Chamber of Commerce 125
Lancaster County (PA) 122, 127
Lancaster Farmland Trust 127
Lancia (car) 283
Landaker, Gregg 86
Landau, Martin 271
Lane, Nathan 284
Lane Community College 20
Langley, VA 181
Lansing, Sherry 210, 212, 214
L.A.P.D. (Hollywood division) 267–268, 269
Las Vegas, NV 209
LaSalle, Mick 271
"The Last Mango in Paris" 134
The Last Shot 273
The Last Temptation of Christ 200
The Last Wave 120
Later with Greg Kinnear 214
Laverne and Shirley 27
Lawrence of Arabia 57
Leach, Wendy 79, 112, 152
Lee, Spike 170, 280
The Legacy 101
The Legend of the Lone Ranger 82
Legends of the Fall 214, 221
LeMatt, Paul 27–28, 53
Lemmon, Jack 18
Leno, Jay 283
Leonard, Elmore 109
Leonard, Terry 82, 191, 192
Levinson, Barry 224
Lexington Ave. (Manhattan) 172
Liar, Liar 243
Library of Congress 30, 187
Lifetime Achievement Award (Academy of Science Fiction, Fantasy and Horror Films) 284
Lifetime Achievement Award (American Film Institute) 285
Lighthouse Reef (Belize) 134
Lincoln, Abraham 8, 242
Lincoln Memorial 253

Little Mary Sunshine 11
The Little Princess 235
Live and Let Die 50
Lloyd, Harold 158
Local 287 (Harrisburg, PA) 123
Lockheed C-118 233
Lombardi, Joe 205
Lombardi, Paul 205
Loncraine, Richard 286
London, Barry 210
London, England 35, 37, 38, 54, 60, 66, 69, 90, 91, 103, 181
Long, Shelly 145
Long House Ruin 157
Long Island, NY 218
Long Island Sound 215
The Long Ride Home (aka. *A Time for Killing*) 18–19, 20
The Longest Yard 56
Los Alamos Reserve Center 203
Los Angeles, CA 3, 13, 14, 19, 93, 98, 100, 113, 148, 172, 186, 198, 202, 203, 204, 210, 219, 228, 237, 267, 269, 270, 273, 274, 275, 281
Los Angeles Film Critics Award 99
Los Angeles International Airport (LAX) 16, 202, 239
The Los Angeles Lakers 130, 270
Los Angeles Police Academy 268
Los Angeles Times 46, 55, 61, 117, 137, 250
Los Feliz, CA 93
Los Ranchos Clinic (LA) 170
The Lost World 243
Lost Worlds: Life in the Balance 278
The Louvre Pyramid 217
Love, American Style 21
"Love and the Former Marriage" 21
Love Story 189
Love Thy Neighbor 121
Loving 63
Lucas, George 25, 26–27, 28, 29, 30, 31, 33, 34, 35, 36, 37, 38, 39, 40, 41, 42, 43, 45, 46, 50, 52, 53, 62, 63, 69, 70, 71, 74, 75, 76, 83, 101, 102, 106, 107, 108, 109, 115, 129, 150, 151, 152, 157, 160, 186, 191, 208, 241, 244, 256, 286
Lucas, Marcia 40, 74
Lucasfilm (Ltd.) 39, 67, 75, 76, 77, 103, 104, 106, 111, 152, 153, 156
Luedtke, David 252
Lumenick, Lou 260
Lunar Embassy 277
Lupone, Patti 121
Luv 18
Lynch, David 101, 235
Lyne, Adrian 89

Macao (Portugal) 112
Macgregor-Scott, Peter 191, 192, 194, 195, 199
MacInnes, Angus 121
MacLean, Allistair 51
Macy, William H. 235, 240, 244
Madame Tussaud's (wax museum) 287
Madonna 284
Magnolia 258
Magnum Force 26
Magnum P.I. 75
Magnuson, Ann 202, 210
Mahal, Taj 249
Maharaja 111
Mahoney, John 140
Main Street (Vineyard Haven) 218
Malibu, CA 15, 75
Malkovich, John 198
Malta 52
Mamet, David 258
Mammoth Mountain, CA 115
The Man with the Golden Gun 50
Manatee Bar (Belize) 136
Mancuso, Frank (Paramount Motion Picture Group President) 116
Manhattan (NY) 145, 148, 152, 164, 166, 172, 217, 232, 254
Manhattan Surrogate Court 172
Mann, Cliff 115
Mann, Pamela 80
Mann's Chinese Theater 186, 284
Mansfield, OH 239
Mansfield Reformatory (OH) 239
Manson, Charles 138
Manzarek, Ray 24
Marcos, Ferdinand 44
Mardie Murie: Arctic Dance 277
Margaret, Ann 144
Marin County, CA 115
Marineland Park (CA) 184
Mariner II 134
Mark, Lawrence 148
Marlowe, Andrew W. 233, 236
Marlowe, Phillip 91
Marquadt, Mary Louise 3, 10, 11, 12, 13, 55, 60
Marquand, Richard 101–102, 103, 107
Married to the Mob 235
Marsh, Terrence 57, 202, 206
Marshall, Frank 75, 76, 80, 81, 83, 109, 112, 114, 115, 155, 157, 158
Marshall, Penny 138, 148
Martha's Vineyard, MA 218
Martin, Dale 184
Martin, Quinn 188
Martin, Steve 148, 268
Maryland 184, 253
Maryland Avenue (Annapolis Naval Academy) 184

Index

M*A*S*H* 20
Maslin, Janet 72, 232, 250
Maslow, Steve 86
Massachusetts 136, 218
Master and Commander: The Far Side of the World 120
Matheson, Tim 75
Mathison, Dirk 61
Mathison, Melissa 3, 60, 61, 70, 75, 83, 97, 98, 100–101, 110, 113, 134, 138, 139, 142, 148, 156, 168, 174, 196, 217, 219–220, 229, 273, 275, 276, 280, 284
Mathison, Richard 61
The Matrix: Reloaded 271
Matthews, Liesel 235
Maugham, Somerset 133
Mauna Kea Hotel (HI) 74
Mawr, Bryn 147
Maxwell St. (Chicago) 195
May, Elaine 18
Mayan temple 135
Mayhew, Peter 38
McAlister, Mike 114, 156
McBride, Joseph 186
McCann, Roy (*McCanny's Notes*) 14
McCarthy, Todd 232, 255–256
McDowell, Andie 245
McGillis, Kelly 120, 122, 127, 128
McGrath, Earl 19
McInnes, Angus 50
McKinsey, Jim 191
McQuarrie, Ralph 36
McQueen, Butterfly 133
McQueeney, Patricia 24–25, 49, 131, 242, 243–244, 261
Mean Streets 26
"Mechanismo" 88
Medal of Freedom 277
Medellin, Columbia 203
Memorial Day 116, 160
Men in Black 189, 243
Mendes, Sergio 23–24
Menemsha Harbor (MA) 218
Mennonite 123, 124, 126
Mequon, Wisconsin 11
Merrill Lynch 72
Mesa Verde National Park 157
Metropolitan Museum of Art 172
Metropolitan Police (England) 178
Mexican Revolution 206
Mexico 105, 130, 202, 204
Mexico City, Mexico 202
Meyer, Ron 210
Meyjes, Menno 150
MGM Studios 155, 197
Miami, FL 134, 253
Michener, James 22
Middlebury, VT 259
Middlesex 52
Midnight Cowboy 19, 129

A Midsummer Night's Dream 273
The Milagro Beanfield War 223
Military Honor Guard (U.S.) 204
Milius, John 43, 44, 201, 207, 210
Millbrook, NY 172
The Millbrook School (NY) 172
Millson, John 164
Milwaukee, Wisconsin 11
Mini Cooper 269
Minority Report 252
Mirren, Helen 131, 133
Mississippi Burning 228
Missouri 48, 110, 225
Mistress of the Seas 187
Mitchell, Andrew 156
Mitchum, Robert 89
Mo' Better Blues 170, 223
Moab, Utah 157
Moffatt, Donald 200, 203–204
Mojave Desert 183
Mojocar, Spain 154
Molina, Alfred 77
Molitto, Sebastian 206
Monmarte 217
Montclair, NJ 229
Monument Valley (UT) 157
the Moon 277
Moonstruck 140
Moore, Julianne 190
Moore, Mickey 81, 82, 112
More American Graffiti 52–53
Morgan, J. Pierpont 215
Morgan, Louise C. 215
Morocco 'Round the Clock 285
Morris, Brian 215
Morrison, Jim 19
The Moscow Bolshoi Ballet 121
Moscow on the Hudson 235
The Mosquito Coast (film) 120, 128, 129–137, 158, 260, 273, 279
The Mosquito Coast (novel) 129
Most Favored Nation (status) 280
"Most Unexpectedly Believable Psychopath" 260
Motion Picture Association of America (MPAA) 117
Motion Picture Showmanship Award 208
Moulin Rouge 139
Mount, Thom 139, 140, 142, 143
Mt. Rushmore 160
Movieline 224, 241, 260, 261
Mrs. Doubtfire 235
M.S. Meltzer Junior High 6
MTV Movie Awards 270
The Mug 8–9
Mulligan, Robert 89
Murch, Walter 44
Murie, Mardy 277
Murie, Olaus 277
Murietta Coffee Factory (Mexico) 206

Murphy's Law 221
Musante, Tony 22
Museum of Natural History 277
Musselman, Alan 127
Mustang: The Hidden Kingdom 278
My Friend Tony 20

National Association of Film Critics 30
National Association of Stuntmen 7
National Board of Review 33
National Coalition of Television Violence (NCTV) 117
National Committee for Amish Religious Freedom (NCARF) 126
National Film Preservation Act 30, 33, 42
National Film Registry 33, 86
National Geographic Films 264
National Guard 20
National Head Injury Foundation 174
The National Inquirer 230
National Organization of Disability (N.O.D.) 278
National Review 143
National Security Advisor (U.S.) 203
National Vietnam War Museum 278
Native Americans (Navajo, Cherokee, Papago, Hopi, Apache) 57, 157, 194
NATO (National Association of Theater Owners)/ShoWest 208, 220, 284
Natural Born Killers 189
Naval Intelligence 178
NBC (National Broadcasting Corporation) 214
Near Dark 262
Needham, Louis and Brorby 6
Needleman, Harrison 3
Neeson, Liam 198, 262, 265, 284
Nellis Air Force Base 203
Nemec, Joseph II 182, 184
Nero, Franco 50
Neufeld, Mace 57, 176–177, 178, 179, 181, 183, 184, 185, 186, 200, 202, 203, 204, 205, 207, 208, 209, 210, 211, 275
New Brighton, NY 148
New England 129, 130, 258, 259, 273
New Jack City 170
New Mexico 157
New York 3, 19, 79, 92, 106, 110, 147, 166, 172, 173, 174, 218, 219, 222, 223, 227, 228, 229, 232, 234, 253, 254, 265, 273, 277, 278, 284

New York (magazine) 98, 260
New York City Police Department (NYPD) 226
The New York Daily News 271
New York Film Critics Association 30
The New York Post 260
New York Public Library 172
New York Superior Court 162
The New York Times 49, 57, 72, 85, 117, 134, 161, 201, 232, 250, 265
Newark, NJ 164
Newark City Hall 164
Newman, Paul 11, 54, 158, 285
News of the World 174
Newsweek 49, 61, 72, 143, 230
Nicholl Fellowship in Screenwriting (award) 233
Nichols, Mike 144, 145–147, 148, 149, 169–170, 171, 172, 174, 175, 197, 236, 286
Nicholson, Bruce 86
Nicholson, Jack 128, 130, 138, 144, 215, 286
Nicita, Wallis 246
Night of the Iguana 11
Night Ride Down 176
NIKA (Russian award) 235
The Ninth Gate 140
"Nirvana Now" 44
Niven, David 50
Nixon, Richard 26, 32
No Knife 56, 57
No Way Out 176
Nobel Peace Prize 43
Noble, Thom 128, 133
"Nobody Speaks to the Captain No More" 134
Nolte, Nick 34
Nordic Track 281
North, Oliver 204
North America 211, 223, 256, 257, 260, 270, 285
North Atlantic Ocean 265
North Carolina 191
North Reformed Church (Newark) 164
North Wilcox Avenue (L.A.) 269
Northpoint Theater (San Francisco) 41
Northwestern (University) 190
Norton, B.W.L. 53
Norway 64, 66
Norwegian Air Force 65
Nourse, Alan E. 88
Noyce, Phillip 177, 178, 179, 180, 181, 182, 183, 184–185, 200, 201, 202, 203, 205, 206, 207, 209, 210, 261
Nunn, Bill 170, 171, 174
Nunn, Terri 34

The Oak Room 172
Oakland, CA 274

Obradors, Jacqueline 246
Ocean's 11 269
O'Donnell, Rosie 284
Ohio National Guard 239
Old Faithful Visitor Education Center 279
Old Town Bar (NY) 228
Oldman, Gary 234, 235, 239, 240
Oldsmobile 283
Olin, Lena 271–272
Oliveira, Alex 229
Oliver 121
Olmos, Edward James 91
On Golden Pond 85, 151
"The 100 Dumbest Things Hollywood's Done Lately" 224
101 Dalmatians 235
One Life to Live 140
O'Neill, Dick 133
The Optimo Store (Manhattan) 172
Orange County, CA 202, 277
Oregon 185
Orlando, FL 254
Orly Airport (Paris) 139
Ormond, Julia 214, 215, 216, 217, 219–220, 260
Oscar Hammerstein 29
Oscars (Academy Awards) 30, 31, 32, 40, 42, 44, 53, 61, 66, 72, 86, 88, 99, 106, 117, 119, 127, 128, 129, 130, 133, 147, 148–149 162, 171, 180, 181, 198, 201, 202, 210–211, 212, 220, 221, 223, 228, 235, 238, 245, 253, 257, 258, 270, 284
Oslo, Norway 64
O'Steen, Sam 147, 171, 173
The Other Side of the Mountain 119
Otter Creek Falls (VT) 259
Ouija Board 260
Out of Africa 161, 252
Out of Sight 260
Outbreak 187
Outchaneichvili, Levani 235
The Oval Office 234
Oyster Bay (Long Island) 218
Oz, Frank 68

Pacific Coast Highway 40
Pacific Ocean 202
Pacino, Al 34, 61
The Package 189
Pakula, Alan J. 161, 162, 163–164, 166, 167, 168, 223, 224, 225, 226, 227, 228, 229, 230, 231, 232
Palmes d'Or (Golden Palm) 44
Palos Verdes, CA 184
Pan Am Building 172
Panama 223
Pantoliano, Joe 198, 199, 219–220
Papaa Bay, HI 249

Paramount Pictures 75, 85, 116, 117, 119, 120, 121, 122, 123, 124, 125, 127, 151, 160, 166, 172, 176, 178, 180, 182, 184, 185, 186, 203, 206, 208, 210, 211, 212, 216, 217, 218, 242, 255, 264, 270
Paris, France 37, 138, 139, 140, 217, 218, 220, 270
Paris Project 138
Park Ave. (NY) 217
Park Ridge, IL 6
Parkay 6
Parkesburg, PA 125
Parliament 156
Patagonia Park 57
Patrick, Vincent 224, 225, 226
The Patriot 258
Patriot Games (film) 176–186, 201, 202, 203, 205, 206, 211
Patriot Games (novel) 178
"Patriot Games II" 226
Patuxent Research Refuge (MD) 253
Patuxent River Naval Air Station 253
Paull, Lawrence G. 93, 94, 99
PBS (Public Broadcasting System) 278
Pearl Harbor (film) 267
Peck, Gregory 50, 89, 143
Peidole harrisonfordi 285
The Pelican Brief 161
Pembroke Docks (Wales) 66
Pena, Frederico (U.S. Housing and Development Secretary) 210
Penn, Arthur 141
Pennsylvania 126
Pennsylvania Dutch Visitors Bureau 126
The Pentagon 202, 210
Penthouse 34
People 56, 61, 98, 241, 283
People Profiles 48
Peoples, David 89
People's Choice Award 244, 256
Perenchio, Jerry 89
The Perfect Storm 258
Petaluma, California 27, 48
Petersen, Paul 20
Petersen, Wolfgang 234, 236, 237, 238, 239, 242, 243
Petra (Jordan) 157
Petrocelli 21
Pfeiffer, Michelle 257, 258, 260
Philadelphia, PA 106, 195
Philadelphia Police Dept 121
Philippines 44, 60
Philips, Lou Diamond 271
Phillips, Mackenzie 24, 27
Phoenix, River 131, 152, 157, 158
The Pianist 270
Picnic at Hanging Rock 120
Pier 17 (NY) 148
Pierson, Frank 162

Index

Pinewood Studios 181
Pinza, Ezio 29
Piper's Kilt II (NY) 228
Pirates 139
Pirates of the Caribbean: Curse of the Black Pearl 271
Pitt, Brad 221–222, 223, 224, 225–226, 227, 228, 229, 230–231, 232, 269, 280, 286
Pitt, Lou 267
Place de Trocadero 217
"Das Plane" 238
Planet of the Apes 35
Planting Fields Arboretum (Long Island) 218
Platnick, Norman 285
Platoon 200
Playboy 56, 98
The Player 252
Plaza Hotel (Manhattan) 172
Plimpton, Martha 133
Plummer, Christopher 52, 55
Point Break 262
Poitier, Sidney 286
Poland 138
Polanski, Roman 138, 139, 140, 141, 142, 143, 270
The Police (band) 220
Pollack, Bernie 215
Pollack, Sydney 161, 178, 212, 213, 214–215, 216, 218, 219–220, 251, 252, 253, 254, 255
Poltergeist 150
Pont des Arts (Paris) 217
The Pope of Greenwich Village 224
Porter, Cole 110
Posada Tepoztlan (Mexico) 206
Posey Iron Works 123
The Possessed 22
Postcards from the Edge 70, 171
Postlethwaite, Pete 198
Potapsco River (MD) 253
Potomac River 252
Powell, General Colin 210
Predator 221
Predator 2 223
Premiere 271
President of the United States 234, 236, 243
The Presidio 55
Presley, Elvis 15
Presumed Innocent (film) 161–168, 177, 229, 253, 283
Presumed Innocent (novel) 161, 178
Prime-Time (TV program) 174
Prince Charles 117
Princeton (University) 171
Prochnow, Jurgen 235
The Professional 234
Promises, Promises 140
Proof of Life 258
Providence, R.I. 265
The Providence Journal-Bulletin 260

Prowse, David 39, 65, 70
Psycho 30, 260
Publicist Guild of America 208
Puerto Rico 202
Pulitzer Prize 14
Pullman (porters) 176
Pullman, IL 196
Purple Haze (film title) 52

Quan, Ke Huy 110, 116
Queen Street (PA) 125
Queens (NY) 166, 229
Quigley Down Under 119
Quinlan, Kathleen 27
Quiz Show 273

Rabin, Yitzhak 211
Raging Bull 129, 280
Raiders of the Lost Ark 61, 63, 74–87, 89, 91, 101, 109, 110, 112, 114, 117, 128, 150, 151, 247, 284
The Rainbow Room 174
Rainer, Peter 260
The Rainforest Foundation 277
Raisin Bran 241
Rambo: First Blood Part II 221
Ramstein Air Field (Germany) 238
Randall, Glenn 82, 83
Random Hearts (film) 93, 252–256, 260, 283
Random Hearts (novel) 251
Ransom 235
Rapke, Jack 257
Rawlings, Terry 98
Rayfiel, David 213, 252
Reagan, Ronald 99, 204
Reardon, Barry 186
Reaume Park (Ontario) 164
Rebello, Stephen 261
Recorder's Court (Detroit) 162
Red Barn Theater 10
Red Dawn 117, 201
Red Hook, NY 228
Red Sea 185
Red Square (Moscow) 239
Redford, Robert 158, 161, 285
Redwood Forest, CA 105
Regarding Henry 144, 169–175, 200, 212
Regine (nightclub) 141
Rehme, Robert 208
Reitman, Ivan 233, 245, 247, 248, 249, 250
Renaissance Center (Detroit) 164
Renoir, Jean 141
Republican Party 244
Reserve Officer's Training Corp (ROTC) 9
The Return of a Man Called Horse 63
"Return of the Ewok" 105
Return of the Jedi 101–108, 114, 283

Return of the Jedi Special Edition 244
Reuben, Reuben 120
Revenge of the Jedi 101, 106
Reversal of Fortune 235
Revolution Studios 270
Reynolds, Burt 20–21, 109
Reynolds, Debbie 34
Reynolds, Norman 78, 86
Rhys-Davies, John 77
Richard III (film) 286
Rickenbacher Air National Guard Base 238
The Right Stuff 210
Rio Vista, CA 277
Ripon College 3, 8, 9, 10, 159, 280
Ritter, John 121
The Ritz-Carlton Hotel (Manhattan) 172
The River 119
A River Runs Through It 222
Riverkeepers 279
Roach, Pat 81, 113, 115
Robb, Charles (U.S. Democratic Senator) 210
Robbins, Tim 280
Roberts, Conrad
Roberts, Julia 187, 214, 242, 245
Robinson, Phil Alden 251
Robocop 184
The Rock 235
"Rock Around the Block" 27
Rockefeller Center 174
Rockefeller Plaza 148
Rodeo Drive 269
Rodgers, Richard 29
Rogan, Josh 61
Rogers and Wells (law firm) 172
Rolex-Jackie Stewart Celebrity Challenge Shoot 156
The Rolling Stones 19
Rome, GA 136
Rome, Italy 37
Ronald Reagan-Washington International Airport 253
The Roof Terrace (D.C.) 210
Roos, Fred 21, 24, 25, 31, 32, 33, 34, 44, 52, 61
Roosevelt, Franklin D. 233
Rosaling Hotel (Los Angeles) 94
Rosemary's Baby 138
Rossetter, Tom 276
Roth, Ann 147, 173, 215,
Rotunno, Giuseppe 171, 173
Rowan Building (L.A.) 94
Royal Air Force 65
Royal Horticultural Hall (Victoria, England) 156
Royal Navy College at Greenwich (England) 181
Rubes, Jan 121
Rubin, David 214
Rudin, Scott 169, 170, 212

Rue de Ponthieu (Paris) 141
Russell, Kurt 148
Russia 262, 264
Russian Navy 262
Russo, Rene 238, 242
Ryder, Winona 214

Sabrina (1954) 212, 213, 215, 220
Sabrina (1995) 161, 212–220, 232, 252, 260
Sabrina Fair 212
"The Sacred Cow" 233
Sahara Desert 80, 81
St. Amand, Tom 114
St. Aubin Marina (Detroit) 164
St. Barnabus Episcopal Church (NY) 229
St. George (NY) 148
St. James Church 11
St. Mark's Square (Venice) 157
Saint Patrick's Day Parade (Chicago) 194, 195
St. Petersburg, FL 263
St. Stanislaus Kotka R.C. Church 148
Saks Fifth Avenue (NY) 254
Saladino, John 173
Salutation (estate) 215
Sam Spade 91
Sampson Hall (Annapolis Naval Academy) 184
San Francisco, CA 32, 41, 274
The San Francisco Chronicle 271
San Gabriel de las Palmas (Mexico) 206
San Pedro, Belize 134
San Pedro, CA 203
San Rafael, CA 27
Sandell, William 236, 237, 238, 239
Sanderson, William 91
Santa Ana, CA 13
Santa Clara County, CA 285
Santa Clarita County, CA 202
Santa Monica Freeway 271
Santa Monica Superior Court 110
Sarajevo 251
Sarandon, Susan 280
Sarsgaard, Peter 266
Save the Children 278
Save the Tiger 119
Savile Row 173
Saving Private Ryan 198
Savoy Pictures 211
Sawyer, Diane 148, 174
Scacchi, Greta 166
"Scary Gary" (Oldman) 235
Schickel, Richard 250
Schindler's List 198, 202
Schlesinger, John 19
Schrader, Paul 129, 130
Schroeder, Pat (U.S. Democratic Rep.) 210
Schwartsbaum, Lisa 260

Schwarzenegger, Arnold 183, 189, 242, 244, 282
Schwimmer, David 246, 286
Sconyers, Ron, General 238
Scorcese, Martin 147, 229, 280
Scotch (liquor) 195
Scotland 156
Scotland Yard 178
Scott, Debralee 28
Scott, Elliot 111, 152
Scott, George C. 144
Scott, Ridley 88, 89, 90, 91, 92, 94, 95, 97, 98, 186, 187
Scott, Tom 123
Scowcroft, Brent 203
Screen Actors Guild (SAG) 7, 15–16, 34,
Seale, John 125, 128, 133, 135
Search '88 Cancer Trust 156
The Search for Life: Are We Alone? 278
Search for the Nile 101
Searching for Bobby Fischer 202
Searle, Michael 156
Second Guns 51
Segal, Steven 280
Seigner, Emmanuelle 139, 140
Seigner, Louis 139
The Seine (Paris) 142, 217
Seligmann, Peter 279
Selleck, Tom 75, 77, 119
Sellers, Peter 190
Selzer, Will 34
Senate Foreign Relations Committee 280
Sequoia (tree) 105
Se7en 222
Seven Years in Tibet 229, 230
1776 140
Severance Hall (OH) 239
Sex and the Silver Screen 284
sex, lies, and videotape 260
"Sexiest Man Alive 1998" 283
Shakespeare in Love 198
Shakespeare School (IL) 191
Shalit, Gene 148
Shapiro, Bob 129
Shaw, Robert 50, 52
Shaw, Sir Run-Run 89
The Shawshank Redemption 187, 239, 286
Sheen, Martin 44
Shelton, Ron 267, 268, 270, 271, 272
Shepard, Sam 21
Shepperton Studios 37, 52, 157
Shestack, John 234, 241
Shimono, Sab 164
The Shining 66, 98
Shire, Talia 24, 48
Shisgal, Murray 18
Shriver, Maria 242
Shuler-Donner, Lauren 198
Sibun River (Belize) 135
The Sicilian 190
Sid and Nancy 234

Sigma Nu 8
Silkwood 144, 147, 148
Sills, Stephen 173
Silver, Joel 176
Simon, Carly 148, 174
Simon, John 143
The Simpsons 268
Sinatra, Frank 160
Sinbad and the Eye of the Tiger 38
Singer, Bryan 223
Siskel, Gene 117
Siskel and Ebert 232
Six Days, Seven Nights 233, 245–250, 251
60 Minutes 283
The Skin of Our Teeth 10
Skywalker Ranch 69
Slater, Christian 198
Sleepers 224
Sliver 201
Slocombe, Douglas 78, 114, 152, 155
Smith, Charles Martin 24, 27
Smith, John 263
Smith, Will 244
Smithsonian Institution's National Museum of American History 160, 285
Sneakers 251
Snipes, Wesley 199
Snuff (monkey) 83
Snyder, David 99
SO-13 (Special Operation 13) 178
Sobocinski, Witold 143
Soderbergh, Steven 260–261
Solt, Susan 164
"Some Enchanted Evening" 29
Someone to Watch Over Me 190
Somers, Suzanne 27
Sommer, Josef 121
Sommerville, David 24
Son of the Morning Star 134
Sony Corporation 283
Sony Lincoln Plaza (NY) 219
Sony Pictures 226, 227, 230
Sony Studios 203, 239, 255, 259
Sophie's Choice 161
South America 131
South Beach (Miami) 253
South Central (LA) 186
South Houston St. (Chicago) 196
South Pacific 29
South St. Lawrence St. (IL) 196
South Street Seaport 148
Souza, Robert 267
Soviet Union 262
Spain 155
The Spanish Prisoner 258
Speed 252
Spencer, John 164
Spencer, Junius 215
Spencer Tracy Award 284
Spielberg, Steven 29, 41, 42, 50,

Index

61, 74, 75, 76, 77, 78, 79, 81, 83, 84, 85, 89, 98, 100, 106, 109, 110, 111, 112, 113, 114, 115, 116, 117, 129, 138, 150, 151, 152, 153, 155, 156–157, 158, 159, 160, 186, 192, 198, 241, 243, 247, 250, 252, 257, 284, 285, 286
Spradlin, G.D. 44
Sprocket Systems 152
Sri Lanka 110, 111, 112, 113, 116
Stafford, Steve 249
Stallone, Sylvester 198
Star (magazine) 230
The Star Chamber 55
"Star of the Century" 208–209
Star Trek IV: The Voyage Home 185
"Star Wars Canyon" 83
Star Wars Episode I: The Phantom Menace 256
Star Wars Episode IV: A New Hope 30, 31, 33, 34–42, 46, 48, 50, 54, 55, 60, 61, 62, 63, 66, 70, 71, 72, 74, 83, 85, 86, 89, 100, 101, 105, 106, 108, 112, 116, 245, 256, 285, 286
Star Wars Holiday Special 62
Star Wars Special Edition 38, 242, 244
"Star Wars Stage" 68, 103, 157
The Starbright Foundation 284
Starkey, Steve 257
State and Main 258
State Department (U.S.) 203
State Street Plaza 148
Staten Island 148
Staten Island Ferry 145, 148, 228
Statue of Liberty 142, 148
Steadicam 112
The Steel Helmet 110
Steinfeld, Jake 113, 154
Stevens, Inger 18
Stevens Creek (CA) 285
Stewart, Donald 177, 201, 202, 207
Stewart, Jimmy 286
Stick 109
Sting (musician) 220, 277, 280
Stinson (plane) 249
Stockwell, Dean 235, 242
Stone, Oliver 176, 189
Stone, Sharon 286
"Stop Cancer" 219
Stoppard, Tom 263
Storagetek 203
Storaro, Vitorio 44
Stowe School (Buckinghamshire, England) 156
Strange Days 262
Strasburg, PA 123, 125
Streep, Meryl 144
A Streetcar Named Desire 176
Streisand, Barbra 115–116
Stripes 245

Strub, Phil 210
Stuart, Jeb 197, 199
Studios de Boulogne (Paris) 140
Styler, Trudie 277
Subcommittee on East Asian and Pacific Affairs 280
"Suburb Climber" 156
The Sum of All Fears (film) 261
The Sum of All Fears (novel) 178
Sun Valley, ID 275
Sunday in New York 11
Surinam 279
Suspect 140
Swayze, Patrick 148
Sweden 64
Swedish Covenant Hospital 5
Swift (meat packing family) 9
Sydney, Australia 129
Symonds, Craig (Prof.) 184

Table Mountain (WY) 281
TACA (Belizean airlines) 133
Taft/Barish Productions 188
Tahiti 247
Take Her, She's Mine 11
Talk Soup 214
Tandem Productions 89, 98
Tanen, Ned 29
Tanzania 285
Tartikoff, Brandon 176
Tate, Sharon 138
Taurus (Ford) 204
Tavern on the Green 219
Taxi Driver 129, 280
Taylor, Elizabeth 286
Temple University 126
The Ten Commandments 185
Tender Mercies 140
Tennessee 23
Tenth Ward (Chicago) 196
Terminal Velocity 223
Terminator 2: Judgment Day 182
Terms of Endearment 130
Tesco (supermarkets) 157
Tess 138
Testament 121
Teterboro Airport (NJ) 281
Teton County (WY) 281
Teton County Library 276
Teton Wilderness Act 277
Texas 158
Thanksgiving 52
Thelma and Louise 222
Theroux, Paul 129, 130, 135, 137
30th Street Station (PA) 123, 125
Thomas, Kristin Scott 245, 251, 253, 254, 255
Thomas, Marlo 174
Thompson, Jeff 9
Three Days of the Condor 213
Three Men and a Baby 223
Three-Penny Opera 10
THX-1138 26, 43, 106
THX Sound System 106

Tibet 278, 280
The Tibet Fund 280
The Tides Hotel (Miami) 253
Tikal National Park (Guatemala) 40
Tillich, Paul 18
Time (magazine) 57, 61, 98, 137, 250
Timecop 55
Tin Cup 267
Tippett, Phil 114
Titanic 242, 262
To Gillian on Her 37th Birthday 235
The Today Show 148
Tokovsky, Jerry 19
Tomblin, David 106
Tombstone 221
Tommy Tomorrow 35
The Tonight Show 283
Tony Award 140, 235
Tootsie 161, 252
Top Gun 89, 120
Torgerson, Ellen 14
Toronto, Canada 61, 260, 265
Touchstone Pictures 245, 248, 250
Tower Trotters 6
Towne, Robert 138
Tozeur, Tunisia 36, 80, 83
Tracy, Susie 284
Traffic 260
Tranwood P.L.C. 156
Travers, Peter 98
Truman, Harry S 233
The Truman Show 120
Trumbull, Douglas 96–97, 99
Tuckeseigee River 194
Tucson, Arizona 57, 106
Tunisia 36, 37, 81
Tuolomne River 115
Turan, Kenneth 250
Turkel, Joe 91, 92
"Turn 'em Loose Bruce" 162
Turner, Kathleen 252
Turow, Annette 166
Turow, Scott 161, 163, 164, 166, 178
12 Monkeys 221, 228
20th Century–Fox 36, 40, 41, 42, 119, 144, 145, 146, 148, 244
Twilight Zone: The Movie 61
Twins 245
Twister 252
Two Cops 267
2 Fast, 2 Furious 271
The Two Jakes 223
2001: A Space Odyssey 30, 35, 39
2010 55, 235
Tyree, Dr. William 159

U-Boat 235
U-Haul 28
UCLA's Campus Events Commission 284

UH69 Blackhawk (helicopter) 203, 238
Under Siege 188, 189
Ungar, Oliver A 50
Union Square (San Francisco) 32
Union Station (Los Angeles) 93
United Artists 44
United States Air Force 210, 238
United States Armed Forces 239
United States Army Special Operations School 210
United States Coast Guard 203
United States Custom House 148
United States Marine Corps (USMC) 203
United States Naval Academy 184
United States Navy 184
United States of America 115, 121, 142, 143, 178, 181, 201, 210, 217, 229, 233, 235, 238, 243, 260, 262, 264
United States Secret Service 196, 236
United Talent Agency (UTA) 24
Universal Pictures 20, 26, 28, 29, 36, 47, 52, 222, 251
University College (London) 160
University of California at Santa Cruz 274
University of Chicago Hospitals 191
University of Southern California (USC) 26, 29, 43, 50, 63, 274
University of Vermont 259
Upper East Side (NY) 172
Upper West Side (NY) 172
U.S. Marshals 199
U.S. Steel (Chicago) 196
USA Today 232
USS *Kitty Hawk* 203
The Usual Suspects 223

V.I. Warshawski 224
Vadim, David 235
Van Nuys, CA 39
Van Nuys Airport 250
Vangelis 96
Variety (newspaper) 72, 98, 107, 186, 232, 233, 243, 255
Varney, Phil 86
Venice, CA 204
Venice, Italy 157, 159
Venice Canals (CA) 269
Verhoeven, Paul 187
Vermont 258, 259
Viacom Entertainment Group 242
Vickers Aircraft Company 82
Victoria Dam 111
Video Image 182, 183, 204

Vietnam 18, 22, 25, 44, 274
Vietnam War 20, 43, 48, 49, 53
The Villa (Belizean hotel) 134
Villa, Poncho 206
The Village Voice 85
The Villain 57
Vineyard Haven, MA 218
The Virginian 20
Vista Hermosa (Mexico) 206
Vivolo (NY restaurant) 217
Vogel, Harold 72
Vogues Hommes 138
Voight, Jon 19, 128, 157
Volcano 245
Volpe, Bruce 170
Volvo 13
Vvendenskoye Cemetery (Russia) 264

Wade, Kevin 144,
Wag the Dog 245
Wales 77
A Walk in the Clouds 227
Walk of Fame (Hollywood) 16, 270, 284
Walken, Christopher 34, 89
Walker, Polly 178–179
Walkman 122
Wall Street (NY) 144, 146
The Wall Street Journal 203, 260
Wallace, Earl W. 119, 128
Wallace, Pamela 119, 128
Walsh, E. Emmett 91, 93
Walt Disney Motion Pictures Group 5, 250
Walton, Tony 171, 172, 173
War of the Roses (novel) 252
Ward, George 162
Ward, Sela 198
Warner, John (U.S. Republican Senator) 210
Warner, Tim 208, 284
Warner Books 161
Warner Bros. 58, 90, 91, 129, 132, 141, 157, 165, 167, 186, 187, 188, 192, 196, 237, 242
Warner Bros. Distributing Corporation 186–187
Wash, John 182
Washington, D.C. 202, 204, 210, 252, 253, 278, 279, 283
Washington, Dennis 191, 194, 195
Washington, Isaiah 271, 272
Washington Heights (NY) 226
The Washington Post 166
Water Grill (D.C.) 202
Water to Wine 277
Watergate 32
Waterloo 185
Waterworld 221
Watts, Robert 76, 80, 84, 106, 115, 152
Watts Riots 186
Waverly Coffee Shop (NY) 228
The Way We Were 218

Wayne, John ("The Duke") 57, 58
Wayne County (MI) 162
Weathers, Carl 50
Weaver, Sigourney 129, 144, 145, 146, 147, 148
The Weaver Thieves 284
Webber, Andrew Lloyd 140
Weeks, Jimmie Ray 140
The Weight of the Water 262
Weir, Peter 50, 120, 122, 123, 124, 125, 126, 127, 128, 129, 130, 131, 133
West, Kit 86
West Coast (CA) 186, 259
West End (London) 273
Wested Leather Company 160
Westin Hotel (Detroit) 164
Westwood V.A. Hospital 202
"(What a) Wonderful World" 123
What Lies Beneath 257–260
What's Eating Gilbert Grape? 198
"Whelan's Men" 283
White, Timothy 278
The White House 204, 236
White Men Can't Jump 267
White Plains, NY 170
Who Framed Roger Rabbit? 181
Who's Afraid of Virginia Woolf? 144, 147
Wick, Douglas 144, 145
Wilder, Billy 141, 212, 213, 215, 218, 220
Wilder, Gene 52, 56, 57
Wilderness Act 277
Will Rogers Institute 278
Williams, Billy Dee 20–21, 68, 102
Williams, Cindy 24, 27, 29, 32, 34, 53
Williams, John (composer) 40, 86, 117, 220
Williams, Robin 284, 285
Williams, Tennessee 11
Williams, Treat 223
Williams Bay, Wisconsin 10
Williamson, Bruce 56, 98
Willis, Gordon 168
Wilshire Abel Theater (L.A.) 239
Wilson, Rita 148
Wilson, Toby 281
Windsor, Ontario 164
Winfield, Paul 162, 163
Winfrey, Oprah 241
Wingate, Clay 14
Winger, Debra 79, 148, 277
Winkler, Henry 47, 48, 57
Wisconsin 8, 12
Wisniewitz, David 81
Without Remorse (novel) 211
Witness 50, 119–128, 130, 133, 136, 168, 177, 213
The Wizard of Oz 160

Index

W.L. Zimmerman & Sons, Inc. 125
WMTH-FM 6,
Wolfenshohn, James 235
Wolfman Jack 27
Wollman Ice Skating Rink (Central Park) 228
Wood, John 215
Wood, Natalie 110
Woodbridge Tavern (Detroit) 164
Woodlawn, IL 191
Woodrow Wilson Drive 23
Woolsey, R. James 202
Working Girl 144–149, 236
The World According to Garp 172
World Bank 235
World War II 46, 50, 76, 140, 198, 247
World Wide Web 237
Wright, Frank Lloyd 93
Wright-Penn, Robin 214

Wrigley Building (Chicago) 195
Writers Guild of America 61, 227
The Wrong Element 286, 287
The Wurffler (German U-Boat) 76
Wyler, William 141, 166
Wyoming 3, 186, 236, 246, 252, 276, 277, 281
Wyoming Air Patrol 281
Wyoming Citizen of the Century Award 277

Xalapa, Mexico 202
Xerox 220
Xico, Mexico 202

Yauch, Adam 280
The Year of Living Dangerously 120, 120
Yellowstone National Park 279, 281
Yellowstone Park Foundation 279

Yentl 116
Yoakam, Dwight 271
Yoga 248
Yorkin, Bud 89
Young, Sean 91, 92, 96, 98
Young Frankenstein 56
The Young Indiana Jones Chronicles 191
Yugoslavia 50, 51, 60
Yulin, Harris 200, 203
Yuma, AZ 103
Yuricich, Michael 96–97, 99

Zabriskie Point 21
Zaentz, Saul 130
Zaillian, Steve 202
Zatayev, Nikolai (Capt.) 263
Zemeckis, Robert 257, 258, 259
Zeta Tau 8
Zicker, Dick 205
Ziesmer, Jerry 44
Zimmerman, Jim 125